AVIATION'S PROGRESS IS EXEMPLIFIED BY THE DRAMATIC CONTRAST BETWEEN THIS F-86 *SABRE*, A 670-MPH, 9,000-HP JET, AND THE 1912 PUSHER-TYPE, 80-HP, HOME-BUILT, 60-MPH BIPLA

FLIGHT

A Pictorial History
of Aviation,
by the Editors of

YEAR

The complete story
of man's conquest
of the air from
his earliest dreams
to the present
jet age, dramatically
portrayed in over
1,000 pictures.
Foreword by
DONALD W. DOUGLAS

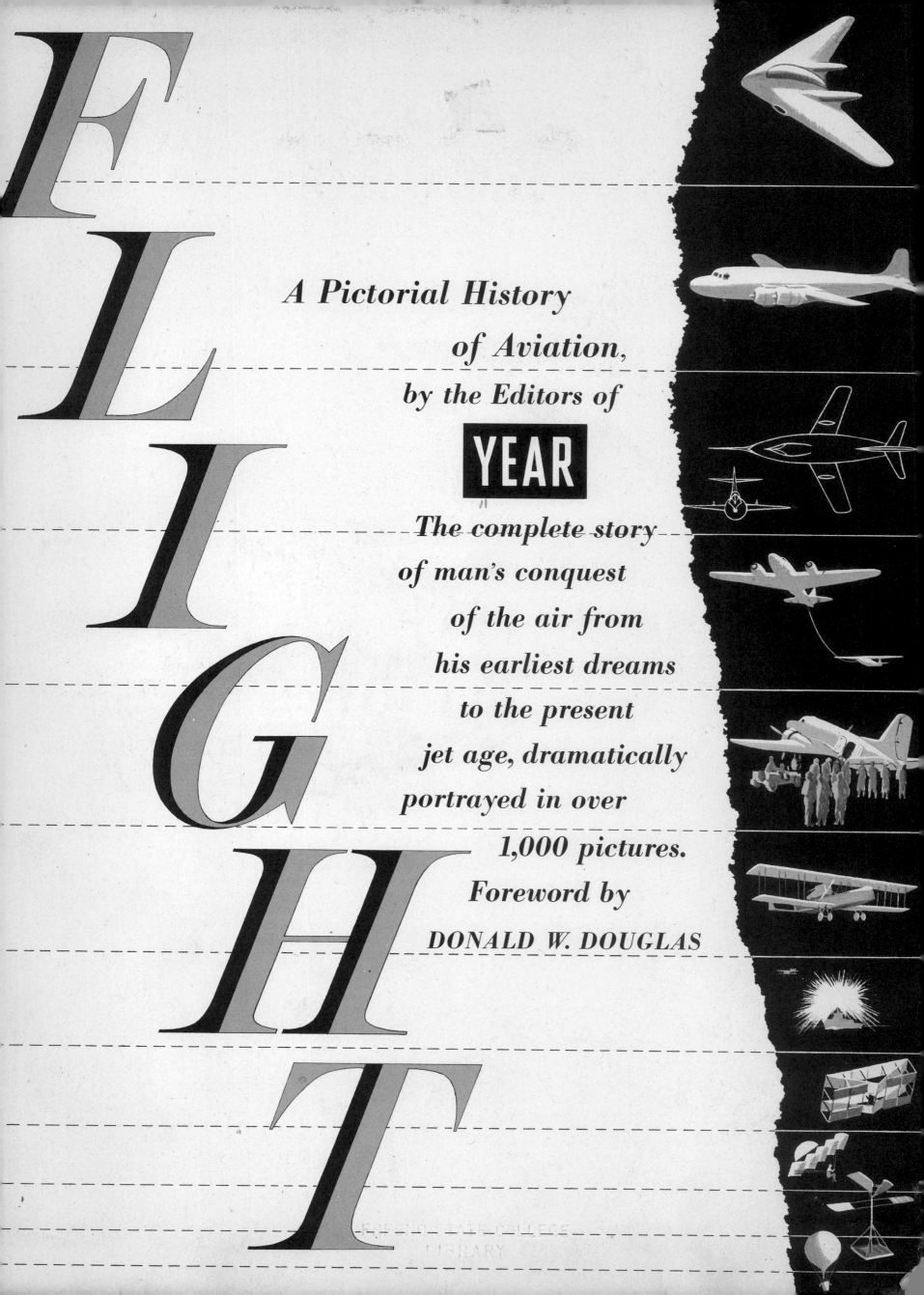

EDITOR AND PUBLISHER
Baldwin H. Ward

MANAGING EDITOR
M. Tugrul Üke

EXECUTIVE EDITOR
Erwin M. Rosen

CONTRIBUTING EDITORS

William Ames	Katherine Daubenspeck	Hugh Harlow	Clyde Parker
Joseph Barry	Richard Daubenspeck	Barbara Kreibich	Peter Rankin
Victor Black	Harry Gann	George Lawlor	Lee Saffo
Warren Bodie	Bernard Goldman	Remi Nadeau	Jules Schwerin
Jack Canary	Michael Hansen	William Orr	John Sloan
Warren Cheney	Robert Hare	William G. Oxx, III	Richard L. Sweeney

Robert Will

EDITORIAL ASSISTANTS

Zelda Cini	Joan Glad	Ethel Parrish
Helen Dillon	Dolly Henkel	Betty Peyer
Ann Funk	Jean Lopin	Lenore Seckler

RESEARCH STAFF

Marie Crummett	Rene La Belle	Euena Matthews	Helen Pickler
Betty Hopper	Jacqueline Major	Anne McCrone	Kathryn C. Ward

ART DEPARTMENT

Philip Berger	Joyce Mayer	Jane Parsons
Sara Jane Marcellee	La Von Moore	Donald Phillips
Sandra Matthews	Sylvia Newman	Clarence Walter

Edited and published by

YOUR LIFETIME IN PICTURES THE ANNUAL PICTURE-HISTORY

11833 Wilshire Blvd., Los Angeles 25, California
Copyright MCMLIII by YEAR, Incorporated
Library of Congress Catalog Card Number: 53-10327
Book trade distribution by Simon & Schuster, Inc., 630 Fifth Ave., New York 20, N.Y.
Printed in U.S.A. by Livermore and Knight Co., Providence 3, Rhode Island
Printed on Wescar Offset paper by Oxford Paper Co., New York 17, N.Y.
Bound by American Book-Stratford Press, Inc., New York 13, N.Y.
Typography by Adtype Service Co.—Los Angeles 15, Calif.

PUBLISHER'S NOTE

FLIGHT—A Pictorial History of Aviation is the second volume in the series of single-subject pictorial history books by the Editors of YEAR, The Annual Picture History. The first volume in the series was *YEAR'S Pictorial History of the Bible and Christianity, and all the World's Great Religions,* and coming volumes will include *YEAR'S Pictorial History of America* and *YEAR'S Pictorial History of the World.* A companion book is *Fifty Turbulent Years* (the pictorial story of the last half-century), the base book of YEAR'S pictorial news annual volumes which each year cover all the world, national and American scene events in 1,000 pictures and 75,000 words.

FLIGHT is not a book with static pictures of planes and dull portraits of people. Between its covers is a fascinating collection of actual news pictures of the dramatic milestones in aviation history ... and candid photographs of the colorful personalities whose heroic exploits have thrilled the world—a book filled with the nostalgia of your lifetime.

Published to commemorate the 50th Anniversary of Powered Flight, this outstanding volume will enthrall you and your family with its 1,300 pictures and 75,000 words ... portraying the complete story of aviation from man's earliest dreams to fly ... to jet planes and rockets. Many rare, unpublished photographs have been included from the world's greatest private collections.

More than two score aeronautical experts have researched scientific and historical documents from all over the world to compile the most accurate and up-to-date pictorial history of aviation ever published. Each section covering an important period of air development is prefaced by statements from key aviation pioneers and leaders.

Edited with the helpful cooperation of the entire aviation industry, *YEAR'S Pictorial History of FLIGHT* records the courage, faith and vision of the men who dared to cut their earthly bonds. It will bring many hours of enjoyable reading and help to define clearly the part aviation has played in modern history.

The Editors faced severe difficulties in editing *FLIGHT.* Much of aviation's early history had passed unrecorded. Source books, references and authorities were regularly in conflict as to date, sequence of happenings and details of events and personalities. Through correspondence totaling more than 3,000 letters to all parts of the world the search for early aviation information and pictures was carried on. Intensive efforts brought over 50,000 pictures and pyramids of literature and source references to be culled and considered. From these, 1,300 pictures were finally selected and some 75,000 words of captions and text written to bring together in one volume the most complete, authoritative picture-history of aviation ever published.

The Editors are deeply indebted to large and small commercial picture agencies throughout the country and to such public institutions and organizations as the Library of Congress (including the Hermann Goering and Gen. Billy Mitchell Collections), National Archives, Smithsonian Institution's National Air Museum, Institute of Aeronautical Sciences (Sherman Fairchild, Harry F. Guggenheim, Hart O. Berg and W. A. M. Burden Collections), Huntington Library, National Advisory Committee for Aeronautics (NACA), and the U.S. Air Force, Navy, Signal Corps and Coast Guard.

The Editors also express their appreciation to those who opened their important private picture collections to *FLIGHT,* such as Adm. Richard E. Byrd, Dr. Wernher von Braun, Cecil B. DeMille, Joseph Nieto, Warren Bodie, Robert C. Hare, George A. Page, Jr., Erik Hildes-Heim, the late A. V. Schmidt, A. M. Rochlen, Jack Frye, J. C. Hunsaker, Alfred V. Verville, George H. Prudden, William P. McCracken, Vaughn Bell, Frank Coffyn, Mrs. Robert H. Goddard, James W. Montee, George Lawlor, John Sloan, Jack Canary, Joseph Barry, and Charles Brown.

Additional significant photographs were made available through the courtesy of the Ford Museum and Greenfield Village from the Ernest Jones Collection, The Union Title and Trust Company of San Diego, National Cash Register Company, *Aero Digest* Magazine, and Aircraft Industries Association.

From foreign countries, including aircraft manufacturing companies and airlines, came the generous cooperation of Historisches Bildarchiv, Bad Berneck, West Germany; Keystone of Munich; L'Aero Club of Paris, France; Iliffe and Sons, Ltd., London; Henry Beaubois, Paris; Imperial War Museum, London; J. Ernie Adams, Auckland, New Zealand; Independent Newspapers, Ltd., Dublin, Ireland; Guido Botta, Naples, Italy; Norsk Telegrambyra, Oslo, Norway and a host of others.

For their editorial suggestions and advice, the editors of *FLIGHT* express special gratitude to Paul Garber, head curator of the National Air Museum, Smithsonian Institution; John F. B. Carruthers, M. A., D.D., of Pasadena; Maj. Lester Gardner, founder of the Institute of the Aeronautical Sciences; Fred Kelly, biographer of the Wright Brothers; John Glennon, librarian of the I.A.S., New York; Basil Littin, Executive Secretary of the Fiftieth Anniversary Committee for Powered Flight; and particularly to the members of the Historical Section of the Los Angeles Chapter of Institute of the Aeronautical Sciences for their unfailing research assistance.

Finally, the Editors wish to express their appreciation to Donald W. Douglas for his keynote foreword and to the aviation pioneers and leaders who so generously wrote out of their experiences and convictions to fittingly preface each era of aviation's history.

BALDWIN H. WARD, Publisher

PILOT (CERTIFICATE No. 93258) DWIGHT D. EISENHOWER

Dwight D. Eisenhower, President of the United States, and Supreme Commander of Allied Expeditionary Forces in World War II, is the first American President in history to hold a pilot's license—Certificate No. 93258. He learned to fly in 1939 when he was stationed in the Philippines as a lieutenant colonel on the staff of General Douglas MacArthur.

"...fifty years that have changed the world"

THIS is a worthwhile project and one which can accomplish good for our country. People on the farm and in the cities all over the land can celebrate with pride the fact that America's free soil gave to the world the miracle of powered flight. Our inventive citizens will continue to develop the airplane into a powerful tool for human progress. Today the security of the free world demands that the United States lead the world in aviation research development and general strength. We shall all have to work together for success.

Dwight Eisenhower

★　★　★

THE flight at Kitty Hawk ushered in what has proved to be the most momentous 50-year period in modern history. During no other half-century have such vast changes taken place in the world. In terms of travel time, the globe has shrunk to a fraction of the size the Wright Brothers knew or could have imagined.

The airplane has served to open up great backward areas. Many countries once isolated by terrain or travel time have been brought within easy visiting range of the rest of the world.

From its frail beginning the airplane has become the predominant instrument of national policy. Today relative air power is the yardstick by which national security is gauged and air supremacy has become the principal deterrent to aggression.

The airplane has been a great boon to mankind in drawing all the people of the world closer together and leading to better understanding. Unfortunately, it has also become an unparalleled medium of destruction but we must never allow the spectre of modern warfare to cloud our vision of the future. The airplane has brought knowledge where it did not exist before. It performs stirring missions of mercy. We must exploit to the utmost the advantage which this great social instrument has given to all of us.

J. H. Doolittle

TOKYO RAIDER AND TROPHY HOLDER JAMES H. DOOLITTLE

Lieutenant General James Harold Doolittle, leader of the famous Tokyo raid in 1942, was an Army Air Service flying and gunnery instructor during World War I. His cross-country speed flights in the 1920's made him famous. He was the first man to take off, fly and land a plane on instruments alone. He holds the Schneider (1925), McKay (1926), Harmon (1930), Bendix (1930), and Thompson (1930) trophies, an unsurpassed record.

DONALD W. DOUGLAS

Foreword

In the last five decades commercial aviation has played a leading role in shaping the world of today and tomorrow.

When historians of the future record in bronze, marble or printed page the saga of the 20th century, they will have to assign to aviation a role of major importance in the story of our times.

The drama of man's struggle for existence and understanding of the universe around him is constantly highlighted by the amazing progress of his conquest of the air.

The first half of this century has witnessed the mastery of many forces known to the ancients only in contemplation and dreams. To those of our own generations whose privilege it has been to share in the first explorations and modest achievements of man-made wings, the distant future is still obscured but the present throbs with accomplishment and promise. Transportation has taken on new dimensions and "wings for the world" have widened its horizons.

New skylanes, new trade routes, new bonds of friendship and commerce, and revised concepts of time and distance are supplanting the old. Their impact on habits of thought and international customs in world trade and politics is strong and unmistakeable.

Today there are no distant ports or mysterious places. An airline ticket is the new magic carpet and seven league boots combined. The airplane is rapidly becoming the new common denominator between racial barriers and far-flung frontiers.

It has been the lot of some of the aviation pioneers, and of those who follow in their footsteps, to witness and help create in their own lifetime global aviation beyond all previous hopes and dreams.

Long, long ago it was written "What is Past is Prologue." Electronics, nuclear and cosmic ray energy, and other modern-day wonders clearly indicate unlimited horizons for the newer wings to come.

Only man's blindness, greed and inability to cope with himself and with his present can halt or destroy aviation's upward progress.

Donald W. Douglas

CONTENTS

A NEW ERA—THE AIR AGE—HAD ITS BEGINNINGS IN 1783 WITH THE ASCENT OF MONTGOLFIERS IN THEIR HOT-AIR BALLOONS, SHOWN HERE BEFORE THE FRENCH ROYAL FAMILY AT VERSAILLES

The Balloon Era

Earliest kites fly as religious symbols; balloons are used in wars and later set records; glider tests open the way to winged flight

One of the most prominent balloonists during the early days of the Twentieth Century, Roy Knabenshue, for his daring feats, was applauded from coast to coast. Now nearing his eighties, Mr. Knabenshue is retired and lives in Arcadia, Calif., where he still is interested in aviation, and is writing his memoirs.

ROY KNABENSHUE FLYING EARLY AIRSHIP

THE business of preparing for a free flight in a spherical balloon was more or less a routine matter. My first ascent was made with a captive balloon. The ascent was 500 feet and the only sensation was that of keen pleasure, no dread or fear. The first free flight was about the same, except that one would speculate as to the manner of landing.

My relatives were against the business and would have no part of it. My friends considered me to be what moderns call a "crack pot" or an idiot. The public held the same opinion.

As I gained experience, I had visions of future airships and felt certain that air travel was just around the corner. Santos-Dumont had distinguished himself by making successful dirigible airship flights in and around Paris, France.

During the period 1900-1904, practically all people I had business dealings with as well as others I had met, including newspaper correspondents, were of the opinion that air travel was out of the question, and that it was a waste

of time and money to attempt to make it a commercial success.

The St. Louis Exposition electrified the world when it offered $200,000 for aeronautic events. This was the first time in history that America made a bid for aeronautic recognition. It provided the impetus that touched off keen competition for the single $100,000 grand prize. And what were the requirements to win?

This event in 1904 was open to any kind of aircraft that was capable of flying over an L-shaped course on three separate occasions and at a speed of not less than fifteen miles per hour. It is with regret that I must report no one succeeded in winning that prize.

On October 25, 1904, Captain T. S. Baldwin's airship, the *California Arrow*, made a flight over the Exposition grounds, making a circle around the big Ferris Wheel, and then to the Transportation building, turning again and heading for the Aeronautic Concourse. When almost over the spot from which the flight was started, the motor failed and a final landing was made near East St. Louis. This was the first time in America that a controlled motor driven circular flight had been successfully performed.

On December 17, 1903 the Wright Brothers had made four flights at Kitty Hawk, No. Carolina. At that time they were concerned only with lateral control and fore and aft stability. They did not attempt to make a turn.

I gave public exhibitions at state fairs, amusement parks and for business houses from 1905-1909. It was during 1909 that I became painfully aware that the aeroplane would supplant the airship in both usefulness and popular acceptance. During 1910-11, I managed the exhibition business of the Wright Company and witnessed new improvements appear almost daily. As far as the public was concerned, the useful day of the airship had passed its zenith.

Roy Knabenshue

Ralph Hazlett Upson became engaged in airship engineering in 1908. He won the International Balloon Race in 1913, 1919 and 1921. He was chief engineer from 1914 to 1918 for the Goodyear Tire and Rubber Company's aeronautical department which produced most of the American balloons and airships used in World War I. He is currently a professor at Univ. of Minnesota Institute of Technology.

AT the turn of the century, the free balloon had been a well-known and usable type of aircraft for over 100 years. Steerable, power-driven balloons, often called dirigibles but more correctly airships, also showed considerable promise in experiments by Santos-Dumont and others. The possibilities of mechanical flight were still considered quite nebulous up to the very time the first flight was actually made.

At about the same time, Germany's Count Zeppelin was developing his famous rigid airship, composed of a metal frame containing fabric balloons and with a fabric outer cover. This development was later merged with that of the Goodyear Tire and Rubber Company in this country, where previous important progress had been made, and is still being made, in advancing the non-rigid type of airship or blimp.

The next logical step in development of the power-driven type, closely paralleling structural development of airplanes, was the all-metal or metal-clad type undertaken in the 20's by the Aircraft Development Corp. of Detroit. A relatively small demonstration unit, the ZMC2, was built for the U.S. Navy, and launched in 1929—

BALLOONIST RALPH UPSON, AT LEFT, AND FRIEND

the hoped-for prototype of much larger metal-clad airships to come.

This ship was eminently successful, out-performing and out-lasting contemporary airships of its size. However, disastrous accidents to several large airships of the older type, together with the rapid development of airplane and helicopter designs, turned away public interest.

A stimulus to all aeronautics was the organization in 1906 of the balloon race for the Gordon Bennett Cup. These were contests for distance in which the free balloon was supreme, and remained so for many years after.

In the meantime, the oldest and most elementary type of aircraft—the free balloon—has staged an inauspicious although meaningful come-back. It has long been recognized that the free balloon is one of the very best means for reaching high altitude in the existing atmosphere. Flights by the brothers Auguste and Jean Piccard, followed by personnel of the U.S. Army Corps, established new altitude records in the 30's which held for many years.

More recent development has mainly been made possible by improved plastic materials and by progress in radio and other instrumentation, permitting full returns from high altitude flights by unmanned balloons. Balloons of similar material have been used to carry messages behind the Iron Curtain, and it is well known that many hundreds of Japanese incendiary balloons during the second world war crossed the Pacific Ocean to this country, with no power whatever except the wind to propel them.

It is an inspiring situation today that in spite of spectacular heavier-than-air advances, the older lighter-than-air type, so far from being counted out, still shows promise of greatly expanded usefulness to come.

R. H. Upson

SOARING FLIGHT of birds symbolizes the inspiration of men to fly. In primitive times, the bird was admired and envied by men who sought the key to the secret of flight. Not possible for himself, man endowed his gods with power to fly.

Giant flying reptiles, bats and dragon-like creatures swept the skies during the Mesozoic Age, an estimated 20 million years ago. The Age of the Bird lasted 40 million years, closing with the rise of the first feathered-bird, the *archaeoptery*.

MAN'S GODS FLEW FIRST

Dream of human flight is displayed throughout art, myths and religion

After the first men walked upright, domesticated wild animals and rode upon their backs; after they learned how to swim and adapt fire to their needs, they paused in their work to envy the flying bird soaring freely overhead. As man could not then master the art of flight he endowed his gods and devils with wings, symbolic of supernatural existence.

The mythology and the archaeological remains of all early civilizations, offer evidence of gods in flight. By 3500 B.C. Babylonian artists engraved the story of *Etana*, a shepherd who flew on the wings of eagles, in cuneiform characters on cylinders of semi-precious stones.

Legends of antiquity abound in astounding tales of flying spirits, scientifically explained today as artistic and religious sublimations of man's frustrated dream of flight. There was Phaethon, son of Apollo, who drove his father's sun-chariot through the sky, lost control and alternately scorched and froze the earth. And

there was the sailor, Sinbad, who flew on the back of a giant bird.

Influenced by the legend of Daedalus and Icarus, earliest of the Greek myths on flight, Bladud, King of Britain (863 B.C.) built himself wings of feathers and leapt from a tower in the Temple of Apollo in London, breaking his neck.

The philosopher-general, Archytas of Tar-

WINGED IRIS, a bronze Egyptian frieze, represented a flying man. Records show that men attempted to fly like Gods before Pyramids were built.

entum in Greece (428-347 B.C.) carved a wooden pigeon that flew by its own power. For two thousand years his exploit, for which no precise scientific explanation survives, was a lively topic of inquiry and discussion. Some scientists suggested that Archytas had employed gas to keep the pigeon aloft; others said he used a lighter wood than any now known, or that he conceived some mechanical gadget remotely related to today's internal combustion engine.

In the rule of Emperor Nero, Simon the magician, publicly exhibited an effort at flight in the Roman forum and was killed. The Saracen of Constantinople (1100 A.D.) flew from a tower in the presence of a great crowd and the Byzantine Emperor Comnenus. He, too, crashed.

So while in myth and history bold men perished, believed by their contemporaries to be punished by the gods for their temerity, others, like Friar Roger Bacon and da Vinci prophesied that human flight would glorify another age.

WAR-GOD MARIS of Japanese mythology, rode a sacred boar to earth. Ancient peoples who gave their gods and devils extra-human power of flight, believed men would be punished if they tried to fly.

FLYING CHARIOT of Ki-Kung-Shi, a legendary prince of China, was a self-powered flying machine driven by favorable winds. Chinese folklore relates many tales of flight by men, dragons and gods.

PERSIAN KING Kai Ka'us, builder of the Tower of Babylon 1500 years before Christ, is claimed to have driven through the skies on a Flying Throne, with four great eagles harnessed to corners of the throne.

OLDEST of flight mythology is the story of Daedalus and Icarus. Icarus disobeyed his father by flying too close to the sun which melted his wings of feathers and wax and without them he plunged into the sea.

KHENSU, a winged god of the Egyptians, was prominent 1,000 B.C. Royalty generously displayed the winged motif on their tombs, thrones and insignia. Hawk symbolized kingly power.

CHERUBIN, the Assyrian winged bull with the human head, was cited by the prophets in the Bible. It was displayed before the palace entrance of King Sargon at Khorsabad, about 708 B.C., to serve as forceful protector.

ASSYRIAN IDOL ASHUR, chief of the deities, had the head and wings of an eagle, the body of a warrior. Carved about 884 B.C., the figure holds a cone and basket in which are stored the divine gifts.

FOUR HORSEMEN of Apocalypse, supra-human allegorical figures, ride the air representing war, famine, pestilence and death (*Book of Revelation* 6. 1-8). Engraving was done by Albrecht Durer, 1528.

FIRST BIBLICAL ACCOUNT of flight described Elijah riding into heaven on chariot of fire: ". . . and Elijah went up by a whirlwind into Heaven. Elisha saw it and he cried father, my father . . ." (*Kings*).

PERSEUS ASTRIDE the Flying Horse, Pegasus, was immortalized in Greek myth. Perseus soars through the air wearing winged sandals and the helmet of Hades which makes him invisible.

MERCURY visits earth as the winged messenger of the Roman gods (the Greek, Hermes); bronze by Giovanni di Bologna. *Victory of Samothrace,* classic female figure of flight was erected 306 B.C. by Poliorcetes on Samothrace Island in the Aegean Sea (Louvre, Paris).

QUEEN BRUNHILDE, heroine of Viking and Teuton legends was a Valkyr (warrior) who led dead heroes from their battlefield skyward into Valhalla.

GIANT KITES were first employed by the ancient Chinese (400 B.C.) as a method of conveying signals during warfare. Later kite-flying developed into a popular social diversion, as in this print of kites representing birds and dragons.

Koreans believe kite-flying originated with lantern flown by a general to inspire his troops, who thought it a divine token. Another Korean general, using cord of a kite to span a stream, is reputed to have given the kite its first real mechanical use.

THE MAGIC CARPET that glided over Bagdad originated in the classic book of Arabic folklore, *A Thousand and One Nights*. Stories by Scheherazade spoke of magical flight, recorded in 900 B.C., telling of this ancient concept of air travel.

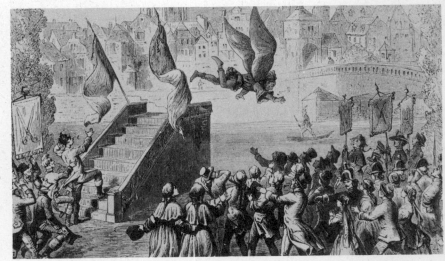

GOODNATURED SATIRES and caricatures of "flying men" were common in the press and theater of 19th century Europe. In 1866, composer Gustav Pressel wrote a comic opera, *Der Schneider Von Ulm* (above) telling of one such exploit.

PARADISE LOST, John Milton's poetic realization of a winged Heaven and Hell (1665), was rendered supremely pictorial by Gustave Dore, two centuries later. The poet's inspired vision of flight and the artist's interpretation of it are among the first such collaborations in literature.

THE PROPHECY of human flight by the 11th century gave way to the building of mechanical inventions which demonstrated the principles of flight. It is recorded that the Caliph of Cordova (right) during time of Moorish occupation of Spain, encouraged building of flying machines.

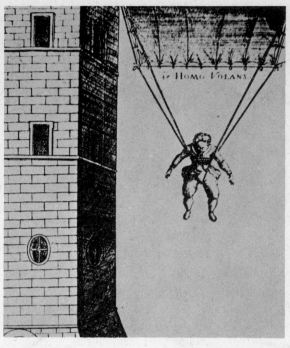

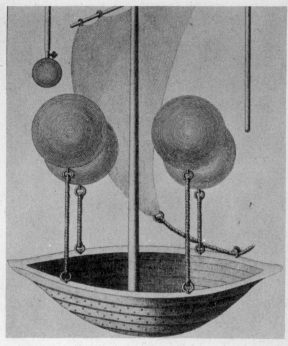

SUPERSTITION and the black arts of sorcery flourished as scientific investigation was banned in the Middle Ages. Men grovelled before an imaginative winged Satan in human form who flew through the air on a dragon charger in a sky inhabited by ghosts.

"FLYING MAN" descends safely to earth from a prison tower by means of a parachute. Upon the original plans drawn by Da Vinci, Fausto Veranzio, a Venetian architect, developed this modification. He printed picture in the book *Machinea Novae*, 1595.

VACUUM BALLOON AIRSHIP was dream of Jesuit Francesco de Lana in 1670. He described a vessel with oars and sails moving through the air suspended from thin copper vacuum globes. De Lana miscalculated force of atmospheric pressure on the globes.

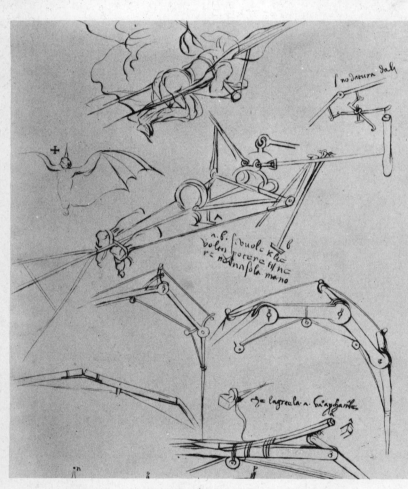

LEONARDO'S SKETCHES SHOW DETAILS OF FLYING MACHINE

FLYING MACHINE MODEL BASED ON DA VINCI'S SKETCHES

Leonardo applies science to his dream of flight

First detailed treatise on the mechanism of flight was written in 1505 by Leonardo da Vinci. The great genius of the Renaissance was fascinated by the idea of human flight. He made endless observations of the anatomy of birds and their movement. "A bird," he wrote, "is an instrument working according to mathematical law, which instrument is within the capacity of man to reproduce in all its movements."

Leonardo finally worked out the first technical design for a flying machine, based on the wing structure of the bat, which he felt would be most efficient. Its operator was to work the machine with his arms and feet by means of ropes passing over pulleys. But despite his scientific approach, Leonardo failed to achieve his dream of flight. He had over-estimated the strength and endurance of human muscles. He did, however, make a major contribution to aviation by demonstrating the principle of the parachute.

The theory of balloon flight was advanced as early as 1250 by Roger Bacon who proposed a "hollow globe filled with ethereal air or liquid fire." In 1670 Francesco de Lana devised an interesting, but impracticable design for an airship suspended from vacuum balloons. It was not until 1776 with the discovery of hydrogen that Bacon's "ethereal air" became a reality. Flight by balloon soon followed, ushering in the Air Age.

LEONARDO DA VINCI

FIRST "BALON" in the Western World rose to a height of 6,000 feet over Annonay in France, on June 5, 1783. Built by the Montgolfier brothers, the balloon, made of paper, was inflated with hot air.

HYDROGEN GAS-FILLED BALLOON by physicist J. A. C. Charles was first launched on August 27, 1783, from Champ de Mars in Paris. The balloon was ten feet in diameter and contained 22,000 cubic feet of gas. It rose to more than a half mile, finally settling in Gonesse, 15 miles from Paris. The awe-struck villagers viciously attacked and completely destroyed the balloon, believing it to be "a devilish visitor from the skies."

BALLOONING ERA BEGINS

First balloon is Montgolfier brothers' paper globe filled with heated air

Invention of the balloon by the French paper makers Joseph and Etienne Montgolfier marked the beginning of man's adventures in the sky. Thousands of people had gathered to witness the scientific demonstrations of the Montgolfiers" at Annonay, France, on June 5, 1783. A huge linen-lined paper bag 35 feet in diameter and filled with hot air, the first "Montgolfier" rose to a height of 6,000 feet. All Europe acclaimed the event. The Montgolfiers were proclaimed "conquerors." Benjamin Franklin, in Paris as U.S. delegate and commissioner, was the first American to witness an air voyage. He declared it to be a "Discovery of great importance . . . which may possibly give a new turn to human affairs."

The first air-borne passengers were a sheep,

a rooster and a duck, sent aloft by the Montgolfier brothers on Sept. 19, 1783. Today, imprinted on the insignia of the U.S. Lighter-Than-Air Craft Division are a sheep, rooster and duck in honor of the first air voyagers. In October of that same year, the Montgolfiers realized their ambition to send human passengers into the air when they sent two men 80 feet high in a captive balloon. And in November, the noted French scientist, Pilatre de Rozier, and the Marquis d'Arlandes sailed five miles over Paris in a Montgolfier balloon. The brave adventurers stood in a three-foot-wide wicker basket, equipped with bundles of straw for fuel and pails of water to extinguish possible fires, and saluted crowd 300 ft. below.

Professor Jacques A.C. Charles, physicist,

using the Robert brothers' discovery of the solubility of rubber, constructed a "globe" of taffeta impregnated with rubber and on August 27, 1783, launched the first hydrogen-filled balloon.

During the 70 years that followed the invention of the first "globe," men experimented continually for a means to direct the course of balloons regardless of weather conditions. In 1851, Henri Giffard of France proved to the world that it was possible to navigate and control the direction of a balloon in flight. He built and flew the first dirigible airship. Motor power for his lighter-than-air craft was furnished by a hundred-pound, one-cylinder steam engine driving a three-bladed propeller designed to run at 110 rpm. The ship attained a speed of six mph.

FIRST HUMAN BEINGS to make a free balloon flight were Pilatre de Rozier and the Marquis d'Arlandes on Nov. 2, 1783. The decorated Montgolfier type balloon rose to more than 3,000 feet, traveling five miles over Paris in 20 minutes. Prior to this, only domesticated animals had been used in flights, thrilling audiences.

TREMENDOUS SENSATION and first progressive steps in aeronautical science are credited to balloon flight of Prof. Charles and the elder Roberts on Dec. 1, 1783. Aloft for two hours, landing 27 miles from Paris, the team introduced the use of hydrogen gas, barometer, valve, net, suspension car—all items still in use.

FIRST SUCCESSFUL CROSSING of the English Channel (Dover to Calais, France) in a gas-filled balloon was made Dec. 7, 1785 by Jean Blanchard and John Jeffries. Fighting to remain on course the pair threw their personal clothing items overboard.

TO WIN FAVOR for balloons as safe medium of transportation, Mrs. L. A. Sage was first English-woman to go up in a balloon. Vincent Lundari took her aloft June 25, 1785. Lundari's attempts to navigate his balloons with long oars proved unsuccessful.

AMERICA'S FIRST balloon ascension was made by Jean Blanchard on Jan. 9, 1793. The air voyage from Philadelphia to New Jersey lasted 45 minutes. Blanchard carried a "passport" from President George Washington asking U.S. citizens to aid the balloonist.

BALLOONS SOON PERFECTED carried men aloft regularly. Scientists, inventors and adventurers strived for a century to find ways to direct a balloon's flight regardless of weather conditions. Experiments were marked by disappointments, misunderstanding and confusion. Balloons, relieved of one disability, fell immediately into another. The ardent balloonists became social outcasts, ridiculed by the press (above) and molested by the public as glory-seeking maddened scientists. Clergymen stated that the Creator regarded as impious man's urge to fly above earth. Nations, however, began to conceive ideas for empires in the sky.

USE OF MILITARY BALLOONS dates to French Revolution. On June 26, 1794, a gas-filled "balon" carrying two French soldiers (above) soared over hostile territory at the Battle of Fleurus in Belgium and confused, demoralized and dispersed the enemy. The balloon "spotters" directed the artillery firing by simple use of signal flags.

HUGE CROWDS thrilled at first parachute jump by Andre J. Garnerin from 3,000 ft. over Paris, October 22, 1797. Original 'chute, made of pure silk, could not be pack-folded. Garnerin jumped in England, Sept., 1802.

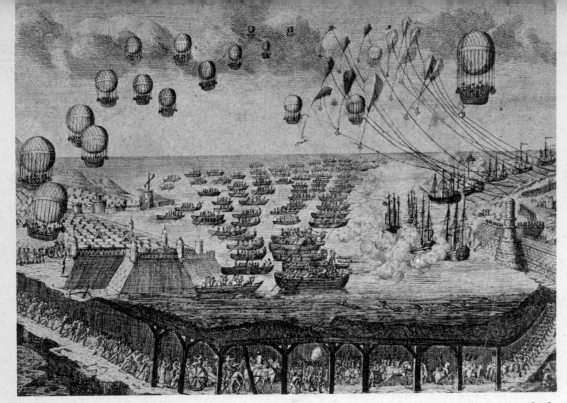

INVASION BY AIR, land and sea, proposed by this anonymous drawing, depicts the ways in which Emperor Bonaparte reportedly schemed to invade England (1804). J. Coutelle, Napoleon's Captain of the Aerostiers, was world's first military balloon observer. His command was disbanded in 1799. Although Louis Napoleon used balloons in Italy, French war balloons languished for 50 years.

MOST PRETENTIOUS conception of a French military balloon was imagined by M. Marey Monge in 1800. Complete in every military detail it could supposedly support an army of 4,000 men for months and voyage to any hemisphere at will.

NAPOLEON BONAPARTE propounded the idea that the English Channel could be crossed with an army conveyed in large transport balloons. In 1805, Thilorier proposed these great balloons to cost 600,000 francs, each designed to carry 6,000 troops.

UNHEARD-OF ALTITUDE of 22,892 feet was reached by Gay-Lussac on Sept. 16, 1804. Gay-Lussac and Biot (above) became pioneers in the new scientific studies of aerostation and the nature of the atmosphere, its magnetism, warmth, humidity.

ENGLAND BEGAN to develop an interest in balloon science and engineering when James Sadler of Oxford, first Englishman to ascend, made repeated efforts to cross the Irish Sea. His final attempt in October, 1812 from Dublin to Holyhead also failed.

WORLD'S FIRST MARTYRS to ballooning were Frenchmen de Rozier and Romain attempting to cross the English Channel in June, 1785. In 1824 Englishman William Sadler (son of James), first to cross the Irish Sea, was killed on his 31st ascent. In the same year, his countryman Thomas Harris (left) supposedly jumped to his death to lighten falling balloon and save his fiancee. France's Mme. Marie Blanchard, as daring as her husband, was killed in 1819 when hydrogen gas became ignited by fireworks attached to balloon. On July 24, 1837 English parachutist Robert Cocking (right) met death when inverted cone parachute failed.

POSSIBILITIES inherent in the science of ballooning stirred the creative ambition of many during the early part of the 19th century. Plans were schemed to transport by air in times of need a whole country from one locale to another. Trips to the North and South Poles and even as far as the moon were advocated. Shown above is the interior of a gondola which was designed and equipped for distance flights.

EARLY CUSTOM of displaying significant balloons during public celebrations was long practiced. ▶ France and England launched balloons at coronation of their rulers and in declaration of war or celebrating peace. China used colorful balloons for religious festivities as did Italian villagers (right) honoring San Guiseppe Day (1828). Gas-filled balloons were common at U.S. fairs, festivals to 1920's.

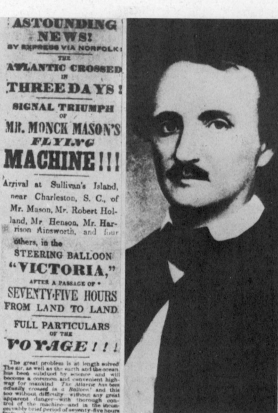

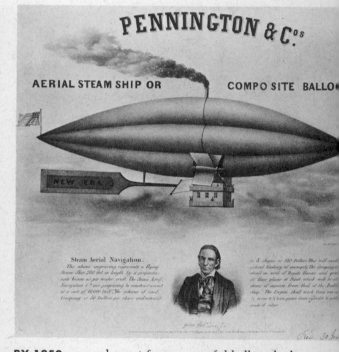

HEATED-AIR BALLOON was launched in England for Queen Victoria's birthday May 24, 1838. It was a Montgolfier type, transported from France. The year before Mrs. George Graham had honored the queen by ascending in the gas-filled *Royal Victoria*.

GREATEST AIR HOAX of the century in America was perpetrated by Edgar Allan Poe. In need of money, Poe wrote an amazing fictitious story of a three-day aerial crossing of the Atlantic. It was printed as a fact in *New York Sun*, April 13, 1844.

BY 1850 every element for a successful balloon had been invented except a way to control its flight with a source of power. In 1852 France's Henri Giffard, "The Fulton of the Air", built and navigated a dirigible airship using a steam-driven engine. Steam motors, however, proved too bulky and heavy, delivering only one horsepower to 112 lbs. of weight. With the advent of power, many companies were formed—all doomed to failure—such as the Pennington Steam Aerial Navigation Company (above).

LOCOMOTIVE AEROSTATIQUE was built by Ernest Petin of France in 1851, but never was tried in flight. Four large balloons attached to a keel sustained the airship propelled by Archimedian screws "to be operated by man or other power."

HISTORICAL FLIGHT was made by Charles Green at the official opening of the London Bridge by King George IV in 1831. Green was the first in England to make novel ascent astride a horse, also was England's first night balloonist.

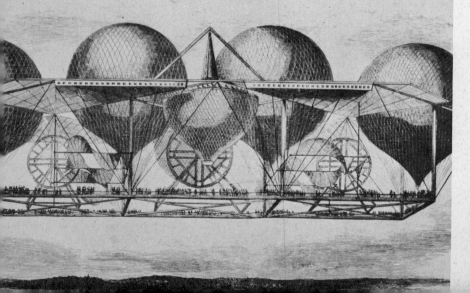

HEAVIER-THAN-AIR CRAFT

Study of birds results in gliders with manually controlled flapping wings

In searching for craft more maneuverable than balloons with which to conquer the air, man's ingenuity reached fantastic heights. Profound study of bird wings, their construction and action in flight, resulted in many birdlike designs, some with flapping wings controlled manually by the operator. Inventive imagination produced rockets, helicopters, monoplane and multiplane models, and gliders of various types. It was mainly from glider experiments that further knowledge of aerial navigation was obtained.

Early gliders were the hang type wherein the operator supported himself on his forearms and his body hung below. Thousands of glides were made in this type craft. In later models a seat was added for the operator's comfort. Octave Chanute, American engineer, introduced truss construction (1898) with struts and stays in his biplane glider, forerunner of the modern airplane.

Flying problems were reduced to three key points: equilibrium, complete control and sustained flight. Wing area was increased to proportions that would sustain the necessary weight,

wings were warped or curved for greater lift value and vertical movable planes or rudders were added for lateral control. Pioneer aeronauts soared higher and further, adding daily to their knowledge of aerodynamics. New inventions also brought tragedies when early airmen were killed in air accidents while testing new equipment.

ROCKET DESIGN using high-pressure steam for reaching moon was caricatured in 1825 in England.

Next natural step in flight progress was to add a power plant to the glider. Steam engines had been used on models with some success but their weight was a basic handicap. Clockwork and rubber band motors, compressed air and steam engines using benzine or carbolic acid gas for fuel were tried. One rocket design specified gunpowder for propulsion. The need of a lightweight engine for further aerial development was acutely felt by everyone experimenting in the field. It materialized at the turn of the century with the invention of the radial type of internal combustion engine.

In 1903 Charles M. Manly, who was chief assistant to Dr. Samuel Pierpont Langley, designed and built a 52-horsepower, 5-cylinder radial gasoline engine weighing 125 pounds. This achievement earned him the title of "father of all radial airplane engines." The engine was built for the $50,000 U.S. government financed Langley *Aerodrome* (see page 29). With the advent of gasoline engines, flying experiments were accelerated and controlled flight was assured.

FOUR CENTURIES OF AERIAL ENDEAVORS exclusive of balloons, are summarized above in this old French chart of 53 designs for human flight. Representing various countries, these designs range from crude bird-like wings and ornithopters to helicopters and multiplanes. Design No. 1 shows world's first flying machine, sketched in 1490 by Leonardo da Vinci, brilliant Italian painter and scientist. In the same year he also drew the first helicopter and parachute design, all preserved in his manuscript *Codex Atlanticus* at the Ambrosian Library in Milan. His drawings greatly influenced air-minded enthusiasts who through the following years contributed greatly to aviation development. Third from the left, first row, is the *Passerola*, elegant aerial machine design of Bartolemo Lourenco de Gusmao of Portugal in 1709, featuring magnetic force. To provide lift and sustained flight, powerful magnets were enclosed in globes. Among other ingenious devices, it contained a huge bellows to furnish artificial wind when air conditions were unfavorable. *Artificial Albatross* in 2nd row, 6th from left, was a birdlike glider built in 1857 by Jean-Marie Le Bris of France. Using a horse and cart for starting power, the *Albatross* was fastened by a rope and when the horse moved forward the glider became airborne. The world's first helicopter, 3rd row, 2nd from left, was built by Gustave de Ponton D'Amecourt of France in 1862. For power he used a steam engine. The Planaphore, 5th row, 3rd from left, was a monoplane model built by Alphonse Penaud, French engineer, in 1872. Featuring his original rubber band motor, it was exhibited in the Tuilleries Gardens in Paris where it soared almost 200 feet. Aeronautics is indebted to Penaud for many inventions including guide-rope brake and a tailless kite.

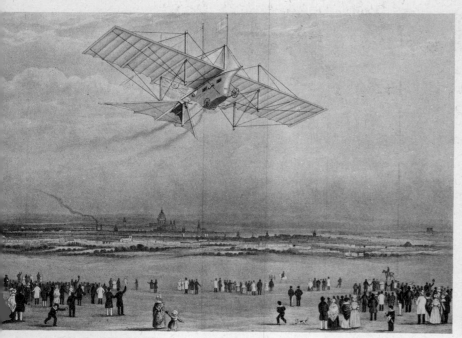

FIRST AERIAL CARRIAGE . . . a monoplane of practical design was patented in England by Wm. S. Henson in 1842. This ship (l.) was a giant for its time with a wing spread of 150 feet, a huge tail, vertical and lateral rudder and 2 six-bladed pusher propellers 20 feet long. All this was to be powered by a 25 to 30 horse-power steam engine. Daringly hoping to organize a world-wide "Aerial Transit Company" with a proposed regular schedule to all countries, he designed the above aerial station. After many discouragements with the models he built he turned everything over to his partner John Stringfellow, and went to America.

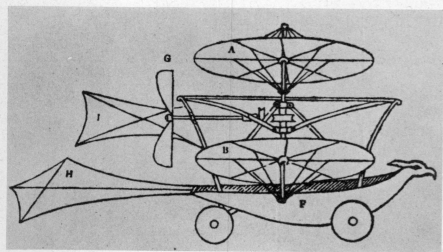

CAYLEY'S THEORY OF POWERED FLIGHT

Cayley's Aerial Carriage (left) by Sir George Cayley (c.), "Father of British Aeronautics", was a heavier-than-air flying machine design of 1842 combining principles of both airplane and helicopter. Lift was obtained by two circular planes termed "elevating fliers", revolving in opposite directions, one rotor above the other on each side of the machine. Two pusher props were meant to propel the ship forward. A broad horizontal rudder was aft the fuselage to assist in ascending or descending and a small vertical one was for lateral control. Canvas-covered fuselage housed steam engine.

Design was influenced by his 1792 toy helicopter (r.), made of feathers, corks and a whalebone bow. Smithsonian Institution at Washington, D.C. proved it to be workable by constructing a model from Cayley's plans.

Cayley approached the problems of flight from the mechanical rather than the ornithopter (flapping of wings) principle. He believed flying required less exertion than was commonly supposed. His theory was "to make a surface support a given weight by the application of power to the resistance of air." Stating that the concave wing provided more lift than plane surfaces, experiments were needed to calculate required engine power.

During the years 1800 to 1810, Cayley considered many problems of mechanical flight questions dealing with initial velocity, propulsion or "first mover", as he called it, leverage on the wings, and strong lightweight construction. He was first to suggest that superposed surfaces as seen in later biplanes, with diagonal wing bracing would add strength without weight. He even predicted future streamlining because in aerial navigation every pound of direct resistance eliminated was found to support 30 extra pounds.

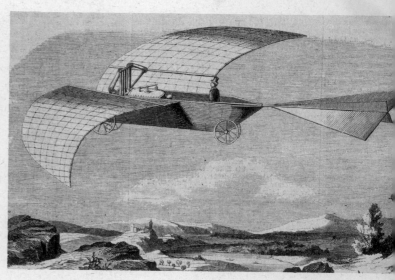

MILLER'S ORNITHOPTER was a self-powered flapping wing designed in 1843 by Dr. W. Miller M.R.C.S. of England. It had wings of hollow cane covered with oiled silk and closely resembled the wings of a bird. It never flew.

A PAIR OF WINGS and a parachute were designed by Retif de la Bretonne of France for paratroopers of the 18th century. The basket carried supplies.

FIRST ROCKET PLANE was a striking design credited to Werner Siemens of Germany, conceived in 1847. It featured two large warped wings and four undercarriage wheels. The explosive force of gun-powder was intended to propel the plane.

AERIAL STOCK CERTIFICATE of 1868 backed a plan for air travel in an aerial steam engine carriage called the *Avitor*. The balloon-airplane, built by Frederick Marriott, a San Francisco editor, flew five mph on its test run but was no match for Pacific winds, so Marriott's ambitious project for international flight tours was abandoned.

◀ **KEY EXHIBIT** at the World's First Aeronautical Exhibition, held at London's Crystal Palace in June of 1868, was John Stringfellow's triplane model, shown suspended. His light steam engine won a prize of 100 English pounds. Also on display were balloons, heavier-than-air models, kites and plans of proposed machines.

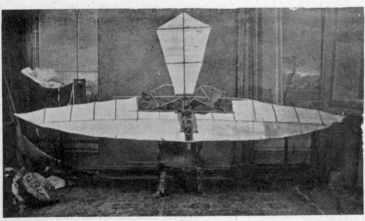

FIRST POWERED FLYING MODEL built by John Stringfellow (center), English engineer, was a monoplane (l.) with a 20-foot wing span, twin pusher propellers and a lightweight steam engine. In June 1848, in Stringfellow's lace factory at Chard in Somerset, England, the model was suspended on a starting wire, releasing itself as it became airborne and flying to the other end of the room. Later, in London it flew again about 40 yards before it was stopped by a canvas barrier erected to break its fall. Heavy costs forced Stringfellow from experimenting further until 18 years later in America when he built the first triplane model (right) using the same type engine as before. Exhibited at Crystal Palace in 1868, the triplane lifted from the wire rigging, thus satisfying spectators that it would have flown had there been suffcient space for free flight. Stringfellow's two flying models proved in performance that his principles of aerodynamics were sound.

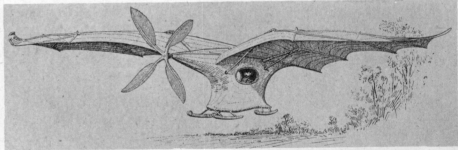

WINDMILL AERIAL STEAMER (above), a huge tethered model airplane was built by Thomas Moy, English engineer, and R. E. Shill in 1868, but no actual trials were made until 1875 at London's Crystal Palace. With two wings, fore and aft, set at a 10° angle and totalling 114 square feet wing area, the machine was powered by a three-hp steam engine that lifted its 120 lbs. six inches from the board track on which it travelled. The windmill effect was created by two air screws set between the wings, each having six blades, each blade with eight planes. The blades were 12 feet in diameter with surface areas of 160 square feet. Tied at the center, the model raced around the circular track and upon reaching the speed of 33 miles per hour it became airborne. Moy described his Aerial Steamer trials in a paper he read before the Royal Aeronautical Society. He theorized that there was little pressure on an object moving slowly through the air but there would be immense pressure if movement were rapid. His startling recommendation that flying speeds of 150 mph should be attempted was incredible for that time. However his *Aerial Steamer* showed the possibility of flying by steam.

ADER'S "EOLE" (above), first motor-propelled airplane, flew its builder, Clement F. Ader (r.), French electrical engineer and inventor of a telephone, to fame on October 9, 1890. Twenty-one feet long with a wing spread of 46 feet, the birdlike monoplane weighed 1100 lbs. and was powered by a 40-hp steam engine with a screw propeller in the nose. It was built in secrecy and privately tested on the grounds of Chateau d'Armainvilliers, near Grets. Ader flew the *Eole* 150 feet but, unable to control it, he smashed the plane in landing. Ader had the same equilibrium trouble a year later with *Eole No.* 2 which flew twice as far but broke a wing when it came to earth. His experiments had cost 2,000,000 francs. With funds from the French War Department, he built the *Avion*. On August 18, 1897 it left the ground several times without mishap, but two days later a heavy wind destroyed it as it was getting off the ground.

BOX CAR HELICOPTER, unusual 1876 design by W. J. Lewis of New York, had four helicopter air screws, twin propellers astern and wings over the car. Lewis planned to build a full-size machine for a roundtrip to Philadelphia at an estimated 100 mph, according to *Leslie's Weekly* of Dec. 30, 1876.

FLYING JUNGLE GYM was designed in 1885 by Dr. W. O. Ayres of New York. The machine featured a four-point landing gear. Dr. Ayres expected the compressed air in the twin drums and tubes to be sufficient to keep his machine aloft. Risking propeller haircut appears normal hazard for operator.

RUSSIAN PLANE CLAIMED "FIRST"

RUSSIA'S FIRST PLANE (photo at top) was built by Alexander F. Mozhaisky, Russian scientist and inventor. His countrymen claimed Mozhaisky's craft had successful take-off in 1882, as portrayed (center) in a contemporary drawing. Portrait at right is of Prof. N.E. Zhukovsky, founder of the Military Aviation Academy in Moscow and called the "Father of Russian Aviation." About 1903, he was reportedly active in early research in aerodynamics, studying the effects of propellers, helicopter rotors and wing construction. Wings he developed were copied by Professor Prantl of Germany who termed them the "Zhukovsky Profile." Professor Zhukovsky is also credited by his countrymen with constructing the first Russian wind tunnel in 1904 at the Kucknisky Laboratory, which the professor had founded for advancement of Russian science. Professor Zhukovsky died on March 17, 1921.

MAXIM'S MULTIPLANE, giant 3½-ton machine of 1893, was built in England by Sir Hiram Maxim. The plane's steel tubing condensed to water for re-use the used steam of the 350-hp steam engine. Hinged planes flanked the 110-foot central plane. Twin propellers measured 17 ft. 10 in. Tested in 1893, it sailed for some distance before the wind blew it over. Maxim is shown here with plane's steam engine which used benzine for fuel. The American-born British scientist worked out in theory complete control of a plane in flight and read his paper before the First American Conference of Aerial Navigation at Chicago, in 1893.

MILITARY OBSERVATION BALLOONS were used effectively by the Union Army against the Confederates in the Civil War. The first aerial military report, disclosing the position of the Confederate troops at the Battle of Fair Oaks,

1862, was telegraphed from a Federal balloon. On May 24, 1862, General Stoneman directed the first known artillery fire from a balloon. Moved from place to place by locomotives, the balloon was inflated (right) before each ascent.

AERONAUTICS IN CIVIL WAR

Balloons used effectively by Union Army in 1861 for military observation

Aeronautics became a branch of the U.S. government during the Civil War when in 1861 President Lincoln and Secretary of War Stanton accepted the services of Professor T.S.C. Lowe and his exhibition balloon for military observation to survey the enemy's lines. Napoleon had been the first to adopt the new science as a part of his government in 1794 and Denmark, Russia and Austria followed suit.

Prof. Lowe became America's first Chief of Aeronautics and made his first attempt at heliography over battle lines at Bull Run. He discovered the position of the victorious Confederates and issued the first aerial military report. On May 4, 1862, Prof. Lowe, high up in his balloon, observed and reported that the Con-

federate Army, under General Magruder, had left its position during the night. Lowe continued his aerial scouting at the battle front in Richmond, May 31-June 1, 1862. By observing, telegraphing, mapping and delivering information on the enemy's position, he enabled General McClellan to save his Federal Army from total destruction. Ascending many times under heavy artillery fire, Lowe made strategical discoveries at the Battle of Fair Oaks, 1862. The Balloon Signal Service, organized by Lowe as a rapid means to forward important information regarding enemy tactics, was first to discover the Confederate Fleet in the James River.

The Confederate Army had watched with envy the Union ballons high up and out of reach of artillery. In desperation, The Confederates gathered together silk from ladies' dresses in the South to make a balloon of their own. The great patchwork ship rose in the air only to be captured by the Northerners.

In the hope that it might shorten the Civil War, the first airship was offered to the government by Dr. Solomon Andrews of New Jersey in August, 1862. After much political opposition

and red tape Congress favored the offer but the war ended before the airship got under construction. With ambitious plans to fly the Atlantic, Dr. Andrews did design a peculiar appearing craft in 1863 and, according to his claim, "flew over New York." There is no record of the flight.

Count Zeppelin, the great German who later developed the modern airship, gained his early balloon experience at the age of 24 as an observer with the Union Army. Balloons were found to be highly effective in military observation and artillery fire was directed from balloons for the first time in history in the Civil War. It was a period—as in all wars—in which great strides were made in developing knowledge and acceptance of aeronautics.

PRESIDENT LINCOLN'S NOTE to Lt. Gen. Scott asking him to see Prof. Lowe "once more about his balloon" evidenced Lincoln's support and confidence in balloons for obtaining military intelligence data.

T.S.C. LOWE, America's first aerial military observer, was the "eyes" of the Union Army, supplying accurate reports on Confederates from his "show" balloon.

BALLOON SIGNAL SERVICE, branch of the Federal Army, was first to disclose the Southern Fleet in the James River, 1862. Prof. Thaddeus Lowe and the Signal Service here telegraph reconnaissance report.

UNION BALLOON *Washington* was released from specially built deck of the steamer, *George Washington Parke Custis* (first "aircraft carrier") to observe enemy's position at Budd's Ferry, November 1861.

"INTREPID," used extensively by the Union Army at the Battle of Fair Oaks, was U.S. government's first military balloon. To complete filling at critical times, the *Intrepid* "nursed" from a smaller balloon.

FRANCO-PRUSSIAN WAR

The Siege of Paris, September 1870 to January 1871, during the Franco-Prussian War, established the balloon as an aid to civilians as well as to the military. Manufactured in a Paris railroad depot (above), balloons were used to carry mail, refugees and messages to link beleaguered Paris with the outside world. Carrier pigeons were also taken aloft and released as message bearers. During the siege, French Premier Leon Gambetta, for first time in history, transferred by air the seat of a nation's government. He ascended (right) with his secretary from Montmarte, October 6, 1870 in a Godard balloon, landing three hours later at Epineuse. They ventured to Tours and set up French Government. On same date of Gambetta's departure, three Americans escaped Paris in another Balloon. Felix Nadar, organizer of the "Balloon Poste" for sending mail out of Paris during siege, participated in history's first air battle. He met a German balloon at an altitude of 10,000 feet and shot his way out of the predicament. Landing in Paris, he was acclaimed by thousands who witnessed first battle in the skies. Some 68 balloons escaped from Paris.

AIR DEFENSE before World War I was little known. However, maneuverable anti-balloon gun, above, was built by famous Prussian munitions manufacturer Alfred Krupp and used in Franco-Prussian war.

STEAM AIRLINER (above) a sensational design by Gabriel De La Landelle, French aeronaut, 1863, utilized the air screw idea, basic principle of the heliocopter. The airliner had large planes on either side of a boat-shaped hull. Atop two masts, each with two revolving air screws, were mounted huge umbrella parachutes, folded except in time of need. Landelle conducted experiments with aeronauts Vicomte de Ponton d'Amecourt and Felix Nadar in an effort to solve heavier-than-air navigation. In 1884, Landelle coined the word "aviation," helped in the organizing of the "Societe D'Aviation."

A PROJECTILE TRAIN (interior, above) carries its passengers in comfort as it speeds through the ether in Jules Verne's great novel, *From the Earth to the Moon*, 1865. Some of Verne's fiction became fact.

PERSONAL RECEIPT (above) signed by Professor Thaddeus Lowe was given to donators aiding Lowe's plans to cross Atlantic Ocean in balloon. At close of Civil War, the balloonist built the largest gas balloon ever constructed, *City of New York*. The balloon, 130 feet in diameter and able to carry 12 persons was destroyed while being inflated.

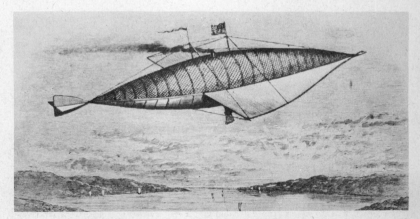

BALLOON-AIRPLANE combination, *Avitor* (above) was constructed by Frederick Marriott in 1869. Trial flight was made over Shell Mound Lake in California (see top p. 20). Marriott had been a partner of Stringfellow in England as press agent for the unsuccessful Aerial Transit Co. of 1842.

TRANSATLANTIC BALLOON VOYAGE was financed by *New York Daily Graphic* to enable John Wise, American aeronaut, to fulfill his ambition of 30 years to cross the ocean to Europe. In 1873 a huge balloon was built having a 400,000 cubic feet gas capacity and a whale boat as a balloon car. A composition was added which Wise believed would render balloon fabric impervious to hydrogen gas, allowing him to remain in air two weeks, if need be. The balloon was launched from New York City and crashed 41 miles away in Canaan, Connecticut. Project was abandoned. New York banner (above) publicized event.

"SKY BICYCLE" was built by Prof. C. E. Ritchell of Hartford, Connecticut. On initial flight, June 12, 1878, it rose to 200 feet altitude and remained in the air for more than an hour. The propeller was driven by the means of pedals, similar to bicycling.

UPPER STRATA EXPLORATIONS into the unknown were made in the late 1800's by the courageous and able French scientists, Gaston Tissandier (photo at right) and his brother, Albert. They made numerous balloon ascents into the higher strata of atmosphere, rising to unheard of heights where extreme cold and direct rays of the sun brought privations and hardships. On one occasion, the entire crew lost consciousness. In 1875, Gaston Tissandier, accompanied by H. T. Sivel and J. E. Croce-Spinelli, rose to a height of 27,950 feet (5½ miles). Only Gaston was alive when the balloon landed. His two associates were asphyxiated. Although balloonists used the most dependable measuring and recording instruments and telescopes of the latest design, equipment for oxygen and for maintaining circulation in the human body was unknown at the time. Scientific ascents came to a halt until such equipment was discovered. Flight of first electrically driven dirigible was made on October 8, 1883 by the Tissandier brothers. Energy for the 92-foot semi-rigid craft was supplied by a Siemens motor of 1½ horsepower. Two test flights were made, each a year apart, over Auteuil, France. The power from the small motor was insufficient against high winds and the project had to be dropped.

HUGE MAN-POWERED DIRIGIBLE was constructed by renowned Naval architect, Dupuy de Lome. Built for France at close of the Franco-Prussian War, the steerable craft had no engines. The four-bladed propeller was powered by eight men and a windlass. Later ships used de Lome's stability control method.

1877 POLAR EXPEDITION was proposed by Commodore Cheyne of the British Navy. He planned the exploration of the North Pole using three balloons to be transported by water to within 20 miles of the Pole. Trailing wire would make possible telegraphic communication from balloons to transports.

"SKY HIGH," "Sky's The Limit," "As High As The Sky," and many more phrases, relating to the art of flying, became a part of the public's everyday vocabulary at close of 19th century. No circus or road show was complete without added attraction of stunt-fliers and famous balloonists. Manufacturers commercialized their items (example above) with "ballooning," which had gained prestige and captured the public's fancy.

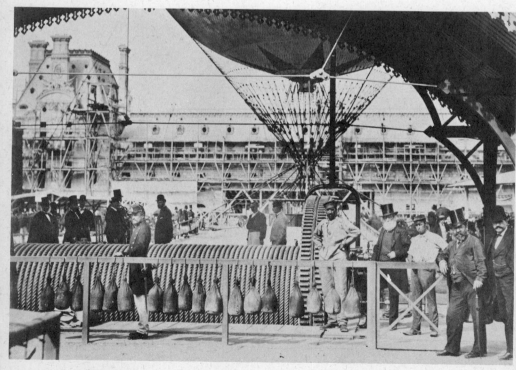

"GRAND BALLOON" (above) was built by the brilliant French engineer, Henri Giffard for London and Paris world expositions in 1876. In 1852, Giffard had built a dirigible airship (see text p. 14), the first practical, steerable balloon in history. It was a 144-ft. balloon in the now-accepted elongated form. He proposed to build a dirigible with the incredible length of 1,970 feet. Because of the tremendous cost involved, actual construction was never started.

POWERED "CIGAR" with incommodious car (above) was one of America's earliest practical airships. Its twin propellers on their single shaft carried its builder, Dr. August Greth of San Francisco, on a successful trial flight over his native city on October 18, 1903. The huge dirigible balloon made two other successful flights over the Bay City and coast on April 23 and 28 of the following year. His ship was non-rigid type.

◀ **DARING GIRL PARACHUTIST** Katchen Paulus of Germany made 516 balloon ascents and 197 parachute jumps in the years between 1893 and 1909. This record established her fame as an aerial marvel of the time despite competition of contemporary male balloonists and parachutists who were setting many new records.

POPULAR HERO AND POPULAR ATTRACTION, Captain Thomas Scott Baldwin (extreme left) and the Hudson Balloon were marvels of the day. Both are shown on Central Park grounds of San Francisco's Market Street in 1893. Baldwin, famed aeronaut, made America's first parachute jump at Golden Gate Park in 1887, built first dirigible balloon in U. S., built and sold Army's first dirigible.

BALLOON-EQUIPPED CAVALRY participated in maneuvers of the Royal British Engineers on White House Hill, above, in 1897. Much later, the British Army adopted kite-balloons—Germany's "Drachen" and France's "Caquot" balloons.

"HARE AND HOUNDS" balloon race, below, at turn of the century was held in England. Hares have departed; hounds start off in pursuit. Each spherical contestant was numbered in this lighter-than-air version of popular English sport.

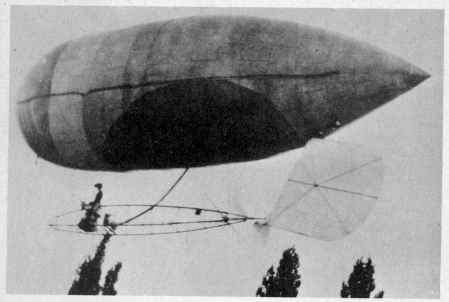

SANTOS-DUMONT ACCLAIMED

It was a brilliant young Brazilian, Alberto Santos-Dumont, who was the first to build and fly an airship in controlled, sustained flight. In wicker carriage of his *No. 9* airship, he rudders leisurely past Paris house-tops (top left.) He ascended in his Santos-Dumont *No. 1* from the Zoological Gardens, Paris, September 20, 1898, and rose to 1500 feet, thrilling the crowd below. Suspended 60 feet below the sausage-like balloon of varnished Japanese silk, the inventor worked the controls from the carriage on which was mounted the 3½-hp tricycle motor operating the two-bladed propeller. Santos-Dumont again stunned Paris, October 19, 1901, when, after two unsuccessful attempts, he piloted his *No. 6* airship around the Eiffel Tower (right) from its starting point at St. Cloud. The nine miles were covered in 29½ minutes. He distributed the prize among his employees and the poor of Paris. In all he constructed and flew 14 airships. To the carriage structure of *No. 14*, he attached a box-kite equipped with an 8-cylinder, 50-hp motor—and flew it on August 22, 1906, receiving official credit for making the first European airplane flight. He next startled Paris in 1910 when he let an American girl, Aida de Acosta, fly a ship of his (at left). She stepped forward to descend, back to climb.

ZEPPELIN — GIANT AIRSHIP

The first rigid dirigible airship to fly was a huge balloon of aluminum framework, 420 feet long, covered with treated linen and silk. Leaving the special floating hangar (right) on Lake Constance ("The Boden-See") near Manzell, she prepares for her maiden voyage, July 2, 1900. The massive aircraft rose 1300 feet and soared at eight miles an hour over the German-Swiss border, making safe landing 20 minutes after take-off. At the controls was her designer-builder, Count Ferdinand von Zeppelin (portrait left) German Lieutenant General of Cavalry, who served in 1862 as official observer of the Prussian Army in the ranks of Lincoln in the American Civil War. It was here, witnessing the direction of artillery fire from the military balloons of Professor Lowe, America's first Chief of Aeronautics, that Zeppelin was awakened to aerial navigation. Upon his military retirement in 1891 he devoted all his time and money to dirigible balloon experiments. On her second flight, Zeppelin's airship lifted and flew in sweeping circles above Lake Constance for an hour and fifteen minutes at speeds up to 20 mph, landing smoothly without mishap. In 15 of 17 hull compartments were balloonets carrying hydrogen gas. Two 16-hp naptha motors, working independently of each other, were housed below, one in each of the easily attachable aluminum gondola cars. Each motor drove a pair of four-bladed propellers connected to the framework. Intercommunication between cars was achieved through the use of speaking tubes and an electrical telegraph system. On her keel was a sliding weight which, when moved forward or back, nosed the airship up or down to steady the craft without throwing out ballast or losing gas.

TANDEM GLIDER EXHIBITION (above) at Santa Clara, Calif., campus on April 29, 1905, featured the monoplane glider, *Santa Clara*. It was built by Professor John J. Montgomery, America's "forgotten" glider pioneer, and demonstrated by Daniel Maloney, professional parachute jumper. Given a balloon assist, the glider was cut free at 4,000 feet by the rider. In a controlled flight of eight miles in 20 minutes it performed amazing spirals and dives and landed on a pre-arranged spot. The poster above advertised Montgomery's "Most Daring Feat." The inventor, shown (hat in hand, below left) with his assistants by the *Santa Clara*, had learned, from his first *Gull Glider* which he tested in 1884, the importance of curved surfaces for lift and hinged wings or rudders, for balance.

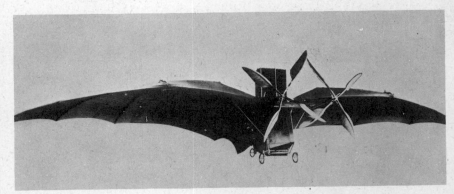

TWIN PROP "AVION," the third and last monoplane built by Clement F. Ader of France, hobbled uncontrolled on its test run August 18, 1897, and crashed, ending Ader's dream of being the first to construct and fly a practical airplane.

TRIPLANE GLIDER was built in 1896 by Octave Chanute, American engineer. Preceded by his 12-plane model and then a five-plane, the triplane in turn was replaced by his popular biplane known as the "Chanute Glider." Over 2,000 flights were made in his gliders without accident. Chanute (portrait above) originated the basic design of truss construction for gliders.

GERMAN FLYING MACHINE was built by Karl Jatho (insert above) of Hanover, Germany, who claimed to have flown it 24 kilometers August 18, 1903 — almost four months before the Wright Brothers made their historic flight at Kitty Hawk, N.C.

READY FOR TAKE-OFF in his first hang-type glider, Otto Lilienthal (above), German scientist and engineer, designed his craft in 1891, using a framework of peeled willow wands covered with waxed cotton cloth. With a wing area of 107 square feet it weighed 40 lbs. He launched himself from a hilltop, soaring aloft to crown 30 years of research by himself and his brother. Otto became the most skilled glider pilot of his time. His flight downhill, shown above, was in 1895. He lengthened his glides to one-quarter of a mile and rose to 75 feet, guiding the craft by shifting his body weight. In less than five years he had standardized his wing spread to 23 feet and made over 2,000 glides. While trying out a new rudder control, he fell and died at the age of 48 on August 10, 1896.

LAUNCHING OF LANGLEY'S STEAM MODEL   GRAND-DADDY OF AERIAL POWER PLANTS   CHARLES MANLY WITH PROF. LANGLEY

SAMUEL LANGLEY The 16-foot tandem monoplane shown above (left), world's largest powered model, was built in 1896 by Dr. Samuel Pierpont Langley, American scientist and secretary of the Smithsonian Institution. Catapulted from a houseboat on the Potomac River, the model, designated as *Aerodome No. 5*, was powered by a 2-hp steam engine and attained a speed of 25 mph in its 3200-foot flight. When the fuel was exhausted the ship made a smooth three-point landing. Langley retired temporarily, feeling he had established the practical principles of sustained flight after years of research and experimenting.

At the request of President McKinley who visualized the use of aircraft in warfare, Langley in 1903 completed his man-carrying *Aerodrome*, four times larger than the model. An appropriation of $50,000 from the War Department helped finance the project which took four years to accomplish. The power plant was a 5-cylinder radial gasoline engine which weighed 125 lbs. and developed 52 hp at 950 propeller revolutions per minute. Forerunner of our radial airplane engines, the great engineering achievement was designed and built by Charles M. Manly, chief assistant to Dr. Langley.

Poised upon its launching track aboard a houseboat (below, left) the *Aerodrome* took off on December 8, 1903, with Manly at the controls. Seconds later the plane hit the Potomac River tail first. Its rear wings and tail assembly had been damaged before the plane was freed of the catapult. The test trial flight of the *Aerodrome* two months earlier (below, right) also had ended in the river after the big ship snagged a guy post on the launching track. Manly was rescued unharmed on both occasions. Langley abandoned aviation and concentrated his efforts on other scientific research but recognition for his basic contributions to flight principles came to him three years later from the Aero Club of America.

FULL SIZE AERODROME SET FOR TEST ON HOUSEBOAT CATAPULT   DISASTROUS PLUNGE INTO POTOMAC RIVER ENDS EXPERIMENTS

FROM THEIR FIRST FLIGHTS AT KITTY HAWK, ORVILLE (r.) AND WILBUR (c.) WRIGHT — SHOWN WITH KING GEORGE V OF ENGLAND — WENT ON TO WIN WORLD RENOWN

Wright Brothers Era

Genius of Wilbur and Orville Wright, Santos-Dumont, Curtiss, Bleriot and valiant efforts of untold others usher in the Air Age

High among the men who have contributed importantly to the growth and progress of aviation is Herbert Hoover. As Secretary of Commerce and President of the United States he secured legislation from Congress for systematic scientific research in aircraft, its first comprehensive safety regulations and, above all, the building of America's national airways. As a private citizen, he has been an unceasing advocate of aviation.

FORMER PRES. HERBERT HOOVER

S OME 30 years ago I visited Kitty Hawk under a Congressional delegation to select a site and build there a monument to Orville and Wilbur Wright. While there the local telegraph operator showed me the original telegram of the Wright Brothers, dated December 17, 1903, to their devoted sister, saying as my note shows: "We have done it. Succeeded in four flights 31 miles an hour against the wind."

Thus began a new era for mankind. Soon, despite public skepticism, there came able men to the support of the Wrights with a vision of fulfillment of man's age-old dream of winged flight.

Year by year these far-seeing pioneers steadied the wings, flew faster, higher, longer and longer, with increasing safety. It has been a long road of brilliant invention and magnificent manufacture from the canvas bi-plane with a 12-horsepower motor of the Wrights to the all-metal monoplane and the gigantic Turbo Jets.

In the span of my generation alone there has come this magnificent revolution in transportation. With it, men's radius, their efficiency and effectiveness have been enormously increased, employment has been expanded, public health improved, and standards of living lifted. Penetration of inaccessible areas is no longer just an adventure; their resources are now added to world supplies.

The development of the military plane has contributed to the effectiveness of the commercial plane. It has become both a gigantic weapon of defense and a danger to our national safety. But the American genius which pioneered its development and its weapons can, with national will, make it our impregnable frontier.

This book records in pictorial form some of the many steps that have led us to a new era of national and international communication and exchange. It is an unfinished story of courage and achievement—unfinished, because today we are on the threshold of new achievements, with airplanes moving beyond the speed of sound and with promise to double that speed.

We now honor the pioneers of controlled flight—not only the Wrights and their determined disciples, but the pioneers who are projecting the airplane into unexplored realms of usefulness.

Herbert Hoover

The first U.S. Army pilot, Brig. Gen. Frank P. Lahm, USAF (ret.), has had a distinguished military career, holding many important posts, including that of Assistant Chief of the Army Air Corps. He brought the first international air trophy to the U.S. by winning the first Gordon Bennett Balloon Cup Race (1906), and was also the first balloon pilot (1905) and the first airship pilot (1908) in America.

O NE summer day in 1907, in my father's house in Paris, I was introduced to Wilbur and Orville Wright, the beginning of a long and treasured friendship. The world at that time had not yet come to recognize fully the significance of the Wright airplane nor the historic importance of their first flight at Kitty Hawk.

The U. S. War Department at that time was cool to the idea of the airplane's military potential, due primarily to the earlier unsuccessful efforts of Professor Langley to construct a plane that would fly. It was only through the farsighted intervention of Teddy Roosevelt — who unearthed a special $25,000 "carte blanche" presidential fund which was ten years old—that the Army was able to contract for its first airplane.

FIRST ARMY PILOT LT. FRANK LAHM (l.) AND FRIEND

The contract provided that the plane attain a speed of 40 miles per hour, carry two persons for one hour, be maneuverable in all directions, be adapted to dismantling and loading on an escort wagon—and that two Army officers be instructed to fly the machine.

In the summer of 1908 Orville Wright delivered the airplane at Ft. Meyer, Virginia, and after a few preliminary trials, gave me the thrill of having my first flight, lasting about six minutes. I had known the excitement of leaving the earth four years earlier, when I engaged in my first balloon ascent, but this introduction to powered flight was a most memorable experience.

The joy of the occasion was marred a few days later, however, when there occurred an unfortunate accident which seriously injured Orville, killed my friend and associate Lt. Tom Selfridge — and delayed even longer the Army's acceptance of the airplane.

The following summer the Wrights fulfilled the government contract, and that fall, under the able tutorship of Wilbur, Lt. F. E. Humphreys and myself were given our training and qualified as airplane pilots.

Since then the world has seen the airplane serve as a weapon of war as well as an angel of mercy; as a means of transporting men and goods speedily and safely to far destinations; and as a hope for shrinking the world so that men may live more closely together as brothers.

Fortunate are those of us who were privileged to participate in the early chapters of aviation history—and to have shared in the realization of man's dream to fly.

F. P. Lahm.

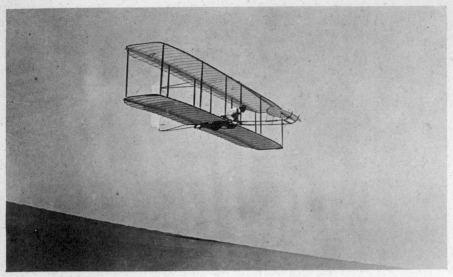

WRIGHTS' THIRD GLIDER of 1902 was flown a thousand times over the Kitty Hawk sand dunes. Wilbur lies prone in glider, above, that had a 32-foot wing spread and movable tail, forerunner of modern controls of aileron and rudder. Successful tests convinced the brothers they were ready for powered flight. All

distance gliding records were smashed by Wrights in previous year with their second glider, double the size of the first one. Experimenting with wing warping, they glided 389 feet, maintaining equilibrium in a 27-mile wind. In 1901 Orville had built a simple wind tunnel at the shop in Dayton for study of air lift.

MAN CONQUERS THE AIR

Wilbur and Orville Wright at last discover the secret of powered flight

On icy-cold, wind-swept sand dunes near Kitty Hawk, North Carolina, five men and a boy witnessed the first successful flight of an engine-driven, heavier-than-air, man-carrying flying machine. The historic date was to become world famous—December 17, 1903.

For the two young men from Dayton, Wilbur and Orville Wright, the successful trial flights that bleak morning were the happy culmination of four busy years of study, patient testing and planning. Sons of a United Brethren preacher, they were reared in a stern late-Victorian atmosphere. From Yankee pioneers who had settled in the Ohio River valleys a century before, the Wright Brothers inherited an aptitude for independent judgment, personal courage and mechanical talents of superior calibre. Two older brothers, Lorin and Reuchlin, and a younger sister, Katherine, went on to college, while Wilbur and Orville, who preferred to putter and invent gadgets, build printing-presses and bicycles, finished only a high school education.

A toy helicopter, made in Paris, awakened their curiosity about flying machines. The brothers flew kites for fun and ultimately mastered the principles and mechanics of glider-launching.

The death of the German scientist, Otto Lilienthal, killed while experimenting with gliders in 1896, was the impetus which impelled the brothers to study the problems of flight. Over a period of four years, they cautiously rejected the findings of previous investigators. In so doing they solved the key problems of flight through their development of wing-warping and the horizontal rudder; experimentation taught them

ORIGINAL WRIGHT ENGINE, a four-cylinder, water-cooled model, without sparkplugs, developed 16 hp. at 1,200 rpm, and used fuel injection system.

how to increase lift and decrease drag. Facts, tested and retested a hundred times, gave them a work-method that provided techniques resulting in developing an airplane that would fly.

First official word that the Wrights had flown successfully was contained in the message telegraphed by Orville from Kitty Hawk to Bishop Wright: "Success four flights Thursday morning all against twenty-one mile wind started from level with engine power alone average speed through air thirty-one miles longest 59 seconds inform press home Christmas." Wright's hometown papers made brief mention of the event, but the U.S. press generally ignored the happening, believing the report merely a hoax.

The years that followed Kitty Hawk were filled with further experiments to build a more air-worthy flying craft and master the techniques of flying. The Wrights' bold demonstrations removed the last vestige of skepticism regarding man's ability to fly a heavier-than-air machine.

For their great contribution to the world, the Wright Brothers enjoyed recognition and financial rewards rarely received by inventors during their lifetime. Their solid scientific methods had set free the ancient dream of human flight.

FIRST AIRPLANE "HANGAR" was at Kitty Hawk, built by the Wright Brothers in 1901 for assembling their gliders. Location was an isolated spot of sand dunes near Roanoke Island listed as having suitable winds by the U.S. Weather Bureau. Nearby were a life saving station and a government weather station.

WRIGHTS' FIRST MODEL was a heavier-than-air flying machine, a biplane weighing 750 pounds, equipped with gasoline motor and two pusher propellers. The wings, six feet apart, had a span of over 40 feet and were 6½ feet wide. The Wrights assembled plane and rebuilt their camp at Kitty Hawk in Sept., 1903.

HISTORIC FIRST FLIGHT of Wilbur and Orville Wright on December 17, 1903 was first free, controlled and sustained airplane flight. Piloted by Orville, plane is lifting off the ground as Wilbur runs alongside. Results of four trials that morning were: (1) 120 ft., 12 sec.; (2) 195 ft., 11 sec.; (3) Over 200 ft., 15 sec.; (4) 852 ft., 59 sec. Gust of wind damaged plane after fourth trial. Photograph was taken by John T. Daniels, coastguardsman, after Orville had set up camera on a tripod and focused it on a point beyond end of the track. When plane cleared the ground, Daniels snapped the shutter, and recorded the first flight for posterity.

CAMP AT KITTY HAWK was built by Wright Brothers to assemble first machine. Weather conditions and mechanical mishaps postponed first test scheduled for Sept. Test on Dec. 14 failed when plane stalled and fell after being 3½ seconds in the air. Two days were required to repair parts.

COURAGEOUS, yet conservative and austere in appearance, the Wrights are pictured in typical attire of the period. They inherited practicality of Yankee forebears.

WILBUR LIES PRONE in normal flying position of early trials. By toss of a coin Wilbur had won first turn to fly. After men from life saving station helped slide the plane up Kill Devil Hill, it took off into the wind. Rising too quickly from the hillside track, it stalled and then settled to the ground.

BIRTHPLACE of the airplane was this bicycle shop on West Third Street, Dayton, Ohio, where the brothers (Orville a bike racer), entered the bicycle manufacturing business in 1895. Here they built their first gliders and a crude wooden wind tunnel.

WIND TUNNEL, at left, proved useful in studying air lift. The first design was made by knocking the ends out of a large laundry starch box. An air blast was supplied by a screw fan at one end. Later, the sides of the wind tunnel were constructed of wood.

WRIGHT FAMILY HOME for over forty years was located at 7 Hawthorne Street in Dayton, Ohio. Here Orville and Wilbur studied all available material on flight. The house was moved and re-erected at the Ford Museum, Greenfield Village, Dearborn, Mich.

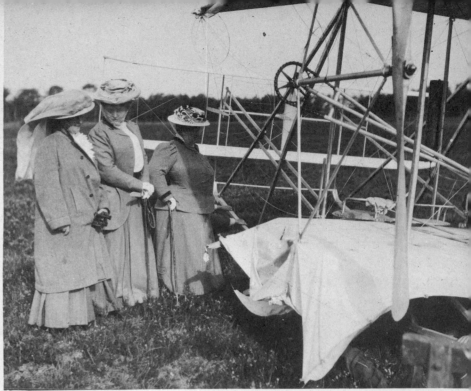

WILBUR GOES TO EUROPE

World interest in aviation had grown tremendously by 1908. The Wright Brothers clung tenaciously to their hard-won aerial prominence in the face of growing competition. During this eventful year, Wilbur devoted most of his time to making record flights. He also sold patent-rights to a French syndicate for $100,000. Orville remained in the U.S. to conclude the Army plane contract with the U.S. government. On Aug. 8, 1908, Wilbur made his first official flight over Le Mans, France. Other flights followed until, in September, he broke the world's record, flying in excess of 52 miles, remaining aloft 1 hr., 31 mins. and 25 secs. On Sept. 21, 1908 he carried a passenger. Not all flights were without accident. Wilbur's trial run on Aug. 13 over Le Mans (the Hunaudieres Race Course) resulted in damage of a wing on landing. In photo at left Wilbur explains to spectators that accident was due to improper leveling-off. American tourists visiting Paris flocked to the Le Mans trial flights. Above, Wilbur's damaged plane is being examined by three famous American ladies: (l. to r.) Mrs. Hart O. Berg, the wife of Wright's European agent, Miss Anne Morgan, and Miss Elizabeth Marbury. Orville and their sister Katherine joined Wilbur in France during December, 1908. Flying operations were transferred to Pau in Southern France where weather conditions for flying were more suitable.

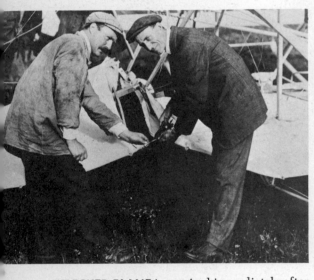

WRECKED PLANE is repaired immediately after the accident on Aug. 13, 1908 at Le Mans. Main damage was to left wing. Wilbur is assisted by Fleury, Hart O. Berg's chauffeur. Berg, as the Wrights' European agent, was contact man.

DISTINGUISHED VISITORS flocked to Le Mans to watch Wright fly for the French syndicate. Pulling on the rope are Comte de Lambert (white collar and cap); Sir Arthur Balfour (long cape); Sir Alfred Harmsworth, later Lord Northcliffe (fur coat). The French Aero Club of Sarthe awarded Wrights a bronze trophy.

FIRST WOMAN PASSENGER to be flown by the Wright Brothers was Mrs. Hart O. Berg. Taking off with Wilbur on Oct. 7, 1908, the courageous Mrs. Berg tied her skirt securely to her ankles with string cord.

TEST FLYING FOR VISITING ROYALTY and government observers and giving flight instruction occupied Wilbur during 1908. To Pau, in France, came England's King Edward VII, Dowager Queen Margherita of Italy, and King Alfonso XIII of Spain (light suit). At left, royalty had deserted their carriages to seek more advantageous viewing positions. Flying with Wilbur is student Paul Tissandier, his French protegé.

WILBUR POSES for a photographer in Auvours woods, adjacent to the racing course at Le Mans, 1908. He concluded an eventful year by winning the prized Michelin Trophy, "The Triumph of Aviation."

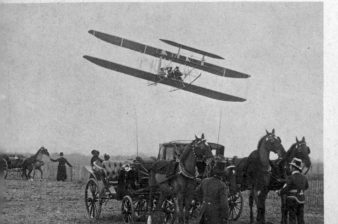

ORVILLE AT FORT MYER

Recognition of the Wright Brothers in the United States came slowly. In December, 1907, the U.S. Signal Corps drew up specifications for an airplane and invited bids. The Wright Brothers submitted a bid for a biplane at $25,000. It was accepted, and while Wilbur was in Europe, Orville built the plane and in the fall of 1908 transported it to Ft. Myer, Va. to make a series of demonstration flights for the government. Photo above shows plane being delivered to Ft. Myer in an Army escort wagon. On September 9, 1908, after many test runs (right), he established three world endurance records. His best flight that day was 1 hour, 2 minutes and 15 seconds in which he circled the drill ground 55 times. Toward dusk, Orville took up Army Lt. Frank P. Lahm in a flight that lasted 6 minutes, 24 seconds. Lahm, himself a famed balloonist, was first air passenger in America in what became the first night flight.

FIRST AIRPLANE FATALITY occurred Sept. 17, 1908 when Orville, in one of the Army trial runs (left) took up Lt. Thomas E. Selfridge, designer of planes with Glenn Curtiss. At height of 125 ft. trouble developed and Orville glided plane down to 50 ft. Then it suddenly fell out of control. Selfridge was killed and Orville, suffering a fractured thigh and broken ribs, flew no more that year. In center photo are Lt. Selfridge and Dr. Alexander Graham Bell, air enthusiast and inventor of the telephone. In the wreck of the airplane (right) Orville lies on the ground in the group to the right. Selfridge is lying under the wreckage at center.

"PIGS MIGHT FLY," an old adage used by debunkers of flight, was contradicted in 1909 by J.T.C. Moore-Brabazon (later Lord Brabazon of Tara). Built from the Wright design by the Short Brothers and likewise launched from a rail, his machine won him the *Daily Mail* prize for first circular flight of one mile made by a British aviator in all-British machine. He also made year's longest flight, 18 miles.

HISTORIC GROUP met at the Short factory in 1908 to negotiate manufacture of Wright airplanes in England. Later, Short Bros. & Harland, Ltd., became a key war and peacetime producer of British aircraft. Seated (l. to r.) J.T.C. Moore-Brabazon, Wilbur, Orville, C.S. Rolls. Standing—Oswald, Horace and Eustace Short, Frank McLean, Griffiths Brewer, Hedges Butler, Dr. Lockyear, unknown.

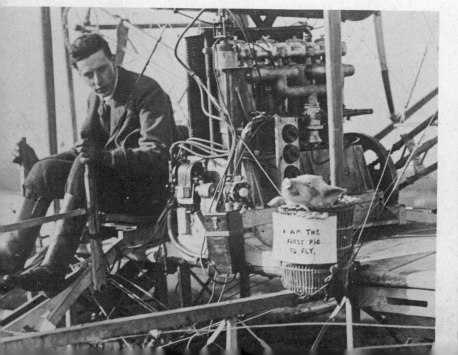

WRIGHT BROTHERS' BID of $25,000 for delivery of an airplane was accepted by the U.S. Signal Corps in February, 1908. In December, when Orville (above, l.) was recovering from his Ft. Myer injuries, he and his sister Katherine joined Wilbur (portrait left) in France where his demonstrations had brought honors to the brothers from many countries and had melted remaining European skepticism, and American indifference. Notified the U.S. Army would expect final tests by mid-June, they sailed for home.

DAYTON HOMECOMING became a two-day tumultuous celebration (June 17-18, 1909) with local business being suspended. Gov. Judson Harmon (left) presents the Wrights with State of Ohio Gold Medal. Behind him sit Wilbur, Orville, Bishop Wright who delivered the invocation, and elder brothers, Reuchin and Lorin. Official U.S. recognition occurred at White House, June 11, when President Taft (above, c.) awarded them medal of the Aero Club of America. In February, 1910, Smithsonian Institution awarded Langley medal to the Wright Brothers, though later their relations with the museum became strained.

CROWN PRINCE of Germany (second from r.) flew with Orville on Oct. 2 when he and Katherine visited Berlin in the early fall of 1909. Orville's plan was to train pilots for the newly-organized German Wright Co. While there, he established new record of 1 hour, 35 minutes, and 47 seconds in the air.

WILBUR DRESSED FOR FLYING in a conservative business suit characterized the Wrights. They accounted for every penny invested in their experiments. Total cost of first *Flyer* was less than $1000. Wilbur kneels at right with friend and early Wright pilot, Frank T. Coffyn, to adjust kite he gave Coffyn's son at Bayside, New Jersey.

Die vom „BERLINER LOKAL-ANZEIGER" veranstalteten Flugvorführungen
Orville Wrights in BERLIN

Kronprinzessin   Hauptmann Hildebrandt   Kronprinz
Orville Wright   Miss Katherine Wright

FIRST ARMY PLANE

Resuming government tests that had been interrupted by the 1908 accident, Orville made first of a series of preliminary flights (left) at Ft. Myer, June 28, 1909. Official Washington poured into the army base to observe the demonstrations, together with Wilbur (doing no flying), Katherine and their Dayton mechanic, Charles Taylor. Standing by the test plane are (l. to r.) Lt. Ben D. Foulois, Wilbur, Lt. Frank P. Lahm, Orville. Fulfilling Army requirements on July 27, Orville broke record for two-man flight, with Lahm as passenger. Time in air was 1 hr., 12 min., 40 sec. On first cross-country flight, July 30, he made speed test with Foulois over a ten mile course, averaging 42.5 miles per hour.

TRAINING ARMY OFFICERS in the art of piloting an airplane was the job of the Wright Brothers, themselves skillful pilots. Among the Army pioneers who flew during the final tests at Ft. Myer were Lt. Ben D. Foulois (later Major General and Army Air Services chief) at left with Orville, and Lt. Frank P. Lahm (right, standing in front of Wilbur). In open hangar at Ft. Myer, Orville (center, l.) is seen with soldier and an unidentified man. Boy is Charles P. Taft, son of the president and brother of Robert A. Taft. Wrights were paid $25,000 for plane plus $5,000 bonus for 2.5 mph speed over Army's 40 mph specifications.

OVER THE HUDSON RIVER from Governors Island to Grant's Tomb and return at an altitude of 200 ft. (left), was the course of Wilbur's dramatic flight on October 4, 1909, during New York City's Hudson-Fulton Celebration. On September 29 he had flown from Governors Island drill field around Statue of Liberty on Bedloe's Island and back.

BEGINNING of the air age brought growing acceptance by governments and the public, both in U.S. and in Europe. The Wrights' *Twentieth Century Flyer* triumphantly beats a passenger train. Such races dramatized man's speed in the air, presaged still distant era of commercial aviation.

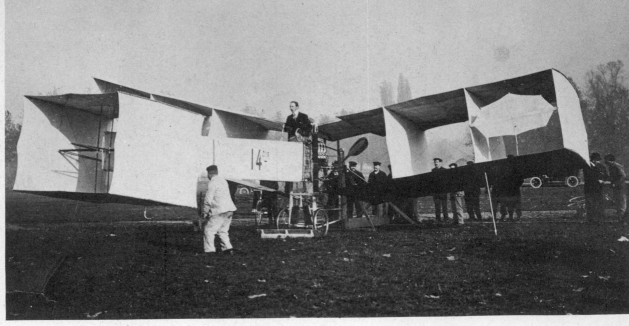

PROPHET OF FLIGHT and controversial pioneer, Alberto Santos-Dumont of Brazil made first airplane flight in Europe. His development of the motorized airship and his exploits with heavier-than-air flying machines assured him a leading place in aeronautical history. Throughout Latin America, Santos-Dumont's popularity surpasses that of the Wright Brothers. From 1898 Paris was witness to his daring flights in airships. In Nov. 1906, he flew his "aeromobile," which he called *14 Bis* (above). It was a Hargrave box-kite airplane with an 8-cylinder motor. Dumont flew it tail first, 685 feet in 21 secs., 10 feet off the ground.

FRANCE BLAZES AIR TRAILS

Santos-Dumont, Farman and Voisin brothers discover new secrets of flight

Alberto Santos-Dumont from Brazil was a courageous pioneer whose name pressed hard on the heels of the Wrights in terms of his aerial accomplishments both with lighter-than-air and with heavier-than-air flying machines. Throughout Latin America his name shines with rare distinction and for years his supporters have valiantly maintained that Santos-Dumont, and not the Wright Brothers, was the first to fly. They assert that the Wrights catapulted themselves into the air, whereas Santos-Dumont rose from the ground by the sole power of a motor.

Undoubtedly there will continue to be a residue of doubt in the minds of some students of aeronautical history as to whom the laurels belong. Surely his sheer flying skill, inventive capacity, continued willingness to personally assume the costs of all his experiments and the qualities of his showmanship entitle Santos-Dumont to world-wide acclamation. Born of great wealth on a Brazilian coffee plantation in 1873, he went to Paris when he was 18 to investigate the inventions of Henri Giffard and the steerable balloon. In 1897 he made his first flight as a passenger in a balloon. Remaining in Paris he began designing motorized balloons.

His early flights often ended in disaster and the courageous, slight of build, sportsman balloonist miraculously escaped death many times. On one occasion when he was fast falling to certain death in his collapsing balloon, he called to some children playing with kites to catch his guide rope. They did as he directed, ran against the wind with the balloon and eased him down to a safe landing. He enthusiastically continued his experiments. It was he who endowed the balloon with "dirigibility." Fitting a gasoline motor

TESTING PROPELLERS of his new aquaplane developed in 1907, Santos-Dumont is the focal point of people's interest on the bank of Seine River in Paris.

and a direct drive airscrew to a gondola swung under a cylindrical gas bag, he was able to fly with speed and direction. In his "little runabout" Santos-Dumont No. 9, he flew about Paris and steered his balloon at tree top level down the Champs Elysees to his home, on June 23, 1903.

From his success in lighter-than-air flight, this "aerostatic sportsman" turned to the designing of a motorized glider that first flew after being released from a dirigible. Subsequently, Santos-Dumont designed and built airplanes that were highly maneuverable, performed reliably in distance flight and maintained constant speed. On Oct. 23, 1906, he made the first airplane flight in Europe. Flying nearly 200 ft. at 25 mph, he won the Archdeacon prize of 3,000 francs offered to the first to fly 25 meters (82 ft.). Later that year he held the official world's record for his flight of 690 ft. in 21-1/5 seconds. In 1909 he built his tiny *Demoiselle* (see picture below) in which he made cross-country flights at speeds phenomenal for that time.

A man of generous instincts, Santos-Dumont relinquished his patent rights on the *Demoiselle*, supplying his designs to anyone interested and thus ended his active flying days. The "Demoiselle" was later placed in the Aeronautical Museum at Chalais-Meudon, near Paris, France.

THE "DEMOISELLE" (Young Lady) and Santos-Dumont are seen in his Paris workshop. This miniature airplane had a wing surface of only 102 sq. feet. Designed for his personal use and sporting pleasure, the machine was Dumont's favorite. On Sept. 13, 1909, he made a 5-mile flight in 12 minutes at a speed of 25 mph from St. Cyr to Buc, to win a bet of $200 made with a friend. Dumont transported his *Demoiselle* to the airfield by lashing it onto a special bed at the rear of his car. The entire plane, equipped with a 24-hp engine, weighed approximately 200 pounds. It gained reputation for its stability as well as speed.

HENRI FARMAN'S ACHIEVEMENTS honored French aviation though he was an Englishman. Originally an artist and champion bicycle rider and race car driver, his flying skill and endurance made him world famous. His first great aerial feat was in 1907 when he flew 770 meters at a speed greater than 50 mph.

CROSSING THE FINISH LINE to win the Deutsch-Archdeacon Prize, Farman was the first to fly a kilometer (.621 miles). The French Aero Club witnessed flight January 13, 1908 on the Army drill field at Issy. Farman flew his Voisin biplane to the 500 meter mark, circled and returned, completing the kilometer.

GABRIEL AND HENRI VOISIN began their fraternal partnership as glider builders before 1903. Influenced by Santos-Dumont, they became the first designers and manufacturers of airplanes in France, supplying pioneers like Farman and Bleriot with biplanes, triplanes, and gliders.

FARMAN FLEW CROSS-COUNTRY from Chalons to Rheims, France, in October, 1908, a flight of 20 minutes. Above, his Voisin biplane skirts the church of a village outside Rheims. Next year Farman broke world's record in the Grand Prix de Champagne at the Rheims international aviation meet, week of Aug. 22, 1909. He receives congratulations (r.) from Madame Sommer whose husband was Farman's racing competitor. In Oct., Farman, Sommer and other French fliers competed in England.

FRENCH PRODUCTION of airplanes under enterprising Voisins paced the rest of the world. Above is a 1908 picture of their factory. Leon Delagrange, once a sculptor, was the first to demonstrate the Voisin biplane in 1907. His friendly rival, Henri Farman also promoted Voisin airplanes and influenced the brothers to replace skids formerly used on under-carriage of their machines with wheels.

"GNOME" ENGINES were used in Voisin planes. Noted for their air-cooling system and whirling cylinders, they produced 50 horsepower.

BLERIOT'S FOLLY was this "contraption" built about 1904 in collaboration with Gabriel Voisin. Combining the structure of the aquaplane and a wind tunnel, it was towed by fast motor boat, nearly drowned Voisin in one test.

WINDWAGON was an early (1904) experiment of motorcycle enthusiast Glenn H. Curtiss, of Hammondsport, N.Y. His ingenuity and daring attracted the eye of telephone inventor Alexander Graham Bell, about to embark on extensive experiments in aeronautics.

AERIAL EXPERIMENT ASSOCIATION, organized in 1907 by Bell to explore problems of flight, included four promising young men, each to design an airplane. Shown at A. E. A.'s Headquarters, Hammondsport, are (l. to r.) F.W. ("Casey") Baldwin, Lt. T.E. Selfridge, G.H. Curtiss, Bell, J.A.D. McCurdy. Pioneer aviator Augustus Post (r.) was not member.

WRIGHTS GET COMPETITION

Motorcycle champion Glenn Curtiss takes to the air—and soars into history

Great is the name of Glenn Hammond Curtiss in the story of the development of the air age in America. He was born in Hammondsport, N.Y. on May 31, 1878, and early displayed a natural bent for mathematics. The pattern of his life began to emerge at the age of 19 when he started to win bicycle races around his home town. He soon experimented with many light, air-cooled engines and turned to motorcycles. By 1904 Glenn Curtiss had gained fame, setting a cycle speed record which stood for several years although frequently contested.

Two years before, the famous balloonist Thomas Baldwin had heard of Glenn Curtiss' remarkable light-weight engines. He approached Curtiss with the thought of using one of these motors to power an airship which the aeronaut was planning to construct. This led to a collaboration between the two men that climaxed in the sale of a Curtiss-powered airship to the U.S. Army—America's first military airship (1905).

With this success Glenn Curtiss gave further thought to aeronautics. When he met the noted telephone inventor, Alexander Graham Bell, it took little persuasion to enlist him in the *Aerial Experiment Association* which Dr. Bell was then organizing (1907).

With $25,000 capital, supplied by Mrs. Bell, the A.E.A. commenced operations at the inventor's home at Baddeck, Nova Scotia. The organization consisted of Dr. Bell, chairman, and Glenn Curtiss, director of experiments, together with three other ambitious young men: Lt. Thomas E. Selfridge, U.S. Army, secretary; Frederick W. (Casey) Baldwin, engineer; J.A.D. McCurdy, assistant engineer.

Not long after experiments began at Nova Scotia, Curtiss interested the group in moving their operations to his home town of Hammondsport, N.Y. where all further research was carried on. After successful glider tests, they enthusiastically turned to the construction of powered aircraft.

Four airplanes were built, each the project of one of Bell's associates. The third, Curtiss' *June Bug*, whimsically named for the month of its completion, was the most successful of the lot. In 1908 it won the first aviation prize to be awarded in America, the *Scientific American* Trophy. The fourth A.E.A. craft, McCurdy's

Silver Dart, was also very satisfactory, and when the group disbanded, McCurdy returned with it to Dr. Bell's home at Nova Scotia, where he continued independent experiments.

After the Association had dissolved, Glenn Curtiss, accustomed to working with others, formed a partnership with A.M. Herring, who had been an interested observer of the A.E.A.'s endeavors. Herring had been Octave Chanute's assistant back in the nineties and claimed to have flown in 1898 a large biplane model, powered by a compressed air engine. The Herring-Curtiss Co. was the first airplane manufacturing firm in the U.S., and reportedly had facilities to produce 100 aircraft annually. Under this arrangement, the *Gold Bug* was built, as well as the famous *Golden Flyer* which won the first international air race at Rheims, France (Aug., 1909).

The partnership lasted only a few months, however, and early in 1910 the Glenn H. Curtiss Manufacturing Co., shortly to be renamed the Curtiss Aeroplane Co., came into being, taking over the assets and facilities of the former firm. The good will was Curtiss' in his own right; he was to keep it the rest of his life.

"RED WING," first powered airplane of the Association, was Selfridge's project. On March 12, 1908, *Aerodrome No. 1*, as it was officially called, was tested in his absence by Baldwin. It proved unmanageable, and was wrecked after an erratic flight of 319 feet. Though a failure, *Red Wing* became pattern for later A.E.A. successes.

"AERODROME NO. 2" or the *White Wing*, was "Casey" Baldwin's contribution to the Association, and first equipped with ailerons. With Baldwin piloting, it flew a distance of 93 yds. on May 18, 1908. In this machine, Glenn Curtiss (in center foreground) made his first flight four days later.

TETRAHEDRAL KITE of 1909 was the final culmination of A. G. Bell's ideas. Though it lifted a man, this machine saw no further development. It was unlikely to reach any noteworthy speed with so much drag. Chief value of Bell's kites was encouragement given A.E.A. men by success of earlier version (1907).

CURTISS' TRIUMPH came with his design for the Association of *Drome No. 3*, the *June Bug*. It flew so well that the group decided to try for the *Scientific American* Trophy to be awarded for the first machine to fly one km officially observed. Up to that time no American airplane had ever flown before the public.

THE "JUNE BUG," with designer Curtiss as pilot, won the *Scientific American* Cup on July 4, 1908. The flight of slightly less than a mile, completed in about 1¾ min., exceeded the requirements and amazed everyone present, even the official observers.

SECRET of the *June Bug's* success, more than any other single factor, was the air-cooled, V-8, lightweight Curtiss engine. Developing about 40 hp, it had been evolved from the remarkable engines of the inventor's motorcycle days.

"SILVER DART" was the name for *Drome No. 4*, McCurdy's effort for the A.E.A. First flown on Dec. 12, 1908, it performed perfectly and eventually completed over 200 successful flights. The *Silver Dart* concluded the Association's experiments; the group soon disbanded.

UNLIKE "LONE WOLF" Wright Brothers, Curtiss always worked as a member of a team, albeit usually the head. Typical of Glenn Hammond Curtiss ("G.H." to his associates) is this picture of him in the center of his group. When the A.E.A. was dissolved, he immediately entered into a partnership with A. M. Herring, another early experimenter. Herring-Curtiss Co. became the first aircraft factory in the U.S. First product was the biplane *Gold Bug* (above, with Curtiss at controls), prototype of Curtiss machines for several years. When it was sold for profit, the Wrights claimed Curtiss' ailerons infringed upon their basic patents.

"GOLD BUG," first Herring-Curtiss product, was built for the Aeronautical Society of New York. It performed so well that before its transfer to the Society, Curtiss used it to win the second *Scientific American* contest, passing the 25-km requirement on July 17, 1909. Shortly thereafter, the machine was delivered to the New York group, Curtiss instructing member G.F. Willard in its operation.

INFLUENCE of the *Gold Bug's* design can be seen in this later Curtiss biplane, flying over the frozen surface of Lake Keuka, about January of 1910. Soundness of the basic configuration is also demonstrated by the *Pfitzner* monoplane (on the ice) which was constructed by Curtiss and followed the same ideas. The latter machine evaded Wright patent with sliding wing tips for varying wing area.

SEAPLANE IDEA had begun to intrigue Curtiss about the time the A.E.A. was breaking up. For his first attempt, he added crude pontoons to the old *June Bug*, renaming it the *Loon*. During November, 1908, many efforts were made to fly the *Loon* off the surface of Lake Keuka, N.Y. Poor float design and insufficient power doomed experiment, but he never gave up hope of flying a hydroplane.

LONG DISTANCE FLIGHT, May 31, 1910, from Albany to New York City, won for Glenn Curtiss the *New York World* prize of $10,000. Above, "G. H." is seen leaving Poughkeepsie, his first stop on the 142½ mile flight, completed in 2 hr., 50 min. flying time. With this achievement Curtiss also won the *Scientific American* Cup for third time, giving him permanent possession of coveted trophy.

CURTISS FLIERS gave the Wright team considerable competition. Outstanding among them was Charles K. Hamilton (above), who made the first long cross-country flight in America, June 13, 1910. The 149½-mile trip, New York to Philadelphia and return, took Hamilton 3 hr., 27 min. flying time, winning the $10,000 prize of the *New York Times* and *Philadelphia Ledger*. Other famous Curtiss

pilots included Bud Mars (right), one of the first trained by Curtiss. With Mars at the old Mineola flying field, N. Y., first airport in the U.S., are (l. to r.) Mrs. Mars, Mrs. Glenn Curtiss, and Mrs. Eugene Ely, whose husband broke into headlines with an abortive attempt to fly from Chicago to New York on October 9, 1910. Ely was to make history in November with his "aircraft carrier" tests.

SEAPLANE SUCCESS was finally achieved by Glenn Curtiss on Jan. 26, 1911, at San Diego, Calif. This first hydroplane flight in the U. S. (first in the world was by H. Fabre in France, March 28, 1910) climaxed many tries following the failure of the *Loon* two years before. "G. H." continued to develop the hydroplane (improved model above) which was a big factor in convincing the U. S. Navy of the practicability of aircraft. Even though three officers had been been assigned to Curtiss' flying class at Hammondsport, the Navy's skepticism persisted. Above at Curtiss' school (1910) are (l. to r.): Godet, Russel, Doherty, Curtiss, Havens, Lt. McClasky, USMC, Lt. Beck, USA, Lt. Towers, USN, Lt. Ellyson, USN and Dixon. Lt. Beck was being trained to operate Curtiss type airplanes for the Army.

NAVY'S FIRST AIRPLANE was Curtiss *Triad* amphibian. Originally delivered (July, 1911) as a seaplane, the craft was named *Triad* (land, sea, and air) upon subsequent addition of wheels. At Lake Keuka, N.Y., are seen Glenn Curtiss at the controls, and Navy Lieut. Ellyson, riding as passenger. Many of the high Naval officers, among them Rear Admiral Richard Wainwright, stubbornly resisted the creation of an aviation service, but others were more far sighted, notably Captain Washington Irving Chambers and Rear Admiral William W. Kimball, and they enjoyed the support of Admiral George Dewey, of Manila fame, who, as President of the General Board of the Navy, was of immeasurable assistance.

CURTISS—FATHER OF NAVAL AVIATION

Ever since the *Loon* fiasco in 1908, Glenn Curtiss had been experimenting with various arrangements of floats and hydro-skis, determined to solve the problem of operating aircraft off the surface of water. Finally hitting on the proper design for a seaplane, he made the first such take-off on January 26, 1911.

"G. H." soon became the world's outstanding expert on seaplanes. The formerly apathetic U. S. Navy was forced to take notice, and the first Navy airplane was finally ordered. Delivered in July, 1911, it was a Curtiss seaplane, for by this time the Herring-Curtiss Co. had become simply the Curtiss Aeroplane Co.

A Navy aviation service gradually came into being, in spite of continued high-level opposition. This was mainly due to the demonstrations of Glenn Curtiss and the untiring efforts of Captain Washington Irving Chambers, U.S.N., who was a strong advocate from the start.

NAVY PILOTS Nos. 1 and 3 were Lts. Theodore Ellyson (l.) and John Towers, eventually Chief of the Bureau of Aeronautics, shown here in a Curtiss biplane at Hammondsport flying school. Pilot No. 2 was Ensign Charles Pousland. In 1911 U.S. Naval Aviation consisted in total of only three airplanes.

AIRCRAFT CARRIERS were born on Nov. 14, 1910, when Curtiss pilot Eugene Ely became the first man to fly an airplane off the deck of a ship. The cruiser *Birmingham,* anchored at Hampton Roads, was equipped with a sloping 28x83 foot platform for this trial. Two months later (Jan. 18, 1911) Ely bested his own performance by taking off from the shore at San Francisco and landing on the cruiser *Pennsylvania.* After a short visit, he flew back to shore. (Ely is seen above, about to leave). For this test, cables were stretched across the flight deck, with sandbags at either end. Cables engaged a hook under the plane, bringing it to a stop.

FLYING VISIT to the *Pennsylvania* by Glenn Curtiss demonstrated to the still doubtful Navy that aircraft and fleet could combine operations. He is seen being hoisted aboard after shore-to-ship flight in San Diego Bay, Feb. 17, 1911. Capt. Charles F. Pond, the cruiser's skipper, stands by (c.) to greet the flier.

A KISS FOR THE CONQUEROR was bestowed by proud Madame Bleriot upon the cheek of her husband upon his return to France following his history-making flight across the English Channel (see text). In the four days which followed his landing at Dover, Bleriot's type XI monoplane was viewed with awe by more than 120,000 people after it had been transported to London by rail car for exhibit.

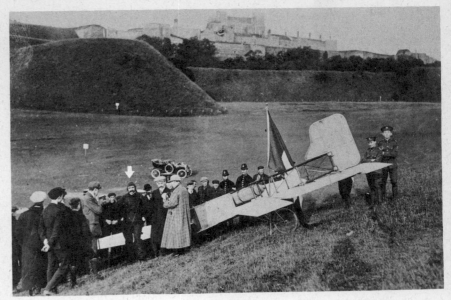

BRUISED BUT HAPPY, Louis Bleriot landed on British soil at 5:20 a.m., Sunday morning, July 25, 1909, the first man to conquer the English Channel by air. He had flown 25 miles over water without guide or compass. Sighting the white cliffs of England and adrift on a southwest wind, Bleriot had followed some boats to Dover and landed on a meadow behind Dover Castle. Friends met him.

BLERIOT FLIES CHANNEL

On July 25, 1909, the world was suddenly awakened to the airplane's promise of becoming more than a mechanical toy. Louis Bleriot of France had flown the English Channel from Calais to Dover, 25 miles, in 37 minutes.

No one could have been more deserving of the ensuing glory than this plucky Frenchman. Bleriot had begun to experiment with aviation as early as 1901 and by 1906 he was as well-known for his crashes as he was for the biplanes he built and tried so vainly to get into the air. Then, in July 1906, he flew successfully in his Bleriot VI tandem monoplane.

Adhering to this configuration, Bleriot succeeded in developing the monoplane further than any other experimenter. But real success came when he won the *Prix de Voyage* for a flight from Etamps to Orleans.

He then set out to win the London *Daily Mail* prize of $5,000 for the first flight across the English Channel. At Calais, popular flier Hubert Latham was also readying for the same flight. Bad weather delayed them all, but early in the morning of July 25, a sleepless Bleriot saw his chance, warmed up his monoplane and was well on his way to the shores of England, despite bandaged injuries from a recent crash, while his rivals slept.

ON THE WAY across the Channel, Bleriot had a number of difficulties: one foot was in bandages from a recent accident and hurt constantly; out of sight of land, he soon lost his bearings; back on course later, his small, three-cylinder engine threatened to overheat. Showers cooled it but dangerously cut visibility.

EARLIER SUCCESS of Louis Bleriot included one of his first monoplanes (top), a canard, or tail-first, type of craft amazingly streamlined for the period. Above, Bleriot is airborne on a cross-country flight totaling 41.2 km over France, with three landings (October 31, 1908). His trial and error crashes finally paid off.

MAGNIFICENT FAILURES were Hubert Latham's attempts at Channel fame. On July 19, 1909, Latham took off from Sangatte, France, in his graceful *Antoinette* monoplane, heading for England. About two miles out, his engine failed and Latham ended in the water. Rescued, the undaunted flier set out again on July 27, arrived within one mile of the Dover cliffs and was once more forced down.

SCULPTOR Leon Delagrange was one of the great French pioneer fliers. A contemporary of the famous Henri Farman, he learned to fly at the same time (1907-08) in a Voisin biplane. After practicing at Issy, the two began exhibition flying. In Turin, Italy, Delagrange took a friend for a ride, and made history, for Mme. Theresa Peltier thus became the first woman plane-passenger (July 8, 1908).

ANOTHER FRENCH pioneer was Robert Esnault-Pelterie whose monoplane designs threatened to rival those of Bleriot. His early (1907) type (above) is interesting for its variable incidence wing and central landing gear with small outboard wheels. Modified, these features have been tested on jets.

ENGLISH pioneers were also busy. One of the foremost was Col. S.F. Cody, transplanted American, whose biplane was the largest craft of its kind in the period 1909-10.

AVROPLANE of A. V. Roe was the first to fly in England (June 8, 1908). The world's first triplane, it used its three wings in an effort to gain more lifting area. After many crashes and mishaps, Roe mastered the design, and his aircraft later became famous in combat in both World Wars.

UGLY DUCKLING of Gastambide-Mengin Co., Paris, eventually developed into the graceful *Antoinette* monoplane. The *Antoinette* motor, a superb V-8 engine which G-M had manufactured for several years, had been employed by Santos-Dumont, Farman, Delagrange, and Bleriot in their first flights, produced for their own airplanes. The first, above, designed by Levavasseur (walking toward camera), was fairly airworthy. Two more were built that year (1908), the last one proving quite successful. Called *Antoinette III,* the first to use that name, it ultimately evolved into a famous type of aircraft used for record-breaking flights.

HUBERT LATHAM, popular after his gallant Channel attempts, was one of the greats who assembled at Rheims, France, for the first international air meet (Aug. 22-29, 1909). Left, he is talking to Mlle. Antoinette Gastambide, after whom his airplane and engine were named. Latham won first prize for altitude (154 meters) and placed second in the *Grand Prix de Champagne* for duration. Pictures show (top) Latham's *Antoinette* monoplane, streamlined and efficient, which he flew exclusively. Below is the pilot's seat, then referred to as "driver's seat," as well as the steam radiators, controls, and typical triangular fuselage.

FIRST INTERNATIONAL MEET

World's great airmen assemble at Rheims to compete for $37,000 in prizes

Climax of the flying year 1909 was the international aero meet at Rheims, France, the world's first aviation competition. When it was announced, fliers throughout Europe began to prepare their crafts for the event. Louis Bleriot, with an eye for the newly-established James Gordon Bennett speed trophy, went to work on a new racer using the E.N.V. engine of 80 hp, an unheard-of force at that time. Others were tuning their airplanes for peak performance. Among the 30 contesting entrants were aviation's top names.

When he learned that there was no American entry, the indomitable Glenn Curtiss petitioned the Aero Club of America to name him its representative in the speed race. With July nearly over and the meet scheduled for Aug. 22, Curtiss had the problem of constructing a plane. In a few weeks he designed and built both airframe and engine, and sailed for Europe, arriving just in time to qualify for the Bennett and other contests which were also scheduled.

Events began on Saturday, the 22nd, when, in spite of inclement weather and an abundance of mud on the field, a huge crowd gathered. They were to gasp at 12 machines flying at once. Even President Fallieres of France came to see records broken, and was not disappointed.

On Sunday, Curtiss set a new speed record for 10 km; Tuesday, Bleriot broke this mark. The

HORSEPOWER, provided by a French trooper's mount, is used to bring Bleriot's *No. 24* monoplane to the starting line at Rheims international meet.

following day Latham established a duration record, only to lose it to Henri Farman, who won the duration prize for his long flight of Thursday, Aug. 27. On the same day, Latham flew to a height of 508 feet, receiving the altitude award. The meet continued Friday with the first James Gordon Bennett speed classic, won by Curtiss. Bleriot then broke all records for speed over a 10 km course, reaching the "tremendous velocity" of 48 mph. On the last day, Farman won a prize for carrying two passengers, and Curtiss set a speed mark for the 30 km course.

The impetus given to flying by the Rheims meet was incalculable, second only to Bleriot's Channel flight. The seemingly insignificant records were unbelievable at the time, and the reliability demonstrated by most of the machines dispelled many of the public's fears and misconceptions about flight. Fortunately, there were no fatalities to mar this good impression.

OBSERVER at Rheims was airplane designer M. Levavasseur, talking to Hubert Latham. The latter's doctors had given him one year to live. He took up flying to live it fully. Several years later, then a famous flier, Latham was killed while hunting rhinoceros on a safari in Africa.

SPEED PRIZE, the *Coupe Internationale d' Aviation,* better known as the James Gordon Bennett Trophy, was offered for top speed over a 20-km course. Gift of James Gordon Bennett (right, in derby), *New York Herald* publisher, the prize created keen interest in the meet. The world's best fliers were drawn to Rheims to compete there for the trophy.

BENNETT CONTEST was the climax of the great air meet. Gallic touch was added by a French army bugler (left), who signaled the start of each heat. The race finally narrowed down to a duel between Louis Bleriot, France, and Glenn Curtiss, U.S. The French aviator had a special airplane for the event, with an 80-hp V-8 engine, the most powerful at Rheims. He blazed around the 20-km course in 15 min., 56 sec., but was six seconds too slow to equal Curtiss' record. The U.S. took the prize. The next day, having lost the Bennett trophy, Bleriot flew his powerful monoplane to a new speed mark, but lost control and crashed. Bursting into flames when it hit the ground, the monoplane was destroyed. The aviator was fortunate in escaping alive. At the right, he and Mme. Bleriot are shown after the accident which nearly ended his career.

AMAZING FEATS astounded the crowds at Rheims. The public had been accustomed to aerial exhibitions where, after considerable flipping of propellers and other preliminaries, an airplane would limp into the air, weather permitting, and fly unsteadily around a small field. Never before had there been performances like these. There was Glenn Curtiss of America (left), whose *Golden* *Flyer* virtually "flew off the drawing board" to the Bennett trophy victory. There were individual contests between the leading airmen, like the race (center) between Louis Paulhan and the victor, M. Tissandier (leading). Low flying, wing-dipping exhibitions brought the spectators to their feet cheering. Best single performance was given by Lefebvre (r.), whose recklessness astonished crowd.

NOT ONLY RECORDS were shattered at Rheims. Bleriot's flaming plane is seen top of page, and many others, like Louis Paulhan's (right) and Henry Fournier's (No. 33 in starting line-up of Voisin planes, below) also crashed. Accidents usually occurred because pilots pushed machines beyond their capabilities. However, no one was seriously hurt. Most of the wrecked planes were of the Voisin design, indicating the inherent weakness of that type. They were improved soon after the meet. Evidence of rapidly growing acceptance of flying may be noted as Renard airship, sailing over the Rheims field (left), hardly draws a glance from the crowd. Three years before, this would have been considered a thrilling spectacle.

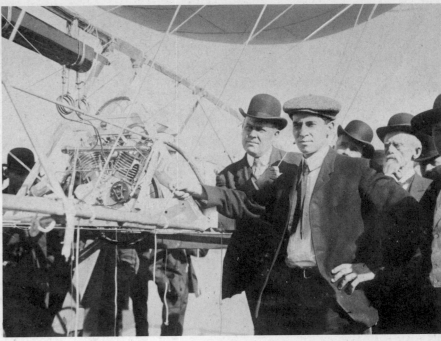

ASTRIDE CATWALK FRAME of an early Baldwin dirigible, Lincoln Beachey, daredevil aeronaut of San Francisco, began his career of exhibition flying at the age of 17 at the Lewis and Clark Exposition in 1905. The following year Beachey joined Knabenshue's troupe of exhibition fliers and became a headliner when he made the first flight around the Washington Monument, June 13, 1906. Curtiss'

motorcycle engine (right) powered America's first dirigible, 52-foot *California Arrow*, built by Captain Thomas S. Baldwin (in derby) of California, and tested by Roy Knabenshue (in cap), August 3, 1904 at Oakland. The first U.S. Army airship was a 96-foot Baldwin with a 20-hp Curtiss engine. The purchase price of $10,000 was paid after it was tested at Fort Myer, Virginia on August 18, 1908.

SKY CRUISERS
Airships herald controlled flight

The airship was the sequel to the balloon in aeronautical history. Free balloons added immeasurably to the science of flight but, being uncontrolled, they were at the mercy of the wind. Experimental research for power to direct their course inspired a variety of methods. First known attempt (1865) was by Hanlein of Germany who used a coal gas combustion engine to power his semi-rigid, elongated balloon. Another proposed manpower, 8 men on a windlass in a boat-shaped balloon car with a propeller at the bow. Benzine power, pedal power, battery-driven electric power, all were tried with some success. The gasoline engine, miracle development that accelerated airplane achievements, also was the answer balloonists were seeking. With this engine lighter-than-air craft could fly against the wind in long sustained, controlled flight. Dirigible balloons became a familiar sight in France and Germany. America's first, Baldwin's *California Arrow*, took to the sky August 3, 1904, and started a period of daring aerial exhibitions and contests. Intrepid fliers, many of whom later became the barnstorming plane pilots of the early flying circuses, rode or ran the narrow catwalk below the aerostat to direct the craft's course. Teenage boys competed with seasoned pilots even to the extent of building their own "balloon sausages". Early ambitious voyages to the North Pole and across the Atlantic were attempted. Many of these expeditions ended in mishaps, but, nonetheless, they added to the rapidly growing general knowledge of aerodynamics.

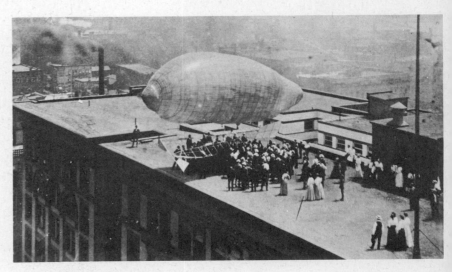

YOUNGEST AMERICAN AERONAUT Cromwell Dixon of Seattle, Washington, and his mother (top photo) formed a team that brought fame to the skilled youth who was only 14 when he demonstrated his airship at America's first air meet at St. Louis, Mo. in 1907. For four years Dixon and his mother, who sewed the 25-foot balloon, travelled the West, exhibiting the cycle airship *Moon* (bottom).

ROOF-TOP LANDING of dirigible balloon, built by Roy Knabenshue, early American flier, occurred on top of the Spitzer Building in Toledo, Ohio, in July, 1905. One of ten ships built by Knabenshue, this airship featured a triangular keel of wooden slats and piano wire, tapering fore and aft. The one-place ship had an aluminum propeller at the bow, driven by a two-cylinder six-hp engine.

ALABAMA BALLOON MEET held at Birmingham, was climaxed by a race between spherical contestants. Large crowds attended these events, most of them eager to go up in the baskets of captive balloons which were tied by guy wires to the ground.

FIRST GORDON BENNETT CUP RACE was won by Lt. Frank P. Lahm of the American Army (l.) in his balloon *United States.* Competing against 16 entrants from seven nations, Lahm and his companion, Major Henry B. Hersey (r.) began their ascent at 4:55 P.M. on Sept. 30, 1906 at Paris and flew 410 miles, landing in Yorkshire, England, in 22 hours, 17 minutes, bringing the first Bennett Cup to U.S.

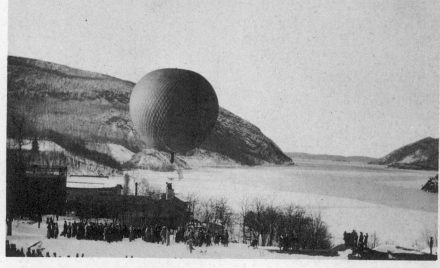

RACING TO ALBANY in early 1900's, Captain Thomas Scott Baldwin, America's early leader in airships, maneuvers his dirigible balloon in an attempt to win the $10,000 prize. He is seen sailing above the crowd of spectators at the start of the race before Grant's Tomb on Riverside Drive in New York City.

ASCENSION OF THE "ALUETTE," the first balloon of the American Aero Club, took place in January, 1906, when it rose from the grounds of West Point Military Academy with Charles Levee, of France, as aeronaut. This, the first balloon ascent made at West Point, was witnessed by cadets and military officials.

ARCTIC AIRSHIP SHED shown under construction at Dane's Island, Spitzbergen, was an arched structure 210 feet long, 85 feet wide, 85 feet high, covered with an acre of canvas and completed in September, 1906 to house the polar airship *America*, second largest in the world. The dirigible balloon, designed by Melvin Vaniman, chief mechanic, and Louis Godard, for the American explorer-aeronaut, Walter Wellman, was powered by an 80-hp motor driving twin steel propellers. Apex of the steel nacelle was a reservoir for fuel. First try for North Pole, September, 1907 ended when a snowstorm forced ship down on a glacier. Two years later, rebuilt with extra motor, *America* tried again but, losing her leather drag, returned to base, towed part of way (r.) by Norwegian vessel *Farm*.

WICKER CAR OF NEBULA, spherical balloon of 1907, left, has for its lone passenger Mrs. Assheton Harbord of Chelsea, England. Ballast bags of sand hang from the edge of the basket. The sensitive balance of weight in a balloon car was vividly demonstrated once when the loss of a lead pencil, dropped overboard, caused the balloon to rocket up 100 feet. The Clouth IV, a large balloon of early 1900's, shown above with Mr. and Mrs. Clouth and party, participated in the long distance race held at Hurlingham, England.

◀ FOUNDER OF ROYAL AERO CLUB Frank H. Butler, English aeronaut, stands by basket car of Spencer spherical balloon which carried him 115 miles, from London to Lincolnshire, England, in 1907, at an altitude from which he was not able to see land. He gave a luncheon in London, May, 1909, honoring the famous Wright brothers and their sister, Katherine, to which every guest had been flown by balloon or aeroplane. Paraphernalia generally used on balloon ascensions, some of which are visible in foreground of photo, included a registering barometer for telling height above sea level at all times, statoscope for recording ascending and descending movements, sand bags for ballast, guide rope, with anchor attached, to grip and hold balloon on descents, a compass, maps and battery-lamps. Many balloonists favored night flights, especially for long trips, because the even nocturnal temperature caused less expansion of the highly sensitive gases in balloon.

PRE-DAWN ASCENSION of A. Holland ▶ Forbes of New York and N.H. Arnold of Massachusetts was made at 3 a.m. (October, 1908) from North Adams, Mass. in *North Adams No.* 1.

VETERAN U. S. BALLOONISTS Alan R. Hawley, left, and Augustus Post in *America II,* set American distance balloon record, 1172 miles in 46 hours, in fifth Gordon Bennett Race at St. Louis, October 17, 1910. Landing in the wilds of Quebec, they were lost for ten days until they met trappers who took them to nearby village.

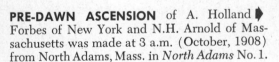

AIR CRASH HEADLINES of America's first airship disaster, left, tells the tragic end of C.A. Morrell's 450-foot, six-engine dirigible balloon over Berkeley, California, May 23, 1908, when she buckled and exploded on her first trip, hurling all 16 passengers, including her inventor, 250 feet to the ground in a mass of twisted rigging. Denied permission to ascend from San Francisco because officials considered the oversized craft unsafe, Morrell ascended from Berkeley, rising slowly as he headed over San Francisco Bay. A sudden buckling mid-ship set off an explosion, fire flared and the envelope split open. Of the 16 broken victims, Morrell, crushed by a prop, was most seriously hurt.

SPORT OF "AEROSTAT AND AERONAT" gained popularity the world over in the early 1900's. Above, balloons are being inflated just before a race. In 1907, leading balloonists Capt. Charles Chandler, James McCoy flew Signal Corps Balloon No.10 473 miles from St. Louis to win the Aero Club Lahm Trophy.

ARMY BUYS FIRST AIRSHIP
August 18, 1908, Captain Thomas Scott Baldwin, America's first airship builder, sold the Army its first airship for $10,000. Named *Signal Corps One*, it was purchased after successful test flight (above) at Ft. Myer, Va. On this flight, Curtiss, outstanding American engineer, in the forward section, operated his engine. Baldwin piloted, astern. The army purchase resulted from government interest shown in Baldwin's achievements. Construction of America's first airship *California Arrow* had begun when Baldwin saw a new motorcycle engine which seemed ideally suited for his ship. After writing to Curtiss, he was invited to visit the Curtiss factory at Hammondsport, New York. Baldwin promptly ordered the motor which powered the *California Arrow* to fame at St. Louis World's Fair, 1904. This was the beginning of a successful team of aerial pioneers. Baldwin was to build 13 dirigible balloons, all equipped with constantly improving Curtiss motors.

Commission for the first ship came when the War Department decided to order a dirigible balloon to be used by the Army Signal Corps. Specifications required a large maneuverable airship capable of continuous flight for two hours at a speed of 20 miles an hour. To meet these requirements Baldwin designed a balloon 96 feet in length, 19 feet in diameter, with a sturdy light-weight framework suspended below where the ship's power plant was installed—the newly-created, water-cooled 20-hp Curtiss engine. On August 18, 1908, the ship was tested at Ft. Meyer with Baldwin as pilot, Curtiss as engineer. Upon acceptance by the Army, the craft became the first to be owned by American Armed Forces.

SPANISH-AMERICAN WAR BALLOONS were housed in this corrugated iron shed at Fort Myer, Va., when the balloon detachment ceased to exist in 1899. It was not until 1907 that an Aeronautical Division was set up in the office of the Chief Signal Officer. It was in charge of "all matters pertaining to military ballooning, air machines, and all kindred subjects." This was start of the AAF.

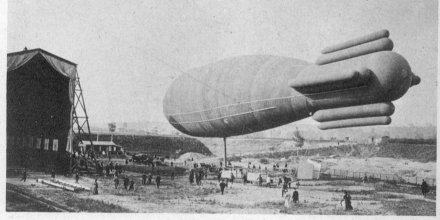

TO THE RESCUE of the French government after its military training balloon *La Patrie* was blown to sea came *La Ville de Paris*, above, donated to French War Ministry by M. Henri Deutsch de la Muerthe, staunch patron of aeronautics and donor of the "Deutsch Prize." The ship was semi-rigid, 190-feet long with stabilizing planes above a 16-foot car rigidly attached below the envelope.

ROYAL ARMY AIRSHIP *Nulli Secundus* was the first English Army ship built in England, in 1907, by Colonel Capper, Royal Engineers, and S. F. Cody, American airman. Semi-rigid, 111 feet long, the ship had a two-propeller motor capable of carrying three men at 20 mph and was used for training of officers.

GERMAN AUTO BALLOON designed by Major von Gross, commander of the balloon battalion at Tegel, near Berlin, was one of a series of airships the German government began building in 1907 under his supervision for troop maneuvers. Two motors, totaling 75 hp, were needed to propel the huge ship.

RELOCATING CAPTIVE BALLOON to a better observation post, the German Army Balloon Corps in 1908 wound the heavy cables around a drum secured to horsedrawn wagon and hauled inflated balloon. Cylinders of compressed gas for inflation were hauled, too, ready for use.

◀ **GLIDER WINGS** were added to improve ballast, landing safety of England's *Nulli Secundus* on her second trial. Pride of Government's Farnborough factory, England's first home-built airship was destroyed in a rain storm, but was important prototype for other balloons of 1907.

HANGAR VIEW OF ZEPPELIN III shows detailed construction of horizontal fins, or rudders, used for changing altitude without necessitating the release of gas or ballast. Built late in 1906 by Count von Zeppelin of Germany, this dirigible balloon in 1908 became Germany's first military airship (No. 1), after Zeppelin IV, which had been intended for army use, tore loose from her moorings at Stuttgart and burst into flames in mid-air.

TWISTED METAL SKELETON of an early Zeppelin airship is mute testimony of the damage done by dreaded fire on board a highly inflammable, hydrogen-inflated dirigible balloon. Zeppelin inaugurated passenger service in 1910 with airships, adding a third, *Schwaben*, the "Swallow", (below), in 1911. By eliminating the forward rudders and using a single set of rudders supported by stabilizer fins at the extreme rear, Zeppelin cut down resistance and skin friction. The streamlined *Schwaben* could fly 43 miles an hour in calm air. More than 100 successful flights covering 6700 air miles were made with 1,675 fares.

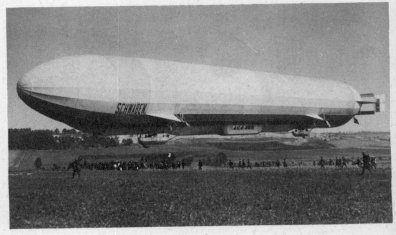

RIDING IN ROYAL CAR with his Emperor, Wilhelm II of Germany, was one highlight of a triumphant August 29, 1909 for Zeppelin. The flight of Zeppelin III over Berlin had brought rousing cheers, royal honors and a day at the palace. Climax was the order of four large Zeppelins for the German Navy.

ZEPPELIN–GERMANY'S "MAN OF THE CENTURY"

The success and honors accorded Count Ferdinand von Zeppelin (1838-1917), famous German inventor who streamlined the airship, were the fruits of an indomitable combination of faith, enthusiasm and persevering energy. He was inspired to study possibilities of powered, directed balloons after flying in free balloons during his military career. At 56, after retiring, he turned to designing a rigid airship.

With contagious enthusiasm and absolute faith in his project, he secured the necessary capital to construct his first Zeppelin airship, tested with fair success on July 2, 1900. Zeppelin aimed for the greatest length in proportion to the diameter of his airship and kept the lines clean and simple. In spite of the great size of his ships, ranging from 410 feet to approximately 680 feet in length, the diameter of an average size airship was about equal to the wing spread of a Wright Brothers biplane. Each succeeding ship added improvements and eliminated faults.

Although 13 early Zeppelins were destroyed through mishaps due to weather conditions or lack of experience in handling big craft, Count Zeppelin never lost confidence and his countrymen continued to back his ventures. His ships served his government in peace and during World War I. They provided passenger service throughout Germany and to North and South America. They became the skyliners of the world. The first airship ever to cruise around the world west-to-east was the Graf Zeppelin with 20 passengers and a crew of 41 men, flying 9500 miles in 21 days, 7 hours, 26 minutes.

GERMANY'S AIR HERO OF 1909, Count von Zeppelin (in white cap), then 71 years old, turned over command of his dirigible balloon, the Zeppelin III, to Dr. Hugo Eckener, his assistant in charge of the passenger-carrying subsidiary, on the dirigible's first historic and eventful flight over Berlin August 29.

INTERIOR CABIN VIEW of *Deutschland I*, Zeppelin's airship, shows the seating arrangement of the aluminum cabin which was lined with rosewood and mahogany. After less than a week in service, the ship crashed over a pine forest and was completely destroyed. Fortunately, all passengers were rescued.

PASSENGERS BOARDING AIRSHIP in Germany, 1910, were eager to try the new mode of transportation. Zeppelin VII, the *Deutschland I*, was Count Zeppelin's first commercial airship. On her maiden voyage the dirigible balloon, largest yet built, included some women among her twenty passengers.

FLYING OVER CROWDS, Zeppelin III, on her historic first flight to the German capital, approaches Tempelhof Field. Bells tolled and Berlin's two million people waited in fields and on rooftops, eager to witness ship's arrival.

FIRST FRAULEIN AERONAUT, Miss Elfriede Riotle of Germany, studied aerial navigation under Captain Telfinger, commander of one of the semi-rigid Parseval airships. Inventive also, Miss Riotle designed and patented several safety devices for dirigible balloons. Major von Parseval, compatriot of Zeppelin, built a series of semi-rigid pisciform ships (above) with sliding cars to control the balance of the ship.

SIEMENS-SCHUCKERT AIRSHIP entering hangar at Berlin, Germany, January 23, 1911, was a product of Siemens-Schuckert Works, one of the many branches of Siemens' Electrical Firm. During World War I the branch plant specialized in airplanes for the German Air Corps.

EARLY RUSSIAN AIRSHIP lifting at Charkov, Russia, near the beginning of the 20th century, was created by Dr. K. Damlewsky. The balloon was designated a "directable flying machine."

PRIMED FOR TEST at Lamotte, France, 1910, *Clement-Bayard II*, French military airship, was the first dirigible balloon to fly from Paris to London in October, 1910. The pisciform ship, non-rigid except for the metal car frame, was built with a box-kite type of rudder and twin muffled motors.

FIRST AERO MEET in the U. S. took place at Dominguez Field near Los Angeles, California. From Jan. 10-20, 1910, it drew huge crowds, offered daily flights and contests, like the quick-start competition won by Glenn Curtiss (above), who made a take-off run of 98 feet in a breath-taking 6-2/5 sec., setting a new record. Curtiss also established new world's record for speed with a passenger by attaining 55 miles per hour.

AIR SHOWS BECOME POPULAR

First U.S. meet held in January, 1910, at Dominguez Field, Los Angeles

After the success of the meet at Rheims, France, the first similar air contest in America was arranged to take place at Los Angeles. While not as spectacular as the French tourney, the American event, under the management of air-minded actor Dick Ferris, aroused a great deal of local enthusiasm. Crowds came daily by streetcar, auto, and even horseback to Dominguez, near present-day Compton, Calif., where the birdmen were performing (Jan. 10-20, 1910).

Before packed grandstands many noted U.S. aviators, as well as France's Maisson, Miscarol and Paulhan, amazed spectators with daring flights and maneuvers. The ubiquitous Glenn Curtiss brought gasps from the observers with his quick starts and speed dashes. Curtiss pilot Charlie Hamilton, former balloonist, complimented his employer by winning $500 for the *slowest* lap (26.83 mph). Charles F. Willard

astounded the audience with the accuracy of his spot landings and won a $250 prize.

The star of the meet was Louis Paulhan. On the third day of the races, the personable French airman set a new altitude record of 4,165 ft. On Jan. 17, he thrilled the crowd with his long cross-country flight from Dominguez to Santa Anita and back. After he had been gone almost two

CARPOWER was employed by Wright flier Arch Hoxsey, hauling his plane to the starting point. Craft was a "B" model, without forward elevator.

hours, a tremendous roar went up from the watchers as his returning plane was seen in the distance. The 75-mile trip took 1 hr., 58 min., 27 2/5 sec., and won for Paulhan the $10,000 grand prize for his achievement.

Another outstanding event of the meet was the race between Roy Knabenshue and Lincoln Beachey, both of Los Angeles, in their dirigibles. The huge porpoise-like shapes wallowed oddly around the course until Beachey, with a slight burst of speed, nosed out his rival at finish line.

Feminine glamor was added to the conclave when popular actress Florence Stone, wife of meet promoter Dick Ferris, went up for a flight with French aviator Paulhan.

A great success, the Dominguez meet established in Southern California an interest in aviation that was later to bring about a concentration there of America's aircraft industry.

RECOGNIZED as one of the great fliers of America, Glenn Curtiss participated in most U.S. air meets. He is shown here with Mrs. Curtiss during the races at Los Angeles.

CROWD CHEERED at spectacles like this: Frenchman Louis Paulhan on his Farman biplane; Roy Knabenshue and daring Lincoln Beachey flying their dirigibles. Knabenshue later became Wrights' manager; Beachey met fame as stunt pilot.

SENSATION of the Los Angeles air meet was Louis Paulhan, whose daring exploits won him almost $20,000 in prizes. He is shown with Mrs. Dick Ferris, who was finally persuaded to fly with him.

LONDON-MANCHESTER RACE

In April, 1910 the *London* *Daily Mail* offered a $50,000 prize to the first airman to cover the 183 miles in 24 hours. It became an international contest when Louis Paulhan, outstanding French aviator (left), and England's Claude Grahame-White (right, in derby —with Henri Farman, in cap) each set out to win. The Briton started first, at 5:19

a.m., April 23, reached Lichfield, a scant 66 miles from his goal. Trouble with his Farman biplane forced him to return to London. Four days later, Paulhan, also in a Farman, took off and landed in Lichfield before dark. In a second attempt, Grahame-White followed, landed 10 miles behind Paulhan, took off again at dawn and was forced down by engine trouble. Paulhan, starting an hour later, successfully flew on to Manchester and won prize for France. Time was 5¼ hrs.

PAULHAN LANDS HIS FARMAN BIPLANE AT LICHFIELD FOR THE NIGHT

GRAHAME-WHITE'S MOTHER TIES A ROSE TO HER SON'S AIRPLANE

GREAT ENGLISH AERO meet at Bournemouth, July 10-16, 1910, saw victory and death. France's Leon Morane (below, with lady passengers) won altitude prize and race around the Isle of Wight. Also competing were Grahame-White and Drexel (U.S.). Tragic death of Hon. Chas. S. Rolls was first British air death.

BRITISH FLIER'S FIRST TRY FOR PRIZE ENDS IN MISHAP

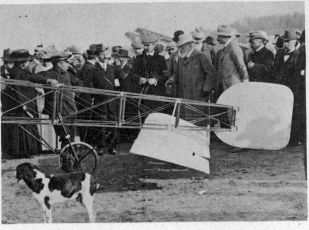

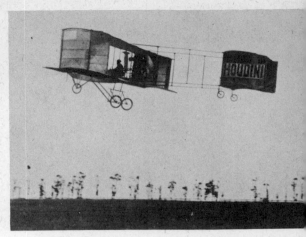

GERMAN AVIATION was beginning to develop by May, 1910, when the first international air meet in that country was held in Berlin. The first German airplane had been designed, built and flown by engineer Hans Grade on Oct. 30, 1909.

ROYAL APPROVAL was given to aviation when King Edward VII of England granted a charter to the Aero Club of the United Kingdom, renaming it the Royal Aero Club of the United Kingdom, (Feb. 15, 1910). Above, France's Louis Bleriot explains plane workings to king.

MAGICIAN Harry Houdini became a flying enthusiast in 1910, regularly piloting his own Voisin plane from city to city, where he was to make appearances. He was the first stage celebrity to utilize flying to meet requirements of a tight engagement schedule.

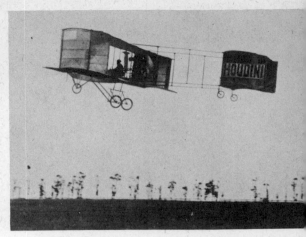

FLYING DUTCHMAN Anthony (Tony) Fokker was only 18 when he built and flew his first airplane (1911). Called the Spider because of its many struts and wires, (above, left), it had no lateral control system, extreme dihedral being employed to ensure stability. Young Fokker (right, in the *Spider*) began experimenting with models as a schoolboy; one of his paper gliders is shown above, center. In World War I, when Fokker offered his services as aircraft designer to Britain and France, they turned him down, maintaining that their own designs were superior. He then made his offer to the Germans who accepted it.

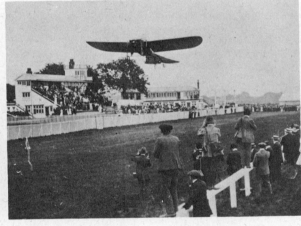

FIRST ALL-METAL AIRPLANES were built by John B. Moisant (pronounced "Moy-sant") in 1910. The second all-metal plane he designed is shown left. A Chicago architect, Moisant turned aviator, learning to fly in Europe. He was a popular performer at Folkestone, England (r.). Then he achieved fame by making the first Channel flight with a passenger in the first Paris-to-London flight, 1910. Because of delays en route, the trip took 20 days.

ORIENTAL INTEREST in aviation was indicated when Commander Saito of the Imperial Japanese Navy went for a ride with Lincoln Beachey in 1910. Japan soon began to develop own aircraft.

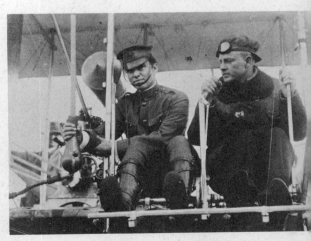

BAMBOO CONSTRUCTION made Santos-Dumont's "Demoiselles" superlight; 18-foot wingspan required small pilots, like Audemars (in seat). Craft attained speed of about 40 mph in 1909.

AIR-SEA RESCUE was first accomplished by Hugh Robinson on Aug. 14, 1911. Rene Simon fell into Lake Michigan in his monoplane during Chicago Aviation Meet. Robinson, flying overhead at the time, quickly landed his Curtis hydroplane ("flying fish") alongside wreck and took Simon aboard.

FIRST AERIAL BOMB was dropped at San Francisco, California, in January, 1911. The bombardier was Lt. Myron S. Crissy, U.S.A. (left, holding bomb) riding in a Wright biplane. He was piloted by a civilian, one of the best Wright exhibition fliers, Philip O. Parmalee.

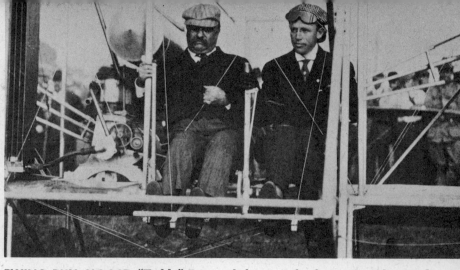

RISKY FLYING over Lake Michigan drew thousands of spectators to the Chicago meet of 1911. Above are two of the fliers at that event, Brindley and Beatty, heading their Wright biplanes out over the water. While this race was uneventful, others ended in tragedy. "Le Croix" Johnstone lost his life, and airman Rene Simon almost met the same fate (see caption at center, bottom, opposite page).

FLYING BULL MOOSE, "Teddy" Roosevelt became the first ex-President to fly on Oct. 11, 1910. "T.R." was attending the St. Louis air meet, and while talking with Arch Hoxsey, persuaded the Wright star to take him up. They were airborne before Roosevelt's horrified aides could stop him. While they banked over crowd, "T. R." waved both hands until even Hoxsey warned him of the danger.

"EGGBEATER," one of Igor Sikorsky's early experimental helicopters, was built in Russia, 1910. Sikorksy became famous for his multi-engined planes, returning to helicopter interest in the late 30's.

STUNT PILOT Lincoln Beachey banks his plane in typical maneuver. Noted balloonist, he took up airplane stunt flying, by 1910 was world's greatest.

AIRCRAFT MANUFACTURER, Britain's Geoffrey de Havilland, sits at controls of his first successful plane, 1910. DeHavilland built military planes for Britain in World Wars I and II; jets, and transports postwar.

Holder of Britain's No. 1 Aviator's Certificate, Lord Brabazon of Tara has been President of the Royal Aero Club since 1943. He made his first airplane flight in England in 1909, following pioneer flights in France.

The charm of aviation, to anyone who has been close to it for fifty years, has been its restless, often turbulent, spirit.

We started off a rail—a biplane with pusher propellers. We added an undercarriage, and ran about. We then found tractors better than pushers. We put our controls aft, instead of in front where the Wrights placed theirs. We next invented the monoplane tractor, such as the Bleriot. Then, for reasons of speed, mark you, we went back to the biplane.

The rotary engine became the radial. The air-cooled engine fought it out with the liquid-cooled, and eventually won—for commercial use, anyway.

Back again we went to monoplanes and carried immense power plants at one time thought impossible, by laying them all along the wing.

MOORE-BRABAZON FLYING IN 1910

Then came the jet. Everything in the melting pot again. Back we went to pushers. The slip stream from the tractors over the wing was gone, and new problems arose. Speeds soared up and up until we met problems never dreamed of in the early days of first gropings.

Petrol has given way to paraffin. By pressurization we have reached astonishing heights and have increased our speed in the rarified atmosphere.

To me, the next fifty years promise advances even undreamed of today. To get where we are has cost much treasure and human life, but such is the restless spirit of man, that gladly he goes forward into the unknown, despising the cost. It is a great story. Let us pray that human wisdom will keep pace with technical advancements, lest we perish by what we have created.

Brabazon of Tara

SPEED was increasing by mid-1910 to a point where airplanes could compete with automobiles. Above is thrilling race between two Curtiss biplanes, piloted by McCurdy (above) and Beachey, and a race car. Although it was a close contest, Beachey won.

ALPS WERE CONQUERED when Peruvian Jean Bielovucic, on Jan. 25, 1911, first flew over the lofty mountains successfully. Four months before, (Sept. 23) fellow countryman George Chavez had made the same crossing, but was killed in a crash landing.

SWEPT-BACK WING, feature of modern jets, was used for stability by England's Frederick Handley Page (later Sir Frederick) shown here in cockpit of his 1909 *Blue Bird*. Plane was only moderate success, but it pointed the way for later improvements.

W. STARLING BURGESS, BUILDING WRIGHT BIPLANES UNDER LICENSE, DEVELOPED A SPECIAL TRAILER TO HAUL PLANES FROM FACTORY TO FLYING FIELD

HARVARD-BOSTON MEET

At Boston Harbor, Sept. 3-13, 1910, a huge throng, including many celebrities, watched English and American fliers compete for nearly $100,000 in prizes, largest yet offered at an air meet. From England came Claude Grahame-White, A.V. Roe, and T.O.M. Sopwith (who was to design some of Britain's finest fighting planes during World War I). Americans competing were Glenn Curtiss, Ralph Johnstone, Walter Brookins, Charles F. Wil-lard, Earle Ovington, and Clifford B. Harmon, who on Aug. 20 had won a prize for a 25-mile flight over Long Island Sound. In the Boston meet, Johnstone captured the duration prize; his record: 3 hr., 5 min., 40 sec. Brookins took the altitude award by climbing to 4,732 ft. Star among these world champions, however, was England's Grahame-White. He not only won the speed prize (5¼ miles in 6 minutes) but just nosed out Curtiss, who was flying one of his biplanes, in the great race around Boston Light for the *Boston Globe's* $10,000 prize.

SPORTSMAN CLIFFORD B. HARMON (STANDING)

GRAHAME-WHITE, SOPWITH, AND OVINGTON

TRANSPORTING AIRCRAFT from factory to flying field, as well as from one meet to another, presented quite a problem. Airplanes were cumbersome and at the same time did not readily lend themselves to disassembly, with their maze of struts and wires. W. Starling Burgess (top of page), whose "Burgess Co. and Curtiss" was the first in the U.S.A. to be licensed to use the Wright patent, solved the difficulty by mounting the partly folded machine on a special trailer. Flying enthusiast and trophy winner Augustus Post (below) moved his Curtiss biplane about, packed in crates. The Curtiss, however, was originally designed to be very quickly disassembled.

FIRST FLIGHT INTO WASHINGTON by an airplane occurred a month after Harvard-Boston meet when its star, Claude Grahame-White of England, flew his Farman biplane from Benning Race Track to the capitol, October 14, 1910. On landing, he received a near-royal welcome. From left to right above, are Mr. Barr; Maj. G. O. Squier; Brig. Gen. Arthur Murray; Brig. Gen. J. A. Johnston; Maj. Gen. W. H. Carter; John Barry Ryan; Brig. Gen. W. H. Bixby; Maj. Gen. Leonard Wood; Asst. Sec'y of War Robert Shaw Oliver; Brig. Gen. James Allen; Grahame-White; Admiral George Dewey; rival flying champion Clifford B. Harmon; Mr. McDonald; and Maj. Gen. J. F. Bell. After visiting War and Navy Departments, in background, the Briton took off again (r.) down W. Executive Ave.

LAST GREAT AERO MEET in America before World War I was the world-wide tourney held at Belmont Park, Long Island (Oct. 22-31, 1910). Most of the noted fliers of both hemispheres were present at this most spectacular of international air events—also the scene of the U.S. defense of the Gordon Bennett trophy, captured by Curtiss the year before at Rheims. Above, a French Farman biplane takes off in front of parking area. Fliers' hangars are tents in far background.

GREAT AERIAL TOURNAMENT

Belmont Park meet in 1910 becomes top society sporting event of decade

America's answer to the splendid Rheims aero meet of 1909 was the Belmont Park event, Oct. 22-31, 1910. Managed by Mr. Allen A. Ryan of New York, it was the climax of the great pre-war series of international air shows. In the year since the French tourney, airplane speeds had increased by almost 75% and their reliability had improved amazingly. Future progress would be made, to be sure, but no air meet for many years was the equal of this one both in its success and its outstanding social significance.

The last-mentioned feature was the special distinction of Belmont Park. In attendance were some of the most fashionable people in America, such as Clarence Mackay of New York, Miss Eleanora Sears of Boston, Harold McCormick of Chicago, Lt. Governor Woodruff of New York state, and many other prominent persons.

To entertain this brilliant assembly, the most distinguished airmen of the time were brought together. Claude Grahame-White upheld the prestige of Great Britain by wresting the Gordon Bennett speed trophy from the United States, October 29, at over 60 mph. French glory was boosted by the new speed record of Leblanc, 66.20 mph (he reached 70 during one lap), as well as Count de Lessep's victory in the race around New York's Statue of Liberty for a $10,000 prize donated by Mr. Thomas F. Ryan. America claimed her share of the honors by dominating the altitude events, a thrilling series of contests between J. Armstrong Drexel and Ralph Johnstone. The latter climaxed the meet with a world's record of 9,714 ft. on the last day.

Biggest thrill of the week was Leblanc's spectacular crash after setting his speed mark. Hurtling at more than a mile a minute, he struck a telephone pole, splitting it in two. After a few weeks in a hospital, the gallant Frenchman was as good as new.

Biggest disappointment was the disqualifying, for technical reasons, of America's Moisant after he had won the *Statue of Liberty* race.

"MISS PARIS," John Moisant's mascot, was celebrated participant at the meet, was one of first two passengers flown across English Channel in August.

MASCOT of England's Grahame-White was this puppet, lashed to a strut of his plane, stepping forward, eyes aloft. Many fliers carried such charms.

INTERNATIONAL ECLAT of the contestants was already established when they met at Belmont Park to determine the world's air champions. At left is the British team: (l. to r.) Alex Ogilvie, James Radley, Claude Grahame-White, and A. McCardle. The American team (center), chosen to defend the Gordon Bennett Cup, are: (l. to r.) J. Armstrong Drexel, Walter Brookins, and Charlie Hamilton. At right are four members of the famous Wright Flying Team, first pilots taught by Wilbur Wright: (l. to r.) Frank Coffyn, Brookins, Arch Hoxsey, and Alfred LeChapelle. Also present was a French party: Count Jacques de Lesseps, Alfred Leblanc, Auburn, Roland Garros, Hubert Latham, and Audemars. Nearly all the outstanding airmen of the time assembled to compete for the coveted trophies.

FOUR GREAT AIRMEN maneuver their planes during one of the events at Belmont Park. Aircraft (left to right) were used by France's Hubert Latham, America's Moisant, Walter Brookins, and Ralph Johnstone. Moisant and Johnstone were to die in crashes before the year's end. Moisant's death at New Orleans, December 31, ended a year of distinguished flying achievement by the 35-year-old Chicago architect-turned-flier.

◀ **AMAZING CAREER** of John B. Moisant (left, in suit and tie with sister Mathilde and Count de Lesseps) was exemplified at Belmont Park meet. While testing his Bleriot monoplane just before the *Statue of Liberty* race, he wrecked it and, telephoning Leblanc, who was recovering from his injuries of the day before, he made arrangements to buy one of the Frenchman's extra airplanes just in time to enter race.

CRASH HELMET is worn by J. Armstrong Drexel (right) as he converses with Courtland Field Bishop, then President of the Aero Club of America. Drexel engaged in a dramatic six-day duel with Ralph Johnstone for the altitude prize at Belmont Park meet. They alternately rose higher and higher, Johnstone winning.

IN STUNNED SURPRISE, Count de Lesseps (l.), John Barry Ryan and Claude Grahame-White watch Moisant returning from the Statue of Liberty. All were amazed at Moisant's replacing his own crashed plane at the eleventh hour, and flying the course in the fastest time. Ryan's father donated prize for this race.

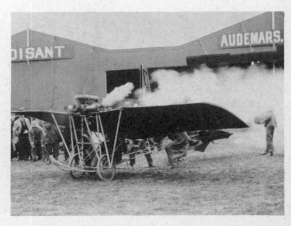

ROUNDING A PYLON is the intrepid Hubert Latham in his beautiful *Antoinette* monoplane. Two weeks later (Nov. 7, 1910), Latham won the *Baltimore Sun's* $5,000 prize for the first flight directly made over the center of a large city (Baltimore).

UPSET came to Moisant when his Bleriot monoplane turned turtle just before he was to take part in the *Statue of Liberty* race. As with most crashes of the time, the aviator was unhurt, but the plane would require extensive repairs before it could fly again.

SPECTACULAR POWER seemed to burst forth when the Santos-Dumont *Demoiselle's* 2-cylinder engine was fired up by flier Roland Garros. Actually, the tiny Darracq engine developed only 35 hp, and the entire plane, less pilot, weighed about 200 lbs.

THE SMART SET took to flying at Belmont Park, not only an important milestone in aviation history, but the outstanding social event of the season as well. A well-known socialite-athlete was Eleanora Sears, who is shown (above, left) about to go for a ride with Grahame-White in his Farman biplane. Air-minded Admiral Dewey, victor of Manila, is seen (center) inspecting the powerful *Baby Wright* racer. Dewey was influential in the high-level controversy over naval aviation. At the right, Cornelius Vanderbilt (with beard), who later purchased his own airplane, is shown as he started on his first flight with Orville Wright.

HIGH FLIER Ralph Johnstone received last minute instructions from the Wright brothers, just before breaking the world's altitude record, flying 9,714 feet on Oct. 31. Johnstone died in a crash less than one month after participating in the altitude contest.

RELAXING for a change, are famous "birdmen" (above, l. to r.) Count Jacques de Lesseps, winner of the *Statue of Liberty* race; Glenn Curtiss, noted for his Albany flight five months before; Hubert Latham, usually unlucky, but an incurable "trier."

NEW JERSEY'S governor, John Franklin Fort, was another distinguished visitor at Belmont Park (above, left, with Arch Hoxsey). Judging by the two men's dress, this was probably a posed publicity photo; there is no record of Gov. Fort having flown.

AMERICA'S HOPE for the Gordon Bennett cup was the *Baby Wright* racer, shown warming up. Fourth from left, in derby, is Wilbur Wright; Orville, in leather jacket, is inspecting the craft before making a test hop. The *Baby* had only a 21-foot wingspan and, with a special V-8 engine, was probably the fastest airplane at the meet. There was no opportunity to prove this, however, since engine failure brought a crash which demolished the racer and seriously injured pilot Walter Brookins. At the time, ironically, Brookins was flying to the aid of Alfred Leblanc, who had wrecked his own ship while breaking the speed mark.

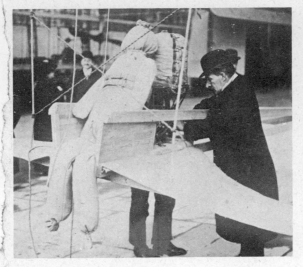

EJECTION SEAT was tested with a dummy in 1910 (above). When in danger, the pilot could trigger a gun which fired him and parachute out of the plane.

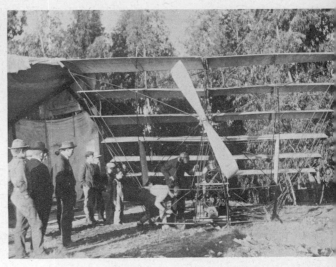

STILL TRYING, Prof. Zerbe and aides added extra wing and switched to a single propeller, but these "improvements" 'didn't bring flight, fortunately for the pilot.

...vented by Prof. J. S. ... Los Angeles, Calif. With its five wing... it had adequate lift, but lacked power.

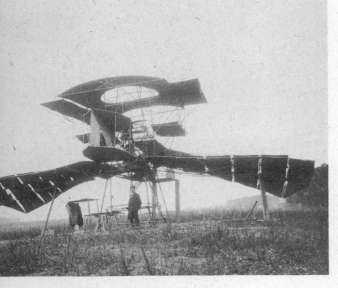

BIRDLIKE flexing wings were tried by German architect Schulz (1910). Like many other such experiments, insufficient power prevented flight disaster.

VALIANT EFFORTS

While the experts like the Wrights, Curtiss, and many others continued to develop their aircraft along proven lines, amateur inventors, crackpots, and some educated scientists were always experimenting with weird ideas. Many of them seemed to ignore completely established principles of physics.

Two favorites of the non-professionals were the multiplane (many wings to get more lift) and the birdwing types (because birds fly so well with theirs). Of course, there were some successes along these lines, notably Roe in England and Etrich in Austria, but theirs were more conventional in arrangement.

Less frivolous was the helicopter idea, but the inefficient power plants of the time doomed even promising types to almost certain failure.

HELICOPTER of Vuitten-Huber was interesting for its 8-cylinder, horizontal engine (45 hp) and the counter-revolving rotors, but it never was airborne.

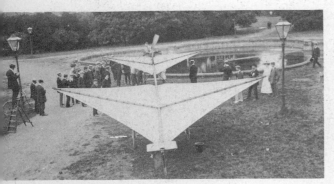

DELTA WING? Captain Wyndham of England designed this one in 1910, based on kite principle.

THINGS TO COME. Famous American cartoonist A.B. Walker, spoofed future aerial age in 1909.

MIXMASTER. The Kimball helicopter (1909) had 20 rotors, all driven by a very elaborate system of pulleys.

TWELVE-WINGED (6 pairs) "Air Yacht" was constructed in 1913 by M. A. Batson for a projected trans-Atlantic flight. It was 74 ft. long and had two airscrews.

AIRSHIP of J. F. Cooley (above, left) was completed in 1910, after two years of building. It was expected to be extremely fast and had a number of novel features. Of special interest were (above, right) the narrow wings, longitudinal radiators, and the twin, intermeshing propellers. Note lack of forward visibility.

SIMILAR to the Vuitten-Huber helicopter (opposite page) was one by G. Newton Williams in 1908, (above, in black hat). Williams utilized the same type Curtiss 40 hp aircooled V-8 engine proven by Aerial Experiment Association.

SIR HIRAM MAXIM, whose steam-powered multiplane had almost flown, back in 1893, is shown above in an improved 1910 version. Using a gasoline engine this time, Maxim failed again, but he continued experimenting until his death.

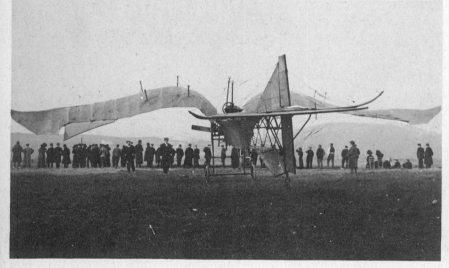

BIRDWINGS were often tried by early experimenters, but few were as startling and ambitious as this. Even many scientists thought birds should be copied.

CORNU helicopter, powered by an early *Antoinette* engine, actually rose into the air, (1908), lifting 2 people as well as itself. But it came down immediately.

AMATEUR SCIENTISTS continued risking their necks. Above, at the opening of the Hampshire Aero Club, (Apr. 9, 1910) the members took turns "learning by doing" in the *Alexander* glider. With no tail, it is a mystery how the craft

had any longitudinal stability. Another brave pioneer is shown above, right, as he launches his crude tandem-wing model into the wild blue yonder. Scene is an outdoor meet in England. Bystanders typify attitude of period; pilot is unknown.

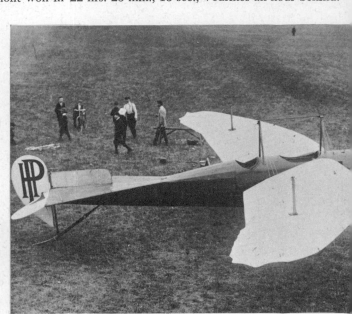

PARIS-MADRID race, for a prize of $30,000, was won by Jules Vedrines (above) on May 26, 1911. One of the premier aviators of the continent, he set a new speed record of 105 mph the next year.

PSEUDONYM "Andre Beaumont" was used by Lt. Jean Conneau of the French Army, a frequent practice among French Army officers when flying in competition. Beaumont won the great Circuit of England race sponsored by the *London Daily Mail*, for a prize of $50,000. Lasting from July 22 to 26, 1911, the contest was 1,010-mile route from Brooklands. Beaumont won in 22 hrs. 28 min., 18 sec., Vedrines an hour behind.

RETURN TO AMERICA of the Gordon Bennett speed trophy was achieved by Charles T. Weyman (July 1, 1911). Pushing his Nieuport monoplane to a speed of 78.77 mph, Weyman crossed white finish line (left) to win the cup. He was only American to enter contest. After this triumph, Weyman made a tour of Europe (at right), meeting Curtiss (r.) in Belgium. Note footgear.

"YELLOW PERIL" was the sobriquet of the Handley Page HP-5, developed from the *Blue Bird* shown on page 57. Built in 1911, the HP-5 was coated yellow; hence the name. Paint was non-corosive which gave plane another name: *Antiseptic.*

DISTANCE RECORDS were shattered by Harry N. Atwood on August 25, 1911, when he flew from St. Louis to New York—1,266 miles in 28 hr., 53 min. flying time. He circles New York's Singer Tower (r.).

"SORRY OLD BOY." A British Army BE-2 biplane was landing at Salisbury Plain when it struck an unseen Farman biplane resting on the ground (1911). A mechanic, starting the Farman's propeller, escaped certain death, falling flat on ground.

GERMAN FLIERS began coming to the fore in 1910-11. The winner of second place in the German Circuit race, Volmöller, lands (left) near Berlin. Right, Obering and Helmuth Hirth (in rear) won the race and a 50,000-mark prize. Both airplanes shown are the Etrich *Taube* (Dove) type as built by the Rumpler Co., Berlin. These birdwing airplanes were very popular in Germany before the war.

"SMARTEST MONOPLANE" ever built was how English writer C.G.Grey referred to the *Antoinette.* On January 7, 1911. Hubert Latham, crack French aviator, was the first to fly successfully across the Golden Gate, San Francisco.

BEGINNING OF AIRMAIL

EITHER rain, sleet or snow that week would have prevented the first U.S. aerial postman from making his appointed rounds. But for Earle Ovington there was no such trouble Sept. 23 to Oct. 2, 1911, when he flew a daily service during the Sheepshead Bay, L.I. air meet. (Sheepshead to Jamaica, L.I.) Above, Frank N. Hitchcock hands Ovington the first air mail pouch on the opening day. Although this was only a stunt, and the mail station temporary (left), it proved the feasibility of air service. Regular U.S. air mail began with Army experiments between Washington and New York in 1918.

ALLAHABAD, India, surprisingly, was the scene of the first air mail flight. On Feb. 18, 1911 during the All India Exposition, French flier Pequet carried mail by plane. A few months later (Sept. 9 to 25, 1911) the *Coronation Aerial Post* was flown daily from London to Windsor.

AIR EXPRESS was first carried by Roy Knabenshue (right), cooperating with the Railway Express Agency. A package to the Morehouse-Martens Co. of Columbus, Ohio, was sent by rail to Dayton, then rushed on to its destination by air. These experiments proved to all the value of aerial delivery. The man with Knabenshue is an Express Co. executive.

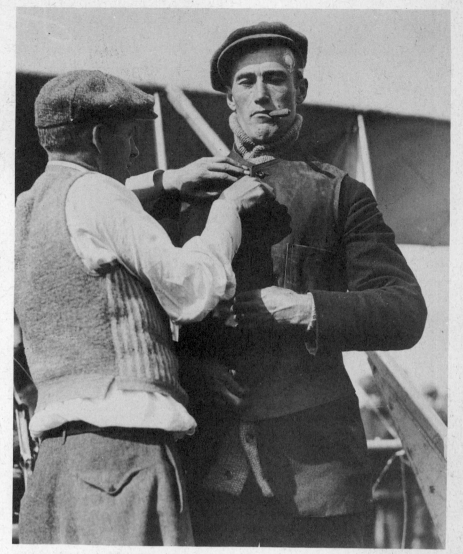

FIRST TRANSCONTINENTAL FLIGHT

Transcontinental flight was finally achieved by Calbreath P. Rodgers, Sept. 17 to Dec. 10, 1911. Inspired by an offer of $50,000 by publisher William Randolph Hearst for the first such flight to be completed within 30 days, Rodgers (above) didn't win but gained international fame for his fortitude. His route is seen below.

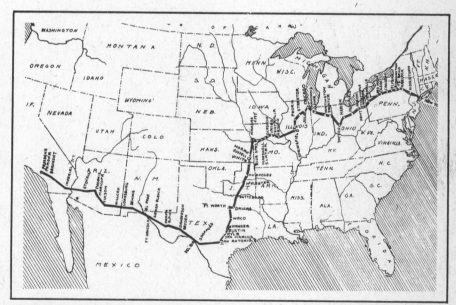

WRECKS along the way from New York to Long Beach, California, caused Rodgers a great deal of grief. Anticipating some trouble, he had provided that a special train follow his course, equipped with spare parts and facilities for making repairs. But he had so many crashes (15 in all) that by the end of the trip his Wright biplane had been rebuilt four times and only the rudder and one strut remained of the original machine. Rodgers was financed by the manufacturers of *Vin Fiz,* a popular soft drink. For that reason, Rodgers named plane the *Vin Fiz.*

INTERIOR OF WRIGHT BROTHERS' FACTORY, DAYTON, OHIO, 1912

FINAL DAB OF BRUSH GIVES ACCURATE BALANCE TO PROPELLER.

EARLY AIRCRAFT MANUFACTURERS

Pioneer aircraft manufacturers built their planes by hand, custom-made. Their methods were in ironic contrast to the huge, intricate assembly-line methods of the future. They fumbled along, devised crude production techniques, and seemingly made only minor headway toward developing the highly-specialized aeronautical designs soon to be demanded.

American manufacturers cast a jealous eye toward European activity where Bleriot and the Voisin Brothers of France, England's Royal Aircraft Factory, and Germany's Etrich Company were producing planes on a larger scale. In the U.S. only a few companies were in operation. Spearheading this group were the Curtiss Airplane and Motor Corporation, the Burgess Company, Aeromarine Plane and Motor Corporation, and shortly afterwards the Thomas-Morse Aircraft Corporation, the Dayton-Wright Airplane Company, and the Wright-Martin Airplane Company.

These companies had relatively little incentive before World War I. First, they were faced with the problem of breaking down popular prejudice against the new invention. The public considered the airplane a dangerous contraption, a plaything of the wealthy—no contribution to progress. It was slow recognizing the plane's utilitarian value. Second, although the manufacturers made some attempt to work together, nevertheless patent litigations and personal jealousies impeded their progress. Finally, although the U.S. had adopted the airplane for military use in 1908-09, it was not actually to be tested until 1916 when Gen. Pershing used scouting planes in his Mexican campaign against Pancho Villa.

Later, airplane designs were to outstrip the development of the motors that powered them. But the flimsy construction of early planes made low horsepowers necessary. Biggest motor at the 1910 Boston air show, rated at 100 hp, was too large for any of the planes on display. Early airplane builders were largely persons with previous experience in automobile building, experimenters with bicycles and motorcycles, etc. Their designs often showed the influence of this prior training.

Full transition from garage-shop and back-yard building of airplanes to regular factory production took about ten years. But it was due to these early experiments, based on training in other fields, that the development of heavier-than-air craft advanced with such tremendous strides.

FINAL ASSEMBLY IN FRENCH FACTORY OF AN *ANTOINETTE* PLANE

W.T. THOMAS PLANE (1911), LOADED ON CAR, READY FOR DELIVERY.

WRIGHT BROTHERS experimented in 1912 with gliders which had arched surfaces, adjustable front rudder, and skids for landing. With the flier prone on the upper surface of its lower wing, this craft could glide more than 600 feet. Orville Wright, shown at left checking glider controls, turned over in a glider at Kitty Hawk, N.C. (right) while testing for satisfactory methods of obtaining automatic stability for their planes.

ROBERT C. FOWLER was first to exhibit an airplane (Hall-Scott, 80-hp motor) on a stage, at the Empress Theatre, San Francisco, Nov. 19, 1912. He made his first transcontinental flight on Jan. 10, 1912, flying from Jacksonville, Florida, to San Francisco, a distance of 2,232 miles in 151 days. In May, 1913, Fowler flew across the Isthmus of Panama and along the Canal.

"GREATEST OF THEM ALL"

"The incomparable Beachey," was the title accorded Lincoln Beachey, considered world's greatest stunt flier. Long before the word "aviator" was used, reporters coined the more appropriate word "birdmen" for such famous men as Beachey, Eugene Ely, Philip Parmalee, Charles F. Willard, John Moisant, Arch Hoxsey. Up to 1908, the only fliers were inventors and airplane builders, cautious and patient men who safely demonstrated their own machines and had long careers. After 1908, however, the "birdmen" appeared. They flew for excitement, tested planes for speed and endurance, lived excitingly for a few months, then died. Crashes seemed useless, but each caused inventor to redesign, perfect his plane.

Beachey started out as a dirigible balloon pilot, a friend of Roy Knabenshue (pilot of the first American dirigible balloon) who convinced Curtiss to train Beachey. Daring, reckless, Beachey soon became famous stunt flier, able to scoop handkerchief off the field with his wing tip. Always sensational, Beachey flew over Niagara Falls through the Gorge on June 28, 1911, and under the Falls Bridge (above). Dressed as "The Mysterious Woman Aviatrix," Beachey (right) played a practical joke on air rival Blanche Stuart Scott, by thus entering a Los Angeles meet. He thrilled crowd by dropping down, averting an accident, and performing revolutions in the air. Beachey was drowned in San Francisco Bay, 1915, when his self-designed monoplane folded in air during World's Fair Exhibition. His death marked the end of "Birdmen Era."

LATE CURTISS PUSHER (left) is flown by Beachey. Plane featured "doughnut" wheels with fat tires, and ring cowling, whose function was to keep the rotary engine from spattering oil. Brother team (center) of early exhibition flying days was Lawrence D. Bell (l.) who later became president of Bell Aircraft Corporation, and Grover E. Bell. Larry, then 18, worked as a mechanic for both his brother and Beachey (1912). Race between an airplane and auto (right) in 1912 resulted in a close victory for Beachey, flying one of first Curtiss planes with ailerons in the wings. In this contest he defeated famous auto racer, Barney Oldfield.

AERIAL SENSATION of 1912 was flight of F. K. McClean through the Tower Bridge in London. He landed in the Lower Pool, then hopped and taxied along the river to Westminster. Stunt was typical of carefree, daring "Birdmen" who created early interest in art of flying.

ROBERT GRANDSEIGNE, wearing shock helmet, daringly flew over Paris and circled Eiffel Tower, on Feb. 11, 1911, at 2:30 A.M., in one of the first night flights ever made. He employed electrical balls to illuminate his plane in dark.

MAURICE PREVOST, famous French speed flier, won Gordon Bennett prize on Sept. 29, 1913, by setting speed record of 126.59 mph. Prevost is standing beside his Deperdussin monoplane, 1912 type, which was similar to plane used in his record flight.

FIRST AERIAL GUNS

The demands of war made many rapid changes in aviation armament. Early weapons (pistols, rifles) proved ineffective, gave way to light-weight machine guns. First gun mountings were awkward, unsatisfactory, had to be set to fire clear of rotating propeller. Capt. Charles DeF. Chandler (left) fired first machine gun (Lewis) June 7, 1912, from a Wright type "B" plane. In 1913 Pilot Manton flew a Grahame-White biplane (center) as Lt. Stellingwerf, Belgian Army, operated machine gun from basket beneath pilot. English mounted Maxim gun (right) on seat of later type French Farman.

FIRST BOMBSIGHT, invented by Lt. Riley Scott, was tested in U.S. in 1911, with bomb held by canvas under the plane. After experiments, Scott won $5,000 Michelin Prize for accuracy in bomb dropping, Jan. 11, 1912.

FIRST SUCCESSFUL RADIO air-to-ground wireless test by the Army was made at Ft. Riley, Kansas, November 2, 1912. At left, Lt. Follett Bradley (l.) observer and radio operator, and Lt. Henry H. Arnold (r.) pilot, are seated in the test plane, a Wright pusher type equipped with a wireless outfit. (The young flier later became famous as "Hap" Arnold, Commanding General of Army Air Forces.) At right, Glenn H. Curtiss (standing, fourth from left) observes the procedure in attaching the wireless apparatus to a Curtiss plane for further wireless experiments.

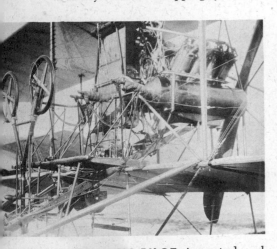

AUTOMATIC PILOT, invented and developed by Lawrence Sperry on gyroscopic principle, was the first in the world. It flew this Curtiss hydro-airplane, Hammondsport, N.Y., 1912.

CATAPULT LAUNCHING of a flying boat (Curtiss) was first made successfully at Wash. Navy Yard, Nov. 12, 1912, two years after the first flight from the deck of a ship. Based on an idea of Navy Capt. W.I. Chambers, the catapult used a cradle, which "went its way" after use.

ARMY WRIGHT "C" airplane, one of seven bought by the Army, was piloted by Lt. Frank P. Lahm (third from left), later Brig. Gen. (Ret.), stationed at Ft. McKinley, Philippine Islands, Feb., 1912. Lt. Lahm won the first James Gordon Bennett Balloon Cup Race among seven nations, Paris, 1906.

CHINESE AND JAPANESE aviators were actively engaged in aircraft operations. Below, left, Lt. C. Nakashima (l.) of Japanese Imperial Navy, is seated with Hugh Robinson in a Curtiss hydroairplane, a late type Curtiss pusher featuring dual control, no forward structure, and aileron arrangement at trailing edge of struts. At right, Capt. Madiot (kneeling in white) explains the mechanism, construction and handling of airplanes to a visiting Chinese Military Mission, plus a group of French military officers.

STRANGE BIPLANE, a mixture of wooden spars, canvas, and bicycle wheels, was created by cross-country flier Col. S. F. Cody, American who became British subject. Shown here readied for flight, 1909, plane made earliest known use of streamers, flags to judge effects of airflow.

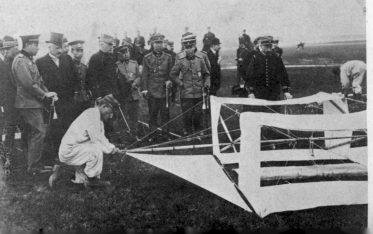

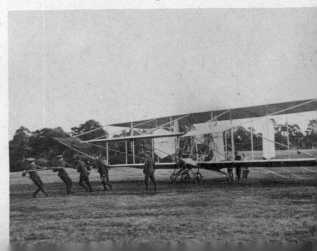

"GRANDDADDY OF NAVAL PHOTOGRAPHY" was title given Lt. Walter L. Richardson (l.), shown holding 5x7 Graflex camera, who made first Navy aerial photograph at Pensacola, Fla., 1914. Photographic reconnaissance became well developed in World War I, produced excellent aerial photos of battlefields.

NAVY LT. T. G. ELLYSON is shown about to launch a seaplane from shore, using novel catapulting method he invented, 1911. Balancing the plane by two wires beneath lower wings, supported by another heavily greased wire, he started engine full speed, held it, made take-off, rising smoothly and rapidly into air.

AMERICA'S EARLY MILITARY AVIATION

Military aviation was still considered a sideline in 1909. The U.S. Army had one airplane, but its two qualified pilots, Lts. Lahm and Humphreys, upon completing their training, returned to their original service branches.

Lt. B. D. Foulois, with only three hours of flight instruction, was left as the Army's only pilot. Dependent largely on his own financial resources, he flew the Army's one plane in winter operations at Ft. Sam Houston, Texas in 1910-11. Pilot training there came out of the one-man class, but after the fatal crash of Lt. G.E.M. Kelly (for whom Kelly Field, Texas was named), further training at the Texas field was prohibited.

A new flying school was built at College Park, near Washington, D.C., with Charles deForest Chandler as Commandant. F.A.I. regulations were adopted as tests for Army pilot ratings.

In 1911 Congress passed the first appropriation for Army aeronautics, $125,000, which permitted the purchase of new planes. The first Army airplane, now in need of repair, was presented to the Smithsonian Institution.

The Navy, in 1912, moved its Aviation Camp from Annapolis to North Island, San Diego, the location of Curtiss' flying school, and the Army's first permanent aviation school was established there early in 1913. At the close of that year the Navy had 9 planes; the Army's 19 were on duty at air fields in the Philippines, Hawaii, Texas and San Diego.

Because of accidents, Curtiss and Wright pushers were condemned early in 1914, leaving the Army with only a few planes. Pilot training came to a virtual standstill while plane rebuilding was underway.

When World War I began, France had the world's largest air force (about 1500 planes), Germany about 1,000, and the U.S. and Great Britain only about 100 each.

EARLY ARMY AIRPLANE (top) was Wright Brothers 1910 type, forerunner of AAF military aircraft. Pilot Lt. Benj. D. Foulois (second from left, later Brig. Gen., Asst. Chief of Army Air Corps) poses with original ground crew, Ft. Sam Houston, Texas. Initial planes used skids for landing, takeoff, and had elevators in front of wings. Later models incorporated wheeled landing gear, moved elevators to rear. Below, U.S. Navy pilots report back from reconnaissance flight over enemy's camp in Mexico.

NORTH ISLAND, San Diego, Cal., was the site of a Navy wooden hangar and headquarters in 1916. Before the Navy took over this site, it was a base for Glenn Curtiss' experiments with hydroairplanes.

ARMY MANEUVERS were conducted at San Antonio, Texas, with airplanes such as the Wright Brothers 1910 type, above, with passenger Lt. Loulois (l.) and Pilot Philip O. Parmalee (who took part in the Army's first aerial bombing operations in 1911).

NAVY'S LARGEST training base, located at Pensacola Beach, Fla. is shown early in 1914. Curly-tailed Curtiss flying boats and hydroairplanes are on the beach waiting to take off from wood ramps in front of tent hangars. Below, Burgess-Wright "coast defense" seaplane, which was sold to the Army in 1913, was used at Corregidor. Lt. Dargue is in the cockpit.

MILITARY AIRCRAFT underwent rapid experimentation and development once its use was appreciated. Early model wind-tunnel (below, far left) was used for testing 6,000 lb. Naval plane, 1915 design, at Wash. Navy Yard. Early Curtiss tractor (left center), military model (winter, 1912-13), was opposite of pusher type. It featured three-bladed propeller, chain-and-sprocket drive, flywheel, tricycle landing gear. Last Wright Brothers training plane (right center) purchased by U.S. Army before World War I was Model F, No. 39, known as "Tin Cow" because of metal covering on its forward fuselage. Curtiss JN-4 (far right) became famous as the Jenny, used to train many World War I aces. It was one of early Curtiss planes to have ailerons in wing instead of being hung from struts.

DARING BIRDGIRLS

In 1909, six years after the Wrights' famous flight, French Baroness de la Roche, flying a Voisin, became the first woman to pilot an airplane. A year later the first American woman pilot, Dr. Bessica Raiche, took to the air in a plane constructed by her husband. However, it was drama critic Harriet Quimby who distinguished herself as the first licensed U.S. woman pilot in 1911, after training at the Moisant Aviation School. Clad in a daring mauve satin flying suit (l.), she was called the "Dresden China Aviatrice." In April, 1912 she flew a Bleriot from England to France to win acclaim as first woman to fly English Channel.

SECOND WOMAN to receive pilot's license in America was Mathilde Moisant, sister of early flier John Moisant. She won own fame as exhibition pilot. At right, she poses with A. Houpert, Moisant school instructor.

BANNERED BANDWAGON announced exhibition by Moisant flying team which toured U.S. and Mexico in 1911-12. Thousands were thrilled by the flights of team stars, Harriet Quimby and Mathilde Moisant. On July 1, 1912, soon after her return from European triumphs, Miss Quimby was killed at an air show in Boston. Miss Moisant discontinued exhibition flying later in year.

◀ **BLANCHE SCOTT** gained the honor of being the first woman flier trained by noted pioneer, Glenn Curtiss. She began flying in 1910 at the Curtiss school in Hammondsport, N.Y. after completing the first cross-country automobile trip made by a woman. Curtiss had objections to her flying, as he felt an accident involving a woman would be detrimental to the budding aviation field. Miss Scott was permitted to continue her training, however, and successfully soloed in the fall of 1910. Although not licensed at that time, she was among first U.S. women pilots.

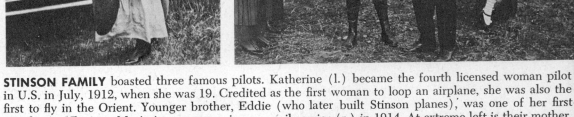

STINSON FAMILY boasted three famous pilots. Katherine (l.) became the fourth licensed woman pilot in U.S. in July, 1912, when she was 19. Credited as the first woman to loop an airplane, she was also the first to fly in the Orient. Younger brother, Eddie (who later built Stinson planes), was one of her first pupils. At 17, sister Marjorie was sworn in as a mail carrier (r.) in 1914. At extreme left is their mother.

OUTSTANDING pioneer woman pilot was France's Mlle. Helene Dutrieu. She appears with wingless trainer version of a Santos-Dumont *Demoiselle* in 1909. Her feats included record-breaking flights and impressive demonstrations in Europe and U. S.

FASHIONS FOR FLYING ran the gamut from the spectacular to the conservative. Louise Glaum's trench coat was in drab contrast to the satin of Harriet Quimby.

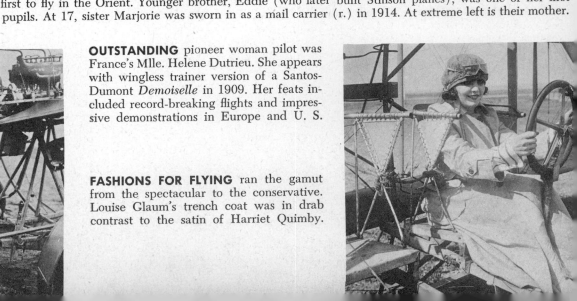

GLENN L. MARTIN

Iowa-born Glenn L. Martin was a successful automobile dealer in Santa Ana, California, when he decided to venture into the new field of aeronautics. Like many others, he began by building gliders. In 1908, he leased a vacant church in Santa Ana and started construction of a Curtiss-type plane of his own design, to be powered by a Ford Model "T" engine. On the morning of August 1, 1909, the plane flew for the first time and from then on Martin became active in all phases of aviation.

By 1910, the self-taught Martin was an accomplished pilot and in 1911 qualified for his F.A.I. aviator certificate. That same year he incorporated the original Glenn L. Martin Co., one of the first U.S. aircraft manufacturing plants.

Until 1917, Martin built civilian and military planes and then merged with the Wright Co. In 1918, he withdrew to reorganize the Glenn L. Martin Co., and then moved to Cleveland, Ohio.

MONEY-MAKING novelty flights, such as Glenn Martin's air delivery of newspapers from Fresno to Madera, California, in 1912 were necessary to finance further development and helped arouse public interest in aviation. Dropping a baseball to a catcher, and taking motion pictures while in flight were typical of Martin's early efforts to publicize aviation.

ENTHUSIASTIC CROWD gathered when, in 1912, Martin flew a float-equipped biplane over channel to complete round-trip flight between Newport Beach, California and nearby Santa Catalina Island.

MARTIN POSES somberly at left, with a group of fellow pioneer airmen. Shown with him are Marine Corps Lt. J. B. McClaskey; early stunt pilot Lincoln Beachey; and Navy Commander Holden C. Richardson. McClaskey and Richardson both were early students of Glenn Curtiss, as was Beachey who advanced to the airplane after a successful career as exhibition balloonist and airship pilot.

At center, popular comedian Joe E. Brown, complete with the familiar "backwards cap" of that period, nervously hangs on to perch behind helmeted Martin. Mrs. Minta Martin sits with her son, at right, in an early Martin plane. Mrs. Martin actively aided in the construction of the first plane which Martin built, and on May 20, 1912, soared with him to 1000 feet over Balboa Beach, Calif.

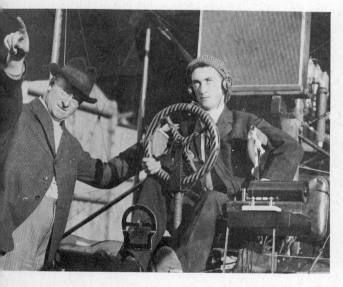

POINTING THE WAY to many was Dr. Wm. W. ("Doc") Christmas, pilot and plane builder. Following his finger is Wm. E. Russell, whose experiments with radio earned him apt nickname of "Wireless Will" (l.). After glider flights in 1905, Christmas made his first public flight in a plane at Fairfax City, Va. in May, 1908. Amid conflicting claims involving origin of airplane control systems, Christmas received a patent on use of ailerons for control.

"GAY NINETIES" adventurer, Charles Rolls, turned to airplanes after triumphs in British motor racing and ballooning. Renowned as "Rolls" of Rolls-Royce, he was taught to fly by Wilbur Wright, was first British air fatality.

CONTEMPLATIVE Walter Fairchild brought steel construction to aircraft in 1911 when he built a monoplane using steel for fuselage structure. It was not until many years later that steel fuselages met with general approval in planes.

CALIFORNIA'S CLIMATE, offering year-round flying weather, appealed to busy Glenn Curtiss, who established aviation base in January, 1911, on the barren waste of North Island in San Diego Bay. The base became an aviation center with planes, including two French *Antoinette* monoplanes (l.), using rough runways cleared through undergrowth. North Island was site of one of Curtiss' several flying schools. In 1912, students were offered free flying-boat instructions as part of the course. Class of early 1912 (c.) had pupils from India and Japan. Student then was Mrs. Julia Clark, America's third licensed woman pilot. Photo at right shows first aero engineer, Grover Loening, (l.), at North Island with the Vincent Astors. North Island later was to become a large Naval Aviation base.

FRANK T. COFFYN, a Wright protege (above, in cap and jacket, with Wilbur Wright), was one of the first six pupils of the famous brothers. In 1912 he fitted the first aluminum pontoons to his Wright model "B". In this, the first Wright hydroplane, he made a number of flights around New York harbor. The first, Feb. 6, 1912, started at the Battery where he took off in spite of floating ice in the Hudson river, flew to Grant's Tomb and back, circling the Statue of Liberty be-

fore returning to his starting point. The following week, Feb. 13, he again amazed New Yorkers by flying under both the Manhattan and Brooklyn bridges (above, top). The year before, famed writer Richard Harding Davis had gone for a ride with Coffyn, afterwards wrote an article called "The New World," for *Colliers,* stating that flying was "the thrill that makes all other sensations stale and vapid." Above, Coffyn stands in front of his Wright model "B" seaplane.

WRIGHT EXPERT by Feb., 1913, Frank T. Coffyn had joined the Burgess firm, licensed builders of Wright designs. By this time Wilbur Wright was dead, and Orville had all but dropped out of the aviation business. It was up to new groups to carry on the Wrights' work. Shown here are: (l. to r.) Lt. Comdr. P. Bellinger, unknown, Starling Burgess, Mrs. Burgess, Coffyn, Lt. Comdr. H. Richardson.

FLIGHT OF FIRST FLYING BOAT (at right) was achieved on Jan. 10, 1912, by Glenn H. Curtiss. Unlike the seaplane which has floats suspended beneath the fuselage, the flying boat lands directly on its hull. With his enthusiasm for water-based planes Curtiss rapidly perfected the flying boat after it showed early promise. Before the end of 1912, he had developed the Curtis F-Boat, several of which

were purchased by both the Army and Navy. Curtiss is seen above, left, standing by one of his *F-Boats* with Henry Ford (r.), whose interest in aviation was being aroused by the achievements of men of imagination like Curtiss. Ford's enthusiasm continued until about fifteen years later, when he ventured into the aircraft business himself, and began the manufacturing of trimotor transport planes.

SIKORSKY BUILDS WORLD'S LARGEST AIRPLANE

On May 13, 1913, Russian engineer Igor Sikorsky first flew the largest airplane of the time. It had four engines of 100 hp each, mounted in two tandem pairs, and wing span of 92 ft. With a gross weight of 9,000 lbs., the *Grand*, as it was called, included accommodations for eight, an enclosed control cabin, was equipped with altimeters, angle of attack, bank, airspeed indicators, etc. Above, the *Grand* is shown during later testing, the original four rudders reduced to two.

At the right, top, the *Grand* is seen as modified in June, 1913. The power plant arrangement was changed to four-in-line. In this form, the airplane was inspected by Czar Nicholas in July, 1913. The *Grand* was wrecked when the engine fell out of an airplane overhead and smashed the *Grand's* wing.

A second four-engined giant, the *Ilia Mourometz*, was flown by Sikorsky, Jan., 1914. It was developed into a bomber, a series of which were quite successfully employed by the Imperial Russian Air Service in World War I. One of these *Mourometz* bombers is shown (right) with Sikorsky (2) opposite his former partner, General Shidlovsky (1.). Sikorsky was decorated by the Czar for his developments.

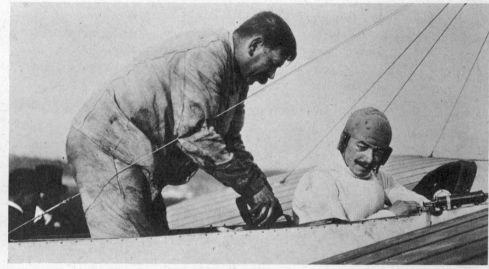

TAUBE OR "DOVE" type monoplane was originally developed about 1909-10 by Igo Etrich of Austria. Basing his ideas on the *Zanonia* leaf, actually a gliding seed pod, Etrich made his first machine tailless, but soon turned to more conventional models. A great success, the *Taube* became the standard German military service type before World War I.

LOOPING AN AIRPLANE was first accomplished by Adolphe Pegoud of France (above, being strapped into his Bleriot) in 1913. Prior to that time, it was assumed that if an airplane lost its normal equilibrium it would almost certainly meet disaster. After Pegoud proved otherwise, daredevils of the sky added new stunts to their repertoires. Meanwhile, another Frenchman, Legagneaux, set altitude record of 20,090 ft., December 28, 1913.

MORANE-SAULNIER monoplane, developed from the Bleriot by Leon Morane (page 55), had become very popular by 1913. One of these fast monoplanes is seen above as it takes off in a cloud of dust. In an identical aircraft, the well-known French airman, Roland Garros, made the first Mediterranean air crossing, Cannes to Bizerte, 558 miles, on Sept. 23, 1913. The longest overwater flight yet attempted, it took 7 hrs., 53 min. flying time. A very progressive company, Morane-Saulnier developed several streamlined racers, one of which, on floats, was a strong contender in the first Schneider Trophy race in 1913. Another of their late developments is shown above. Built about the same time, it featured a completely enclosed 100-hp Gnome rotary engine and a streamlined plywood fuselage.

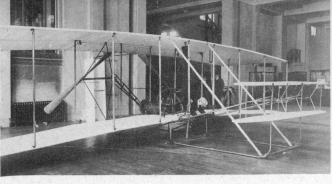

CERTAIN THEY WERE RIGHT, the brothers Orville and Wilbur (left) resented the claim of the Smithsonian Institution that Dr. Samuel Langley had invented the airplane. Refusing to compromise, Orville finally sent the original Wright biplane to the Science Museum, London in 1928, where it remained (above) for 20 years. At last, in 1942, the issue was settled, and the English museum built a replica (right), then returned the machine to the U.S., where it was formally given to Smithsonian Institution Washington, D.C. Dec. 17, 1948.

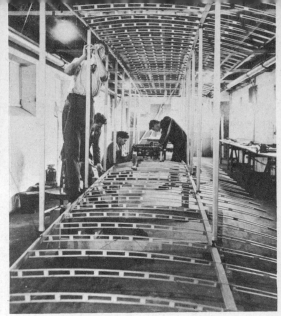

SIDELIGHT of the Wright controversy is seen above. Ruth Law, famous aviatrix who made notable flights in the U.S. and Japan (1914-16) used a Curtiss biplane equipped with a Wright control system, because she had learned to fly with Wright equipment.

NORTH POLE discoverer Admiral Peary took his first plane ride Oct. 12, 1915, piloted by Frank H. Burnside (r.), member of the Aero Club of America.

WRIGHT BROTHERS TAKE LEGAL ACTION

"So long as there is any money to be made by the use of the products of our brains, we propose to have it ourselves." This statement of Wilbur and Orville Wright expressed the feeling that prompted them to bring suit August 18, 1909, against Glenn Curtiss for alleged patent infringement, followed shortly by similar action against a number of other aviation pioneers in Europe as well as in the U.S.

In 1903 the Wrights had applied for a patent on their flying machine. This patent (No. 821,393) was granted on May 22, 1906, allowing 18 claims which to a considerable degree covered the entire field of flying machines. Nearly all who built workable airplanes, therefore, were technically guilty of infringement. In practice, the Wrights never interfered with amateurs or those trying to develop the science. They mercilessly attacked however, those who built machines for profit. This action made the Wrights very unpopular with the aviation press of the time and with the general population in Europe where the heroes of the day, Bleriot and Farman, were defendants.

The real fight was with Glenn Curtiss, since much personal feeling was involved. The first injunction against Curtiss was revoked, then quickly reimposed. A series of court battles followed, with the verdict finally granted in the Wrights' favor, Jan. 13, 1914. Curtiss then altered his aileron design (the main bone of contention), and the Wright Brothers started legal action again. This case continued until August, 1917, when, with the war emergency pressing, the case was dropped.

A study of all the evidence, in the light of present-day knowledge, indicates that the viewpoint of the Wrights was substantially correct.

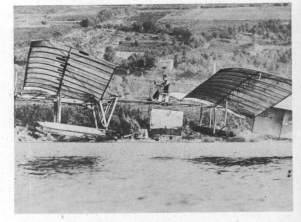

CONFUSION entered the Wright case when Glenn Curtiss flew the Langley *Aerodrome* on June 2, 1914. While many felt that this vindicated the Smithsonian Institution's claims, Orville Wright pointed out that drastic revisions in the machine's structure had been made since Langley's original attempts to fly it. By 1914, sufficient had been learned to make it a relatively simple matter to fly any airplane of basically sound configuration. Eventually, in October, 1942, the Smithsonian stated that it had erred in cooperating with Curtiss, himself involved in litigation with Wright at the time, and that the *Aerodrome* had been so modified that its 1914 test was inconclusive.

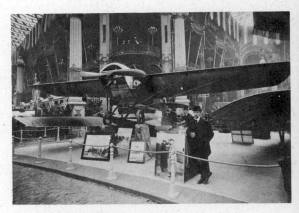

PARIS AERO SALON was held each pre-war year from 1908, attracting most of the European manufacturers. The 1913 Nieuport exhibit is shown above.

PUNITIVE EXPEDITION into Mexico by U.S. Army in 1914 was first use of American airplanes in actual warfare. Most of the aircraft employed were Curtiss JN-4's (below), later famous as the *Jenny* trainers of World War I. The Mexican campaign was valuable in preparing the infant U.S. Air Service for later participation in World War I. Major H. A. Darque, below, kept photographer purposely posing him until mob of Mexicans who had stoned him quieted.

FIRST SCHEDULED AIRLINE

New Year's Day, 1914, witnessed the inauguration of the world's first regularly scheduled air passenger service. The 22-mile route, Tampa to St. Petersburg, Florida, was flown by a Benoist flying boat, similar to the contemporary Curtiss F-boats. Like the latter, the Benoist had room for only one passenger, beside the pilot, and the fare was necessarily high. Nevertheless, the first day's operation was properly heralded as a milestone in aviation history, the opening ceremonies attended by 6,000 people. Scene of the event, at right shows in foreground (l. to r.) Bannister, a local businessman; A. C. Pheil, mayor of St. Petersburg and first passenger; Anthony (Tony) Jannus, pilot; P.E. Fansler, manager; L.A. Whitney, Secretary of the Board of Trade; Thomas (Tom) Benoist, designer of the airplane. After a few weeks of operation, the line was a financial failure, but its operation afforded a brief glimpse into the future of commercial air transportation. Tony Jannus had been a famous cross-country flier (1910-11) as well as having been the first to pilot a plane for a parachute jumper (Captain Albert Berry, during 1912).

SWEPT WING tailless airplane, the Burgess-Dunne was an early preview of mid-century bombers. This 1916 model was well streamlined. Dunne had built his first tailless airplanes in England back in 1910.

FLYING BOAT "AMERICA" was built by Curtiss in 1914 for a projected trans-Atlantic flight. Lt. John C. Porte of England was scheduled to make the attempt, and the entire project was financed by Rodman Wanamaker of New York. Curtiss designed and built the *America* (left) in record time, but the start of World War I prevented the flight at the last minute. Above right, are seen (l. to r.) Lt. Porte; his assistant, George Hallet; Glenn Curtiss; and Miss Katherine Mossan, who christened the *America*. At war's outbreak Lt. Porte was called back to England, where he was instrumental in getting the *America* type purchased by the Royal Navy for coastal patrol duties. From this developed the big H-12 *America* patrol boats and the English-built "F" series and H-16 Porte flying boats.

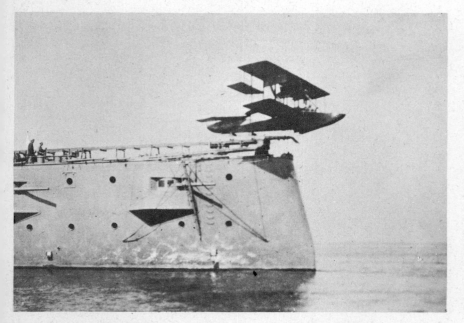

CATAPULT LAUNCHING from a warship was first performed successfully (above) in November, 1915, aboard the *U.S.S. North Carolina*. The airplane was a Curtiss *F-boat*, piloted by Capt. Henry C. Mustin, U.S.N. The launching device, developed from the ideas of Capt. Washington Irving Chambers, U.S.N., was operated by compressed air. A complete success, it was soon put in service.

VERVILLE PUSHER was built in 1916 by Alfred Verville, a former assistant of Glenn Curtiss. Its configuration was typical of the pusher fighters of the time, though the Verville was more streamlined, especially in the neat installation of the 100-hp Curtiss OX engine. By this time, however, the pusher type had already become outmoded and was used only at the beginning of World War I.

GERMANY'S WAR HAWKS TOOK LARGE-SCALE WARFARE INTO THE SKIES, THEN LOST THEIR EARLY DOMINANCE OF THE CLOUDS TO ALLIED PLANES AS THE WAR PROGRESSED

First World War

Despite opposition, airplane role changes from scouting to combat and reveals for first time its power as a weapon of destruction

With a record of 26 air victories that has never been equalled for the time in combat, Capt. Eddie Rickenbacker was America's first "ace." When the U.S. entered World War I, he enlisted and went to France with General Pershing as a staff driver, transferring shortly thereafter to Gen. Billy Mitchell's Air Command. As Commanding Officer of the 94th Aero Pursuit Squadron—the famous "Hat-in-the-Ring" Squadron—he won lasting fame for his exploits.

WHEN World War I broke out there were only a few score men in the United States, and only a few hundred in the entire world, who had ever flown a plane. The first airplanes to appear at the front were frail little linen-and-bamboo "pushers," much like the primitive plane in which the Wright Brothers had achieved man's first powered flight scarcely ten years before.

Under the impetus of war, the mechanical development of airplanes and engines was astounding. Within two years we had fighter planes that could fly more than 100 miles an hour and carry not only the pilot, but one or more machine guns as well.

The art of mastering these aircraft developed with equally astonishing rapidity. There was so

TOP U.S. WAR ACE EDDIE RICKENBACKER

little known of flying, that once we grasped a few fundamentals, we just took off and taught ourselves the rest. We were concerned principally in getting as much as we could out of our planes and getting down alive.

We could not see very far into the future, but I had watched the plane grow from a rickety "kite" to a fairly stable machine which, by the end of the war, was capable of carying several men and as much as a ton of bombs.

Because I knew engines and saw constantly more powerful motors being produced year after year, there was no question in my mind but that military aviation would be the deciding factor in another war that was sure to come.

Even then I felt the real potential of the airplane was in transportation. I could see it revolutionizing our entire way of life.

With the tremendous development that has taken place since World War I, the airplane is today the most important single factor in our life. Even so, it has only begun to demonstrate its unlimited ability to serve mankind. I am confident that men of goodwill can, and will, turn it from the most destructive weapon God ever let man create into the Angel of Peace that, in His wisdom, He originally intended it to be.

Eddie Rickenbacker

Colonel Jesse G. Vincent, former vice-president of engineering of the Packard Motor Car company (1912-15), co-designed with J. G. Hall of the Hall-Scott Motor Co., and guided into production the Liberty Aircraft engine of World War I, first aircraft engine with standardized parts to be mass-produced.

LIBERTY ENGINE CO-DESIGNER J. G. VINCENT

MASS production of aircraft engines with standardized parts first came to the U.S. with the Liberty engine of World War I. No engine since that time has probably had more influence in aircraft development. From 1914 to 1917, 15,131 were built, 6500 of them by Packard Motor Car Co. which largely guided the engine production program from its inception.

In February, 1916, we produced a 12-cylinder engine with cylinders set in blocks of three and in banks of six at an inclined angle of 60 degrees, and in April, 1917 a 12-cylinder engine, three times the size of the earlier engine and with 905-cubic-inch piston displacement. These two engines were largely the basis of the design approved by the Army and Navy Aircraft Production Board for sample production June 4, 1917.

The new engine was called the "Liberty" because the first test model was inspected by government officials on Independence Day, 1917, only 33 days after we had begun the first drawings for it.

Although the government asked for five 12-cylinder engines and five 8-cylinder engines on a test run, the project to supply the Allies with an engine that could be mass-produced quite possibly would have died had not England promptly cabled an order for 1,000 of them as soon as the endurance test on the first 12-cylinder model was completed. Actually, the order to build production Liberty engines for the Army and Navy was not definitely given until September, 1917. The first production-built motor was sent to Washintgon on Thanksgiving Day that year. By May of 1918, we were producing at a rate of 15 per day and reached a total of 900 during the month of October.

By October 1918, total Liberty engine production by six manufacturers was over 5000 and would have reached 10,000 by April 1919 if the war had continued.

The fighter planes in use by the Allies were not designed to take such a heavy engine as the Liberty. In January 1918, a two-seater fighter, the *LePere*, was authorized for development by Packard, equipped with the Liberty 12-cylinder engine. It was flight-tested in May and production of 25 was authorized. The Armistice came before the order was completed. Predictions at the time were that it would have become one of the principal U.S. combat planes had the war continued. Later this bi-plane with supercharged Liberty engine set an altitude record of 34,509 feet.

J. G. Vincent

FLEDGLING GERMAN pilots learned to fly in a variety of aircraft including this *Albatross* two-seater trainer. One of the most satisfactory school machines in the world, its design stemmed from aircraft used by the pioneer German pilots Hirth and von Loessl to establish records for altitude and endurance just before the war. German aircraft were heavier, higher-powered than Allied planes.

FRENCH AND ENGLISH flying services freely exchanged airplane designs and ideas with the result that both had fairly standardized types in August, 1914. This lineup of French Farman "pusher" trainers could have been duplicated in England where the same model was called the *Longhorn*. Early French air equipment included the Zodiac class blimp airship. One is shown in flight.

WAR TAKES ON NEW DIMENSION

Belligerents experiment to discover wider military uses for the airplane

Long before the first shot was fired in World War I, a battle had been raging in army headquarters of many nations. That fight was over the part the airplane, or the "air arm," would play in any future international military conflict.

Die-hard military conservatives looked at aviation either as a branch of the signal corps or of the cavalry. They acknowledged that aircraft could range farther and see more of the enemy's movements than cavalry and that airplanes were useful in messenger work. But here their confidence in the value of an air arm ended.

The airplane, they claimed, was limited to flight in fair weather during daylight hours. Where one man could care for five horses, one airplane required the attention of at least five ground crewmen plus the flying crew.

Supporters of air power painted a much more useful future for the airplane, but all in theory. They said planes could be employed for tactical and strategic duties: they could direct artillery fire in support of ground operations, and fly hundreds of miles to drop bombs on distant targets, thus multiplying the range of artillery. The truth was, neither group correctly called the turns that military aircraft would take when it was to be widely used for the first time in warfare.

Both groups thought of the airplane only in its relationship with ground action: neither anticipated that it would be developed to participate in warfare against opposing air forces and thus present an entirely new concept of the airplane as a military weapon. This pattern was recognized first by the proponents of military aviation who scrambled to experiment with innovations, but had no formulas to implement or prove the value of their ideas.

WINSTON CHURCHILL, First Lord of the Admiralty in 1914 and a qualified pilot, is here starting from Portsmouth on an inspection of the British fleet.

In general the schemes trying to make the airplane a dominant weapon in 1914 and 1915 were sound. Air-ground rockets developed by the Frenchman, Le Prieur, prophesied the "Tiny Tim" rocket of World War II. Water-cooled infantry machine guns were modified to air-cooled models for aircraft, to save weight and take advantage of the cold air in which they operated. Aircraft cannon, originally various calibre infantry pieces, were taken aloft and tested.

As a result, aircraft of all types—anything capable of flying—were pressed into service. Out of this chaos of theory versus experience finally came a pattern: aircraft for purely scouting purposes were developed as light, fast, short-range types; weight-carrying planes with longer range were employed as bombers; and similar types substituting additional fuel for the weight of bombs were developed to reconnoitre and photograph enemy installations. Grouped together such duties made the "air arm" a useful aid to ground operations.

Although specific duties were recognized, the true fighting airplane was still to emerge—that type of plane which would embody a fighter pilot facing the enemy through whirling propeller blades armed with a synchronized gun.

ZEPPELIN RAIDS on French cities and English coastal towns began soon after war was declared. More terrifying than damaging, these night raids were first to bring fear and inconvenience of modern warfare to non-military populations. The action caused the Allies to withdraw men and equipment to satisfy the clamor for more home protection. Anticipating aerial bombing attacks from airplanes as well (which did not occur in England until 1916) the British government in 1915 authorized publication of German and English airplane silhouettes to help citizens identify friendly and enemy airplanes overhead. The Zeppelin service, which mainly cruised with the German fleet, received a substantial blow in November, 1914, when Wing-Cmdr. E.F. Briggs, D.S.O., bombed one of its bases.

PUBLIC WARNING

The public are advised to familiarise themselves with the appearance of British and German Airships and Aeroplanes, so that they may not be alarmed by British aircraft, and may take shelter if German aircraft appear. Should hostile aircraft be seen, take shelter immediately in the nearest available house, preferably in the basement, and remain there until the aircraft have left the vicinity: do not stand about in crowds and do not touch unexploded bombs.

In the event of HOSTILE aircraft being seen in country districts, the nearest Naval, Military or Police Authorities should, if possible, be advised immediately by Telephone of the TIME OF APPEARANCE, the DIRECTION OF FLIGHT, and whether the aircraft is an Airship or an Aeroplane.

GERMAN AIRSHIPS	BRITISH AIRSHIPS
AEROPLANES	AEROPLANES

FIRST BRITISH PLANE to land in France was this B.E. 2B, an unarmed, two-place observation type. The pilot, Major Harvey-Kelly, D.S.O., was officer of the Royal Irish Regiment attached to the Royal Flying Corps and is seen reading a map near the haystack (r.). He landed at Amiens on August 13, 1914, with 36 other British planes. This was first mass movement of airplanes in history.

PRIZE OF WAR was this Rumpler *Taube* monoplane captured by the French in September, 1914. A widely used German plane, its wings and tail were shaped like those of a dove, hence its name. Sturdy and reliable, the two-man *Taubes* scouted for the German armies advancing through Belgium. At height of the drive, Immelmann in a *Taube*, dropped pamphlets over Paris urging surrender.

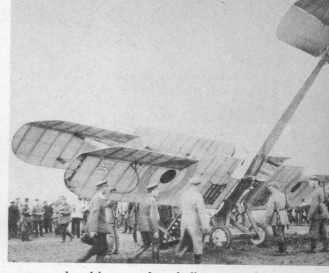

BOMBS DROPPED by hand were part of the guesswork of early military aviation. By 1915, the inherent dangers of operating primitive planes were increased by frequent exchanges of machine gun or small arms fire by opposing planes. Every known means of destruction that could be carried by an airplane was tried, including skyrockets developed by the French (c.) for use against German balloons. Ineffective, they were replaced by incendiary bullets. Mutual respect for dangers of early air fighting led to the development of unwritten rules of chivalry among enemy airmen, not unlike that of knights of the Middle Ages. German pilots who downed English plane (r.) virtually undamaged took delight in entertaining the crew at their headquarters, toasting their ability as aviators.

AERIAL ARTILLERY appeared in many strange forms, clearly pointing out that the turn of events in the air was not foreseen by airplane designers or military strategists. Guns were added to existing types haphazardly and with little regard for efficiency, safety and comfort of the airmen. The French gunner (left) literally "stood up" to the Germans in order to fire his rifle. His only protection was a thin metal shield and warm clothing. Infantry weapons, such as the 3-inch cannon shown mounted on a Voisin bomber (center) gave more trouble to the airplane's crew than they did to the enemy and late in 1915 were abandoned in favor of smaller rapid-fire cannon and machine guns. Lieut. Antoine Marchal French aviator (r.), demonstrated the possibility of bombing Berlin by flying from France to drop leaflets on the German city. Scheduled to continue across Germany to Russia, engine failure forced him down in Austria to be captured.

ANTHONY H. G. FOKKER, Dutch airplane designer (l.) in 1915 added the machine gun synchronizer to his list of aviation achievements. Although he claimed Dutch neutrality to escape military service in Germany, his factories there turned out some of the best planes in the German Air Service. Among them was the 1915 Fokker E-III monoplane (center) which carried many early German pilots to victory until its capture revealed to Allies the secret of the German synchronized gun. The first practical synchronized gun in history was a hastily modified Parabellum machine gun (r.) mounted ahead of the cockpit on the fuselage of a one-place Fokker scouting plane.

FOKKER BUILDS SYNCHRONIZED GUN

As inevitable a military development as the airplane itself, the synchronized machine gun had for years eluded the best efforts of armament engineers to perfect it into a practical air weapon. Inventors knew what they were after: a simple device which would regulate the fire of a machine gun so that its bullets would pass through the revolving blades of a plane's propeller without striking them. August Euler, a pioneer German pilot and plane builder, received a patent on such a device in 1910, but did not develop his invention. By late 1914, the English Sopwith-Kauper system was still unperfected. Then France's Roland Garros, famed pre-war stunt pilot serving at front, together with plane builder Raymond Saulnier worked out a substitute device. To the propeller of a Morane-Saulnier scout monoplane they attached steel guards to protect the propeller from bullets

fired through it from a free-firing Lebel automatic rifle. But on a flight in March, 1915, when Garros fired at a German plane, the vibration from bullets striking the steel guards shattered the propeller and he had to land in German territory. Garros' captured plane, and what was left of the propeller, were turned over to Anthony Fokker who was asked to perfect it. Citing the analogy of a Dutch boy throwing stones between the revolving blades of a windmill, Fokker developed a practical synchronizer. Applied to Germany's best scout planes, the device gave her pilots a temporary advantage over the gun-toting French and English planes. Immediately, Allied single-seat scouts retaliated with machine guns mounted above their upper wings, firing freely over the revolving propeller. Almost over night, militarists who had ridiculed the value of aircraft in war reversed their opinions, and begged manufacturers for better planes with which to meet the enemy in the skies. Air warfare had become a reality. At once the belligerents began redoubling their efforts in the development of the airplane as a weapon.

PILOT ADJUSTS GARROS-SAULNIER DEVICE

GERMAN TOWS BRITON IN BOASTFUL CARTOON

EARLY NIEUPORT XVII USED AN OVER-WING GUN

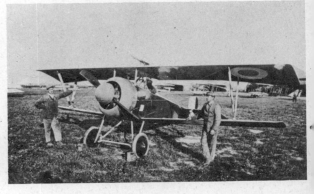

CARTRIDGES ARE READIED for machine gun whose synchronizer is built into the engine of this French Spad-VII. Allied synchronizers worked on the hydraulic principle rather than on Fokker's mechanical system. The hydraulic system, invented by Rumanian engineer Georges Constantinuescue, worked much like automobile brakes. A pump sent pulses through a tiny tube of oil, interrupting the gun's fire when the propeller was in the way. Propeller did not affect the gun's rate of fire as it did in the Fokker system, where gun was run by cams on propeller shaft; slow-moving propeller meant slow fire.

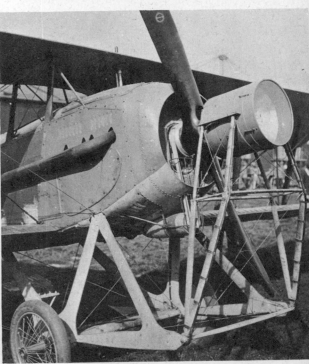

NIGHT FLYING in 1916 resulted in a number of odd innovations, including this searchlight mounted on a French Spad. Its purpose was to light up ground targets and to help the pilot find his home landing field in the dark. Night fliers were generally aided by crudely-constructed oil or gasoline flares set along the airport runway.

LAFAYETTE ESCADRILLE was formed in 1915 when American youths in the French Foreign Legion gained transfers to the French Air Service, then petitioned to form an all-American squadron under French Command. The Lafayette, officially named Squadron No. 124, gave an outstanding performance, became a symbol, returning Lafayette's aid to the Americans during the Revolution.

U. S. AIR BUILDUP began when America entered war, April 6, 1917. Training schools were enlarged and new flying fields were established, bringing a flood of applicants for pilot training. Successful candidates were taught rudiments of flying, then held in reserve until squadrons were sent overseas for final instruction. On September 1, 1917, the First Aero Squadron began its operations in France.

U.S. ENTERS WAR

STUDENTS BEACH SEAPLANE at Yale's air patrol station, Huntington L.I., a prominent example of the many college and university reserve squadrons which helped speed up the war-time growth of U.S. air strength. Members of Yale's reserve group were assigned to coastal patrols. Yale's program, embracing both Army and Navy, included one of few units.

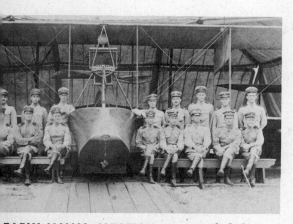

EARLY NAVAL AVIATION group included many pioneers and aviators who later were to be known for outstanding record flights. Front row, left to right: Sufley, Bellinger, Towers, Mustin, Read, Johnson, Cunningham, Evans, Haase. Back row: Paunack, Spencer, Bartlett, Edwards, Bronson, Carry, Norfleet, McDonnell, Scofield, with Curtiss flying boat.

STRICT CENSORSHIP imposed on neutral U.S. kept American plane makers in the dark regarding late European developments. Early 1917 Wright-Martin "R" biplane, complete with motorbike, was a serious conception in the U.S. of a military airplane.

Declaration of war on the Central Powers by the United States threw a tremendous production and manpower potential to the side of the embattled Allies. In the air, America was ridiculously weak, with only 35 pilots, 55 second-rate training planes that had seen service along the Mexican Border, and 1,087 enlisted men. Equally weak was America's technical knowledge and experience in combat plane design and construction. As an ally, the U.S. soon was visited by English, French and Italian missions laden with up-to-date engineering data. Hasty meetings with Aircraft Production Board resulted in a Congressional appropriation of $675 million in July 1917, the largest amount ever voted for a single purpose up to that time.

This sum provided for construction of 22,500 airplanes, expansion of aviation personnel to nearly 10,000 officers and 87,000 enlisted men, development of the "Liberty" engine, and establishment of new training fields.

Lacking modern fighting plane designs, U.S. manufacturers built training planes by the thousands and taught young men to fly them in both contract and military schools. Successful foreign airplane designs, particularly the British De Havilland-4's, were adapted to U. S. methods of production. In a matter of months, almost every branch of American industry was involved in building some part of U.S. aerial might.

American pilots reaching France at first were assigned to English and French squadrons. The first American pursuit squadron to go into action —the 103rd, on February 18, 1918,—was formed from the Lafayette Escadrille. The all-American squadrons which came to the Front shortly after were outfitted exclusively with aircraft purchased from the Allies. The first American-made combat plane to join the A.E.F. was a Liberty-engined DH-4 on May 11, 1918. From then on, Germany felt U.S. air power in action.

PROMINENT PERSONALITIES took an active part in the drive to build interest in U.S. air preparedness. Socialite Mrs. Charles A. Van Rensselaer served as chairman of the National Aero Committee. With her (above), is Walter Camp, famous Yale athletic coach, originator of the "All-American" football selections and the "Daily Dozen" exercises. Pioneer girl flier, Katherine Stinson, below, proved women had a place in aviation. She flew thousands of miles in her own plane recruiting, selling Liberty Bonds and dropping leaflets, such as printed appeals for the Red Cross, on principal cities in the U.S.

AMERICAN PILOTS often learned to fly the hard way at French flying schools. After several hours' instruction on pre-war French trainers like the Caudron G.3 "flying bathtub", below, it was said a student pilot could fly anything, even a barn door.

HIGH ALTITUDE flights were everyday fare for No. 139 Squadron, R.A.F., in operations against Austria from Italian bases. This squadron often crossed the Alps and ranged as far north as Switzerland with its two-place Bristol F2-B fighters. Commanded by Major William Barker, No. 139 and other Allied squadrons gained air mastery from Austria, who previously overwhelmed the Italians.

NO. 85 SQUADRON, Royal Air Force, with American pilots, English and Canadian commanders, including top Aces Col. Billy Bishop and Major Mickey Mannock, flew 130-mph SE-5a pursuit planes. U.S. squadrons which trained in combat with French, English, Italian forces, later provided commanders for A.E.F. units.

DANGEROUS JOB for ground crews was starting an airplane engine by hand. Crews took pride in the combat performance of planes in their care, worked long hours tuning them up to perfection. Engine mechanics, riggers and repair men were specialists, well-trained as the pilots whose lives depended on their skill.

FIRST AMERICAN-BUILT combat plane received in France by the A.E.F. (June, 1918) was this DeHavilland-4, based on a successful English design but powered by the 400 horsepower "Liberty" engine built by U.S. automobile manufacturers. Although not as modern as many 1918 foreign military designs, the DH-4 was an outstanding observation and bombing plane. English Sopwith "1½ Strutters" seen below at a supply field, were named for their peculiar wing bracing, and were also used in large numbers by American and French forces. A low-powered, late 1915 design, this plane started out as a two-seat fighter and served out the war in artillery spotting, light bombing and photo reconnaissance.

OBSOLETE PLANES used by some U.S. squadrons in the spring of 1918 gave added danger to normal hazards of air fighting. French Nieuport 28's of the 95th Pursuit Squadron, A.E.F., above, occasionally shed wing coverings in a dive, often kept American pilots from going after enemy. Spad 13's later replaced them.

HUGE AIR TRAINING BASE was established by the U.S. at Issoudon, France, to teach basic military flying techniques to American pilots who had learned to fly in the States. Here these fledglings got their first taste of air fighting tactics.

BREATHTAKING TERROR of air combat was impossible to capture with a camera but imaginative artists brought its horror to the public with powerful realism. The 1918 Liberty Loan painting by John O. Todahl (c.) depicts a French Spad XVI battling with a German Albatros C-III. Continued interest in air-war during the post-war period developed aviation art specialists who drew planes more accurately in vividly-imagined situations. Dime novel air-war pulp magazines of the Thirties carried covers by artists like William Blakeslee. Highly accurate were his paintings of English Sopwith "Camels" and Vickers "Vimy" bombers (l.) attacking German artillery positions and (r.) the pilot of a German Pfalz D-III meeting swift death from the guns of a British DeHavilland-4.

AERIAL PHOTOGRAPHY in 1914 utilized conventional cameras and techniques but by 1918 had become an entirely new branch of photographic science. Photographic maps, made from photos taken straight down, were used to determine position and strength of the enemy. Photos taken at a slant gave a perspective view of the ground. By late 1916, areas to be bombed were photographed and specific targets chosen by a new art, "photo reconnaissance." Wrecked plane (l.) carried a movie camera to photograph aerial activity for newsreel audiences. Movies of flight formations, aerobatics or squadron procedures were used in indoctrination and training. Aerial photos taken of battle progress, like French gas attack on the Western Front (c.), were dropped to processing units on the ground where, in a few minutes, an army commander could judge the success of the operation. Aerial cameras (r.) came to be widely used during 1918.

LOW FLYING ground attack planes were developed by the belligerents, particularly Germany. Strikingly modern was the all-metal Junkers CL-I of 1918, a design of Professor Hugo Junkers, pioneer German metal airplane specialist. Attack planes shot up troops and installations, were armored to protect their crews.

PLATED SECTION of a downed German A.E.G. ground attack plane is guarded by a British soldier. Machine guns, in addition to those for the pilot and gunner, protrude from bottom of fuselage. Armor made planes heavy and awkward.

FOKKER D-VIII was a late 1918 German pursuit plane with a plywood-covered cantilever wing developed by the Dutch designer. The Fokker wing tapered in thickness from the center toward its tips. It did not require external wires or struts, which created wind resistance, to give it strength. Fokker used this principle on several wartime and post-war types.

DEFEAT OR VICTORY for slow, cumbersome observation or bombing planes depended on the pilot's skill and the gunner's marksmanship. By 1918 aerial gunnery in training and in combat had become an art. Materiel-starved Germany used paper miniature planes on a reel (l.) to give student gunners, equipped with wooden "machine guns," practice in tracking moving objects. The Allies were better off, trained aerial gunners in real airplanes (l., center) shooting at real flying targets, but with a "machine gun" that took pictures of "hits." Allied gunners used a standardized brace of two machine guns (r., center) that could be turned to shoot in almost any direction. The gunner of his German Halberstadt CL-II fighter (r.) was well equipped to carry out his ground attack duties. His Parabellum machine gun was fitted with a telescopic sight, a rifle stock, and he was surrounded by grenades and signal flares. This plane is named for pilot's girl friend.

MILITARY AIRSHIPS AND BALLOONS

Lighter-than-air craft, the first means by which men were carried aloft, were put to a variety of uses during World War One. "Rigid" types—those with a framework made of wood or metal to hold their shape—were made famous by Count Ferdinand von Zeppelin, whose name the type bore as a classification. Of the 120 Zeppelins built by Germany from 1914 through 1918, a mere half-dozen survived the war, only to be sabotaged by mutinous German naval troops at Nordholz Zeppelin station. Twelve others were dismantled as unfit for further service. The rest were destroyed by enemy action or operational accidents. The L-49 (above), one of the few captured intact, was shot down in France during the night of October 19, 1917, perhaps becoming the largest prize of war on record. Tremendous size of the Zeppelins dwarfed the tethered observation balloons which carried one or two men assigned to observing enemy activities. When the balloon was attacked, the defenseless observers jumped to safety (r.) equipped with the earliest practical parachutes, while balloon was pulled to earth.

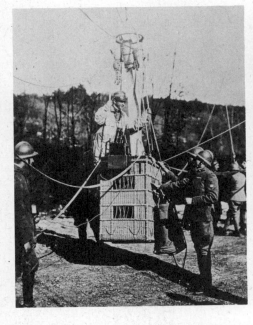

L-40 CLASS Zeppelins were 643 feet long, 79 feet in diameter, carried 30 tons of fuel, equipment and bombs. Holding a crew of 22 men, it could cruise for four days, travel 62 mph, and climb to 21,000 feet. It was the most widely utilized Zeppelin class; 17 of them were constructed in 1917.

ITALIAN OBSERVER prepares to go aloft in captive balloon (l.). Allies called captive balloons "sausages" because of their shape. Germans, transporting a balloon by its cables (above), named them "Drachen" (kites). Crews communicated to ground posts by phone, radio.

◀ **EXPLOSION** of the highly inflammable hydrogen gas used to inflate captive balloons was ever-present danger to their handling crews. American "sausage" (l.) blows up, and burns as static spark ignites gas.

PARASITE FIGHTER, an airplane attached to a ▶ "mother" airship for its protection, was tried by the English. A Sopwith *Camel* pursuit was attached to the dirigible R-33 experimentally in an attempt to find a means of defending British airships from German attack. Although device was not used in combat, Lt. R.E. Keys, R.A.F., was successfully released from the R-33 and piloted *Camel* to a safe landing.

ANTI-SUBMARINE patrols were carried out on the Atlantic Coast by U.S. Navy non-rigid "blimps," built by the Goodyear and Goodrich rubber companies. Airship crew training began with spherical "free" balloons and small, powered "blimps" (below). Goodyear school class of July, 1917 (l.) saw Atlantic service. Crew car was attached (r.) to "blimp" by ropes and "finger patches."

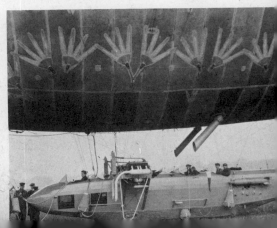

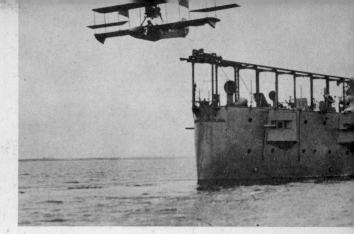

DEADLY COMBINATION for Allied shipping was the German Raider Wolf and its seaplane, Wolfchen. The Wolf launched its seaplane to scout targets for its guns and torpedoes. The Wolfchen was not armed, but carried radio to direct mother ship.

DOWN AT SEA, an English Felixtowe F-3 flying boat burns fiercely on the foggy waters of the North Sea following an air battle. Flying over the scene is the victorious German Brandenburg W-29 seaplane piloted by Lt. Christiansen, top German naval ace.

SEAPLANE CATAPULT, developed by Capt. W. Irving Chambers, U.S.N. in 1912, was made standard equipment on capital ships of the Atlantic Fleet in 1916. First battleship outfitted was the North Carolina. Catapult operated by compressed air.

NAVAL AVIATION

Flying boats and seaplanes carry air war to the oceans

Aircraft capable of operating from the surface of the water were developed only a few years before World War I, yet they became as important to the world's navies as their land-based cousins had been to the belligerent armies.

Evolution of the naval air arm followed the land pattern: first, as the scouting "eyes" of the fleet; second, as a weapon to intercept and destroy intruding enemy long-range seaplanes and flying boats. At first, water-operated aircraft were frequently adaptations of tried and proven land designs. Ultimately, the science of flight from and over the seas became a specialty.

English sea-air developments dominated those of the Allies and Germany because of tradition. Her best patrol-bomber flying boats, the "F" boats, were based on American Curtiss designs, stemming from Wanamaker's *America* built in 1914 to cross the Atlantic. English seaplanes did yeoman duty in many sea battles, keeping an eye on Germany's fleet and attacking the Zeppelins Germany depended upon for scouting help.

England's tradition, however, proved to be a disadvantage. While she favored long-range flying boats, Germany tended to rely on short range, speedy and maneuverable twin-float seaplanes. Italy, surrounded by water as was England, utilized seaplanes to a great extent in her operations against Austrian Naval and air forces. U.S. Naval air forces performed effectively with the Royal Navy and the French in their seaplane operations. All belligerents adapted certain types of seaplanes to carry torpedoes. But the weight of this potential missile reduced flying ranges to an impractical point.

RETURNING after making raids, landplane *Camels* alighted in the water next to the nearest Allied surface ship. Most pilots were saved, but planes usually sank. Later, planes were equipped with balloon-like bags that inflated to keep plane and man afloat. The experiments inspired aircraft carrier.

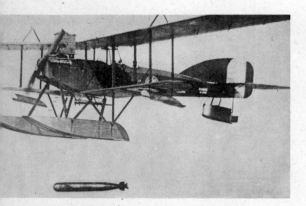

ENGLISH SHORT model 320 seaplane, above, was an early successful torpedo plane. All belligerents developed similar types. Tiny Brandenburg flying boat, below, could be broken down and stowed on German submarines, scouting surface ships to sink.

ALL METAL construction, low set wing and sleek lines made the Dornier Cs-1 seaplane strikingly modern in appearance. Fast and maneuverable, German seaplanes were superior to clumsy Allied types.

SHORT RANGE English *Camel* fighters were towed to the North Sea, took off from lighters to meet German naval air power. In 1918 one such flight bombed and destroyed Zeppelin base at Tondern.

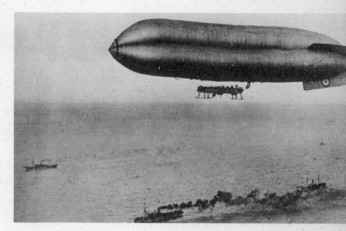

ENGLISH BLIMPS patrolled British coastlines, guarded convoys, occasionally bombed submarines. Italians used a "mother ship," below, to fuel seaplanes at sea, make repairs and provide living quarters for the crews. Ship was called the *Europa.*

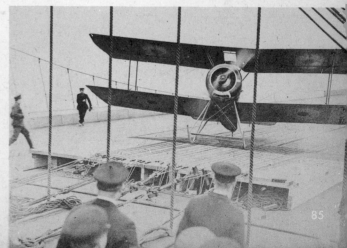

U. S. NAVY experiments included launching a giant Italian Caproni bomber from a speeding sea sled which carried the bomber close to its target. Deck flying experiments, below, were carried out by the English in 1918 aboard a converted cruiser, *H.M.S. Furious,* the first aircraft carrier. Rope barriers and "haul down" straps were tried to halt landing planes. Some planes had skids, as below, instead of wheels.

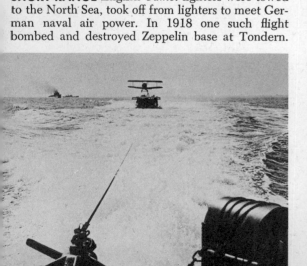

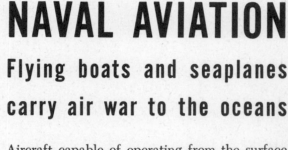

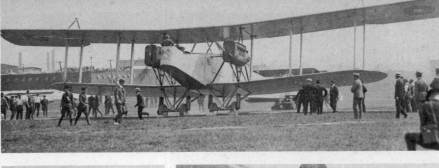

FIRST HEAVY BOMBERS

Giant bombing planes, capable of carrying a thousand pounds of bombs to targets as far as 400 miles behind the battle lines were in regular use the last year and a half of the war. Outstanding bombers were the English Handley Page, above; the German Gotha and Friedrichschafen; the French Farman and Letord; and the Italian Caproni. The Handley Page was scheduled for production in the U. S., as well. The first model, built by Standard Aircraft Corp., was christened *Langley*, and made its first flight (top right) July 6, 1918. These planes carried bombs ranging from the 1,650-lb. British "S.N." (named for Essen, where it was first dropped), to the tiny "B.I.B." (Baby Incendiary Bomb), 6-inches long (both standing, right). Closeup of Handley Page "nose" (middle right) shows the pilot at his controls and the gunner with his Lewis machine gun and bag to catch cartridges. With a 100-ft. wing spread, the Handley Page was an excellent weight carrier, took forty persons aloft shortly after the war (bottom right). Bomber was converted for passenger transport.

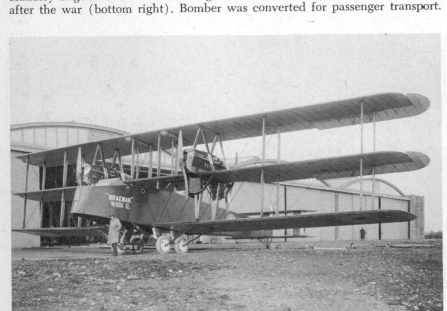

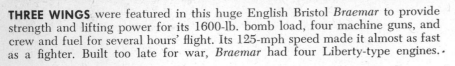

THREE WINGS were featured in this huge English Bristol *Braemar* to provide strength and lifting power for its 1600-lb. bomb load, four machine guns, and crew and fuel for several hours' flight. Its 125-mph speed made it almost as fast as a fighter. Built too late for war, *Braemar* had four Liberty-type engines.

CHURCH SERVICES for troops and R.A.F. personnel sometimes were conducted from the cockpit of a plane by a Royal Air Force "Padre." Chaplains often flew from field to field delivering several short sermons on a Sunday morning. Although welcoming spiritual guidance, fliers generally were fatalistic, superstitious.

BOMBER AND ESCORT prepare for a daylight raid on Germany. Armorers attach a demolition bomb to racks on the lower wing of a British De Havilland-4 bomber (l.) which will be escorted on its mission by the British-owned French Nieuport fighter (r.). Although bombers carried forward and rear guns for their defense, fighters usually accompanied them to discourage attacks by enemy formations and to engage the enemy if attacked. Single-engined bombers were assigned to short range missions, leaving the heavy multi-engined bombers for long range work. Except where single plane hit-and-run missions were carried out, bombers worked in close flying groups composed of elements of three planes each.

FAMOUS CARTOON CHARACTER "Jiggs," with a bomb under his arm, was the insignia of the 11th Aero Squadron, Day Bombardment, A.E.F. Assigned to the front September 5, 1918, it saw brief but vigorous action in the Lorraine, St. Mihiel and Meuse-Argonne sectors in France. The 11th was one of the many all-American squadrons to reach the front during the hectic closing weeks of the war. Its planes were the American-made, "Liberty"-engined De Havilland-4, capable of a 125-mph top speed, an air endurance of two or three hours, and altitude of 19,500 ft. Fully loaded, the DH-4 bomber weighed only 3,582 pounds.

APOSTLE OF BIG PLANES was the Italian pioneer airplane builder, Gianni Caproni (top, with a group of allied officers). A thorough scientist, Caproni researched all aspects of aerodynamics before building first plane in 1912 which served as a flying laboratory from which Caproni gained data enabling him to build, in 1914, a large tri-motored biplane intended for passengers and freight. His biplane was converted to a bomber in 1915, carried a crew of four (lower left). Ultimate in Caproni development were the giant triplane bombers (right), some models of which had wings spanning 130 feet, were capable of carrying a ton and a half of bombs. Able to fly long distances, they frequently went out in force, climbing over the Alps to bomb Austrian cities. Several French bombing squadrons used Caproni biplanes and triplanes. The Caproni was one of the types selected for U.S. construction in 1919; however, only five of these were built.

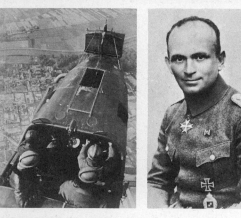

METHODICAL GERMANY developed bombing airplanes and bombing techniques to a high degree of perfection. Her designers came up with planes like the Siemens-Schuckert R-1 (upper left) with engines, enclosed in the body, driving by chains or gears the propellers located between the wings. Even the Zeppelin Company, while recognizing the shortcomings of its monstrous airships, developed equally monstrous airplanes, some with five engines and wings spanning 150 feet. In these bombers, engines could be repaired in flight and the plane commander and his operational officers sat together (extreme left) in a compartment suggesting the bridge of a ship. The German Third Bombing Group, whose radius of action extended from the Lowlands to include all of England, was commanded by Captain Ernst Brandenburg (portrait above), distinguished aeronautical engineer and airplane designer. While interested in development of Germany's huge R-class bombers, he preferred to use the smaller Gotha G-class bombing plane (r.) in his raids. Here armorers attach bombs.

LARGER BOMB SIZES to increase effectiveness of ▶ raids, complicated the problem of stowing missiles aboard airplanes. Bomb at right is nearly as long as the airplane, a Farman, which was used through the war for a variety of purposes, including training. The French did not develop large bombers in sufficient numbers to compete with German production.

◀ **ANTI-BRITISH POSTER,** in which German labor used quotation attributed to English syndicalist Joynson-Hicks, testifies to the effectiveness of Royal Air Force bombing of Germany's industrial centers. Headlined "What England Wants!", the poster credits Joynson-Hicks with urging, in effect, repeated bombing day after day of German industrial zones, using hundreds of airplanes, until destruction was complete. Syndicalists objected to war to effect social changes because of its destruction, advocated general strikes and violence instead. Planes illustrated are intended to represent Handley Page bombers.

TOP AMERICAN ACE was Capt. Edward Vernon Rickenbacker, prewar idol of American automobile racing. When U.S. entered the war he joined the infantry, became Pershing's chauffeur. Later he transferred to the Air Service for pilot training and eventually was assigned to the 94th "Hat-in-the-Ring" pursuit squadron March 4, 1918. Rickenbacker showed outstanding qualities as a leader, was made commander of Number 1 flight, 94th, in May and became commanding officer of the squadron on September 24, 1918. Flying with a caution born of years on the race track, he neither took chances in air battles, nor did he expect his men to. It has been acknowledged that if Rickenbacker had not paid so much attention to the welfare of men in his command, he could easily have raised the total of his victories—25 airplanes and balloons—to a higher score. His record was made in eight months flying at the front.

FIRST FRENCH ACE, Georges Guynemer, a sickly youth, was rejected by the French draft before he enlisted as an air cadet in 1915. A proficient pilot, he was shot down in September, 1917, with 53 victories to his credit. His body was never found. A member of "Les Cigognes" (the "Storks") squadron, he fought fearlessly, had been shot down eight times before his death. Twice he downed enemy planes with only one bullet each, an unequalled record.

PRECISION FLYING helped Paul René Fonck (r.) to become the highest-scoring Allied Ace to survive the war. In one air battle, he downed six German planes, used only 56 bullets. With him is Santos-Dumont, who made first airplane flight in Europe.

FAMED CANADIAN ACE was Lt. Col. William A. ("Billy") Bishop. On March 25, 1917, he shot down a German *Albatros,* his first victory. This flight almost proved to be Bishop's last when his engine stopped at 1500 foot altitude and he managed to glide to Allied territory. During the next six months Bishop destroyed 45 German planes. In September, 1917, he returned to Canada on leave a national hero, made whistle-stop speeches from rear of train. (L. to r.): Bishop's mother, Bishop, Margaret Burden, his fiancee, Maj. Worth Bishop, his brother.

He married Miss Burden in October, returned to France early in 1918, and in May took command of No. 85 squadron. He started a carnival of destruction never equalled in aviation. In 12 days he shot down 25 German planes, five of which he downed his last day at the Front. With a total score of 72 German planes, he was assigned to the British Air Ministry in June, with no opportunity to increase his score.

MAJOR RAOUL LUFBERY originally served with the Lafayette Escadrille, became commander of the U.S. 94th Aero Squadron. He gained 17 victories, was killed in May, 1918 when his plane caught fire in a flight. He jumped rather than burn to death.

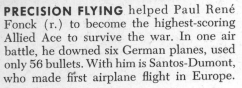

A FEARLESS FLYER, Lt. Charles Nungesser was third-ranking French Ace with 43 victories. Wounded 17 times, he also suffered many broken bones in crashes. He disappeared in May, 1927, attempting Paris-New York flight.

FOUR PLANES, 14 BALLOONS shot down in 17 days was the record of Lt. Frank Luke, Jr., of the 27th Aero Squadron, A.E.F. Often A.W.O.L., he disliked discipline, fought a one-man war against German observation balloons. A native of Phoenix, Ariz., Luke was shot down on September 29, 1918.

ONE WHEEL LANDING in an English Sopwith *Camel* was almost disastrous for Capt. Elliott White Springs (c.), ace of the U.S. 148th Squadron, serving with the RAF. Credited with 12 victories, he became popular writer in 20's.

ACES OF W.W. I

France originated the "Ace" system early in the war to stimulate the efforts of her fighting airmen. The system was copied by other nations who expanded it, publicized outstanding airmen and pictured the successful pilot out of all proportion to his counterpart in the trenches.

Under the French system, an ace was a pilot who had shot down five German planes. In Germany, ten planes were required. Among the Allies, all adapted the ace system except England, who did not officially count air victories. England did, however, single out Albert Ball (43 victories) for public honors and later widely acclaimed Canada's William Bishop (72 victories) as the British "Ace of Aces."

After Bishop was assigned to non-combat duties in June, 1918, Edward Mannock succeeded him·to command of No. 85 Squadron. Mannock was killed a month later, in July. In all, Mannock downed 73 planes during his fighting career. While alive, his achievements were kept under wraps, in line with Britain's policy of not publicizing her aces. Excessive publicizing of aces made them prime enemy targets. In addition, they were led about like circus attractions to build morale, and make speeches lending importance to official functions. The aces resented this, as it took them away from their fighting jobs.

All belligerents required confirmation of claimed victories from ground or air witnesses. To show the effect of confirmation on a pilot's record, René Fonck of France, claimed 127 victories, but received credit for only 75. He shot down 52 planes in Germany that were not confirmed by French ground forces. Bishop or Mannock may have had 20 more victories than they were granted. Yet von Richthofen claimed 80, and none of these were contested.

COLORFUL GERMAN ACE, Capt. Eduard von Schleich, shot down 35 Allied planes, at one time led the famous Bavarian "Blue Tail" Squadron. On September 27, 1918, U.S. 17th and 148th Squadrons shot down 13 *Blue Tails,* put them out of action.

ALL-TIME "ACE OF ACES" Capt. Baron Manfred von Richthofen downed 80 Allied planes, was killed April 21, 1918 by Capt. A. Roy Brown, a Canadian. In July, 1917, an Allied bullet, which creased the Baron's skull, hospitalized him for more than month.

DANGEROUS TRIO as far as Allied pilots were concerned was (l. to r.) Capt. Bruno Loerzer, plane designer Anthony Fokker and Lt. Hermann Goering. Loerzer led the Third German Pursuit Squadron, gained 44 victories. Goering claimed 22 victories.

NATIONAL HERO at time of his death, Lt. Franz Max Immelmann was first highly publicized German ace, invented "Immelmann turn." Arrogant, but master pilot, he gained 15 victories before his death, June 18, 1916 in a mysterious twilight dogfight.

SQUADRON TEAMWORK was developed to a state of perfection by Capt. Oswald Boelcke, a school teacher before he joined the German Air Service. Credited with 40 victories, Boelcke was killed October 28, 1916, in collision with pupil, Lt. Boehme.

COMPARATIVE SCORES

von Richthofen (Ger.)	80	Menckhoff (Ger.)	39
Fonck (Fr.)	75	Gontermann (Ger.)	39
Mannock (Eng.)	73	Gilmore (Eng.)	37
Bishop (Can.)	72	McCall (Can.)	37
Udet (Ger.)	62	Bolle (Ger.)	36
Collishaw (Can.)	60	von Muller (Ger.)	36
Barker (Can.)	59	Boyau (Fr.)	35
McCudden (Eng.)	58	Wollett (Eng.)	35
MacLaren (Can.)	54	Buckler (Ger.)	35
Guynemer (Fr.)	53	Doerr (Ger.)	35
Loewenhardt (Ger.)	53	von Schleich (Ger.)	35
Fullard (Eng.)	53	Veltjens (Ger.)	35
Voss (Ger.)	48	Koennecke (Ger.)	35
Little (Eng.)	47	Coiffard (Fr.)	34
McElroy (Can.)	46	Quigley (Eng.)	34
Rumey (Ger.)	45	Baracca (Ital.)	34
Berthold (Ger.)	44	Brunowski (Aus.)	34
Loerzer (Ger.)	44	Coppens (Belg.)	34
Ball (Eng.)	43	Wolff (Ger.)	33
Baumer (Ger.)	43	Fromherz (Ger.)	33
Nungesser (Fr.)	43	Kroll (Ger.)	33
Jacobs (Ger.)	43	Thuy (Ger.)	32
Madon (Fr.)	41	Carter (Can.)	31
Larkin (Eng.)	41	Sachsenberg (Ger.)	31
Jones (Eng.)	41	Osterkamp (Ger.)	31
Boelcke (Ger.)	40	Billik (Ger.)	31
von Richthofen (bro.)	40	White (Eng.)	31
Claxton (Can.)	39	Jordan (Eng.)	31
Dallas (Eng.)	39	Hazel (Eng.)	31

OFF-DUTY GERMAN pilots relaxing between air battles, are (l. to r.) Loewenhardt, Schaefer, Udet, Mayer, Bodenschatz. With 62 victories, Lt. Udet was the highest scoring German pilot to survive the war, afterwards became world-famous stunt pilot.

FIRST SIMON-PURE American ace, Lt. Douglas Campbell of the U.S. Aero Squadron, enlisted, trained and fought with Americans. Campbell was shot down June 5, 1918, but survived war.

AUDACIOUS 19-year-old Capt. Albert Ball became England's first great ace, gained 43 victories before his death in May, 1917. With him are his father, sister, mother and friend at Buckingham Palace for bestowal of D.S.O.

HIGH SCORING English Maj. Edward "Micky" Mannock is said to have downed 73 planes, one more than Col. Billy Bishop whom he succeeded as C.O. of No. 85.

AUSTRALIAN PILOTS served England with distinction. Capt. Andrew H. Cobby, with 26 victories, was top ace from "Down Under," flew colorful Sopwith.

FIRST SCHEDULED AIRMAIL IN U.S.

On May 15, 1918, when the war in the air in Europe was at its peak, scheduled air mail service was inaugurated in the U.S. between Washington, D.C., and New York City, via Philadelphia. Army pilots and Army planes (modified Curtiss JN-4H *Jennies*) were used. Maj. R. H. Fleet was the officer in charge. The Army flew the mail until August 12, when the Post Office Department, with Assistant Postmaster General Otto Praeger in charge of the air mail, took over the Army routes and began new ones. In the photo above are (l. to r.) Assistant Postmaster General Praeger, M.O. Chance, Postmaster of Washington, D.C., A.L. Burleson, Postmaster General and President Woodrow Wilson awaiting departure of Lt. George Boyle on first lap of North-bound mail flight. Lt. H. P. Culver was to meet him in Philadelphia, carry mail on to New York. In similar relays, Lts. Torrey Webb and James C. Edgerton flew mail from New York to Washington (218 miles) in three hours, 20 minutes.

VON RICHTHOFEN KILLED

Captain Baron Manfred von Richthofen typified German military might in the air as Tirpitz, von Hindenburg did on sea and land. Above left are the famous ace and his squadron mates: (l. to r.) Festner, Schaeffer, the Baron, his brother Lothar, and Wolff. Germans thought Richthofen invincible—a demi-god. But on April 21, 1918, he took off from the squadron field at Douai (above right) in his all-red Fokker Dr-I triplane (replica, extreme top) and was shot down about 11 a. m. just behind the Allied lines by Capt. A. Roy Brown (l.), 209 Sq'dn, RAF. Respected by his enemies, he was buried with full military honors. His funeral was attended by men of nearby Allied squadrons, who covered his casket with floral tributes. In effort to preserve legend of his invincibility, German officials released an official report that the great hero had been killed by ground fire.

LT. GEORGE L. BOYLE received instructions from Maj. R. H. Fleet before taking off for Philadelphia. As Boyle started, his engine stopped. Someone had forgotten to put gasoline in his plane's tanks. Finally under way, he became lost, broke his propeller landing on a Maryland farm. Next day, Lt. H. P. Culver picked up mail and flew it to New York.

FIRST VICTORIOUS A.E.F. pilot, Lt. Allan Winslow (l.) shot down a German plane April 14, 1918, the first day of operation for his squadron, the 94th pursuit. Lt. Quentin Roosevelt (r.), son of President Theodore Roosevelt, flew with the U. S. 95th pursuit, was killed July 14, 1918. Brave to a fault, he shot down one German plane. Commander of Army Air Service activities at the Front was Col. William ("Billy") Mitchell (below, with cane), fearless in battle. With him is Gen. Pershing.

AIR MAIL PLAN was described to President Wilson (l.) by Maj. Fleet. Lt. Torrey Webb, flying from New York, was to relay mail to Edgerton in Philadelphia.

BELMONT PARK was the New York air mail terminal. Lt. and Mrs. Torrey Webb are shown before his take-off for Philadelphia. He carried 150 pounds of mail.

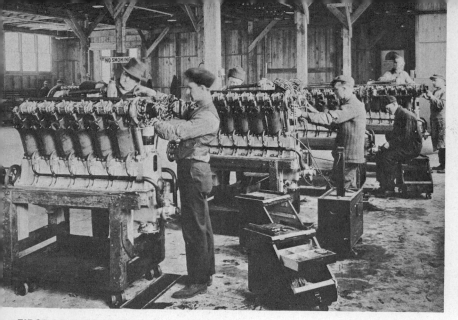

FIRST LIBERTY ENGINE was delivered July 4, 1917, six weeks after engineers Vincent (Packard) and Hall (Hall-Scott) began designs. Originally an eight-cylinder engine, it was developed into a V-12 of 375-to-400 hp. America's automobile makers undertook their manufacture, built thousands. Part of the Packard Motor Co. shops are seen here with workmen preparing "Liberty's" for final tests.

AIRCRAFT PRODUCTION in U.S. reached astounding totals by mid-1918. The Dayton-Wright Airplane Company, organized in April, 1917, produced 400 training planes and 2,703 DH-4 battle planes by November 11, 1918. On July 31, 1918 the one thousandth DH-4 fighter from this company was shipped to France. By the end of war, 2000 Dayton-Wright DH-4's had arrived overseas.

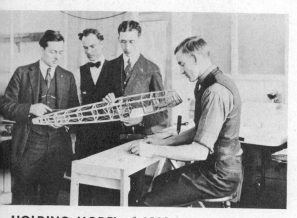

MARTIN BOMBER designed in 1918, was scheduled for production during 1919. Powered by two Liberty engines, its speed was approximately 120 mph, its range 300 miles. It carried a 1500-pound load of bombs. The later Navy version carried torpedoes.

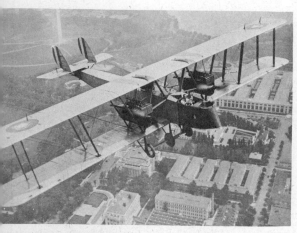

HOLDING MODEL of 1918 Martin Bomber are Donald W. Douglas (l.) and Glenn L. Martin. Douglas was Martin's chief engineer (1918), later formed his own huge company. Lawrence Bell, founder of Bell Aircraft in 1939, was Martin protege.

IN GUARDED PLANT of Boeing Airplane Co., World War I aircraft were built for both the Army and Navy in 1917. Company was founded July 15, 1916. First Boeing aircraft, a seaplane, flew November 15. Similar training types were built during the war.

SCIENTIFIC AIR DEVELOPMENTS

U.S. catches up with Europe

From August, 1914 to April, 1917, U.S. plane development lagged behind that of Europe. It was lack of money, not creativeness, that prevented many excellent designs from ever leaving the drawing boards.

With the declaration of war came appropriations that let American manufacturers prove what they could do. During its building of standard European plane types at close to mass production rates, the industry brought out many prototypes of planes that were to rank among the world's best for many years.

Some of these U.S. designs included the 175-mph Christmas *Bullet*; Curtiss 18-B and 18-T two-place fighters in the 160-mph class; L.W.F. G-2, a 138-mph fighter-bomber and single-seat fighters: J.V. Martin K-3 with retractable landing gear; Thomas-Morse MB-3, a 150-mph type produced in quantity during 1921-22 as the Boeing MB-3A; the Orenco D, built by Curtiss and the huge Curtiss NC flying boats.

America's mechanical ingenuity during World War I also accounted for such developments as the high altitude engine turbo-supercharger, gyroscopic air navigational aids, air-to-ground radiophone sets, air crew oxygen masks, electrically-heated flying clothing, automatic cameras and helium gas.

UNUSUAL FIGHTER monoplane below was designed by Grover C. Loening in 1918. Loening was an ingenious aero engineer who developed many aviation patents. Where most designs were improvements on standard types of the day, Loening started from scratch, made his monoplane as efficient as possible. It had a top speed of 146 mph and could climb to a 26,000-foot altitude, carrying two men—a better performance than most single-seat fighters. Its engine was a 300-hp American Wright model "H", based on the French Hispano-Suiza. If the war had lasted into 1919, the Loening monoplane undoubtedly would have gone into quantity production.

PIONEER AVIATOR Glenn Curtiss devoted the production of his factories almost exclusively to training airplanes, produced over 3,000 JN-type *Jennies* for U. S. government from 1916 to 1918. JN-4 model B, above, was widely used by the Allies during war.

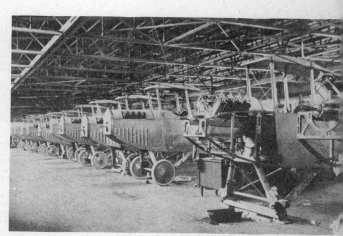

COMPLETED AIRPLANES as well as Liberty engines were produced by Packard Motor Car Co. in 1918. Designed by Capt. G. Lepere, French Air service engineer, the Packard-Lepere fighter could go 136 mph, carried two men. Production ceased with peace.

ODD LOOKING aircraft below, designed and built by Sperry Gyroscope Co., was the ancestor of the guided missile or "flying bomb." Developed during 1916-18 for the U.S. Navy, these automatically-controlled craft were intended to carry explosives.

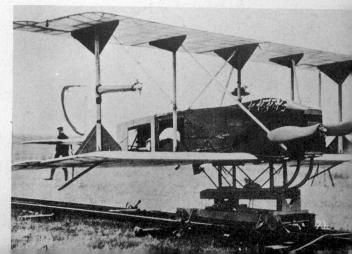

TYPICAL OF COURAGEOUS FLIERS IN '20s WERE SPEED KING AL WILLIAMS, ATLANTIC'S "LONE EAGLE" CHARLES LINDBERGH, AND ARMY'S DARING JIMMY DOOLITTLE

Courageous Twenties

Dramatic flights, technical pioneering focus world's attention on aviation, lift it from barnstormer's domain to industry status

After contributing early to aviation's safety with the invention of navigational aids, Richard E. Byrd headed the world's first flight to the North Pole (1926), flew the Atlantic (1927), and conquered the South Pole (1929). Information obtained from his polar flights brought vast areas to the known world.

IN the early days there were many difficulties to overcome and new things to develop to make flying possible.

Never, for example, will I forget the day in the spring of 1918 while on duty at Naval Air Station, Pensacola, Florida, when I received orders from Washington to train, as rapidly as possible, 100 pilots in night flying with sea planes. We had no landing lights on the water and no blind flying instruments as we know them today. For the first test flights we used lights on the beach for landing. We finally used buckets of gasoline on rafts as landing lights.

We did not have in early 1919 instruments necessary to navigate a seaplane out of sight of land, so for the Navy NC trans-Atlantic flight an instrument had to be developed to obtain the height of the sun above the horizon and another instrument to measure the drift of a plane over the water from wind.

While we (Floyd Bennett and myself) were exploring between the North Pole and the North Magnetic Pole (the north magnetic pole is approximately 1200 miles south of the north geographical pole), the magnetic compass simply did not work. I had to get our direction from the sun compass which Bennett and I used the following year to reach the North Pole.

We had a tough time with skis for the first North Pole flight in 1926. We had to use a larger plane so as to be able to carry enough survival

CMDR. RICHARD E. BYRD PREPARING FOR POLAR FLIGHT

equipment to give us some chance in case of forced landing. We had to take off down hill.

Because of the short run-way, and because we knew practically nothing about skis for the type of Fokker plane we were using, (the skis were too small and too weak) we cracked up several sets and our plane went over on its nose on the first attempt to take off for the Pole.

Commander George Noville and Captain Mike Brennan designed and constructed a set of skis that did the trick. On flights of this kind I acted as navigator and took turns at the wheel. Bennett deserves the major credit for the success of our first two years of Arctic flying.

In connection with our trans-Atlantic flight of 1927, I was most interested in demonstrating the practicability of regular commercial trans-Atlantic flights and constructed the plane accordingly—a specially built Fokker that could and did carry the equivalent of a passenger, a pay load, and U.S. mail. We were not racing, but had planned this flight so far ahead of other contestants that we would have been the first across had not the plane crashed on the first test flight. Noville suffered internal injuries, I broke my arm in

two places, and Floyd Bennett's injuries were so grievous that they were the indirect cause of his death some months later.

When we took off for France after the plane was repaired, we went through three storms, one of which blew us off the course 200 miles. When we reached the vicinity of Paris in weather too thick to land, we returned to the coast of France and landed in the sea, our survival equipment working. We had been in the air 42 hours.

We have had four South Pole expeditions and have built four Little Americas, each of which was promptly covered with snow. Our expeditions have been mainly scientific and included dozens of flights of exploration and survey with a number of surface trail parties organized. Our many difficulties arose from the fact that the bottom of the world averages at least 40° (Fahrenheit) colder than the top of the world.

Our plane, the *Floyd Bennett*, did not have cruising radius enough to make a nonstop flight to the Pole, so we had to set down a refueling base where we could land and refuel on our return from the South Pole.

Bottom of the world is an untouched reservoir of natural resources which the nation will one day desperately need. We therefore are proud that on our South Pole undertakings we were able to discover thousands of square miles of area never before seen by man and delineate hundreds of miles of hitherto unknown coast line.

Richard E Byrd

A Naval aviator in World War I, Harry F. Guggenheim, President of the Guggenheim Fund for the Promotion of Aeronautics, continues the work of his father in encouraging aviation toward achieving highest potential.

HARRY F. GUGGENHEIM

WHILE the history of aviation, from the earliest efforts at flight to the present, is a fascinating story, to my mind the most exciting period was that of the 20's. It was then that the foundations for today's commercial and military aviation were laid down. High adventure and daring were still the common order, and personal accomplishment was still the flier's most effective and frequent stimulus.

My family and I have been fortunate enough

to be intimately concerned with the development of aviation, and other forms of flight, such as rockets, since the First World War. It was my father, the late Daniel Guggenheim, who made funds available in the early 20's for the establishment of the Daniel Guggenheim Schools of Aeronautics, and who, through the Daniel Guggenheim Fund for the Promotion of Aeronautics, supported studies in instrumentation and instrument flying, aircraft safety and commercial passenger-carrying aircraft design.

It was in those days that such aviation greats as Orville Wright, William H. Durand, Rear Admiral Richard Byrd, Lt. Gen. James H. Doolittle, and Col. Charles A. Lindbergh were making their dramatic early contributions.

In 1927 the first regularly scheduled commercial air line in the United States began its service, with the aid of money loaned by the Daniel Guggenheim Fund and technical assistance provided through the Fund. The first weather reporting service for passenger planes was established in 1928 with the Fund's aid.

Lt. Gen. James H. Doolittle (then a lieutenant) on September 24, 1929, made history when he flew an airplane at the Fund's Full Flight Laboratory, with covered cockpit, taking off, flying and landing entirely "blind"—a breathtaking feat for that time.

We also had a great deal of interest in airplane safety in those days—an interest that is still gathering momentum. Under the auspices of the Daniel Guggenheim Fund, an International Safe Aircraft Competition was held in 1929, which resulted in dramatic gains in aircraft safety.

But possibly our most important activity of those days, from the long range point of view, was the establishment of the Guggenheim Schools of Aeronautics in six leading American universities. These schools ushered in the developing of modern engineering in aeronautics.

Harry F. Guggenheim

JOURNEY'S END for NC-4 was mooring at Plymouth, England, May 31, 1919. Headed by Lt. Cmdr. Albert Cushing Read, piloted by Lt. Walter Hinton and Lt. Stone, the brilliant feat of this U. S. Navy seaplane aroused world's admiration. Totally unprepared for their reception at Plymouth, the crew won praise for the successful way in which they had conducted the flight. Read is carried on shoulders of admiring doughboys and sailors at Paddington Station, London, June 1, 1919. Wiring Navy, Washington, Admiral Plunkett said, "Regret loss of NC-1 and damage to NC-3, nevertheless information of utmost value gained."

NAVY SEAPLANE SPANS OCEAN

One of three NC's is successful in attempting first Atlantic crossing

Authorization by the U.S. Navy for the construction of NC flying boats was signed by Secretary Josephus Daniels in Dec., 1917. Work began at the Curtiss Engineering Corp. in Garden City, Long Island during Jan., 1918, and the first plane, the NC-1, was successfully flown Oct. 4, 1918. Planned as anti-submarine weapons, they were also designed for possible Atlantic crossing.

The Armistice on Nov. 11, 1918 curtailed aircraft procurement, and only four of the Curtiss seaplanes were built. The idea of an ocean flight was part of the thinking behind the preliminary design and construction of the NC-1 and was revived with new intensity in December, 1918,. when the London *Daily Mail* made its offer of 10,000 pounds for the first crossing. Navy sentiment was, in effect, "If there is to be no fight, there will at least be a flight!" Plans were laid for an attempt to fly to Europe in May of 1919 using all four NC boats ordered.

After considerable training and technical preparation, during which the NC-2 was dismantled to provide parts for the other three craft, the NC-1, NC-3 and NC-4 left Rockaway Beach on May 8 for Halifax, Nova Scotia. Thus began the first attempt at a crossing of the Atlantic by heavier-than-air machines.

By May 15, all three seaplanes had flown from Far Rockaway, L.I. to Trepassey, Newfoundland, a distance of 1000 nautical miles. On May 16, with the promise of a full moon to help them, the three seaplanes took off into the gath-

LIMPING into Ponta Delgada, Azores, the NC-3 is shown ending a 52-hour, 205-mile journey on the ocean's surface. Damaged by heavy swells while alighting for bearings May 17, she could not take off.

ering darkness of the unflown Atlantic ocean.

Lost in dense fog, the NC-1 and NC-3 both alighted on the open sea on May 17 to obtain bearings. Hindered by high seas, neither plane could take off again and the severely damaged flagship NC-3, commanded by Towers, managed to taxi under its own power to port at Ponta Delgada in the Azores. The NC-1, after taxying for five hours, was discovered by the destroyer *Ionia* and the crew removed. The huge seaplane sank off Corvo on May 20, 1919.

The NC-4 reached Horta on May 17, continued to Ponta Delgada May 20, and on May 27 made a brilliant crossing to Lisbon, Portugal.

There remained only one more accomplishment—the flight to Plymouth. Here on May 31, 1919, a pilot of Massachusetts birth set foot on the shores of the harbor from which the Pilgrims took ship for the New World three hundred years before. During the flight of 3,936 nautical miles in a flying time of 52 hrs. and 31 min., Commander Read and crew had demonstrated the quality of Naval organization that made possible the first spanning of the Atlantic ocean by air.

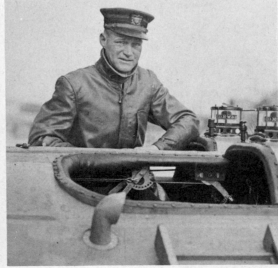

ARRIVAL AT HOBOKEN of officers and crew of the three seaplanes aboard the transport *Zeppelin* shows, right to left, Lt. Cmdr. A. C. Read of the NC-4, Cmdr. John H. Towers of the NC-3 and Lt. Cmdr. P. N. L. Bellinger of the NC-1. Center photo is of Lt. Cmdr. Mark A. Mitscher, pilot of the NC-1 and later a distinguished Admiral of World War II. He is standing in left cockpit of NC-1, which illustrates extent of pilot exposure to elements. Welcome of flying crews by Navy Dept. was highlighted by visit to office of Secretary of Navy, Josephus Daniels. Shown are Secretary Daniels and on his left Asst. Sec. Franklin D. Roosevelt. Standing immediately behind are Bellinger, Read and Towers. The success of Read and crew stands out as marked example of well-planned flight.

FIRST NONSTOP ATLANTIC FLIGHT

At 4:13 p.m. on June 14, 1919, a heavily-laden Vickers-Vimy biplane took off from St. Johns, Newfoundland, and headed east across the Atlantic. At 8:40 a.m., the next day, 16 hrs. and 27 mins. later, the same plane glided to a nose-down landing in a bog near Clifden, Ireland. Out of the crushed nose scrambled pilot Capt. John Alcock and navigator Lt. Whitten-Brown, concluding the first direct non-stop Atlantic crossing in aviation history. With them came a dog, a cat, and a four-pound sack of mail.

As congratulations to these two courageous airmen poured in from all the world, they journeyed to London and were given the 10,000-pound prize for the flight, awarded by the London *Daily Mail*, and were knighted by King George V. When the breathless pair were at last able to recount the experiences of the crossing, they disclosed the nightmarish weather they had encountered. Losing control of the plane because of icing during the night, they narrowly escaped crashing into the sea.

In a civic welcome by the Royal Aero Club of England, vice chairman Sir Capel Holden remarked he did not think the men as yet appreciated what they had done.

Pictures above show Alcock storing food for flight, and the dramatic moment of takeoff. At right, Alcock and Brown, now famous for their flight, reach London.

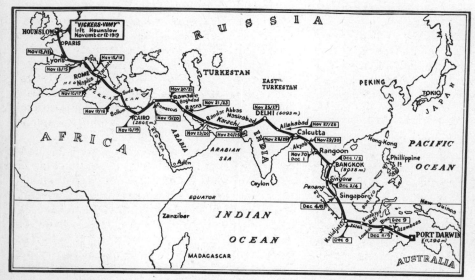

ENGLAND-AUSTRALIA FLIGHT
Starting from Hounslow, England on Nov. 12, 1919, Capt. Ross Smith and a crew of three headed a Vickers-Vimy bomber southwest towards Australia. On Dec. 10, the same plane, with its original engines, landed at Darwin, thus completing the first recorded direct flight between Great Britain and Australia. The route over which they traveled is shown above. Awarded a 10,000-pound prize by the Australian government for their feat, Capt. Ross Smith and his companions had given the world another striking demonstration of the fact that the airplane was a practical vehicle and not just a plaything or instrument of war. Pictured left to right in front of their gallant Vimy bomber are Captain Keith Smith, co-pilot (brother); Captain Ross Smith, pilot; Sgt. J. M. Bennett and Sgt. W. H. Shiers, mechanics.

ALASKAN FLYING EXPEDITION of the Army Air Service began June 15, 1920, from Mitchell Field, Long Island, N.Y. Four DeHavilland DH-4 biplanes equipped with Liberty engines made the flight under the command of Capt. St. Clair Street. They arrived at Nome, Alaska on August 25, in 56 hrs. flying time, after passing over rugged uncharted country. The group returned to N.Y. on Oct. 20, having covered a total of 4,345 miles in 112 flying hours. Capt. Street is shown at left, with his fellow pilots.

SOUTH AMERICAN FLIGHT of the *Samaio Correia* started Aug. 17, 1922 from N.Y. to Brazil. Piloted by Lt. Walter Hinton, the large twin-engined F-5L flying boat flew 5,880 miles in 100 hours and arrived at Rio de Janeiro on Feb. 8, 1923. Flight's purpose was exploration of air routes to So. America. L. to r. are T. Baltzell, cameraman; Lt. Walter Hinton, pilot; Dr. P. Martins, co-pilot; G. T. Bye, historian; J. Wilshusen, mechanic.

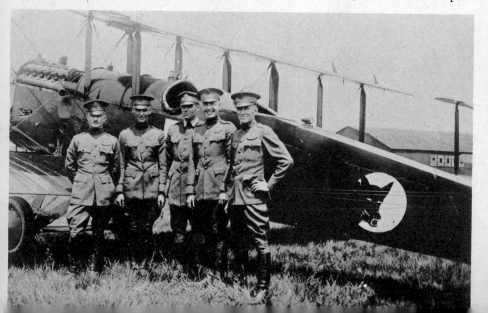

ARMY ROUND-THE-WORLD FLIERS IN 1924 WITH GEN. MASON PATRICK

DOUGLAS WORLD CRUISER "NEW ORLEANS" BEING REFITTED AT BOSTON

U.S. ARMY AIRMEN MAKE FIRST COMPLETE ROUND—THE—WORLD FLIGHT

Taking off from Lake Washington at Seattle early in the morning of April 6, 1924, four sturdy biplanes of the U.S. Air Service started their history-making flight around the world. Arriving back at Seattle on Sept. 28, the world fliers had girdled the globe in 15 days, 11 hrs. and 7 min. flying time. Two of the planes were lost during the flight, the *Seattle* on a mountainside between Seward and Chignik on the Alaskan Peninsula, and the *Boston* in the Atlantic after a forced landing on the flight to Iceland. Named after U.S. cities, the Douglas World Cruisers were specially constructed for the flight, had cruising speeds from 53 to 103 mph and were equipped with 400-hp Liberty engines. The *Seattle* was flown by Major F. L. Martin who was commander of the flight. The *Chicago* was flown by Lt. Lowell Smith who took over the flight after loss of the *Seattle*, the *Boston* was flown by Lt. Leigh Wade and the *New Orleans* by Lt. Erik Nelson.

DESIGNER DOUGLAS, MOTHER, AND FLIERS

THE "CHICAGO" AT KUSHIMOTO, JAPAN, JUNE 1, 1924

LT. L. H. SMITH GREETED BY PRESIDENT COOLIDGE

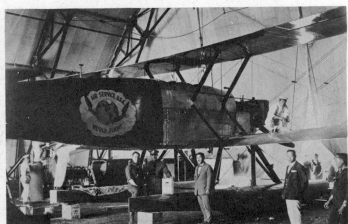

COAST-TO-COAST flight of the Army Fokker T-2 on May 2-3, 1923, broke all existing non-stop distance and speed records. Piloted by Lt. John A. Macready and Lt. Oakley G. Kelly (c. and r.), the Liberty-engined monoplane made the flight from Roosevelt Field, New York to Rockwell Field, San Diego in 26 hrs. and 50 min. Loaded to a gross weight of 10,850 lbs. and 735 gals. of fuel, the Fokker T-2 had great difficulty in becoming airborne. After 20 miles of flight the plane had reached a bare 400 ft. of altitude and later the next morning near the Rocky mountains, gorges and passes had to be followed to get through to Phoenix. Crowd of 100,000 greeted fliers at Rockwell Field. Base Commander Maj. Henry H. Arnold, later chief of USAAF said, "The impossible has happened."

INTERNATIONAL AIRMAIL had its birth at Seattle, Wash. on Mar. 3, 1919 when Eddie Hubbard and William Boeing (r.) flew the first load of mail to Victoria, Canada in the *B & W*, a two-place open cockpit flying boat. It was first plane built by Boeing at Seattle factory.

HERO OF THE FIRST day and night coast-to-coast airmail flight by U.S. Postoffice Dept. was Jack Knight (r.). Originally scheduled to fly Omaha-North Platte leg of the flight, he saved the future of air mail by flying unfamiliar North Platte-Chicago leg, as well, over unlighted airways, when relief pilot failed to arrive. This heroic demonstration by Postoffice fliers Feb. 22, 1921, brought appropriations for continuation of air mail, installation of beacons. Converted war planes, like one below, flew early mail.

PAN AMERICAN FLIGHT of five Loening OA-1 amphibians of the U. S. Army Air Service set new distance records for this type of aircraft and also promoted much good will in the twenty foreign nations of Central and South America which were visited. Starting from Kelly Field, Texas, on Dec. 21, 1926, the group flew as far south as Valdiva, Chile, before returning to Washington May 2, 1927. Commanded by Maj. Herbert A. Dargue, three of the amphibians are shown in formation (left) as they approached Colombia. Photo at right shows Capt. Ira Eaker (r.), Lt. Fairchild standing on *San Francisco* after landing at Rio de Janero.

NAVY PACIFIC FLIGHT from San Francisco to Honolulu was attempted on August 31, 1925. While ▶ neither of the planes completed the flight, one of them, under the command of Cmdr. John Rodgers, flew 1,992 statute miles before alighting at sea for lack of fuel. Ripping fabric from lower wings of their Navy PN-9 flying boat, crew rigged sail between wings, headed for Nawiliwili, Hawaii. Here plane enters harbor.

BRUTE POWER of Packard engine in Army's Eng. Div.-Verville R-1 racer provided margin of victory for Lt. Corliss Mosely, winner of first Pulitzer Race. Average speed was 156.5 mph.

FAMOUS CURTISS HAWK line descended from the Navy-Curtiss CR-2, was the winner of the 1921 event. Bert Acosta proved superiority of the small, streamlined racer over powerful type some favored.

SPEED RECORDS FELL when manufacturers, encouraged by Gen. "Billy" Mitchell, produced fast planes like the Curtiss R-6 of 1922. Lt. R. L. Maughan averaged 205.8 mph to win events.

PULITZER TROPHY RACES

Nationalism and a strong desire to promote American aviation prompted the Pulitzer brothers to establish a prize fund for speed achievements. U.S. aviation development was lagging. Aircraft production had nearly ceased. It was apparent that establishment of a competitive event to succeed the International Gordon Bennett Race, which ended in 1920 when France won permanent possession of the trophy, was of prime importance. The Pulitzer Trophy Race became the premier aviation event in America for six years.

The initial speed event was held at Mitchell Field, Long Island, on Thanksgiving Day, 1920. Many military and civilian entries participated, but the 638-hp Army-built Verville R-1, an entry in the final Gordon Bennett event, was the only true racing design present. By 1922, development costs and design progress had taken their toll, and civilian entries no longer appeared. A seesaw battle between the Armed Services lasted through 1925, fighter development benefiting.

OVER 100,000 PEOPLE watched Lt. Al Williams average 243.7 mph in his Curtiss R2C-1 racer at the newly-built St. Louis airport. He led three Navy teammates to victory over weak Army competition.

MID-AIR DISINTEGRATION of the old Curtiss R-6, killing Lt. Burt Skeel, marred the Pulitzer record. Lt. H. Mills (above) won the trophy in an R-3 monoplane racer.

FINAL WINNER of the Pulitzer Trophy was Army pilot Cy Bettis, flying a Curtiss R3C-1, Oct. 12, 1925. Lt. James Doolittle triumphed in the Schneider Trophy Race a few days later with same plane.

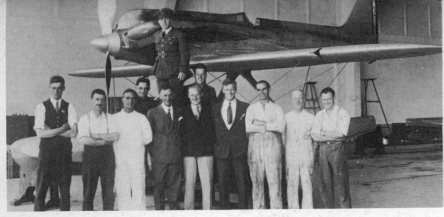

SUPERMARINE S-5 flown by Flight Lt. S. H. Webster (standing on float) and designed by R.J. Mitchell (center, in light trousers) won the 1927 Schneider Contest at Venice, Italy at an average speed of 281.65 mph. This contest marked the first official participation by the British Government in the races and started the team of Supermarine and Mitchell on the basic design features which finally culminated in the famous "Spitfire" prototype (above) which first flew on Mar. 5, 1936. In mass production at start of World War II this superb fighter was eloquent testimony to the wisdom and genius of R. J. Mitchell who died in 1937.

SCHNEIDER RACES

Trophy fosters speedier flight

In Dec. 1912, at a dinner given in Paris by the Aero Club de France, came the first announcement of the Schneider Trophy. Donated by Jacques Schneider, this trophy was intended to encourage the development of seaplanes. Under the rules of the F.A.I., the Trophy was to be awarded permanently to any nation who could win the trophy three times in succession.

Starting as a sporting event in 1913 at Monaco, France, the Schneider Contests assumed such international stature that in 1923 the U.S. Navy sent a crack team of men and machines to Cowes, England and won the trophy decisively. From that time on, the prestige of entire national aircraft industries hung in the balance at each race and the competition which resulted had a tremendous influence on the design of ensuing aircraft and engines.

It has been said that no single international contest in aviation history so profoundly affected the development of high speed aircraft as did the Schneider Contests.

Much pioneering was done in superchargers and doctored fuels to obtain more power from the engines then available. The winner of the 1913 contest was powered by a 160-hp engine, while that of the 1931 winner received its power from an engine developing 2,350 hp.

Italy, missing only the first two meets, prepared three Macchi MC-72 racers for the 1931 meet. These seaplanes were equipped with twin Fiat engines in tandem, each driving a propeller in opposite directions on the same axis. Development of this 3100-hp coupled engine had not reached the flight stages in time for the 1931 meet, but continued effort on the design by Regia Aeronautica enabled Italy, in 1934, to establish a three-km absolute speed record for seaplanes, still unchallenged after 19 years.

In all, twelve contests were held in the U.S., France, Italy and England during the period 1913 to 1931. England, by winning in 1927, 1929 and 1931 was awarded permanent possession of the Schneider Trophy.

ROLAND GARROS had difficulty becoming airborne in his 80-hp Morane-Saulnier seaplane at the 1913 meet at Monaco, France. For this reason Garros, later one of the aces of the first war, did not compete.

FIRST WINNER of a Schneider Contest was Marcel Prevost who piloted his Deperdussin seaplane to victory in the 1913 meet at Monaco, France. His speed was 45.75 mph. Plane had 160-hp engine.

NEW SPEED RECORD for seaplanes of 86.78 mph was set by this Sopwith *Tabloid*, fitted with a 100-hp engine. The tiny biplane, flown by Howard Pixton of Great Britain, won the 1914 contest at Monaco.

AMERICAN VICTORY came with the superb flying of Lt. David Rittenhouse of the U.S. Navy (below). Flying a Curtiss CR-3 racer in the meet at Cowes, England, Rittenhouse won at a speed of 177.38 mph.

FINAL CONTEST for Schneider Trophy occurred in 1931 when Flight Lt. John Boothman piloted his Supermarine S-6b to victory with average speed of 340.08 mph. Rolls-Royce engine powered plane.

LT. JAMES DOOLITTLE passed the 200-mph mark in the 1925 meet at Baltimore, Maryland, by flying his Curtiss R3C-2 racer, powered by a 600-hp Curtiss D-12 engine, to a brilliant victory at 232.5 mph.

CAPT. A. FERRARIN sits atop his Macchi M-52 (1,000-hp Fiat A-S3 engine), one of the Italian entrants for the 1927 contest at Venice, Italy. Forced down by engine trouble, he did not complete race.

ROLLS ROYCE furnished Supermarine with an engine developing 1900 hp. Installed in the new S-6 and flown by Flight Lt. H.R.D. Waghorn at the 1929 contest, this British entry won easily at 328.63 mph.

ITALY'S HOPE for the 1931 meet was the twin engine Macchi MC-72. Engine development problems prevented its competing, but in 1934, flown by W/O Agello it set a seaplane mark of 440.68 mph.

DEATH OF A BATTLESHIP, in aerial tests supervised by Gen. Mitchell in 1921, proved that an under-water burst close to a ship's hull was more deadly than a direct hit. Tests illustrated vulnerability of warships to attack, a main issue of Mitchell's prophecy that future wars would be settled by air power. Mitchell strongly criticized military policy that overlooked the key role of aircraft.

INVESTIGATING TRAGIC DISASTER of dirigible *Shenandoah* in 1925, a Naval Air Board of Inquiry summoned deposed Brig. Gen. Mitchell, (seated, c.), wearing his permanent-rank insignia of Colonel. Through his attorney, Rep. Frank R. Reid, Illinois (standing), he refused to testify to "protect his rights"—with a view to his own impending court-martial, Oct. 28, 1925, which found him guilty.

"BILLY" MITCHELL

Ignored prophet battles for independent air force

William E. "Billy" Mitchell, the father of American military aviation, struggled valiantly for the development of air power in the U.S., but ironically remained a prophet without honor. A pioneer in revolutionizing warfare techniques, he reached a bitter climax to a colorful, heroic life when a court-martial deposed him as Assistant Chief of Air Service. Yet after great loss of lives and money, most of his predictions about future warfare were to come true and his recommendations be adopted.

His military career was long and distinguished. In 1898, at the outbreak of the Spanish-American war, he enlisted at 18 as a private, served in Cuba, Philippines, Mexico, and won a commission in the Signal Corps the same year. He was the youngest officer to be appointed to the Army General Staff (1913).

In World War I, he was the first American to fly over enemy lines, becoming chief of U.S. air service at the front, later commanding all allied aviation services. Emerging from the war a Brigadier General, Mitchell was appointed Assistant Chief of U.S. Army Air Service.

In this post, from 1919 to 1923, the "stormy petrel" became the focal point of a controversy as to whether bombs could sink battleships. Mitchell argued for a separate air arm, an air-secretary equal with the Army, Navy secretaries, and a wider acceptance of the airplane as a defensive, aggressive weapon rather than merely as a "scouting service." But more important, in aerial tests he exposed the vulnerability of warships to air attack.

In 1925, he became an outspoken critic of the country's aviation policy, figured prominently in newspaper headlines when he accused the Army, Navy of "incompetency, criminal negligence, and almost treasonable administration of national defense." Court-martialed for insubordination, violation of good order and military discipline (96th Article of War), he was found guilty, suspended from rank, command, and duty for five years without pay or allowances. Gen. Mitchell resigned before the sentence could take effect. Later, Pres. Coolidge upheld the suspension, but restored the allowances and granted him one half of his monthly pay. In 1945 he was posthumously restored to service with the rank of major general and awarded the Congressional Medal of Honor . . . "in recognition of service and foresight in aviation."

RETURNING TRIUMPHANTLY to the Philippines in 1924, Mitchell landed at Clark Field (top) during nine-month survey of Pacific aerial defense. There, he met again Emilio Aguinaldo (below,) and gave thrilling flying lesson to the leader of the 1899 revolt, whom General Mitchell had helped capture.

HOMESPUN HUMORIST Will Rogers (left), was a strong friend of Mitchell. An aviation enthusiast, later to perish with Wiley Post in an air crash, he made several excursion flights with Mitchell the year of his court martial. Another close associate was pioneer plane builder Glenn Curtiss (center, standing, left, next to Mitchell, by the Curtiss "Military Eagle" plane of 1920). Convinced early of inevitability of U.S. entry into World War I,

Mitchell had enrolled in the Curtiss Company's flying school at Newport News, Va. in the winter of 1915-16. He also encouraged Curtiss to establish an additional training center in Miami. Dapper, dashing, socially prominent Mitchell (right), resigned from the Army, February 1, 1926, took up farming in Middlebury, Vt., until his death in New York City, Feb. 19, 1936—too soon to see his ignored predictions realized in World War II.

SHOT INTO AIR by catapult, this observation biplane is typical of those used through the 20's by world's navies. Naval chiefs considered aircraft mostly as "spotters" for surface fleets, were unwilling or unable to comprehend fully Billy Mitchell's demonstration of bomber sinking a battleship. Battleships and cruisers catapulted biplanes equipped with floats, retrieving them by crane from the ocean.

TIN FISH, as torpedoes were called, is sped on its way by a Douglas torpedo bomber of the 20's. Of all Navy theories, that of torpedo planes stayed almost the same in principle through and past Second World War. First patent on a torpedo plane was granted Rear Adm. Bradley A. Fiske in 1912. Another air technique pioneered by the Navy was dive bombing which was tried in 20's, developed later.

WAR PLANES NEGLECTED IN 1920's

Military aviation held back by opposition of old-line generals and admirals

The cessation of hostilities in 1918 left the warring nations with thousands of planes and fliers, neither with a military future.

Facing extreme cutbacks, the world's air forces abandoned those who learned to fly in the service, retaining career men who had climbed the regular service ladder. This played a large part in shaping military air policies of the 1920's.

There was little or no money to develop new aircraft types. Existing World War I planes were modified to perform new duties. Experimental aircraft seldom got beyond the prototype stage. In all major air forces, there were fewer than five changes in standard combat models of each type.

In the U.S., the military were busy with other specialties: flying-mail, fire patrols, setting speed and altitude records.

In 1921, the Italian, Gen. Guilio Douthet wrote his "The Command of the Air," in which he said air power should—indeed *must*—be a co-equal with armies and navies. He went so far as to say wars would be fought entirely in the air, and that strategic bombing fleets would be the

key to victory in the next war. However, his theories were not well received by the powerfully entrenched army and navy men of the world, who kept aviation under their control for years as an adjunct to their services.

PLANE-CARRYING SUBMARINE was another Naval idea which in the long run proved impractical for combat use. The plane is the Cox-Klemin XS-1, a tiny craft designed and built for a U.S. Navy sub.

The British modified their W.W. I planes to patrol and keep peace in their new Middle East domains. They advanced their designs in the combat field, while clinging to biplanes with liquid-cooled engines as standard aircraft.

During the 1920's, naval air arms experimented with and made a success of catapults. Various other ideas were tried and discarded, such as plane-carrying submarines.

The French, leaders in aircraft development during the war, stagnated. The Germans, blocked by the Versailles Treaty from producing military planes in their own nation, built and operated war-plane plants in other nations, such as Sweden and Russia. In Germany, they concentrated on getting high performance from low-powered civil planes, used gliders for training.

Red Russia inherited a few obsolete foreign planes from the Czar. The Bolsheviks invited foreigners to build planes in Russia and bought their military planes in Europe.

Tired of war, the world paid little attention to military aeronautics in the 1920's.

FIRST U.S. CARRIER was the *Langley*, which had been converted from the collier *Jupiter*. First used October 26, 1922, the carrier was approved by Navy men remembering the success of Eugene Ely who took off from the deck of the *USS Birmingham* Nov. 14, 1910. Two battle cruisers were converted next. Finished in 1927, they became the *Lexington* and *Saratoga*, famed carriers of World War II.

WAR BIRDS FOLD WINGS for storage aboard a carrier, where space was at a premium. Martin torpedo planes shown were among first U.S. Navy aircraft in regular service to use land-type gear which became standard later on in 1920's. Some catapult-design scout planes continued to use floats for years, but almost all other types, like flying boats and utility craft, were landplanes or amphibians.

ENGINE FAILURE due to water which had escaped from crude filter to gas tank, was blamed for this crash of a torpedo plane in June, 1920. Many fatal crashes suffered during the 1920's were due to incomplete trial-and-error maintenance techniques.

◀ **AERIAL EYES** were stressed in the Air Service during the 1920's, when cameras and camera planes underwent intensive development. Shown here is a group of cadets learning to operate a camera mounted in rear cockpit of an observation airplane.

DEADLY FIGHTERS in their day were these Boe- ▶ ing P-12's, typifying the small open cockpit biplanes which were standard equipment in all air forces during the 1920's. Higher speeds were attained by increasing the horsepower; it was not until the 1930's that designs were improved to gain efficiency. Guns still fired through propeller blades.

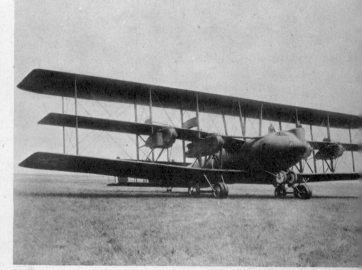

EARLY HEAVY BOMBERS like these U. S. Keystones, were service standards from the 1920's until late in next decade. Carrying crew and engines out in wind reduced planes' speed, range, bomb load. Airstream pressures against guns also gave defenders difficulty.

FIRST COMMANDER of the Navy's Bureau of Aeronautics was Rear Adm. William A. Moffett. Under him, Navy pushed development of radial engines, the Norden bombsight, and metal hulls for flying boats. He died in 1933 *Akron* crash.

LUMBERING FREAK of the early 1920's was the first of all "superbombers," the six-engined triplane Barling Bomber. Although it flew, the engine horsepower of the day was inadequate for such a huge plane. The Barling ended its life as a target for strafing practice.

THRILL FOR BRITISH crowd at the Handley Page airfield in England was the relatively closeup view people had of samples of their bombers. In 1919, Winston Churchill cut RFC from 30,000 officers, 300,000 men, to only 3,000 officers, and 30,000 men.

UNLOADING IN CHINA, this British plane was one of the fleet England kept there during 1920's to protect her subjects and their property. Britain used World War I planes extensively in foreign areas to keep peace and to insure control in the early 1920's.

BRITISH EXPERIMENTED with their catapults on the ground, with a large flying field ahead of the plane. This was done before catapulting plane at sea. Royal Air Force, like other air services, conducted tests of some unlikely devices during the 1920's.

CHARLES A. LINDBERGH poses beside his plane prior to his take-off from Roosevelt Field May 20, 1927. The *Spirit of St. Louis* (above, right) is being wheeled from the hangar for the start of the perilous journey which no man had yet successfully completed. As the young flier buttons his flying togs (lower, right), his face is set and grim. Immediately after this photo was taken, a drizzling rain began. Anxious officials pleaded with him to wait until the skies cleared, but he refused. Climbing into the cockpit, he looked out with a tight smile, pointed the nose of his plane into the overcast sky, and took off across the stormy Atlantic.

LONE EAGLE FLIES ATLANTIC

Young Lindbergh makes "impossible" New York-to-Paris nonstop flight

In May 1919, Raymond Orteig, a wealthy Frenchman, offered a $25,000 prize for the first nonstop airplane flight from New York to Paris. Several attempts were made by French and American fliers without success and with some tragedies. It remained for a then unknown American youth to win the prize and the admiration of a world grown smaller by his adventure.

Taking off in light rain, the quiet, slender 24-year-old flier attempted what veteran airmen termed "impossible"—to fly the Atlantic alone. His courage and daring caught the public's fancy. Around the globe people sat with their ears glued to their radios and a prayer in their hearts for some news of his progress. For twelve hours there was only ominous silence, and then came the heartening news that his plane had been sighted off the coast of Ireland. Ten hours later he made a perfect landing at Le Bourget

airfield, near Paris, and climbed out of his plane. "Lindy" had succeeded in his bid for fame.

A huge crowd had gathered to greet him. When he landed, they give him one of the great-

GASOLINE GAUGE on instrument board of the *Spirit of St. Louis* did not show 60 gals. left in tank at flight's end. 370 gals. were used, 11.1 per hour.

est exhibitions of adulation the world has ever known. Lindbergh, his face drawn and tired from the ordeal, smiled shyly and waved at the shouting multitude. It took the better part of an hour plus several stalwart policemen finally to get him safely from the field. He had covered the 3600 miles between New York and Paris in 33½ hours. His average speed was 107½ miles per hour in his $13,000 Ryan monoplane.

In the days and weeks that followed, Lindbergh was feted and idolized wherever he went. He was lauded by kings and nobility. He received 35 million pieces of mail, countless citations and medals, and was awarded the rank of Colonel in the Air Reserve. He recorded his own story of his lone flight in the *Spirit of St. Louis* in a book entitled *We*. It was highly successful and widely reprinted. Through all the ovations, however, his magnificent poise never deserted him.

FRIENDLY RIVALS in the trans-Atlantic attempt (l. to r.), Lindbergh, Comdr. Richard E. Byrd and Clarence Chamberlin wish each other success. Although Lindbergh was first to fly solo across Atlantic, Clarence Chamberlin, a few days later with Charles Levine, made first nonstop flight from New York to Germany.

DETAIL DIAGRAM of *Spirit of St. Louis* shows the single-engine Ryan monoplane designed especially for Lindbergh. Performance of plane's 220-hp Wright Whirlwind radial engine proved value of air-cooled engine in era of liquid-cooled types. The famous plane was later placed in Smithsonian Institution on exhibit.

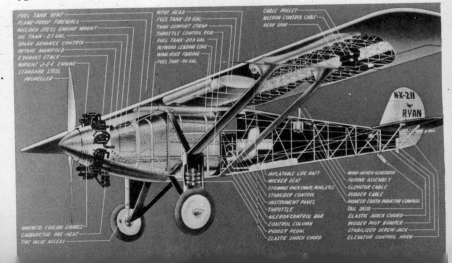

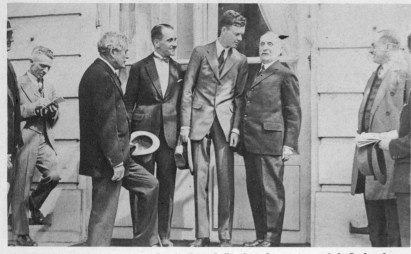

MARSHAL FOCH congratulates "Lindy" after his successful flight from New York to Paris. While in France, the young hero was decorated by the President of the French Republic with the Cross of the Legion of Honor. He visited mother of Charles Nungesser, lost in Atlantic attempt in May.

HERO'S WELCOME greeted Lindbergh on his return to the United ▶ States. In the photo at right he is shown during his triumphant parade down New York's Broadway. Tons of confetti, ticker tape and torn newspapers and telephone books showered the parade in the unbridled demonstration.

YOUTHFUL PRINCE OF WALES poses with Lindbergh in the Royal Box at the Derby Ball in London. This was but one of the dozens of parties held in the flier's honor in the U.S. and abroad in the weeks following his flight. Lindbergh is wearing the Air Force Cross which King presented him at Buckingham Palace.

CHEERING THRONGS surge forward eagerly as the *Spirit of St. Louis* circles for a landing at Croyden Field, England. Their welcome was so vociferous a police cordon had to be thrown around the plane to keep "Lindy" from injury.

CALVIN COOLIDGE praises Lindbergh's courage at ceremonies held in the flier's honor at Washington Monument. Following his speech, the president awarded Lindbergh the D. F. C.

FLYING LESSON in piloting an old "pusher" biplane is given Lindbergh by Al Wilson, the plane's owner, before he took off in the 1910 Curtiss replica at 1928 National Air Races. Lindbergh later joined an airline, also served as adviser to aeronautical branch of the United States Department of Commerce.

"THE LONE EAGLE," alone no longer, is shown here in one of the first photos with his new bride, the former Anne Morrow, who was also an aviation enthusiast. With them at Mitchell Field, N. Y., is Harry Guggenheim, president-trustee of the David Guggenheim Fund for the Promotion of Aeronautics.

PILOT AND CO-PILOT, Lindbergh and his wife are pictured ready for the take-off on one of their many flights together. Following his surveys for early passenger lines, the two made trans-Pacific good will flight, a tour over Central America, and a 30,000 mile trip during which they landed in 21 countries.

ANTHONY FOKKER was aviation's "Rover Boy." Born in Java in 1890, he was a licensed pilot in Germany at 21. A year later he opened his first plant near Berlin and added one in Schwerin in 1913. Fokker contributed importantly to much of Germany's air might in World War I. He invented a synchronizer for firing machine gun past moving propeller blades. After the war Fokker developed many worthy aircraft types in Holland. He brought his first tri-motor, the F-7, to U.S. in 1925. It gained immediate acceptance. The *Josephine Ford*, above, was name given Fokker tri-motor Byrd flew to North Pole in 1926.

AUTO PRODUCTION GENIUS Henry Ford joined forces with William B. Stout to manufacture the first Ford Tri-motor in 1925. The famous "Tin Goose" of the airways was based on the 1924 Stout Air Pullman, a Liberty-powered monoplane with a corrugated metal body. First of these planes to be built by Ford was the *Maiden Detroit*, above. Ford planes were never mass-produced with the energy of his automobiles. Only 135 were in use by October, 1929, a year after full production. Ford, seen here with Col. Charles Lindbergh (r.), gave impetus to aviation by his mere presence in it during the 20's.

AIRCRAFT MANUFACTURERS
Postwar designs slow to emerge

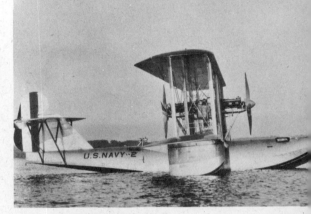

Large quantities of surplus war planes held back production of new types in the U.S. after World War I. With modifications, the DeHavilland DH-4 could carry 500 pounds of mail; its sturdy Liberty engine gave it a top speed of 120 mph.

In European countries, where airlines were developing as passenger carriers, more was expected of the airplane. Junkers all-metal monoplanes were in production in Germany immediately following the war.

In France, Farman and Breguet began manufacturing transports of original design in 1922. Early British transports were mostly modifications of Handley Page, Vickers-Vimy and other World War I bomber types.

Anthony Fokker smuggled plane parts and machinery from Germany, then made his own escape to Holland in his first passenger plane, the F-2. He built planes there until coming to America. Pan American's order of six Fokker F-10 transports in 1928 was the largest single order for passenger airplanes up to that time.

Lockheed's manufacture of fast transports associated its *Vega* (1927) and the *Sirius* (1929) with many record flights.

At the 1929 National Air Races in Cleveland, several trends reflected the advances in the decade. Single-purpose planes (i. e., trainers, sports, racers) were noted for the first time in large number. Among passenger planes, the Boeing B-80A stood out, indicating the emergence of large transports in the U.S.

CLAUDE RYAN built the *Spirit of St. Louis*, the plane Lindbergh flew across the Atlantic, one year after he built the *Bluebird* (top photo), which had caught Lindbergh's eye. Operator of an airline between Los Angeles and San Diego, Ryan became one of nation's foremost plane builders. Ryan is shown with George Prudden (l.) who in 1929 designed first low-wing tri-motor transport built in U.S.

1920 AIRLINER was built by Remington-Burnelli and labeled the BR-1. It was later placed in the Smithsonian Institution. The most notable feature of this early giant aircraft was its introduction of the airfoil contour on fuselage, an innovation in design.

MOST PROLIFIC BUILDER of Army and Navy aircraft in U. S. during 20's was the Curtiss Factory at Garden City, N. Y. Firm provided fighting planes for China, So. America, other countries. Curtiss planes won majority of the Pulitzer Trophy races.

BOEING PLAYED KEY ROLE in both military and passenger transport. PB-1 (above), called the *Flying Dreadnaught* was experimental craft built in 1925. Though never manufactured in quantity, it provided Navy with valuable experience in operation of metal-hull flying boats. The Boeing B-40A (below) was built in 1927. It was earliest transport to use "Wasp" engines, still had open cockpit for pilot.

"WASP" ENGINES, manufactured by Pratt & Whitney, were successful competitors of Wright *Whirlwinds*. P. & W. was formed in July, 1925, by Frederick Rentschler, former president of Wright, and George Mead, who developed the *Whirlwinds*.

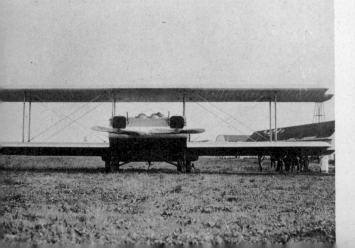

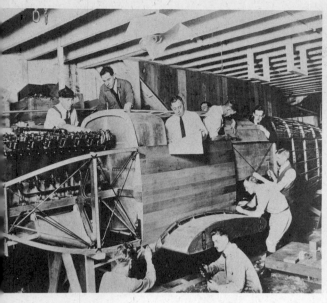

MAN AND DESTINY were wed when Donald Douglas was one of the spectators to watch the Wrights demonstrate their plane to the Army in 1909. Then but 17, Douglas was so enthusiastic he resigned from the Naval Academy after three years because the Navy was not yet sold on aviation. After completing his education at MIT, he became Jerome C. Hunsaker's assistant in aerodynamics, worked on first U.S. wind tunnel experiments. Aerodynamic theory was not dynamic enough for Douglas, who became chief engineer of Glenn L. Martin Co. in 1915.

Five years later, with $600 capital, he went to work for himself in the rear of a Santa Monica barber shop (right). Douglas is at left in photo. There he designed *Cloudster* (l.), first plane to lift its weight in payload. Four years later, he secured an Army order for the DWC, first plane to circumnavigate the earth. As young men have grown up, so has aviation. Douglas' sons, William E. (center, l.) and Donald Jr. both joined the Douglas firm. William became missiles coordinator, Donald Jr., vice-president in charge of military sales, a company director.

SHERMAN FAIRCHILD'S first plane, the FC-1, hauled his newly invented cameras aloft in 1926. By 1929 the Kreider-Reisner Co., Inc. had become the Fairchild Aircraft Corp. The FC-1, which won the Scientific American Trophy Award, became the model for the famous *Challenger* transport, which Hagerstown, Maryland plant turned out at rate of one-a-day, 1929. Fairchild cameras pioneered in making air maps.

RUSSIAN REVOLUTION can be thanked for Count Igor Sikorsky's residence in the Western World. A native of Kiev, by 1914 he had produced four-engine plane which flew 1600 miles. Sikorsky built the first heavy (4-engine) bombers ever used and held almost every aviation record in Russia before he fled from that country in 1917. In 1923 on Long Island he built his first aircraft organization, and a year later turned out the twin-engine, 14-passenger S-29, left. Sikorsky (left) poses with engineer G.O. Noville and co-pilot Homer M. Berry of the unsuccessful Rene Fonck trans-Atlantic flight in 1926. Sikorsky's S-38 amphibian is shown (right) at its 1928 debut.

THE "ARGOSY," first airliner of the Imperial Airways, boasted three radial air-cooled Armstrong-Siddeley-Jaguar engines of 385 hp each. Proud asset to the early British line's far-flung service, the *Argosy* soared on the London-Karachi-Delhi trip, ranging from Croydon to Salonika on the first leg of the flight. The vast London-Cairo-Capetown route was also on the *Argosy's* schedule and the plane was later to fly the final hop in the enterprising Australia-to-Britain mail experiment in 1931. Modern luxury service was hinted by the built-in bar and meals served on the *Argosy* while in flight.

WINTRY WASTES of Northern Europe made skis a practical landing gear in the early days of commercial transport. In use in 1929 by Finnish Air Lines was this ski-equipped Junkers F-13, the *"Oh-Ali."* Junkers planes inspired many aircraft designs. First Junkers, Fokker, and Ford tri-motors appeared in 1925, all within a few months of each other.

THEA RASCHE, German aviatrix, advanced the feminine role in aviation when she flew this Italian Savoia-Marchetti 14-passenger transport in 1929. Plane was in the regular New York-Boston service of "Airvia." This aircraft was unique in its twin floats, each serving as a cabin, and in the puller-pusher power which was still favored by some designers. By criteria of that day, this was a "huge" plane.

ONLY "OVERSEAS" AIRLINE in U.S. after World War I was the Key West-Havana route of Aeromarine. Originally a carrier between New York City and resort towns, it used converted Navy flying boats. Small mail subsidy forced dissolution in 1923.

COMFORTABLE WICKER had added advantage of light weight in Fokker F-3 built for Royal Dutch Airlines (KLM) in 1920. Travel comfort, government subsidies gained KLM key European routes; lack of both caused failure of early airlines in Britain.

PEACE CONFERENCE PAPERS and personnel, hoisted across the channel on RAF Communications Flights resulted in sanction of civilian air trips to Paris—and birth in August, 1919, of Air Transport & Travel, Ltd., Britain's first real passenger airline.

FIRST AIRLINES
Europe builds world routes while U.S. develops air mail

"Back to Normalcy," the cautious covenant that won Harding the presidency in 1920, threatened to eclipse the battle cry of the postal service: "The *Air* Mail Must Go Through!"

Valuable as training for Army pilots during the war, air mail had not proved itself vital or necessary since taken over by the Post Office Department in August, 1918. Even though regular service between Chicago and New York had opened within a year, the high death toll exacted by this "Graveyard Run" over the Alleghenies was not the "normalcy" the country was seeking.

Civil aviation was having its biggest development abroad. Paris Peace Conferences sparked Europe's air travel; Prohibition gave the U.S. its major "airline"—the Key West-Havana run of Aeromarine subsidized by a government contract to carry mail to Cuba. Barnstorming daredevils gained few adherents to passenger transport, and the country's air mail future looked dim —until an audacious exploit saved the day.

Mere days before Wilson departed the White House, the first night mail was flown across the country by daring Post Office fliers, whose only beacons were bonfires lit by farmers. That night, a "lame duck" gave wings to commercial aviation—and air mail pilots ranked with war aces as America's new heroes. In 1924, most of the 1,886 miles of airways were lighted.

Final collapse of every British airline in 1925, through lack of government subsidy, was followed by the founding of Imperial Airways with a ten million pound grant to spend over 10 years. In the U.S., 1925 marked the passage of the Kelly Bill, inviting bids from private companies for delivery of mail over "feeder" lines called Contract Air Mail Routes by the Post Office Department.

In 1926, 14 routes (CAM-1—CAM-14) were put in operation by forerunners of today's airline companies. But passenger travel still lagged, until Lindbergh's solo hop across the Atlantic encouraged the nation to fly. At once airline stocks rose as aviation barnstormed its way into American big business and the boom.

MUSHROOMING FRENCH LINES gained confidence of passengers with Farman *Goliaths*, derived from World War I bomber. Government subsidies enabled French to undersell British airline services until the birth of England's Imperial Airways in 1925. Air France airline did not emerge until 1933.

CROSS-COUNTRY FLIGHT over unlighted airways by ten air mail pilots Feb. 22, 1921, brought $1,250,-000 appropriation by Congress for continuation of air mail, provided funds for lighting the airways. Jack Knight (above), saved the flight (see p. 96), which secured the future of commercial aviation.

ENERGETIC BEGINNINGS of air express were reflected in loading of a Handley Page World War I bomber at Mitchell Field, N. Y., November, 1919 for attempt to fly nonstop to Chicago. When the airplane was forced down because of engine trouble, the delivery had to be completed by train. Early shipments generally traveled by combined air and rail express. Regular Air Express service started on Sept. 1, 1927.

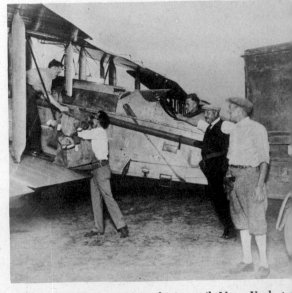

FIRST NIGHT FLIGHTS of air mail New York to Chicago were possible in August of 1923. Revolving searchlights connected emergency landing fields spaced 25 miles apart. A year later, lighted airways reached to Rock Springs, Wyo., and coast-to-coast night flights began. Biggest hazard was now in the planes themselves—converted war time De Havilands, available at cost due to post-war surpluses

CONTRACT AIRMAIL ROUTES OPEN

U. S. airline patterns can be traced to the "feeder" lines opened to private bids in 1925. On April 6, 1926, Leon D. Cuddeback (upper left), flew the Elko, Nev.-Pasco, Wash. run for the first of the five original Contract Air Mail Routes to begin service. Operated by Varney Air Lines, it was known to the Post Office Department as CAM-5. Western Air Express flew Douglas M-2's from converted movie studio at edge of Vail Field (lower left) east to Salt Lake City over

CAM-4. Hazardous DeHavillands were vanishing as owners of the "feeder" lines bought planes of early manufacturers like Claude L. Ryan (above, r.), whose early planes flew the Los Angeles-Seattle route won by Pacific Air Transport. PAT's owner, Vern Gorst, appears with Ryan after the two set a record of 7 hours, 3 min. in San Francisco-Seattle survey flight. Contract air routes "fed" government's "main line" transcontinental air mail route until bids were opened on this route in 1927. San Francisco-Chicago leg, won by amazingly low bid of airplane manufacturer William Boeing, laid early foundation of United Air Lines.

TONY FOKKER'S ESCAPE to Holland from Germany following World War I gave enormous impetus to development of Dutch KLM. With the Fokker F-7 in 1925, it became first airline to use air-cooled rather than water-cooled engines. KLM, world's second oldest airline, was formed in 1919. Denmark's DDL, world's oldest, was founded just a month before war ended.

BOSTON-NEW YORK route of Colonial Air Transport's CAM-1 was opened June 18, 1926, by (l. to r.) pilots Leroy Thompson, H.I. Wells, Maj. T.O. Freeman. They hand mail to general manager Juan T. Trippe, who later organized Pan American Airways.

FIRST SCHEDULED FLIGHT of passengers over the contract mail routes was inaugurated by Colonial Air Transport the night of April 4, 1927, on its Boston-New York run. Holder of Ticket No. 1 was Mrs. Gardiner Fiske, standing. Colonial was earliest forerunner of today's American Airlines.

TRANSPORT PLANES had greatest development in Germany due to Versailles restrictions on military aircraft. This 15-passenger Junkers G-31 with three compartments, two berths, was used by Deutsche Luft Hansa.

NON-ALCOHOLIC CHRISTENING of a Ford Trimotor by Amelia Earhart and smiling Grover Whalen in New York Penn. Station July 7, 1929, launched first coast-to-coast air line. Passengers flew by day, took train at night; trip's 48 hours cut cross-country travel time in half.

AMERICA'S HORIZONS WIDENED with flights to South America in 1929 by Pan American Airways following survey flight by Col. Charles Lindbergh (in helmet). Sikorsky flying boats were developed in 1928 for Pan American, formed in 1927 to fly 110-mi. Key West-Havana route, once Aeromarine's.

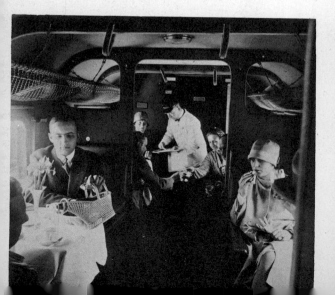

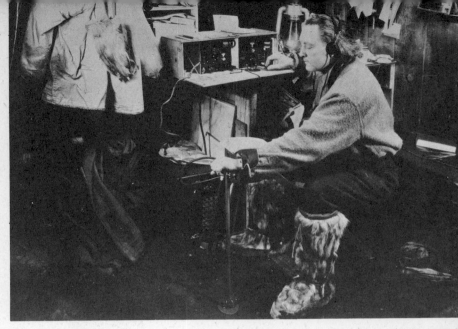

FIRST OVER BOTH POLES was Lt. Comdr. (later Rear Adm.) Richard Evelyn Byrd. He conquered North Pole at 9:02 a.m. May 9, 1926 in trimotor Fokker *Josephine Ford* (above), named for daughter of auto-magnate, sponsor of flight. Pilot for 15 hour, 30 minute flight was Floyd Bennett, for whom Navy (L.I.) air base is named. At right is Byrd as he appeared during his six-month stay alone at Advance Outpost during 1933-35 Antarctic expedition. Overcome by gas, he almost lost his life during lonely vigil as weather observer, but was rescued in nick of time. Byrd's South Polar trips resulted in discovery of valuable mineral deposits and gave U.S. backing in Antarctic territorial claims. His projected third expedition to Little America was canceled by the beginning of World War II.

POLAR FLIGHTS

SOUTH POLE AIRCRAFT, a Ford Trimotor, is dug out of its snow covering at Byrd's "Little America" base camp prior to flight across pole Nov. 28, 1929. Bernt Balchen was the pilot, Harold June was radio operator and Capt. Ashley McKinley, U.S. Army, was the photographer. Development of sun compass for polar navigation aided Byrd on both his flights.

RAOLD AMUNDSEN used semi-rigid airship *Norge* to follow Byrd over the North Pole by two days. With Amundsen were Col. Umberto Nobile, airship commander, and Lincoln Ellsworth. When Nobile and crew of the airship *Italia* were lost returning from a flight over the North Pole May 24, 1928, Amundsen flew by plane to give aid. Nobile was later rescued; no trace of Amundsen was found.

Years before man ever reached the North Pole on foot, he assaulted the frozen wastes through the air, only to die in his first effort.

The initial attempt to reach the pole by air started July 11, 1897 when Solomon Auguste Andree, Nils Strinberg and Knut Frankel took off in a free balloon from Kings Bay, Spitzbergen. They covered 200 miles in three days, coming down on White Island, where they eventually perished. Strinberg, who was buried, apparently was the first to die, followed by Andree and Frankel who died together on the icy ground. Their bodies were found almost exactly 33 years later, Aug. 6, 1930, in the spots where they fell.

Lt. Comdr. Richard E. Byrd, who retired from the Navy in the early 1920s after an injury hurt his chances for advancement as a deck officer, flew to the North Pole May 9, 1926. He was followed two days later by the Nobile-Ellsworth-Amundsen group in the dirigible *Norge*. The airship hovered around the pole for two hours of scientific observation, then flew 2,200 miles farther to land at Teller, Alaska.

Byrd also was first to reach the South Pole by air, on Nov. 28, 1929.

Lincoln Ellsworth, wealthy explorer, put money into the airship expedition which followed Byrd over the North Pole. Later Ellsworth also flew extensively over "Little America," as Byrd named the Antarctic regions where he made his headquarters.

Sir Hubert Wilkins and C. B. Eilson became the first men to fly from North America to Europe by the polar route on April 15, 1928. They made the 2,200-mile flight from Pt. Barrow, Alaska, to Spitzbergen in 20 hours, 30 minutes.

HUGE AREA of Antarctic was claimed for the United States after one of the exploratory flights made by Lincoln Ellsworth and Bernt Balchen in 1929. Pictured are (left to right) airplane builder John K. (Jack) Northrop, Balchen, Ellsworth and a Mr. Jay, the designer of the Northrop airplane (behind) which made the long aerial voyage. Some 77,000 square miles were claimed as a result of this flight. Balchen went on to become one of the foremost polar fliers in America, earning special recognition for his services during World War II.

Ellsworth, an Army pilot during the first World War, made several Antarctic flights. On one of these he was forced down at the Bay of Whales with his pilot, Herbert Hollick Kenyon, while on a flight from Dundee to "Little America." Though the two fliers landed safely, their radio would not operate. They were believed dead until found upon providential arrival of the Royal Research Society ship *Discovery*.

INTO ICY HANGAR at Kings Bay, Spitzbergen, crewmen tow the *Norge* just before she carried Amundsen, Ellsworth and her Italian commander, Col. Umberto Nobile, over the North Pole two days after Byrd. Instead of flying to the Pole and returning directly, the *Norge* hovered more than two hours at the top of the world to take scientific readings and then flew on 2,200 miles to Teller, Alaska. Map shows course taken by the *Norge*, and that taken by Byrd.

NOTED EXPLORER Sir Hubert Wilkins (r.) pioneered technical developments on his flights over both the North and South Pole regions. Wilkins' efforts earned him knighthood from King George V of England. He had hoped to prove the feasibility of commercial air transportation in the Arctic and exploration in the Antarctic.

"ZR-1 SHENANDOAH," modeled after the German military Zeppelin, was the first American-built rigid dirigible. Other Navy dirigibles included *USS Los Angeles*, built by Germany as World War I reparations payment and shown at left moored to the *USS Dakota*, mother ship of Navy's dirigible fleet, *USS Akron* and *USS Macon*. All met disaster but *Los Angeles*, which was dismantled. The *Shenandoah* made 15 successful flights in 1923. Damaged by a storm Jan. 16, 1924, she was restored, only to crash (r.) Sept. 3, 1925 in a storm 35 miles from Marietta, O., killing 6 officers, 9 men.

BALLOON JUMPING originated as a publicity stunt in a U. S. newsreel. Having to overcome only about four pounds ▶ of gravity, a balloon jumper giving average leap might soar 40 feet high, cover as much as a quarter of a mile. English parachutist E. A. Dobs tested the new sport in England (at right), was electrocuted when he landed on a 3000-volt line.

AIRSHIPS
Dirigible's end forecast

After World War I the victorious Allies sought to surpass the capacities of German military Zeppelins. During the hostilities appearance of the German giants over London and Paris in night raids had brought new and terrifying dimensions to war. London had been bombed 12 times by Zeppelin airships. The Zeppelins spelled annihilation in the minds of a war-wracked civilian population. But in the 1920's France and England learned the unreliability of the rigid dirigible. Loss of the *Dixmude*, which disappeared over the Mediterranean without a trace in 1923, caused France to abandon dirigible flights. The English had bad luck with the *R-33* and the *R-34*, each of which suffered damage during rough weather. By 1930, the *R-101* had crashed and burned, carrying 47 persons to their death. Only the U.S. remained seriously interested in the military possibilities of the rigid dirigible.

FIRST TRANSATLANTIC crossing by a dirigible was in 1919 by *R-34* (moored in background), of England's RAF. Lt. Comdr. Zachary Lansdowne, USN (extreme left), later killed in *Shenandoah* disaster, was aboard as American observer. With gas capacity of 2,000,000 cu. ft., ship amazed world with miraculous crossing. Accidents blighted later history of *R-34* and sister *R-33*. First crossing of *R-34* took 75 hours.

FIGHTER AIRPLANES were first launched from a dirigible by England's Royal Air Force. The *R-33*, sister ship to the *R-34*, is shown rising from an English aerodrome preparatory to a mid-air launching of attached aircraft. In 1930, the U.S. Navy successfully launched Lt. R. S. Barnaby in a glider from the underside of the dirigible *Los Angeles* at an altitude of 3000 feet over the shores of Lakehurst, New Jersey.

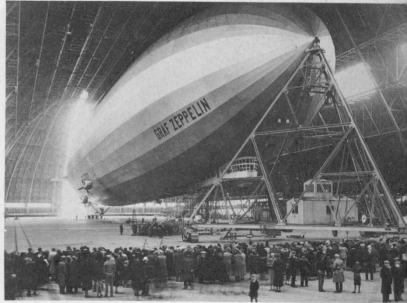

"THE ROMA," designed by Umberto Nobile and built in Italy in 1919 for the U.S. Army, exemplifies semi-rigid construction of the dirigible. Like *Norge* built in 1926 and the *Italia* built in 1928, the *Roma* had a keel structure at the bottom of a boneless hull. Compare the *Roma's* lumpy contours with the sleek lines of the fully rigid *Graf Zepplin*. The *Roma* hit a high tension wire and fell in flames in 1922. Here, the *Roma* is shown completing test flight at Langley Field, Va. Its loss speeded change to use of helium.

DR. HUGO ECKENER, famed German dirigible expert, receives congratulations of President Herbert Hoover (l.) after completing, in 1929, round-the-world-flight in the *Graf Zeppelin* (shown refueling above, after 1933 flight from Germany). Dr. Eckener was the key figure in post-W.W. I development of rigid dirigibles for long range civilian transport. The *Graf Zeppelin* carried 24-35 passengers. Its outer envelope was completely supported, independent of the lighting gas, by an intricate skeleton of girders. Germany led the world in development of the rigid dirigible, ostensibly for passenger transport only. German activity centered about Count Ferdinand von Zeppelin, whose company at Friedrichshafen built nearly 130 airships for both military and civilian use between 1900 and 1930. Goodyear Rubber at Akron, O. was prime U.S. exponent of airships. America's monopoly on helium, only adequate non-inflammable lifting gas, severely hampered German efforts. Dr. Eckener tried to obtain helium, but U.S. refused, fearing misappropriation for military purposes.

WORLD'S FIRST practical rotary-wing aircraft, the Cierva C-4, was created by Juan de la Cierva. Getafe Airdrome at Madrid, Spain, was site of first successful flight, Jan. 9, 1923. A four-minute flight around a closed course was made on Jan. 31. Cierva talks with noted aviatrix Thea Rasche by 1929 autogiro.

DANGEROUS METHOD of starting engines by swinging propellers by hand was eliminated by use of the electric starter. Early type shown on a Liberty 12 engine in Martin MB-1 was direct-cranking starter. Batteries were unreliable, so inertia starter was developed using energy stored in flywheel.

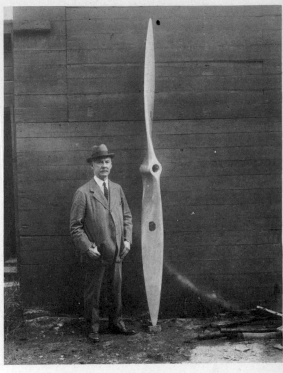

DURALUMINUM PROPELLERS, perfected by Dr. S. Albert Reed, provided improved performance and reduced weight. First Curtiss-Reed propellers were made by twisting duraluminum. A forged duraluminum propeller helped James Doolittle win 1925 Schneider Cup Race. Reed received Collier award.

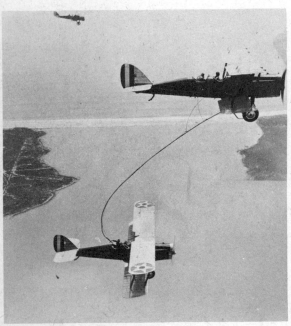

FIRST MID-AIR REFUELING of an airplane was accomplished by Army pilots in modified versions of famous DeHavilland DH-4BM. Lts. L. H. Smith and J. P. Richter stayed in the air four days over San Diego, Calif., in June, 1923, establishing world's duration mark. Smith took part in Army's World Flight.

SCIENCE ADDS SAFETY

Speeds rise, hazards fall; war's lessons utilized

The science of flying had progressed almost beyond man's comprehension in the decade ending in 1919. The simple box-kite craft of 1910 had yielded to streamlined monoplanes and biplanes with metal structures. Duraluminum, first made in Germany, was developed during the years 1903 to 1914. Dr. Claude Dornier designed the first German plane to be built of duraluminum. By 1919, smooth stressed-skin construction was progressing from the experimental stage to the development stage. Pioneers in the production of all metal airplanes in the U. S. were Stout Engineering Laboratories and the Thomas-Morse Aircraft Co. Stout built the first U.S. plane with stressed-skin metal construction, a Navy torpedo-bomber monoplane with two engines.

While American manufacturers developed many exceptional airplanes and components, funds for their production were not appropriated. As a consequence, America fell behind France, Great Britain, Italy, and other nations in the fields of commercial and military aviation up to 1927. Lindbergh's flight ended U.S. apathy.

In spite of the problems connected with the obtaining of appropriations, significant design progress was made during this historic period. Radio communication between airplanes in flight and ground stations, and radio navigation aids became realities. Flight instruments such as the turn-and-bank and rate-of-climb indicators came into widespread use. Air-cooled radial engines captured the position formerly dominated by the V-type liquid-cooled engines. Wooden propellers were rapidly being replaced by new duraluminum propellers. By 1929, aviation was well established as a major industry.

STRATOSPHERE FLIGHTS of Lt. J. A. Macready helped establish value of turbo-supercharger for high altitude flying. Lt. Macready (l.), standing next to Dr. Sanford Moss, inventor of the engine supercharging method, piloted this Packard-LePere LUSAC-11 in 1921 to altitude record of 34,509 feet.

FIRST EXPERIMENTS to construct metal-covered aircraft in U. S. were at Stout Eng. Labs. Early test of high-speed riveting, above, (conducted for George H. Prudden, designer of plane later to become Ford Tri-motor) led to developing of pneumatic rivet guns.

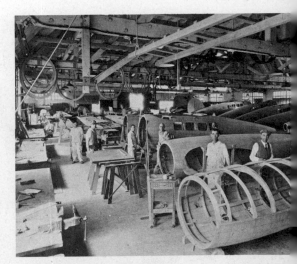

IMPROVED METHODS of aircraft manufacture included Lockheed-developed molded plywood fuselage construction, shown above. The innovation was first used in 1927 in manufacture of the *Vega*, a high speed cabin monoplane designed by Allan Lockheed and John Northrop. First *Vega* was *Golden Eagle*

WINNER of the Guggenheim Safe Aircraft award in 1929 was the Curtiss *Tanager* biplane. Prizes totaling $150,000 were awarded by the Guggenheim Fund for the airplanes making the greatest advance in safety without loss of efficiency. The Curtiss used slots and flaps, as well as wing-tip floating ailerons.

SPECTACULAR TAKEOFF of Handley Page *Gugnunc* was typical of top entries in the Safe Aircraft Competition. Sir Frederick Handley Page invented the automatic wing slot, a device for controlling the flow of air over a wing at low speeds. Slotted landing flaps were also invented by this Englishman.

CONTEST COMMITTEE for Daniel Guggenheim Safe Aircraft Competition included financier Harry F. Guggenheim and famous Col. Charles Lindbergh (center). Harry Guggenheim, as president of the Fund for the Promotion of Aeronautics established by his father, conducted safety plane contest.

WAR DECLARED on the boll weevil! Department of Agriculture experiments, conducted as early as 1920, proved that crop dusting by airplanes was the most effective and economical method of fighting pests. A Huff-Daland *Early Bird* dusts cotton fields with calcium arsenate.

HELICOPTER EXPERIMENTS made headlines when young Henry Berliner demonstrated his vertical lift machine for the U.S. Navy in 1922. Meanwhile, the Army-built DeBothezat helicopter was successfully flown for 1 min., 42 sec. at McCook Field, Ohio. Height attained was 15 feet. Pescara and Breguet were among designers of vertical lift machines.

TOO RADICAL for its time, this tiny Gordon Bennett Trophy Race entry was abandoned before it was fully developed. This small 1920 speedster was Dayton-Wright RB-1. Advanced features included retractable landing gear, variable-camber wing, full flaps, enclosed cockpit.

SUBJECTED TO RIDICULE in the aviation press of 1922 for its novel features, the Verville-Sperry R-3 racer was prophetic of future fighter design. Ancestor of all succeeding low wing, retractable-landing-gear aircraft, the R-3 had the first rubber-spool engine shock mounting, and landing gear position indicator. In 1924, a modified version won the Pulitzer Trophy.

MAN'S CONQUEST OF DARKNESS became a reality in 1929 when Lt. James Doolittle, using the Sperry Gyro Horizon and Directional Gyro, made first complete "blind" flight. Piloting a Consolidated NY-2 while under a hood, Doolittle took off from Mitchell Field, navigated over a 15-mile course, and made a successful landing. This public demonstration of air progress was made on Sept. 24, 1929. Lt. Ben Kelsey was check pilot.

ROCKET PROPULSION for aircraft first appeared in 1929 when Fritz von Opel experimented with powder rockets attached to a glider. Max Valier of the German Rocket Society was pilot for first flight on Sept. 30. Flight was made as part of a publicity scheme.

FIRST NONSTOP FLIGHT to Germany from New York was made by Clarence D. Chamberlin (second from right) June 4, 1927, in a Bellanca monoplane owned by Charles A. Levine (right) who hopped aboard at last minute to become first Atlantic air passenger. The original plan was to try for New York-to-Paris Orteig Prize, but after Lindbergh's flight a new goal was chosen—Berlin. With

Chamberlin and Levine in this photograph taken prior to the flight are (l. to r.) C. S. "Casey" Jones, pioneer instructor, test-pilot and engineer; Lloyd Bertaud who had been chosen tentatively as the pilot; and Will Rogers, the American humorist so intimately associated with aviation. Arriving in Berlin June 7 after forced landing 118 miles away, fliers received welcome rivalling Lindbergh's.

RECORD FLIGHTS IN THE LATE TWENTIES

FOKKER TRI-MOTOR "AMERICA" was procured for Richard E. Byrd by Rodman Wanamaker for a flight to demonstrate the practicability of regular trans-Atlantic flights. When dense fog prevented a landing at Paris, the plane was crash-landed in sea off Ver-su-Mer, Normandy, at 2 a.m., July 1, 1927.

ROUSING WELCOME greeted Lts. Lester J. Maitland (l.) and Albert F. Hegenberger, with Mayor Rolph of San Francisco, upon their return to the Bay area after historic flight from Oakland to Hawaii June 28, 1927 in an Army plane. They completed the 2,400-mile, over-water flight in 25 hrs., 49 min.

CREW MEMBERS of the *America* were (l. to r.) Bert Acosta, pilot who replaced Floyd Bennett, injured in a test-flight accident, Comdr. R. E. Byrd, George Noville, flight engineer; Bernt Balchen, relief pilot. They stayed aloft 42 hrs., flew 4,200 mi.

AMERICAN PILOT, William S. Brock and Edward Schlee, Detroit business man (r.), left Newfoundland August 28, 1927 in their Stinson monoplane *Pride of Detroit* to try for a world-girdling speed record. After 18 days they reached Tokyo, having covered 12,995 miles in 145½ hours flying time. Dissuaded from continuing the flight across the Pacific, the two fliers returned to New York City by steamer.

FIRST CIVILIANS to fly from the U. S. to Hawaii were Ernest L. Smith and Emory B. Bronte (r.). Fog obscured the ocean during the entire 2,340-mile flight. They reached Molokai July 15, 1927, 25½ hrs. after take-off, with barely enough fuel in tank.

LONG DISTANCE FLIGHTS from England to India, Africa and Australia during 1925-26 flown in a single-engine De Havilland won knighthood for Alan Cobham. In 1927 he made a 20,000-mile flight around Africa in twin-engine seaplane (below) with wife.

RACING THE MOON around the world, John Henry Mears and Capt. Charles B. D. Collyer (r.) used a Fairchild cabin monoplane and planned their schedule to coincide with fast ocean liners on which to cross the Atlantic and Pacific. Taking off from New York on June 29, 1928, they completed the 19,275 mile circuit in 23 days, 15 hrs., 21 mins.

INTERNATIONAL GOOD-WILL FLIGHT from New York to Bogota, Colombia, in November 1928 earned Lieutenant Benjamin Mendez (below) the distinction of being the first South American to receive the U.S. Distinguished Flying Cross. He made the 4,600-mile flight in 435-hp Curtiss Falcon Seaplane.

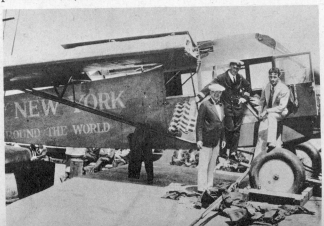

FIRST EAST-WEST CROSSING
Herman Koehl, James Fitzmaurice and the Baron Guenther von Huenefeld (l. to r.) left Baldonnel, Ireland for New York City on April 12, 1928, in a Junkers all-metal monoplane. Bad weather, shifting winds blew them north of their course and they crash-landed on Greenly Island, Labrador after 36½ hours. Floyd Bennett flew to their aid but caught pneumonia en route and died. Bernt Balchen flew them to N.Y. for heroes' welcome.

THE CREW OF THE "SOUTHERN CROSS" were (l. to r.) James W. Warner, American, radio operator; Capt. Charles Kingsford-Smith, Australian, commander and pilot; Capt. Charles T. P. Ulm, Australian, co-pilot; and Lt. Harry W. Lyon, Jr., American, navigator. They made the first flight across the Pacific Ocean from the United States to Australia in May, 1928, flying from Oakland via Hawaii and the Fiji Islands to Brisbane. The *Southern Cross* (above photo, autographed by Fokker) was built from two Fokker planes which Capt. Sir George H. Wilkins used during his first disastrous year in Alaska. In December of the previous year, Capt. Kingsford-Smith (wearing helmet, at right) used the huge monoplane (then named *Spirit of California*) in an attempt to beat the world's endurance record. With him is co-pilot, Lt. George R. Pond. After approximately 49 hours and with less than three hours to break record, they had to land due to lack of fuel.

FLYING FROM MAINE TO SPAIN, Roger Williams (l.) and Lewis Yancey (r.) broke the world's record for overwater flying July 10, 1929. Their Bellanca monoplane completed the 3,400 miles in 31½ hours. Only one month earlier, Armeno Lotti (2nd from l.) and Rene Lefevre (c.) made similar flight.

CHEERING CROWDS waving red banners broke through police cordons at Curtiss Field, L.I. to greet the four-man crew of the Russian-built seaplane *Land of the Soviets* on their arrival November 1, 1929. Departing Moscow August 23, the plane made the 12,500-mile trip via Siberia, Alaska and Seattle.

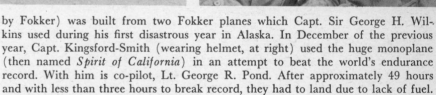

AIR-TO-AIR REFUELING was employed to keep the U. S. Army Fokker C-2 tri-motor monoplane *Question Mark* in the skies over Los Angeles for new endurance record set January 1-7, 1929. Headed by Maj. Carl Spaatz, commanding, and Capt. Ira C. Eaker, chief pilot (also on Army's first South American goodwill flight), the crew stayed aloft 150 hrs., 40 mins., before being forced down by engine trouble. They travelled approximately 11,000 miles at average speed of 70 mph. Flight required 5,205 gallons of gasoline, 202 gallons of oil. Refueling crew, shown at left with hose, were (l. to r.) "Red" Woods, "Scottie" Duthie, and Lts. Moon, Solter and Hopkins. The *Question Mark's* crew were (l. to r.) Sgt. Roy Hooe, Lt. Elwood Quesada, Lt. Harry Halverson, Capt. Eaker, Maj. Carl Spaatz.

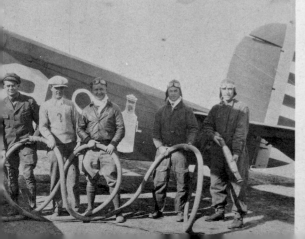

SEARCH FOR FRENCH ACE, Capt. Charles Nungesser, and Maj. Francois Coli followed their disappearance May 8, 1927, attempting to fly Atlantic nonstop. Seaplane *Jeanne d'Arc* (above) was flown in search by F. Sidney Cott, Cy Caldwell. In 1923, Nungesser wed American, Consuelo Hatmaker (l.).

CARRIER PIGEONS, shown here being taken on ▶ plane, were used to report location, size of fires by Aerial Forest Patrol, established in 1919 in the West.

HEADLINE MAKERS

Trans-ocean flights, cross-country records make famous heroes of courageous pilots

ATLANTIC FLIGHTS gained impetus by arrival in New York, April 27, 1927, of Capt. Rene Fonck, decorated French pilot. His crew and their wives christened specially-built Sikorsky plane. Nungesser was preparing his Levavasseur; Chamberlin his Bellanca; Lindbergh's quiet preparations made no headlines.

TRANSCONTINENTAL RACE began Oct. 8, 1919 when 64 planes left both coasts to cross country and return in Army contest to lay air routes. Maj. Carl Spaatz (third from l. with parents, sister to r.) was first to reach East. By him is Col. Miller, C.O. of Roosevelt Field. Spaatz did not complete return lap.

GLENN MARTIN (wearing helmet), shown in scene with Mary Pickford, got $700 a day for performance with his plane in *The Girl From Yesterday*, 1915 Famous Players movie. Martin had opened Los Angeles factory in 1912. In 1918, he built new factory in Cleveland, O., to produce Martin bombers.

POPULAR LEADING MAN of the twenties was Lt. Omer Locklear, one of the movies' first stunt fliers. He appears above with Francelia Billington in *The Great Air Robbery*, an early sky thriller. Locklear flew in first film made at DeMille Field, Los Angeles, was later killed there while stunting in a film.

GRANDLY EXPLOITED, spectacular aviation films had wide popularity. In addition to Omer Locklear, stunt fliers like Paul Mantz and Dick Grace were also in demand. Mantz flew planes in *Hell's Angels*, most famous air movie. In 1951, he filmed *Cinerama* footage from his specially modified B-25 plane.

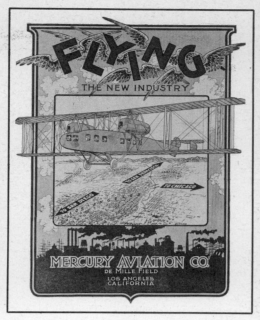

PIONEERING TWO INDUSTRIES, Cecil B. DeMille, while directing motion pictures for Famous Players-Lasky, Inc., went into aviation business in late 1918 with eight *Jennies* (Curtiss biplane trainers) and one Army DH-4 (far r., with De-Mille). Sites of DeMille's two fields were in present West Hollywood section of Los Angeles. In August, 1920, the first all-metal cabin plane seen on the West Coast—a Junkers monoplane (above, left)—was delivered to DeMille Field No. 2 from the John Larsen Junkers agency by Capt. Eddie Rickenbacker. Above photo was made prior to departure of four businessmen on luncheon trip to San Diego, Sept. 9, to illustrate ease of air travel. Pilot Thompson holds door for Harry Chandler, editor Los Angeles *Times*, in cabin with John B. Miller. Guy Cochran and J. H. Fisher stand next to DeMille. Cover of catalogue, center photo, indicated scheduled flights to San Diego and San Francisco, unscheduled trips East.

CLOUD SEEDING was successfully demonstrated late in 1924 by Captain A.I. Eagle (above), who sprinkled electrified sand from plane to eliminate fog and control rainfall. Early weather-making process was developed by Dr. E. Francis Warren.

EARLY SKIS built for an airplane turned up in a movie, *Unseeing Eyes*, filmed in Canadian Rockies in 1923 by Ed Griffiths, extreme left, talking with pilot Casey Jones. Skis are said to be those Cmdr. Richard E. Byrd duplicated for history-making flight from Spitzbergen to the North Pole, headline event of 1926. This film-making venture helped chart Canadian air-paths, typified parallel growth of motion pictures and aviation.

FLAPPER ERA saw fulfilled the prophecies made in Gibson days by James W. Montee, America's oldest licensed pilot. Wampus star Doris Posson holds arm of man who learned to fly in his sixties, was champion of legislation fostering vital air safety laws.

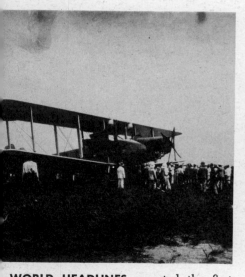

WORLD HEADLINES reported the first flight from Belgium to the Belgian Congo in 1925. Headed by Edmond Thieffry, the flight of over 8,000 km. began Feb. 12, was completed (above) April 3, when plane, a British Handley Page built in Belgium, finally arrived at Kinshasa. Passenger flights to the colony soon began.

AIR HEROES OF 1927 honored at White House by President Calvin Coolidge Nov. 14 are (left to right) Lt. Lester Maitland, first to fly non-stop to Hawaii with Lt. Albert Hegenberger; Clarence Chamberlin, who flew to Germany nonstop with Charles Levine; Art Goebel, Hawaii flier; Lindbergh; Ruth Elder, forced down in Atlantic attempt with George Haldeman; Hawaii fliers Paul Schluter and Emory Bronte; Hegenberger; Geo. Noville of Byrd's crew; Byrd; Haldeman; Levine; Bernt Balchen of Byrd's crew; W. S. Brock, E. F. Schlee, round-world fliers.

FLYING FISHERMEN Earle Ovington and J. W. Forse racked up 77 mph and a fair catch in test of Curtiss seaplane in 1919. Called *Seagull*, it was designed as pleasure craft. Aviation's first fisherman, Ovington was also first air postman, delivered mail in Long Island air meet Sept. 23-Oct. 2, 1911. Private plane use would come years later.

BOMAR OVER THE BATTERY was typical of air thrills provided by daredevils like Billy Bomar (above), in New York and elsewhere. Dick Johnstone's loops were air-meet staple of 20's.

WING WALKERS had heyday in twenties, were replaced by precision acrobatic flying in 30's. Al Williams headed international stunt team at 1930 National Air Races; "Tex" Rankin was notable precision flyer; Lindbergh was member of a Navy stunt team.

ROPE LADDER enabled relief pilot to reach plane in which Clyde Schleiper, Harley Long attempted, in 1938, to pass endurance record held by Key Brothers, New Orleans.

TOP TWA OFFICIALS in the 30's, Jack Frye and Paul Richter (r.) set altitude record in 1928 for multi-engined aircraft in Fokker F-10. Richter died in 1949. Frye later became head of General Aniline.

LT. JAMES H. DOOLITTLE was greeted by his baby daughter at fuel stop in Texas during 22 hr., 35 min. flight from Florida to San Diego, Sept. 5, 1922— first time the continent was spanned in under 24 hrs.

TRAGIC HEADLINES told of Eddie Stinson's death on Jan. 26, 1932. The "Dean" (for his 15,000 flying hours) crashed demonstrating Stinson *Detroiter*. He appears with aircraft designer B. F. Mahoney (l.).

HAIR-RAISING PROPOSAL by "Society for Promotion of Aviation" was offer of prize to youngsters under 18 flying cross-country in 1926. Though unrealistic, group gave good training.

SOARING was long neglected in U. S. Then in German-built Pruefling glider (above), Navy Lt. Ralph S. Barnaby made record U.S. soaring flight of 15 min., 6 sec., Aug. 18, 1929 at Cape Cod, winning first U.S. "C" Soaring Certificate. In soaring, pilot climbs; in gliding, he loses elevation.

INTERNATIONAL AIR CONGRESS delegates in Washington, D.C., 1928, included (l. to r.) Wm. P. McCracken, Ass't. Commerce Sec'y.; W. Glover, Ass't. Postmaster Gen.; Edw. Warner, Ass't Navy Sec'y.; Lindbergh; Wm. Whiting, Commerce Sec'y.; Ford; O. Wright; and H. Guggenheim.

TROPHY-LADEN BIPLANE, used to hunt coyotes in So. Dakota, illustrates unique use of airplane in the 20's. Most states passed laws as early as 1919 forbidding use of airplane in actual game hunting. "General uses" of airplane—rice-sowing, insect dusting, etc.—were widely publicized at first. All during the 20's headlines such as "planes seeking fleeing fugitives," occurred frequently.

DWARFS AND GIANTS of early aircraft sit side by side on Curtiss Field for "Aviation Day," held Oct. 16, 1921 by Aero Club of America to spur interest in flying. Remington-Burnelli "airliner" (r.), with maximum seating capacity of 25, towered above other machines, especially Mummert's "streamlined" 30 hp.-2 cyl.-engine biplane next to it. Thirty planes took part without any accident.

NATIONAL AIR RACES (Aug. 24-Sept. 2, 1929) saw first use of "race-horse starts," i. e., planes on a line (above), urged for three years by Cy Caldwell. Aircraft design showed development of single-purpose planes. Star was "huge" Boeing transport "whose three Hornet engines were above reach of tallest man."

STALIN'S FERVOR was bestowed on crew members of Moscow-U. S. flight over North Pole in June, 1937. The three pilots flew 5,288 miles non-stop, were in the air 63 hrs. and 17 min. until crash landing in a field in Oregon. Wild enthusiasm greeted return of aviation "stakanovites" (pace-setters); Molotov beams at right.

FLYING BICYCLE was bizarre brain-child of W. F. Gerhart, aeronautical engineer at McCook Field, Dayton, Ohio—better known for serious experimentation. Gerhart, however, built this apparatus in 1923, giving it six wings and mounting it on the frame of a bicycle. Propeller was driven by foot pedalling. In its first flight, it rose three inches from ground for a run of 20 feet. The inventor gave up.

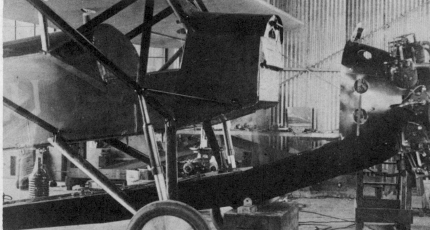

"BAIL YOUR fuel tank and engine if in trouble," was theory underlying Abreu "detachable" plane, seen above intact, below as it could be transformed in mid-air in emergency. Turned into a glider, plane floated to earth. It was successfully demonstrated, as were tests with detachable fuselage whipped to struts of Martin bomber. "Detachable" pilot (in parachute) remained best emergency remedy.

DIRIGIBLE ERA ENDS WITH DISASTROUS EXPLOSION OF ZEPPELIN "HINDENBURG" AT LAKEHURST, N.J., MAY 6, 1937

Commercial Aviation

Stable commercial air transport era dawns during the thirties amid build-up of warplanes and rehearsals for large-scale war

Russian-born Igor Sikorsky, who designed and flew the world's first four-engined plane in 1913, continued working with multi-engined aircraft during the 1930's, gaining fame with his trans-oceanic flying boats. He failed in a 1909 design for a helicopter, but in the 1940's won wider fame by developing the first successful helicopters in the U.S.

M Y activities in aeronautics started in 1908 in Tzarist Russia. During 1909 and 1910 I constructed two helicopters which were not successful, but later produced several types of airplanes. The most important of these was the first successful airplane with four engines which was constructed and test flown in 1913. This craft was followed by a series of large airplanes which were the first four-engined bombers ever used by any country.

Following the Russian Revolution, I came to America in 1919 and in 1923 organized my own aircraft company which, in 1929, after certain reorganizations, became a division of United Aircraft. Among the different types of aircraft produced by this organization there were sev-

IGOR SIKORSKY, FLYING BOAT AND HELICOPTER BUILDER

eral which enjoyed world-wide acceptance and use. In 1928, we produced the first successful twin-engine amphibian, the S-38, which was extensively used by Pan American Airways and several other airlines.

In 1934 came the first long-distance Flying Clipper, the S-42, which established 10 world records and the following year pioneered the

commercial air route across the Pacific and, later, across the Atlantic. In 1939 we manufactured the first successful helicopter, which I test piloted and established the official world record for endurance. Subsequently a number of aircraft were ordered by government services. In the concluding years of the Second World War, these aircraft were the first American helicopters to be used on the battlefront. The following years saw a gradual improvement of the helicopters and during the Korean War they were able to demonstrate their value in full.

Helicopters have been responsible for saving thousands of lives and have rendered many other valuable services to our military forces. Their future role will link them with the world's business and industry and other important phases of peacetime living.

President of Academy of Aeronautics, La Guardia Airport, New York, Charles Sherman "Casey" Jones, served in the U.S. Army Air Service in France during the First World War and in the 1920's entered many of the national air races successfully. He was a vice-president of Curtiss-Wright Corporation and a director of the Curtiss-Wright Flying Service during 1930's and holder of transport pilot's license No. 13. His keen interest in aviation started after his first flight in 1911 as a passenger.

T HE 1930's in the U.S. may be considered as a period of readjustment and consolidation for both the aircraft manufacturers and the airline operators throughout the country.

The airlines which began carrying the mail in the late Twenties were virtually forced into passenger-carrying service when the Post Office Department readjusted payments. The result was the development of much more efficient airplanes—notably the DC-3.

Shortly after the election of President Roosevelt, all mail contracts were cancelled on the ac-

C.S. (CASEY) JONES, AT LEFT, AND FRIEND

cusation by the Postmaster General that there was collusion among the lines. The Army Air Force was ordered to carry the mail, resulting in a sorry performance and death of a number of military pilots, principally because the Army aircraft were not fitted with adequate instru-

ments or navigating equipment. The ultimate outcome was a complete reorganization of the airlines, and from that time on progress and expansion characterized airline operations.

During the early Thirties the manufacturing industry was at a low level of operation with military orders almost non-existent. Around 1935, when it became apparent that trouble was ahead, orders started to come in from foreign governments. Shortly thereafter war broke out in Europe, and within the short span of three years the President was to ask for—and get produced—a total of 50,000 airplanes a year. Thus was the beginning of an almost inconceivable increase in the aircraft industry which finally culminated during World War II in the largest business the world has even seen.

EXPANSIVE ERA in aviation that came with the "Lindbergh Boom" was typified by the Fokker F-32 transport, garlanded for its christening, above. With this super-liner Western Air Express hoped to woo passengers in large numbers, duplicating the success of its early contract air mail routes. Its twin-engine mounts, each with two motors back to back, presaged the four-motor transports of the forties, while its interior (l.) reflected tastes of the day (tapestried panels, curtains, "indirect" lighting). Internal wing construction was of wood.

AIRLINES BECOME BIG BUSINESS
Mergers add strength until halted by New Deal

Following Lindbergh's trans-Atlantic hop, aviation stocks outsold all others in a ballooning market. A tangle of disconnected lines far exceeded the demand for air travel. Only cohesive routes would attract steady passenger revenue.

Thus, Boeing Air Transport, with its San Francisco-Chicago line, found a logical partner in National Air Transport, operating the Chicago-New York segment of this "Main Line" route. By June 30, 1930, Varney Air Lines and Pacific Air Transport, too, were under the Boeing wing, all under the name United Air Lines.

The other big merger of 1930 had a more complicated origin. Its earliest roots were in Colonial (CAM-1) and Robertson (CAM-2); its more immediate parent was an unwieldy holding company called Aviation Corporation. Formed as a subsidiary of Fairchild Aircraft, it, in turn, soon boasted many subsidiaries among widely scattered airlines. The most important of these merged Jan. 25, 1930 into American Airways.

Another operator of early contract routes, Western Air Express, merged with Transcontinental Air Transport (TAT), which had been formed in 1929 primarily as a passenger carrier. The result was Transcontinental & Western Air (TWA), organized February 13, 1931.

Favoring these mergers was Postmaster General of the Hoover Administration, Walter Folger Brown. Passage of the McNary-Watres Bill in April, 1930, gave him almost unlimited control of airline operation. He was empowered to juggle existing routes and add many new ones, often forcing the companies to accept them.

Even so, the first act of the new administration in 1933 was to investigate these so-called "Spoils Conferences," with the result that all air mail contracts were cancelled Feb. 9, 1934.

Within ten days the Army was flying the unfamiliar routes. Resultant death toll forced the government to re-open bids April 20, but on terms of complete reorganization of the airlines.

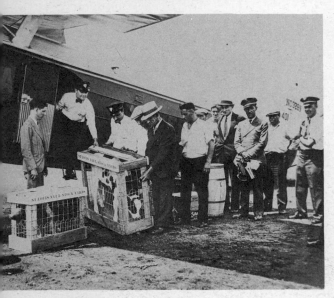

LIVESTOCK, pioneering for the newly-formed TWA, was photographed on arrival in Newark from St. Louis stock yards August 6, 1931, the beginning of scheduled airline freight service in the U.S. In 1929, the first cross-country air passenger service had been opened by TWA's immediate parent, TAT. (p. 107).

PRIMITIVE AND MODERN methods forged Canadian airpaths. Canoes share bank with Fokker and Fairchild seaplanes in 1931 scene on Great Bear Lake, Hunter Bay. Colonial Airlines, in 1928, was first airline to contract for flying mail from U. S. to Canada.

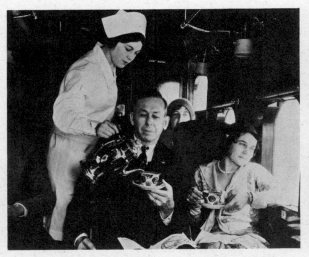

PILOTS GRUMBLED AT FIRST at prospect of having to look after distaff crew members in new Boeing 80-A's. But officials of Boeing Air Transport planned to try proposal of young Iowa-born Ellen Church that trained nurses be employed as flight attendants. On May 15, 1930, the world's first airline hostess (r. above) appeared on San Francisco-Chicago route. Miss Church (third from l.) designed first uniforms. Sometimes regular nurses uniforms (l.) bespoke training that quickly won the gratitude of public and pilots alike.

SKYPATH TO THE ORIENT received vital link when Pan American's *China Clipper* flew past uncompleted Golden Gate Bridge to deliver the first trans-Pacific air mail to Hawaii and Manila. Alternate plan to reach Orient by Alaska Great Circle route led Pan American to form Pacific Alaska Airways in 1932, with a base at Fairbanks (bottom, left). But the route from San Francisco to Hong Kong was surveyed in 1933; bases on Guam, Wake and Midway were built in 1935; and on November 22, 1935, Postmaster General James A. Farley (above, r.) turned over the first trans-Pacific air mail to Capt. Edwin C. Musick, atop the ladder, who flew it to Hawaii and Manila. The first passengers were flown to Hawaii, Oct. 21, 1936. Hong Kong Clipper flew mail to China in 1937.

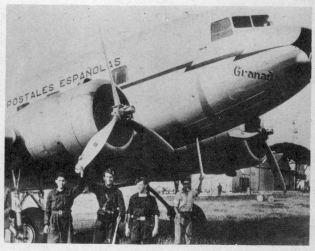

PATH OF BEACONS to Seattle was followed by Northwest Airways, expanding into leading airline. In 1933, Amelia Earhart helped survey difficult route from Chicago.

NEW YORK'S GOV. ROOSEVELT predicted "rather gradual growth year by year" for aviation while making industry's first political flight, with his family, on American Airways, to accept Democratic nomination.

CIVIL WAR IN SPAIN halted commercial aviation there. Above, a Douglas DC-2 is guarded by government soldiers and civilian volunteers at Barcelona air field. It was originally delivered to Spain for use as a transport.

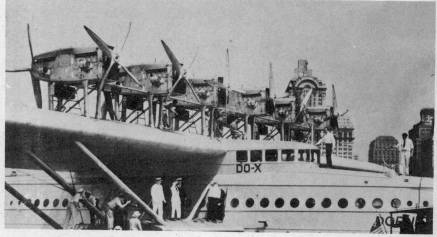

TWO GREAT AIR PATHS linking France to her colonies were flown by *Air France* after its emergence in 1933. One led to Africa and Brazil. The other, to Indo-China, was route of the *Emeraude*, pictured during early trials in which she chopped England's Channel record in half. Pilot Launay (third from r.) flew her to Saigon, January, 1934. On return, plane crashed, killing all aboard.

MAMMOTH "BARNSTORMER" DO-X was built in Switzerland by Dornier under auspices of Germany's Luft Hansa airline. On 1930-31 "demonstration tour," it lumbered over four continents, finally reaching New York (above) after 9 months. Mounting pylons for its 12 engines atop the wing contributed to drag that kept it within 50 ft. of water for eight hrs. after New York take-off.

GREATER GROWTH of the three transcontinental airlines followed re-bidding on air mail contracts in 1934. Split up of airlines and aircraft companies meant best facilities were available to all. United, which had introduced Boeing 247 (lower, r.) in 1933, flew Douglas DC's, as well, on its "main line" route, pio-neered during the Twenties. Rambling southern transcontinental route of American Airways emerged as the cohesive pattern of American Airlines, also flying DC's (l.) in 30's. Central route, operated by TWA, was widely known as the "Lindbergh Line" (top r.), recalling his 1929 survey of the cross-country route.

MODERN AIRLINES EMERGE

1934 re-bidding brings new lines, new routes

Airlines both suffered and gained from the re-organization and re-bidding on routes demanded by the Black-McKellar Bill of June, 1934.

Capital Airlines, known then as Pennsylvania Airlines, gained the Detroit-Milwaukee route in the 1934 re-bidding but lost its Washington-Detroit route to Central Airlines. Afterwards, the two merged to form Pennsylvania-Central Airlines, later known as Capital.

Chicago & Southern Air Lines, Inc., born in 1933, received the Chicago-New Orleans route in 1934 and operated between Detroit and Chicago, Houston and New Orleans in the Thirties.

Continental Air Lines, Inc. succeeded Western Air Express and Wyoming Air Express in operation of routes linking El Paso and Denver. Called Varney Speed Lines at the time of the re-bidding, it took the Continental name in 1937.

Delta Air Lines, Inc., which had been absorbed by American in 1930, reorganized in 1934 with a Charleston-Dallas mail contract. Later expansion of Delta Airlines included Cincinnati and two Chicago-Miami routes.

Mid-Continent Airlines, Inc. was the name adopted in 1938 by Hanford Tri-State Airlines. It won Winnipeg-Chicago-Kansas City route in 1934, later added routes to St. Louis and Tulsa.

National Airlines, Inc. began operating in Florida in 1934, won a New Orleans route in 1938, and later flew Miami to New York. Northeast Airlines, Inc. began operation on hazardous New England routes on its own in 1937.

Northwest Airlines, Inc. expanded steadily. In 1945 New York was added; Honolulu came in 1948; and in 1950, Formosa and Hong Kong.

Western Air Lines (name adopted by Western Air Express in 1941) formed a strong bond with United in 1934. "Oldest U.S. Airline," Western faced an uphill struggle to regain her former prominence, and did so under the United wing.

EASTERN AIR LINES became one of America's most successful airlines when Capt. "Eddie" Rickenbacker (4th from l.), formerly v.p. of North American Aviation, took reins. Left is James H. Kindelberger, of North American; Mrs. Rickenbacker wears corsage; on steps is Mrs. Woodrow Wilson, President's widow.

"GREAT LAKES TO THE GULF" became route of Tom and Paul Braniff's airline when service was extended to Corpus Christi in 1935. Rebidding on air mail contracts in 1934 gained Chicago-Dallas route. Deriving chief revenue from mail, line strove successfully to attract passengers, as above 1939 photo testifies.

HIGH WINDS AT SOUTHAMPTON force passengers of English flying boat *Capella* to go ashore by launch. High tariffs on foreign landing rights, rising Pan American competition, Air Ministry restrictions, and increased air mail requirements forced dissolution of Britain's Imperial Airways in favor of government-operated British Overseas Airways Corp. (BOAC) on eve of World War II.

SOUTHERN SKYPATHS of the Pacific were charted by Pan American in 1937. Capt. Edwin Musick arrived at Auckland Bay, New Zealand, on March 29, 1937, in Sikorsky flying boat, above. Musick lost his life flying the second scheduled flight to Auckland, December, 1937. This New Zealand route later proved vital when war's outbreak choked routes to Orient. It formed vital link with Australia.

BUSHWACKING "TACA," short-haul airline in Central America, began in 1932 with flights by New Zealand-born Lowell Yerrex in a four-place *Stinson, Jr.* In 1934, Yerrex received an air mail contract from the President of Honduras for his help in Honduran revolution. Above, single-engine Bellanca is loaded from cart. Trans Aereos Centrale Americanos extended routes to So. America.

AIRLINE WAS BORN when C. D. Howe, then Canadian Minister of Transport, tendered official send-off to first Trans-Canada Air Lines Lockheed 10 to survey the transcontinental route on July 7, 1937. The first commercial service undertaken by TCA, off-shoot of Canadian National Railways, was between Vancouver and Seattle, 122 miles. Canadian Pacific opened Canadian Pacific Air Lines.

COLD WEATHER PROBLEMS, ably solved by Finnish Airlines (Aero O/Y), provided invaluable experience for turning back Russian invasion of 1939-40. Prior to this struggle, Finnish Airlines, in common with other European airlines, flew *all* first class mail. Called "all up" policy in Britain, it was straw that broke the back of England's Imperial Airways.

BACKBONE OF KLM, Royal Dutch Airlines, was line from Amsterdam to Batavia in Dutch East Indies, opened in 1934, and flown by Douglas DC's after delivery of first DC-2 above. Donald Douglas (third from right) made delivery to KLM officials. Only one of the DC-3s survived German bombing of Schipol airport in May, 1940. It escaped to London.

MAIL BY AUTOGIRO was first carried regularly by the Eastern Air Lines in 1939, when this KD-1B received load at Camden, N. J. airport, flew to top of 30st St. Post Office in Philadelphia. Richard C. du Pont formed All American Aviation, 1939, to fly mail over Pennsylvania-N.J. circuit. Lacking even roofs to land on, planes had hooks to pick up cargo.

DOUGLAS DC-4, first successful four-engine transport, was delivered to United Air Lines in 1939, above. Left of Scottish piper is William E. Douglas, father of manufacturer Donald Douglas (extreme r.)

◀ **GLENN MARTIN,** in 1933, built the *China Clipper* (model on desk). His B-10's met government needs for high-altitude bomber in 1934 and improved B-12's served British in N. Africa to 1940.

GLENN CURTISS flew his new 20-passenger Condor from Albany to New York City in 1930, duplicating history-making flight he had made over the same route 20 years earlier. He died July 23, 1930. ▶

BUILDERS OF THE THIRTIES

Expansion in transport, threat of war bring new speeds, comfort, designs

The progress and goals of the world's leading nations in the thirties were reflected in the character of their aircraft manufacture.

Rebirth of Germany's Luftwaffe came in 1933 with the appointment of Hermann Goering as the Reich's "Minister of Air Transportation." Transports were designed with an eye toward their eventual military use. Junkers Ju-52/3m's, for example, were to become the backbone of Germany's "lightning" paratroop warfare and cargo supplier for Rommel's troops. Slight modification of the Heinkel He-111 was to make it the dread He-111K of the Luftwaffe's bomber arm. Messerschmitt's Bf-108 of 1935, was the direct ancestor of the Me-109.

France was tragically weak in the mass production of modern aircraft. Nationalization (state control) of her aircraft industry in 1937-38 resulted in a large force of obsolescent types. A change in government brought a resurgence of civil aviation in 1938—but too late.

Italy's geography dictated production of large flying boats and seaplanes. In 1931, she demonstrated her progress to the world by the flight of 12 Savoia-Marchetti S-55 flying boats from Rome to Rio, and flight to U.S. in 1933. By 1936, the tri-motored bomber was king in

Italy, though a critical shortage of materials forced composite construction (wood, metal, fabric), which placed her behind other nations in the development of all-metal aircraft.

Russia, in contrast, had many all-metal monoplanes in use during the 30's, and production of new types was progressing rapidly. The first Russian aviation "Five Year Plan" was instituted for the years 1928-32. At the end of this period, some 1,500 planes were in use. A goal of 8,000 war planes and 20,000 engines was set for the second "Five Year Plan," 1933-1937.

Japan successfully shrouded its developments from foreign observers. This and the uninformed argument that Japanese planes were merely second-rate copies of American types, succeeded in convincing Americans erroneously that Japan was not to be strongly counted among the aviation powers.

In England, many new military types began appearing in 1936, such as the *Hurricane* and *Spitfire* fighters, and the *Blenheim* bomber. To accelerate production of new designs, England developed its "shadow" scheme in 1936. Under this plan, auto manufacturers built "stand-by" aircraft factories at government expense. A modernized air force grew out of this foresight.

In U.S., growing popularity of air travel brought construction of commercial aircraft. In 1933, Boeing produced the Model 247, first U.S.-built modern transport of all-metal construction. Its prominence was overshadowed in 1934 by the appearance of the first transport in the Douglas DC series which was soon to gain world-wide airline acceptance.

North American Aviation, formed in 1934 from an aviation holding company, entered the production picture. Observation and experimental bombers followed its successful BT-9 of 1936. The NA-73, designed in 1939 for the RAF, was to become the U.S. Army's P-51.

Boeing's concentration on four-engine bombers produced, in 1939, the Model 307, or *Stratoliner*, first pressurized, four-engine transport.

As war came to Europe, Lend-Lease contracts began changing the production picture in U.S. The Curtiss "Mohawk," built for France, fought the Messerschmitt; a later design, the P-40, gained famed with the Flying Tigers in China. Boeing built improved models of its *Flying Fortress*. Martin's *Maryland* bomber served the British in the Middle East. These and other planes were to form the sinews of U.S. air might, in the global struggle ahead.

ANTHONY FOKKER, seen below in craft he built and flew in 1911 to get his license, saw his planes eclipsed by all-metal transports after 1931 CAA ruling required periodic inspection of internal wooden wing construction. Fokker died in 1939.

YOUTH PREVAILED at Lockheed after reorganization in 1932, following its purchase by the Gross Brothers. Pictured here are: Ronald P. King, assistant treasurer; Carl Squier, vice-president, sales; Lloyd Stearman, president; Robert Gross, chairman of the board and treasurer; Cyril Chappellet, secretary; Hall Hibbard, vice-president and chief engineer. First transport designed and built by Lockheed under its new leadership was the *Electra*, which appeared in 1934, distinguished by its high speed and all-metal external construction. The Electra was developed into the Model 14 (1936) and the Model 18, the *Lodestar* (1938). In 1939, the first model of the P-38 was turned out, and the first *Hudson* bomber was delivered to the British.

CLAUDE RYAN, (left) and O. J. Whitney stand beside the first Ryan S-T trainer. This was prototype of later Army Air Corps PT-20 and PT-22 and of Navy's NR-1, all used well into World War II. In 1939, he built YO-51 observer plane.

BARBER SHOP BACK ROOM operation of Douglas had expanded into this sprawling Santa Monica plant by 1938. Installation of 5,000-ton hydropress (right), which could stamp out 100,000 parts a day, bespeaks the development in production techniques. Domination of transport market with DC-3 gave Douglas firmest non-military backing of all planemakers. Navy torpedo bombers and dive bombers, plus B-18, gave Douglas prominent military position.

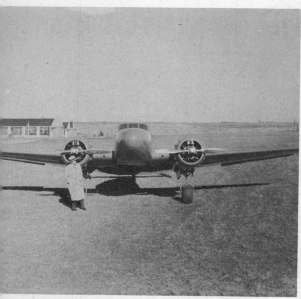

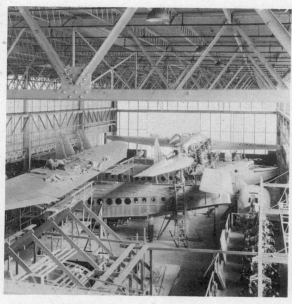

BEECH AIRCRAFT made history in 1932 with Model 17 biplane, combining comfort with high speed and performance. Later Model 18 (above with Walter Beech) was used as the basic training plane for 90 per cent of navigators and bombadiers in W.W. II.

VOUGHT-SIKORSKY, formed in 1939 by consolidation of former Chance-Vought and Sikorsky divisions of United Aircraft, was chiefly engaged in construction of multi-engined amphibians and flying boats, such as four-engined S-42 in 1933 and S-43, 1935.

LAST BOEING TRANSPORT before production of revolutionary *Stratoliners* in 1939 was Model 247, above, which appeared in 1933 while Douglas was developing the DC line. Comparison with the stick-and-wire craft shows aviation's impressive strides.

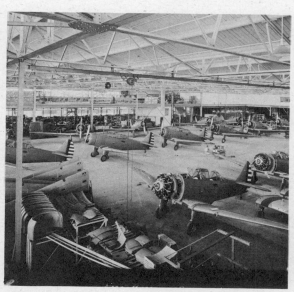

CONSOLIDATED AIRCRAFT Corp. moved from Buffalo in 1935, built plant at Lindbergh Field on land filled from California's San Diego Bay (in background); obtained largest U.S. order since 1918 for 60 flying boats, forerunners of PBY-1 *Catalinas*.

NORTH AMERICAN AVIATION started manufacturing operations at a new factory in Los Angeles in 1936, began production of the BT-9A trainer for the U.S. Army Air corps, later developed the model into famous AT-6 used by all allied nations in W.W. II.

JOHN NORTHROP formed a new company, Northrop Aircraft, Inc., in 1939 to work on military contract for development of XP-61, famed "Black Widow" twin-engine night fighter; built N-3 PB, twin-float attack bomber for Norwegian Air Force.

VERSAILLES TREATY provisions forbade air armament in Germany after World War I. But in the mid-30's, France became alarmed at the impressive fleet of "civilian" planes which had been produced since Hitler's rise to power. It was noted these aircraft had more than an accidental similarity to bombers, and that German technical achievement had not been impaired by military defeat. It was widely rumored that planes like those above could be converted to military use within 12 hours. Left, Dr. Claude Dornier, one of the leading figures in German plane production, edifies the young by absorbed whittling on a chestnut.

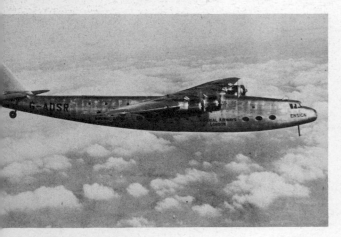

CIVILIAN PRIDE of Imperial Airways in 1938, the *Ensign* became a vital instrument of the British Transport Command under the pressure of early war days. Plane saved hundreds of men at Dunkirk.

KING'S CUP was won in 1933 by Captain Geoffrey De Havilland in his DH *Leopard Moth*. With De Havilland (c.) are Captain Hubert Broad (l.), 1926 winner, and Alan Butler, former chairman of firm.

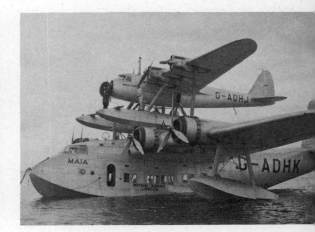

PICKABACK experiments were made extensively by Imperial Airways of Britain. Photo shows composite craft, *Maia* and *Mercury*, in Ireland. Idea never proved to be commercially feasible for airlines.

TWA SET transcontinental record in 1935 with flight of 11 hrs., 5 min. from Los Angeles to New York City. Record was made in Douglas DC-1, forerunner of the respected DC commercial transport series.

LOCKHEED "ORION," fastest transport of its day, was built in 1931. Popular among speed pilots, plane set many marks. With it, Swissair set 8½-hour record from Zurich over Mediterranean to Tunis and back.

FAIRCHILD BUILT this Model 82 in its Canadian plant. Plane's high payload, ease of maintenance and low-cost operation made it a quick favorite with "bush" operators, who still used plane years later.

FLYING WING TYPE of plane was one of first produced by newly-formed Northrop Aircraft in 1930. It was test-flown by Eddie Bellande (r.), standing next to Jack Northrop, creator of advanced designs.

LAUNCHED IN 1939, this Boeing 314 was the largest flying boat ever put in service by Pan-American Airways. It served in both oceans during war, was replaced in 1945 by Douglas and Boeing landplanes.

LOCKHEED ESTABLISHED itself as builder of high-speed transports with Model 14. Howard Hughes flew this forerunner of famous Lockheed Hudson around the world in 1938 in 3 days, 19 hrs., 14 min.

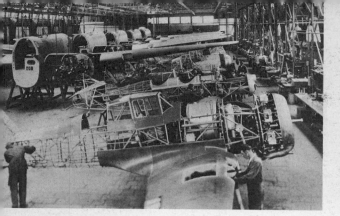

DUTCH PRODUCTION of aircraft, while of top quality, could not halt the Nazi push. This Fokker plant served as a Luftwaffe repair depot after surrender. Shown are lines of T-5 bombers, D-21 fighters and an S-9 trainer.

BOMBER air crews of the French L'Armee de L'Air learn the perplexities of the specialized equipment for releasing bombs on enemy forces.

EARLY BORDELAIS B-20 bomber, despite its ungainly appearance, was ahead of its biplane contemporaries. France lost its aviation lead and could offer only minor resistance when the Germans launched their crushing air-ground attack.

FRENCH, ITALIAN AND DUTCH PLANES

The French Armee de L'Air resistance against the World War II German march on Paris was ineffective. Yet, the French aircraft industry, with residual forces of the first World War, had continued development of military aircraft through the 1920's and 30's. A single explanation for the failure of the French defenses cannot be given. A world-wide lethargy to the German political expansion coupled with a 1936 socialization of the French military aircraft industry played a major share in the downfall.

When the persistent territorial encroachment of the Reich finally aroused the world, the curtain had already begun to descend for France. An attempt was made to re-equip her air force with top-line airplanes by ordering American built warplanes; however, too few of these were delivered before the German push.

Many of the French patriots escaped after the fall of their homes and, adopting the red "Cross of Lorraine" as an insignia, fought shoulder to shoulder with the RAF against the Germans.

Better craftsmen than warriors appeared to be the character of the Italians of World War II. Entering the hostilities when the Allied Powers were reeling under the German onslaught, Italy expected a quick victory. However, the Allied air forces refused to concede battle to the Fascists, and the Regia Aeronautica was mauled by the more aggressive Allied air crews.

Prior to the outbreak of war, Mussolini had instigated an ambitious program of news-making record flights. While these records encouraged technical progress, they only clouded the effect of the combat worth of the Italian air arm. Basing their strategy on obsolete concepts, the Italian General Staff dictated the design requirements to the industry. They, in turn, produced planes that could not adequately compete with the rigorous tactics of the Allied pilots. The morale of the Italians dropped with each crushing defeat until, resisting the Nazi order to prolong the hostilities, they complied with the Allied unconditional surrender demand on Sept. 8, 1943.

CRUSHED by the blitzkrieg of Hitler's invasion, the Belgian government quickly surrendered to the attackers. SABENA, the Belgian airline, moved its headquarters to the Belgian Congo and continued to operate. One of Europe's most efficient airlines, SABENA used fast, three-engine transports to fly on its routes between Europe and Africa. Pictured is an Italian-built Savoia-Marchetti SM-73 transport, shown with airline, government dignitaries.

FIRST LINE FIGHTER of the French at the outset of battle was the cannon-firing Morane-Saulnier MS-406C.

FREE FRENCH airmen and these Potez 63 bombers joined the RAF to assist in the smashing of Rommel.

ADVANCED design was the Dutch Fokker G-I fighter-bomber. Appearing in 1936, the *Reaper* popularized the twin boom configuration. Anthony Fokker, famous for his warplanes used by the German air services of World War I, produced many worthy designs at his Amsterdam plant. The other major Dutch aircraft plant, Koolhoven, joined with Fokker to equip their country's air services with capable warcraft. Too few were produced to be effective.

LENDLEASE Curtiss Hawk 75A's reinforced French Dewoitine D-520's and Morane-Saulnier 406C fighters.

FRENCH BOMBERS, Amoit 143M's, awkward appearing, typified antiquity of most prewar French combat craft.

BOASTFUL MUSSOLINI proclaimed that his *Regia Aeronautica* was invincible. However, the lack of raw materials and mass production techniques impeded the Italian aviation industry and Il Duce's vaunt could not be sustained. Above is shown the opening of an airport near Turin where more than two hundred Fiat CR-32 fighters were lined up for inspection. Italy's poor showing caused Nazis to take over Italy's air force.

THREE-ENGINE aircraft, disclaimed by most countries, were used in great numbers by Italy. Shown is Fiat G-12.

WORLD'S FASTEST seaplane was this Italian Macchi MC-72, but Fascists could not produce top combat planes.

MANY ITALIAN FIGHTERS were mated with German engines to obtain higher speed. One was this Fiat G-55.

FASCIST BOMBER, showing Italian development of twin-engine design, was the Fiat B.R. 20, built during '40.

F.D.R. CONGRATULATED 1933 Collier Trophy winner, Frank W. Caldwell, for his part in developing controllable pitch propellers. This "greatest achievement in aviation in America," as it was termed by the award committee, was produced by the Hamilton-Standard Propeller Co. under Caldwell's direction. A "full-feathering" propeller developed by Curtiss-Wright Corp. operated electrically.

VERTICAL FLIGHT was tried among other experiments in the earliest days of powered aircraft. Helicopters like the Berliner and DeBothezat machines of 1922 managed to rise a few feet, but none of them were fully controllable. First of the practical helicopters was Germany's Focke-Achgelis Fa-61 of 1937. Igor Sikorsky produced first commercially-useful helicopter, VS-300 (above), 1940.

AIR SCIENCE COMES OF AGE
Engineering research and inventions bring solution to many flight problems

While aircraft production fell sharply from the heights attained following Lindbergh's flight, the depression-born competition was instrumental in changing aviation from its former loosely experimental character into a practical science. Many inventions which appeared during the early scramble for publicity or financial gain reappeared in the thirties and were developed for commercial and military use.

For example, the tricycle landing gear, first used by Glenn H. Curtiss on the *White Wing* of 1908 began to appear on American production models in 1937. But not until the advent of World War II did this landing gear gain general acceptance in foreign countries.

It is not widely known that Dr. A. A. Griffith of England's Royal Aeronautical Establishment was conducting serious experiments with gas turbine compressors for aircraft as early as 1927.

However, it remained for Prof. Ernst Heinkel of Germany to develop the first practical gas turbine engine. The HeS-3B produced 1,100 pounds of thrust and first flew in the Heinkel He-178 jet monoplane on August 24, 1939.

The importance of research organizations such as America's National Advisory Committee for Aeronautics and Great Britain's R.A.E. in developing inventions into useful mechanisms was paramount. These organizations possessed elaborate facilities for conducting exhaustive tests to prove the reliability of an invention.

Aviation progress was inseparably tied to power-plant developments, including engines, propellers, cowlings, fuels and metallurgy. Rapid advances attained in airplane performance during the 1930-40 era definitely reflected the importance of research and progress in power-plant engineering. The N.A.C.A. developed low-drag

cowling for air-cooled radial engines in the early months of the decade. Prestone high temperature cooling systems, developed in the United States, soon replaced bulky water-cooling systems in aircraft throughout the world. In 1932, Pratt & Whitney Aircraft and Wright Aeronautical, working in conjunction with the Navy Bureau of Aeronautics, developed twin-row air-cooled radial engines which were to set an unsurpassed record for reliability. Frank W. Caldwell and the Hamilton-Standard Propeller Co. produced the first successful, controllable-pitch propeller in 1932, and demonstrated the first constant-speed propeller in 1934 as one of the most significant developments in aviation history. The rapid advances made during this creative period were indicative of subsequent progress. The 1930-40 decade, ushered in with the stressed-skin monoplane, departed with the futuristic jet.

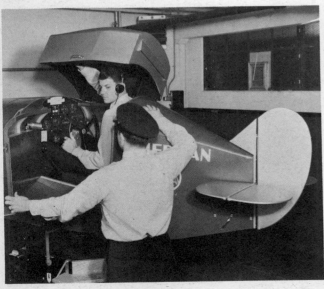

MAN UNDER THE HOOD could make a successful instrument flight without leaving the ground in Link trainer. Night flights, once the airman's nightmare, became routine when instruments like Sperry's gyro-horizon were adopted. New blind-flight aids included two-way radio, airway lights, radio compass, gyroscopic instruments, radio beams.

FLYING WING plane designed by Dr. Alexander Lippisch in Germany was grandfather of World War II tailless, rocket-powered Messerschmitt Me-163B. The Westland "Pterodactyl" was later designed, built in Great Britain.

MAN FROM MARS suit worn by Wiley Post was pressurized for stratosphere flights. His famous supercharged Lockheed Vega, *Winnie Mae*, was used in pioneering high altitude research flights in 1934. The Collier Trophy was awarded to the Air Corps in 1937 for developing the Lockheed XC-35, first successful pressure-cabin airplane.

MODERN DESIGN was exemplified by the smooth lines of the Northrop *Alpha* transport. Designed by ingenious John K. Northrop about 1930, its performance surpassed that of most fighter aircraft of the period. The *Alpha* was first used by National Air Transport to replace obsolete biplanes. U. S. pioneered modern commercial aircraft.

BENDIX TROPHY WINNER Laird *Super Solution* was typical 1931 racing plane. Laird engineers combined an N.A.C.A. cowl, the Hamilton-Standard adjustable propeller, and clean-design *Wasp* engines enabling Jimmy Doolittle (above) to establish new Bendix race record.

IRON MIKE, the Sperry automatic pilot, shown here in the control cabin of the Martin 130 *China Clipper* of 1934, allowed pilots to rest on long flights. This device enabled Wiley Post to undertake his solo flight around the world in 1933. Martin *Clippers*, when constructed, were the largest all-metal flying boats ever built in the U. S. Twin-row radial, air-cooled engines were installed for the first time on a commercial flying boat. Low-drag N.A.C.A. cowlings contributed to flying ship's high performance.

A NEW GENERATION of aluminum-skinned monoplanes replaced the fabric-covered biplanes of the 20's. The Boeing Aircraft factory, shown producing 247-D transports in 1934, pioneered in this field, built B-17 *Flying Fortress* in '35.

RED AIR FLEET demonstrated giant ANT-20 eight-engine monoplane, built ▶ under second "Five Year Plan," and flown in 1934. Named *Maksim Gor'kii*, this 58-ton plane had 206-foot wing spread. Shown (right) over Red Square in 1935, it was wrecked minutes later in mid-air collision. *Gor'kii* carried crew of eight.

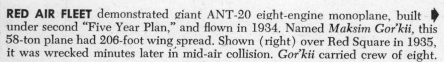

◀ **AUTOMATIC LANDING** was achieved by coupling Sperry Gyropilot to Instrument Landing System radio beams. This Air Corps General C-14B made many such landings in 1937. ILS was developed by U. S. Bureau of Standards for directing plane landings during darkness.

WINGLESS AUTOGIRO, ▶ developed in Britain by Juan de la Cierva in 1933, was followed by direct take-off 'giro in 1934. Kellett KD-1 is shown with earlier type having conventional system of directional control. U. S. Army purchased seven Kellett machines in 1938 for experimental use.

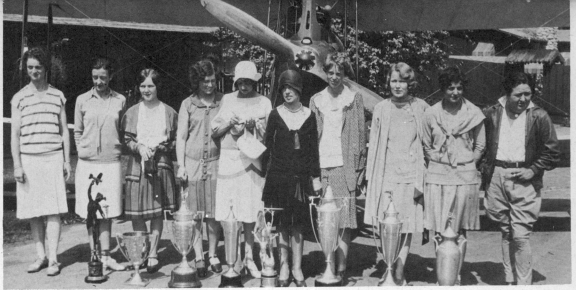

FAMOUS WOMEN FLIERS assembled at Santa Monica, Calif., preparing to fly First National Women's Air Derby to Cleveland in Aug. 27 event of 1929 National Air Races. From left they are, Louise Thaden (first), Bobbie Trout (forced down), Patty Willis, Marvel Crosson (killed), Blanche Noyes (seventh), Vera Walker, Amelia Earhart (third), Marjorie Crawford, Ruth Elder (fourth), and Florence Barnes. Amelia Earhart (left photo) flew Atlantic as first woman passenger June 17, 1928, and was first woman to solo Atlantic May 20, 1932. She and navigator Fred Noonan were lost in Pacific during 1937 flight.

WOMEN IN AVIATION

Air heroines spur popular acceptance of flying

The roaring twenties brought many changes to the women's world. Women smoked, voted, wore one-piece bathing suits, and took to the air in ever-increasing numbers. Before World War I only a handful of women had piloted aircraft, but the tremendous impact of aviation during the 1914-19 period had made this new sport attractive to women the world over. In 1918, at the age of 20, Katherine Stinson established a new non-stop record, flying 610 miles from San Diego to San Francisco in the fantastic time of 9 hrs., 10 mins. During World War I she and her sister Marjorie trained Army pilots.

The first postwar woman's pilot license went to Laura Brownell (1919), and the race for international honors was underway. In 1920 Louise Favier (France) established a woman's international altitude record of 21,325 feet. The year 1925 saw Ruth Gillette as the first woman entry in the National Air Races at Mitchell Field, N.Y

In 1926 Viola Gentry startled New York City by flying under Brooklyn and Manhattan Bridges.

Lady Mary Heath, flying as co-pilot for Royal Dutch Airlines, between London and Amsterdam, became the first woman pilot in passenger service, July 28, 1929. On June 29, 1929, at Los Angeles, Phoebe Omlie set an unofficial altitude record of 24,000 feet, and during October, 1934, Dr. and Mrs. Jean Piccard ascended to a height of 57,979 feet in a huge stratosphere balloon at Dearborn, Michigan.

From 1930 to 1940 flying became a pastime for more and more women. Instead of one or two names appearing in the headlines, a veritable avalanche of women flashed before the public. Winifred Spooner, Laura Ingalls, Beryl Markham, Jean Batten, Frances Marsalis, Anne Lindbergh, Maryse Bastie, May Haizlip — all made their various contributions to history and established records for women in aviation.

BRITISH AVIATRIX Amy Johnson established record flights from England to Australia, Japan, and Cape Town, South Africa, during 1930-36. With her husband, Capt. Mollison, she was first woman to make nonstop east-west Atlantic crossing July 28, 1933.

MRS. LOUISE THADEN was first woman to win New York-Los Angeles Bendix race (1936). With Frances Marsalis, she established an endurance record of 198 hours in 1932. In 1936 she received Harmon Trophy for being the most outstanding woman pilot.

QUAKER RUTH NICHOLS was holder of early pilot's license. Her Atlantic flight in 1931 ended in crash in Newfoundland. She held women's altitude record of 28,743 ft., women's 3-km speed record (210.6 mph) in 1931. She organized Relief Wings, air's Red Cross.

MISS ELINOR SMITH, at age 17, set women's endurance record at 26 hrs., 21 min. in August, 1929. In December, assisted by Bobbie Trout, she boosted this to 45 hrs., 5 min. She appears above at the National Air Pageant, Roosevelt Field, in 1933.

MRS. KEITH MILLER was first woman to fly London to Port Darwin, Australia (1928). Flight took five months and covered 12,500 miles. In 1930 she held U.S. women's transcontinental record. Above is German glider she flew in New York Glider Meet, 1931.

WOMEN'S AIR DERBY (Santa Monica, Cal.-Cleveland, Ohio, August, 1929) brought winner Louise Thaden $4,400 prize money. Derby girls participated in other events of Cleveland Air Races, first time women fliers competed on equal basis with men.

Statement by Jacqueline Cochran

I celebrated the Fiftieth Anniversary of the first powered flight by man by becoming the first woman to pass the sonic barrier and by setting in a *Sabre* jet some new world's speed records. These speed records will not last long because aviation, notwithstanding the progress made, is just in its infancy.

For over twenty years I have been flying, having flown enough miles during this period to take me to the moon and back eight or more times.

In 1934 I started in the London-Melbourne Air Race expecting to win in a plane that had a top speed of about 225 mph. That was before the days of ocean air transports. In 1938 I won the Bendix air race with a speed of 250 mph from Los Angeles to Cleveland. In 1948 it required 446 mph for me to place third. And in June 1953 I made 675 miles per hour over a 15 kilometer course. Such has been the march of aviation.

In 1941 I flew a Lockheed bomber from Canada to England, and it was quite an event, taking twelve hours. During the summer of 1952 I flew my Lockheed *Lodestar* to Europe just to have it for transportation purposes while on the continent. From the aviation standpoint this flight in the *Lodestar* was no longer an event but just in a day's routine.

Breaking the speed of sound on May 18, 1953 was an unforgetable experience but it took a vertical dive from 48,000 feet to do it. Planes are now able to beat the speed of sound in level flight. They will be testing Mach 2 before long.

It took man about 25,000 years to decide to fly. Thereafter, it took man only 50 years to surpass the birds in their own realm.

And the end of such progress is by no means in sight. Rockets and guided missiles are taking over. Air freight will soon be cheaper and, of course, much faster than ground freight. Only the commuter will know about the inside of a train. Already we have penetrated the outer atmosphere and are on our way to conquer space.

The trouble is that we of the present generation were born too soon. But that will also be said by the next generation, for the flight of man is endless. Each goal is but a camp for the night.

Jacqueline Cochran

GLAMOROUS JACKIE Cochran, holder of five of the eight world speed records, was awarded Distinguished Service Medal and the French Legion of Honor. She won 1938 Bendix Trophy Race, and in 1953 broke sound barrier in Canadian-built *Sabre*.

RUTH ELDER, unsuccessful Atlantic flier, bids Thea Rasche, noted German aviatrix farewell as Miss Rasche starts flying tour of New England, Sept. 25, 1927. Ruth deserted aviation soon after Air Derby to score as a Hollywood movie queen in the thirties.

WOMEN IN THE WAR

On Dec. 7, 1941 "Rosie the Riveter" of World War II stepped into the place of the pioneer aviatrix. Women, aside from early-day stewardesses, had little place in commercial aviation prior to the forties, and only a handful had the chance to distinguish themselves as famous fliers. During the years 1939-41, over 2,200 women were trained in the CAA Pilot Training Program. At the start of the war there were 1,200 women with commercial licenses and 25 with instrument rating. A total of 3,050 women had private pilot's licenses. Although civilian flying was strictly curtailed during the war, these women served as engineers, control tower operators, sales managers (right), assemblers, riveters (left) and instructors. The office of Civilian Defense employed hundreds of women as aircraft spotters and radio-teletype operators. Thousands of women, working with aircraft for the first time, gained knowledge and love of the air.

WORLD'S LARGEST FLYING BOAT, the Dornier DO-X, took off from Friedrichshaven, Germany, in November 1930, flew to Amsterdam and then to Calshot, England, where the Prince of Wales went aboard and piloted the huge 169-passenger ship for ten minutes. Delayed by fire damage at Lisbon and by storms at the Canary Islands, the big plane arrived at New York August 5, 1931. The DO-X had a span of 157 ft., weighed 105,000 lbs. fully loaded; 12 engines in tandem pairs gave it cruising speed of 130 mph.

FLIGHTS IN 1930's

REFUELING IN AIR for a nonstop flight from London to India, Sir Alan Cobham handles the fuel hose while keeping position behind the twin-engine airliner. Later in the day, the refueling plane crashed near Aston Clinton, caught fire and was destroyed. The crew of four was killed instantly.

While Dr. Claude Dornier's mammoth DO-X capable of carrying 169 persons, was attracting world-wide attention, another Dornier-designed seaplane, piloted by Captain Wolfgang von Gronau, was making pioneering flights across the northernmost routes of the Atlantic Ocean. After the third Atlantic crossing, Von Gronau continued around the world by easy stages.

Meanwhile, the Russian-born American pilot, Boris Sergievsky, test-pilot for designer Igor Sikorsky, established four seaplane records in 1930. In 1934 he set ten speed and altitude records for seaplanes, and four additional world records for amphibians in 1936.

Henry T. (Dick) Merrill, veteran pilot, and Harry Richman, noted New York entertainer, attempted a nonstop flight from New York to London in September 1936 using a Vultee airplane called "Lady Peace." They crossed the ocean safely, but were forced down in Wales by

fuel shortage just 175 miles short of their goal.

The transcontinental speed record was broken repeatedly in the early thirties as Capt. Frank Hawks, James Doolittle and Roscoe Turner raced from coast to coast at ever-increasing speeds. In January, 1937, sportsman pilot Howard Hughes, holder of the world's landplane speed record of 352 mph, won transcontinental honors with a flight from Los Angeles to New York in seven hours, 28 minutes.

On March 17, 1937, the huge Sikorsky S-42 *New Zealand Clipper* took off from San Francisco with Capt. Edwin C. Musick in command. This was a survey flight to link the United States, Hawaii, and New Zealand. Musick had commanded the first trans-Pacific air mail flight to Hawaii, Guam, Manila and return in 1935. On a later survey trip, Musick and his entire crew were killed. The Musick Trophy was established in honor of this trail-blazing flier.

SHOWING THE STRAIN of a record-breaking flight around the world in 8 days, 15 hours, 51 minutes in June 1931, Wiley Post and Harold Gatty landed their Lockheed monoplane *Winnie Mae* at Roosevelt Field, L. I. After stops in England, Germany, Russia, they lost 14 hours "weathered in" in Siberia before continuing via Alaska and Canada. In July 1933, Post made a solo flight around the world in *Winnie Mae*, flew the 15,596-mile trip in 7 days, 8 hrs. 49½ min.

NEW NONSTOP DISTANCE RECORD was made by Russell Boardman and John Polando who flew their 300-hp Bellanca from New York to Istanbul, 5,011 miles in 50 hours, 8 minutes. They flew over Paris en route to drop letters. Seated between the fliers is Capt. Dieudonne Coste whose record the Americans broke.

"WRONG WAY" DOUGLAS CORRIGAN caused a sensation by flying his nine-year-old airplane from New York to Dublin "by error." He stoutly maintained his intended destination was Los Angeles. He served a five-day flying suspension aboard ship returning to New York, was given hero's welcome.

THREE-TIME WINNER of the Thompson Trophy, Roscoe Turner (shown receiving the award from Mary Pickford) set transcontinental speed records in 1932, '33, '34. His greatest competitor was Capt. Frank Hawks (right) who made a record transcontinental round-trip flight in August 1930, flying east-west in 14 hours, 50 minutes, and returned in 12 hours, 25 minutes. Two years later, Turner beat the east-west record flying to Los Angeles in 12 hours, 33 minutes. In July 1933 he established eastbound record of 11 hours, 30 min. Capt. Hawks, at his death, 1938, held more inter-city speed records than any other pilot.

PRESIDENT ROOSEVELT congratulates Maj. Alexander P. de Seversky in 1941 on winning the Harmon Trophy for many innovations and improvements in aircraft design. The Major, who lost right leg in World War I, designed the first all-metal, low-wing basic training plane, and the P-35, one of first pursuits in 300-mph class.

FLAGSHIP OF THE ITALIAN SQUADRON from Rome to Rio in January, 1931, rests in the harbor at Rio de Janeiro as Gen. Italo Balbo, leader of the first mass flight across the South Atlantic, prepares to go ashore. In July, 1933, Gen. Balbo led a flight of twenty-four twin-engine Savoia-Marchetti planes from Orbetello, Italy, via Holland, Iceland, Labrador, New Brunswick and Canada, to the Century of Progress Exposition in Chicago. Stopping at New York on the return flight, the Italian eagle visited Wiley Post who had recently returned from seven-day solo flight around the world. Balbo was Italy's Air Minister.

PROF. AUGUSTE PICCARD (left, with brother Jean) made the first stratosphere balloon flight in May, 1931, rose to 51,775 ft. In August 1932, he bettered record to 53,153 ft. Both flights were for research testing of equipment.

THE BALLOON, "EXPLORER," climbed to 60,613 feet in July, 1934, for the National Geographic Society. During descent, the bag tore and Maj. Wm. Kepner, Capt. Albert Stevens and Capt. Orvil Anderson parachuted safely from gondola.

$25,000 PRIZE for flying to Dallas, after their arrival in New York nonstop from Paris, was awarded to Capt. Dieudonne Coste (3rd from left) and his co-pilot Maurice Bellonte (l.) The prize was offered by Col. W. E. Easterwood. In photo are Mme. Doret and Marcel Doret, French flier.

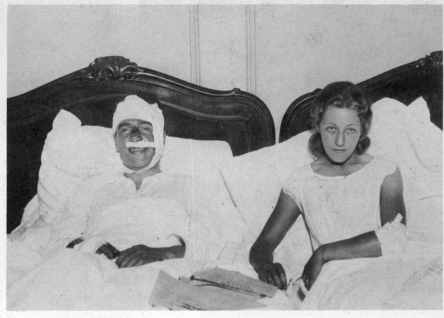

THE FLYING MOLLISONS still wore bandages when they and Amelia Earhart visited President and Mrs. Franklin Roosevelt at Hyde Park in July, 1933. One week earlier they had taken off from Wales in their twin-engine DeHavilland to fly nonstop to New York. Thirty-nine hours later they were forced down in fog at Stratford, Conn., and sustained painful injuries when the plane crashed on landing. Capt. James Mollison made the first solo westward crossing of the North Atlantic in 1932. The following February, he made a record flight from West Africa to Brazil. Amy Mollison soloed London to Capetown and back, 1936.

ACCURATE AERIAL NAVIGATION with sextant, stars, timepieces and compass marked Howard Hughes' record flight around the world in 3 days, 19 hours, 14 minutes July 10 to 14, 1938. With weather obscuring visibility during much of the trip, the twin-engine Lockheed *New York World's Fair 1939* was never more than a few miles off course and always within a few minutes of the planned schedule. A triumphal parade for Hughes and his four-man crew was led by Mayor LaGuardia (who was an aviator in World War I) and Grover Whalen, president of World's Fair which flight publicized.

WINNER OF THE 1932 THOMPSON TROPHY race, the famous Gee-Bee racer, piloted by Jimmy Doolittle, roars past a pylon. Doolittle won the Schneider Trophy Race in 1925; in 1929 he made the first "under the hood" blind flight; and in 1931 he made a record transcontinental flight. In 1932, he set landplane record of 294.4 mph.

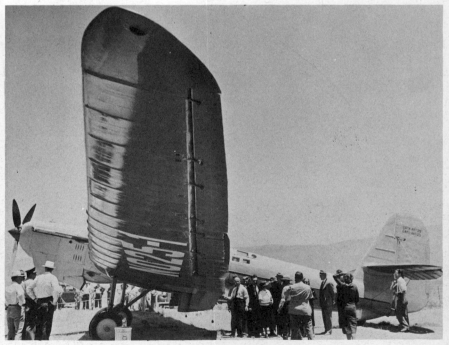

NORTHERN SEA ROUTE ADMINISTRATION was the official title of a Russian expedition which set up a base on an ice floe 13 miles from the North Pole as the first step in establishing air communication between Russia and America via the Polar regions. The expedition was headed by Dr. Otto J. Schmidt (center), shown with Ivan Papanin (l.) chief of arctic stations, and M. V. Vodopyanov (r.), chief pilot. In June, 1937, a few weeks after the Polar base was established, a Soviet airplane flew from Moscow to Oregon. In July, a second plane piloted by Mikhail Gromov and a crew of three, left Moscow bound for San Francisco. Passing the intended destination, it landed in a pasture near San Jacinto, Calif., to set a new long-distance flight record of 6,262 miles in 62 hours. Gromov had made a longer flight in 1934: 7,707 miles using a Russ ANT-25 plane. This was not officially recognized as Russia was not member of International Federation.

STABLE AIR PLATFORM is provided by the non-rigid blimp with its hard nose-cup. The Goodyear Co. made this type of airship for the U.S. Navy. Blimps served as offshore observation posts in submarine hunts. Radar operated efficiently from this aerial platform and depth bombs could be dumped from blimp's gondola.

GET-TOGETHER of the majority of U. S. Navy's lighter-than-air fleet, in 1930, appears above. Four types of "gas bags" can be seen. In the left background rests the rigid dirigible *USS Los Angeles*. At right appear five free balloons. In middle, two non-rigid blimps nudge the earth. Above them floats a captive "sausage" balloon, still useful for hanging air nets to trap or baffle approaching enemy craft.

DIRIGIBLE "HINDENBURG" (above) represented Germany's final bid to lead the world in use of the dirigible as a passenger transport. Largest rigid airship ever built, the *Hindenburg* was 803 feet long from nose to tail, and 135 feet through its thickest diameter. She could cruise 8,000 miles. Of the 97 aboard when she met her sudden end at Lakehurst, N.J., in 1937, 35 persons were killed.

ILL-FATED AIRSHIPS

Storms, flaws and explosions destroy the dirigible

Three tragic disasters were to eliminate the dirigible from aviation. The first tragedy struck the cruising *USS Akron* shortly after midnight, April 3, 1933, some 2,000 feet above a stormy Atlantic, off the New Jersey coast. A down draft plunged the *Akron's* tail into the sea. Aboard were 76 officers and men, including Rear Adm. William A. Moffet, chief of the Navy Bureau of Aeronautics. The admiral had said of the *Akron*, "She's the safest dirigible ever built anywhere." Moffet was not among the three survivors.

On February 12, 1935, a blast of wind ripped away the upper fin of the *USS Macon* at 1,250 feet altitude, off Point Sur, California. Lt. Comdr. Wiley, survivor of the *Akron*, maneuvered the *Macon* to the sea's surface, tail first. As her tail slipped into the waves, two over-anxious crewmen leapt from the *Macon's* nose, still 125 feet above the waves, and were killed by the impact. Surface ships saved the rest of the crew, while the Pacific swallowed the *Macon's* breaking hull.

At 7 : 20 p.m., May 6, 1937, at Lakehurst, New Jersey, the *Hindenburg* dropped her lines for mooring after an Atlantic crossing. At 7:25 p.m. she lay a flaming skeleton when her highly-flammable hydrogen gas caught fire. Among those who died were Capt. Ernst Lehmann, pioneer Zeppelin booster. Germany built one more dirigible after the *Hindenburg*, the LZ-130. Flown in 1938-39 during tests, her exact fate was unknown, but she was believed destroyed in an air raid on Friedrichshafen during the war.

PROFESSOR PICCARD remains the most famous of the free balloon experts. He appears hatless, in dark suit, above. Piccard's ascents exceeded ten miles in altitude. Gondola here is a replica of the one used during the world's initial balloon ascent in 1783.

TRAGIC CLOSE to U. S. attempts to use the rigid dirigible for Navy purposes appeared in the fates of the *Akron*, shown at left under construction, and the *Macon*, the aft section of whose control car is seen at right. In both cases, turbulent air striking their tail assemblies left the huge airships helpless. The *Akron* went down off the New Jersey coast in 1933. The *Macon* broke up in California coastal waters. The three survivors of the *Akron* tragedy are shown (center) delivering official disaster report to Navy Secretary Swanson and staff. Lt. Comdr. Wiley (offering report) had also survived the disastrous end of the *USS Macon*.

JAPAN FOUGHT almost continuously during the 1930s, in Manchuria, China and against the Russians in Manchukuo. Picture at top left shows Japanese fighters ready to take off against the Russians in 1939 during the "border clash" which nearly led to war between the two. Superior aircraft led the Japanese to exaggerate greatly their aerial victories claimed against Russians. Bottom left

shows a Japanese pilot and gunner set to go into action against Chinese in then-standard two-place biplane of 1933. Picture at top right shows the terrific death toll of a Jap raid on Shanghai, taken in 1937 by an American. At bottom right is pictured the wreckage of an American Curtiss *Hawk* fighter plane purchased by the Chinese to fight Japs, whose air superiority was unchallenged in Orient.

PLANES FIGHT AGAIN IN 30's

World's warplanes undergo tryouts in China, Ethiopia, Spain and Finland

After more than 10 years of rest following World War I, airplanes again took wing in far-flung battles early in the 1930's.

First in Manchuria, then in Ethiopia, followed by Spain and China and Finland, warplanes showed their weaknesses and strengths, and designers learned what might yet be needed for

W.W. II. During these wars, airplanes were thought of and used as auxiliaries to armies and navies. The independent air force, in practice in Britain, did not get its first battle-test until W.W. II, nor did strategic bombing, both advocated by Italian Gen. Giulio Douhet in 1921. His theories were vindicated, however, during the big war.

In Manchuria, warplanes played a slight role in the Japanese conquest. Both there and in Ethiopia, they were used primarily as scouting equipment. A little bombing was done, but it was not of a magnitude meant to influence the outcome of the wars.

Warplane types which were to be used in World War II first tried their wings in Spain. Italy and Germany utilized their latest and best, while Russia contributed fighter planes which proved successful against Fascist bombers in fair proportion to their numbers. However, they failed miserably against Hitler's Messerschmitt fighters. Large-scale bombings were used at Barcelona and Madrid, but were not carried out long enough or hard enough to show their true potential. Japanese raids against undefended Chinese cities proved nothing militarily.

Russia, using the first of her native-designed-and-built warplanes against the Finns, found them completely obsolete when pitted against

the modern types which Finland bought from other nations and used in combat. A complete overhaul of Communist air power and techniques was initiated shortly thereafter.

After the "rehearsal wars" were over, Europe set the pattern for the role warplanes would play in the impending Second World War.

ITALY, UNOPPOSED in the skies over Ethiopia, gave the first tryouts to plane designs later to fight in Spain and W.W. II. Farewell parade for Marshall De Bono shows tri-motored Italian bombers.

HEAVILY OUTWEIGHED in the air Abyssinia had only a few obsolete airplanes with which to fight the up-to-date air offensive used by Mussolini. Here, Ethiopians load one of their two-seater biplanes

OVER SPAIN, the Italians were close to being unopposed since Fascist planes far outnumbered polyglot Loyalist craft. Shown are Savoia-Marchetti bombers making bomb run without flak or fighter defense to bother them. Germans, too, gave Franco's Rebels aircraft, although bulk came from Mussolini.

MOROCCANS were flown to Spain to aid Franco, in these Junkers Ju-52 transports (top), which later were mainstays of the Luftwaffe in W.W. II. Bottom picture shows remains of Loyalist aircraft downed by Rebels. The Loyalists bought planes from everywhere, but Russia supplied most of craft.

REBEL OUTPOST goes up in smoke, hit by Loyalist bomb. While Fascists had more and newer planes, Loyalists made excellent records with what they had, especially Russian fighters which were modernized versions of older U. S. craft. Despite damage, Rebel bombing didn't seem to hurt Spanish Loyalist morale.

RUSSIA ATTACKED Finland in 1939, just as W.W. II broke out, and found her air fleet left much to be desired. Finns, using Italian, American, British planes, put up a valiant fight, in which Stalin learned his aircraft designs were almost completely obsolete. Russia started extensive program of new designs after war with Finns, which bore fruit in the middle of World War II. At left is shown a downed Russian bomber, at right, a Finnish biplane used as bomber.

FINNS USED SWASTIKA long before Nazis adopted the emblem, having started in 1918. Shown above is up-to-date Finnish light bomber, a British *Blenheim* bought from England and used against the Russians.

RUSSIAN ANT-6 BOMBERS like those above, appearing over Helsinki early in the morning of Nov. 30, 1939, told the Finns Russia had attacked without declaring war. Despite Russian fighters' success in Spain, in the Finnish war her planes proved inadequate when up against those of other nations.

MOLOTOV BREADBASKET, a container which revolved as it fell and spewed 60 incendiary bombs in all directions, wrought brutal havoc on wooden homes and buildings in little Finland's cities.

FIRST SUPERBOMBER was the Boeing XB-15, of 1937. Its four 850-hp Pratt-Whitney engines gave 35-ton, 149-ft.-wingspan giant a speed of 200 mph, ceiling of 20,000 feet.

MANY RESCUES were effected during 30's by Coast Guardsmen using Douglas Dolphins. Amphibians made sea-to-land flights.

MODERN ATTACK plane was the Northrop A-17A of 1937. Designed to strafe troops, export versions were used in W.W. II, until fighters took over ground support tasks.

STANDARD FIGHTERS for the Navy were these biplane Grumman F3F's, replaced just before W.W. II by *Wildcat* monoplanes.

GHOSTLY FACES were not those of men from Mars, but members of the First Pursuit Group in high-altitude garb. Wearing oxygen masks and fur-lined leather coveralls, they flew open biplane fighters. In 1931 they made nonstop 400-mile flight from Selfridge Field, Mich., to Bolling Field, Wash., D. C., at 20,000 feet.

WARPLANES
Fascism's rise spurs military designs

Had it not been for the rise of Fascism in Germany and Italy, the progress of military aircraft in the 1930's might have been nil. As it was, innovations appeared at mid-decade which played an important part in W.W. II.

Restricted by the Versailles Treaty until Adolf Hitler came to power and denounced it, Germany in a very short time built an aerial juggernaut which almost conquered all of Europe. The Luftwaffe would have succeeded had it operated on the tenets of a sustained war, but the theory of Blitzkrieg, with breathing space between campaigns to replace lost aircraft, won out, and Germany went into W.W. II with many, excellent planes, but no spare parts or reserve planes. She also had no heavy bombers.

Britain pioneered in new models and refined airplanes, but did not produce them. She set up a "shadow factory" system, wherein automobile manufacturers built aircraft under government subsidy, providing the nation with enough new designs to hold her own against an aggressor.

America developed excellent aircraft, once she saw the shape of developments in Europe. The nation also had two years of producing airplanes for the anti-Nazis before she became embroiled at Pearl Harbor.

Soviet Russia, having disposed of foreign aircraft producers and designers, made progress too, but it was difficult, under a regime which might sacrifice an aircraft designer and his design to political thought.

France, torn by political intrigue, made her aircraft factories government property. She turned out nothing significant in design, and had few airplanes in production. She had no chance when the Luftwaffe struck.

The decade started with biplane fighters and unwieldy bombers. By the time war had begun, wires were gone, landing gears retracted and engines had high powers. Speeds were four times that of 20 years before.

NEW, FAST BOMBERS like these Martin B-10's, shown as they prepared for a mass flight from Bolling Field, Washington, D.C. to Alaska, were replacing biplanes by 1934-35. The fast craft had excellent handling characteristics with their full combat loads. Succeeding the Martins later in the 1930's were the Boeing *Flying Fortresses* of W.W. II fame, along with other improved designs.

SKYHOOKS for fleet scout planes like this *Vought* of 1920's vintage, were dirigibles *Akron* and *Macon* on which the idea was tested in the 1930's. Primary purpose was to have planes scout for fleet. Idea died when crashes caused abandonment of the dirigible.

STORMY PETREL of the 1930's was Maj. Alexander de Seversky, whose book *Victory Through Air Power* did little to enhance him with Army authorities. His company produced fighters which set speed records and were ancestors of W.W. II *Thunderbolts*.

AIR CORPS COMMANDER during expansion in the critical 1935-38 period was Maj. Gen. Oscar Westover (left), who moved into General Headquarters Air Force, air corps' combat element. With him are (c.) Col. H. H. Arnold and Major Carl Spaatz.

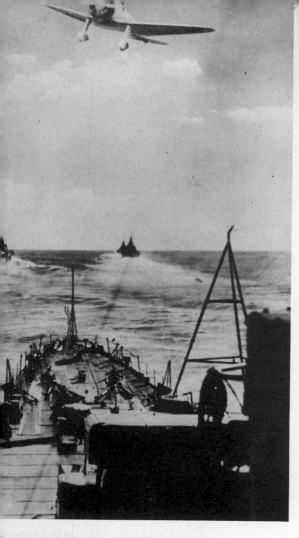

PARATROOPS FOR OFFENSE were a Russian idea, and battalions of 400 to 500 'chutists were trained as early as 1932. Picture above shows paratroops dropping from late-1930's Russian bomber while, at right, a mass-drop is shown. Failure of Russia to use 'chutists to any extent in W.W. II was blamed on purges which cost the lives of men who knew how to use paratroops, and struggles inside the Red Air Force over whether to build bombers or transports, resulting in not enough construction of either type. In 30's, paratroops were stationed in Far East, Japan then being considered more a threat than Europe.

◀ **PREPARING FOR WAR,** a Japanese fighter plane of the late 1930's circles over line of battleships. The Japanese paid strict attention to aircraft as sea weapon, then proved their efficiency at Pearl Harbor. Accused of copying designs, Japanese actually used only best of foreign ideas in their planes.

BIG GERMAN SHOW of huge Luftwaffe ready to strike was put on during tour of Col. Charles Lindbergh, shown with Air Marshal Hermann Goering, in 1936. Nazis later proved their power.

GERMAN GENIUS, during the days before the Versailles treaty was scrapped and rearmament openly begun, turned to getting high efficiency from low power. Picture is of Feisler *Storch* (Stork), an observation plane using slots, flaps and other design features to get it in and out of very small landing fields. At the same time, Nazi chemists were perfecting variety of synthetic fuels.

GUIDING BRAIN behind the Luftwaffe development before he met with fatal "accident" was Ernest Udet, W.W. I ace. Had his plans been followed, England might have been taken.

BRITISH BATTLEPLANES of the 1930's were typical of the day, but with some improvements over other nations'. At left below is the Blackburn *Skua*, Britain's first naval dive bomber. Shown in center is a formation of biplane bombers containing revolving gun turrets in nose, a British innovation. At right are Hawker fighters using Rolls-Royce Kestrel engine, forerunner of famed W.W. II Merlin power plant. British pioneered many excellent types of aircraft in pre-World War II days, including the *Spitfire,* and then put them into production in numbers sufficient to use when they were needed in 1939. Notable British design of 1931 was the *Gloster SS-9,* a biplane which had guns mounted in the wings outside the propeller arc and carried 1,600 rounds of ammunition per gun, more than was carried per gun in W.W. II fighters. The same plane had supercharger on engine, early use of what later became standard equipment.

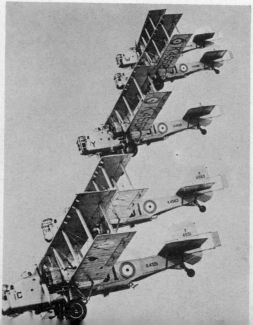

DECEMBER 7, 1941—SNEAK ATTACK ON PEARL HARBOR BY 360 CARRIER-LAUNCHED JAPANESE PLANES PARALYZED U.S. PACIFIC FLEET, JOLTED WARFARE INTO THE SKIES

World War II

Allies defeat German and Japanese air fleets; first jet planes are put to use by both sides as U.S. produces 96,000 planes in 1944

A pioneer military flyer, Carl (Tooey) Spaatz, who flew his first operational mission in Pershing's 1916 expedition into Mexico, rose to become commanding general of the Army Air Force before his retirement after World War II. He is best known as commander of the Eighth Air Force during its build-up from a small group of bombers to the strategic weapon which hammered Germany into defeat.

GEN. CARL SPAATZ

ON April 16, 1945, it was within the power of my command to announce the end of the strategic air war in Europe. A weekly average of 4,000 tons of bombs had rained on Austria and Germany from the day of the Normandy landing; a two-weeks' toll of 3,484 Nazi planes had been the final coup de grace to the famed Luftwaffe.

While the statistics of destruction, slowdown and failure of the enemy could be recorded in volumes, the actual measure of achievements of military aviation in World War II is perhaps best found in the words and official records of our former enemies in Europe and the Pacific.

Dr. Albert Speer, Reichmeister of Armaments and War Production, estimated Germany could have produced from 30 to 50 percent more fighter planes, but for our bombing. "We had new blueprints every few months and then had to tear down the buildings," he reported. "If a program lasted longer than three months it was a miracle."

Dr. Speer stated that about a million men were employed in the removal of bomb damage, excluding those engaged in reconstruction or manufacturing materials for replacement. Taking production underground to escape air raids compounded the Germans' difficulties. Bad ventilation caused headaches, working area temperatures were too low for comfort, and sanitation remained an unsolved problem. Dr. Speer summed up, "One cannot win aerial warfare through cement and tunnels."

Despite military necessity, Germany was never able to allot more than approximately 60 percent of its raw materials to armament production. The demand for consumer goods remained inordinately high because of the continual air attacks with their resultant destruction.

An official morale report in March, 1944, said, "Morale has reached a low point never before observed since the beginning of the war. One can hear even from trustworthy citizens that one ought to make an end of the war . . . The air terror proves to be the crux in the molding of morale."

Such words have the taste of bitter experience. Compare them to the report of the Japanese Diet on September 4, 1945, by the Premier, in which he stated, "In the days just preceding the termination of the war it seemed almost impossible to carry modern warfare further for any long period of time. The manufacture of modern war materials, principally aircraft, by mass production methods such as we had adopted before, would shortly have to face insurmountable difficulties as a result of the destruction of transportation and communications facilities caused by air raids . ."

These words assume even more significance when we realize that the attacks which laid waste to more than 42 percent of urban industrial areas had begun only eight months before. In 1944, not more than 100 bombers attacked Japan in a single operation; in early August, 1945, 801 *Superfortresses* attacked in a single night's operation. The bomb load per aircraft had increased from 2.6 tons per aircraft to 7.4 tons in the same period.

The combat efficiency of the B-29's enabled us to reduce Japan more economically than Germany. Fewer bases were required than in Europe, and in all the attacks on urban industrial areas, the loss ratio, due to all causes, was only 1.22 per cent of attacking aircraft.

The heartless statistics of total war alert us to the limitless possibilities or airpower applied to peace. Is there a better, saner use for the greater ranges and altitudes now at our command?

Carl Spaatz

PROF. WILLY MESSERSCHMITT

Starting as a gliding enthusiast in 1921, Willy Messerschmitt became one of the world's foremost airplane designers. During his work with the Bavarian Aircraft Co., he designed the Me-20, 10 place, all metal transport, and various sports planes including the 2-place Me-23 which won the Continental Races in 1929 and 1930. His Me-109, standard German fighter during World War II, still holds the world's speed record for propeller-driven planes, 469.22 mph. Ruled out of aircraft work by the terms of the World War II armistice, he is now in housing construction.

THE history of the German aircraft industry teems with such outstanding personalities as Otto Lilienthal who conducted the first successful flights as early as 1893, and Grade, Rumpler, Dornier, Junkers, Heinkel—just to name a few air-minded men who furthered the cause with idealism combined with that other important element—technical vision.

The contributions of the Messerschmitt firm consisted principally of W.W. II fighter planes: the standard fighter Me-109, the heavy fighter Me-110, and the jet fighter Me-262, first mass-produced jet aircraft in the world, which paved the way for future development both in Germany and elsewhere. The demand of the military for more armament was generally in contradiction with the technician's wishes, but was of necessity included in the design. Prior to World War II the achievements of special prototypes of the Me-109 attracted world-wide attention, as, for example, the speed record for land aircraft in 1937, and the absolute speed record of 755 km/hr for propeller-driven planes in the summer of 1939.

Always a glider enthusiast, in 1921, with a continuous flight of 21 minutes in a motorless plane, I established a world record. The sailplane was, in those days, the only testing means for the German aircraft builder, since the Versailles Treaty had forbidden the construction of motor-driven aircraft. Only after the conditions of the Treaty had been relaxed could the German aviation industry take a further step forward.

Preceding and during World War II, the well-known military models were created. In addition to the previously-mentioned jet fighter Me-262 with two turbojet propulsion systems, I designed, in cooperation with Dr. A. Lippisch, the tailless Me-163. This model was equipped with rocket propulsion and could reach a height of 10,000 meters (32,500 feet) in three minutes. Little known is the fact we were successful in exceeding a speed of 1000 km/hr (621 mph) as early as 1941 with the Me-163.

By 1945 a fighter with jet propulsion and swept-back wings had been developed. This plane, the P-1101, was already characterized by many of the features common in present day aircraft.

Following World War II, the writer, like other German aircraft manufacturers, was forbidden by an allied edict to make airplanes. It is hoped that the lifting of this restriction will permit us to work in our field once more, contributing with other manufacturers toward the benefit of all.

Messerschmitt

FIRST BRITISH JET flew May 15, 1941 at Cranwell. It was an E28/39 design, initiated in 1939 by Gloster Aircraft Co. under direction of George Carter. It used an 850-lb. thrust W-1 Whittle engine.

WORLD'S FIRST successful gas turbine jet aircraft was built by the Heinkel Co. under the auspices of Dr. Ernst Heinkel. Known as the He-178, this jet plane served as a flying test bed for the HeS 3B engine, also being developed by Heinkel. First flight of this revolutionary design was on August 27, 1939 at Rostock, Germany, when Capt. Warsitz made the first circuits of the field. Thrust of the HeS 3 B engine was rated at 1,100 lbs. and marked the culmination of gas turbine development dating from '36.

CAMPINI CAPRONI N-1 showed rise of interest in jet propulsion in Italy. First flown in August of 1940, this novel plane was powered by a 900-hp reciprocating engine driving a three-stage ducted fan. It went 110 mph.

DAWN OF JET PROPULSION

Advent of World War II accelerates gas turbine research and development

In 1934, a blood-red seaplane roared across a measured 3-km course in Italy to break all existing records for aircraft at a speed of 440.68 mph. In 1939, in Germany, a Me-109-R flown by Fritz Wendel increased the record to 469.22 mph. Each of these records, while an admirable feat of engineering and flying skill, was, in effect, a defeat to designers who realized that there were certain limiting factors which prohibited much appreciable increase in aircraft speeds. These factors were the loss of propeller efficiency as blade tips reached sonic speeds and the power limitations of the piston engines themselves. It was obvious that if technical developments in the air were to continue, a new propellerless engine with much greater power must be produced.

In 1928 an Englishman, Frank Whittle, wrote an examination thesis on the possibilities of gas turbines as airplane engines and of jet propelled flight. By 1930 he had taken out his first patents. Simultaneously a German, Hans von Ohain, was doing research in the same field and applied for his first patents in 1935. Official interest of the British government in Whittle's efforts led him to form Power Jets Ltd. in 1936 to develop his basic ideas on turbojet engines. His efforts were so promising that in 1939 the Air Ministry awarded

a contract to Power Jets Ltd. for a flight engine and, at the same time, commissioned the Gloster firm to build the special airframe necessary to flight test this new propulsive device.

In Germany, Dr. Ernst Heinkel added a gas turbine engine division to his airframe plant, and, in collaboration with von Ohain, produced a turbojet suitable for flight. Known as the HeS 3, this engine flew in the He-178, also built by Heinkel, on Aug. 27, 1939, thus making the He-178 the first turbojet aircraft in the world to fly. On May 15, 1941, almost two years later, the Gloster E28/39 was flown in England powered by the first flyable Whittle engine, the W.I.

Of historical interest was the Italian Campini Caproni N-1 which, because of wartime secrecy clamped on jet developments in England and Germany, was long thought to be the first jet to fly. Developed in 1939 by Ing. Secondo Campini and first flown in 1940, this plane used a system of propulsion known as a *ducted fan* where an Isotta Fraschini 900 hp piston engine drove a three-stage compressor. The airflow through the compressor took up the heat radiated from the engine, the exhaust gases were added, and, finally, fuel was burned in the tailpipe. The project's performance was disappoint-

ing, and caused it to be abandoned in late 1942.

Development in Germany, after Heinkel's success, spread to the Junkers and B.M.W. engine factories. As a hint to the vast potentialities of the turbojet realized by the German High Command, it is noteworthy that no less than 5,000 Junkers *Jumo 004* turbojet engines were built before the war's end, and production was at the rate of 1,500 units per month. A total of 1,294 Messerschmitt Me-262's were built to utilize this output during late 1944 and early 1945, in spite of heavy bombings and material shortages.

By the end of the war Britain was in full production on the Gloster F9/40 *Meteor*, which first flew on Mar. 3, 1943. In the United States, with the aid of the Whittle W-IX turbojet, General Electric produced the first American turbojet, the I-16, and flew two of them in the Bell XP-59A on Oct. 1, 1942, at Muroc, Calif. On January 9, 1944, the Lockheed XP-80 also made its first flight with a British Halford turbojet.

Jet aircraft had arrived. Driven by the impetus of war, the German Me-262 was climbing to operational heights at speeds faster than U.S. bombers could reach in level flight. The turbojet had defeated the propeller—and seemed hardly to have touched its own potential.

AMERICA'S FIRST gas turbine powered aircraft was the XP-59A, first flown by Robert Stanley at Muroc, Calif. on Oct. 1, 1942. Built by Bell Aircraft at Buffalo in a brief 12 months, it was powered by two I-16 jets developed by General Electric from Whittle prototype W-1X, secretly sent to U.S. in June, 1941.

JET PIONEER Sir Frank Whittle (right) is shown with Mr. G. Strauss of the British Ministry of Supply and Mr. Don Bliss of the U.S. Embassy in November, 1949, when the W-IX engine, loaned to the U.S. in 1941 to aid American research, officially was given to the Smithsonian for permanent exhibit.

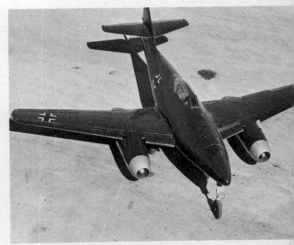

MESSERSCHMITT ME-262 became mainstay of German Fighter Command in closing months of the war. Powered by two Junkers *Jumo 004B-1* axial flow jets of 1,980 lbs. thrust each, these aircraft displayed marked superiority over propeller-driven craft and showed extent of German research in jet propulsion.

FOR HEROIC PILOT, CREW NAMED THIS DB-3 "GALLANT"

"STURMOVIK" ATTACK PLANES WERE SCOURGE OF NAZIS

YAK-9 FIGHTERS WERE EQUAL OF NAZIS' AND ALLIED CRAFT

RUSSIAN PLANES IN WORLD WAR II

Overwhelmed and practically wiped out in 1941 by the great numerical and technical superiority of the attacking Nazis, the Soviet Air Force was able to more than close the gap by 1943.

After a thorough overhaul of its air command following the Finnish War, the Soviets were producing large numbers of good planes by 1943.

However, the Communists completely subordinated their air power to army command. Red aircraft flew in support of ground attacks.

Ignoring the use of strategic bombing until very late in the war, the Soviets never were able to mount an attack of more than 100 planes. Their standard TB-7 was no match for American or British long-range bombers. Best-known Red plane was the IL-2 *Sturmovik* attack plane. Heavily armored, it made the first wide use of air-to-ground rockets, which hurt Nazi morale more than it damaged German war machines.

The Reds lost about 5,000 aircraft in the fall and summer of 1941, most of them obsolete. Their best fighters defended Moscow and other principal cities. By 1944-45 the Russians had 20,000 warplanes operational at one time, including Lend-Lease American and British planes.

Hampering Russian operations throughout the war was a complete lack of radar and almost no radio navigational aids. As they acquired U.S. planes, the Reds built a navigation system, though never equal to that of the Allies.

Maintenance and supply for the Russian air forces were poor during the first year of war, but by 1943 they became adequate.

YAK-3 PRODUCTION BEHIND URALS INCREASED RAPIDLY

THESE TU-2 BOMBERS MADE MOST RAIDS UNESCORTED

MASS-PRODUCED RUSS ENGINES EQUALLED OTHER NATIONS'

MITSUBISHI TYPE "O" NAVY FIGHTER (ZERO)

MITSUBISHI TYPE KI-462 FIGHTER

KAWASAKI TYPE KI-61 ARMY FIGHTER (TONY)

JAPANESE PLANES

On December 7, 1941, it was with considerable chagrin that Allied airmen discovered their best fighter planes were being out-run and out-maneuvered by the Japanese Navy fighter known as the *Zero*. Powered by the 1,100-hp Mitsubishi Kinsei engine, the *Zero* had a speed of 340 mph and a service ceiling of 34,000 ft. No U.S. or British fighter could match that performance. It was two years before the old P-39's and P-40's were replaced with the P-38's and P-47's that provided some equality between Japanese and Allied fighter pilots. And although the Japanese never mass-produced four-engine heavy bombers, their twin-engine planes kept abreast of and in some categories ahead of the Allied counterparts until close to the end of the war.

Japanese twin-engine bombers reached a superior performance level, several types being in the over 300-mph class: the Mitsubishi Army Type 4 heavy bomber, *Peggy 1* in the Allied code, rated at 346-mph; Mitsubishi's reconnaissance bomber, *Dinah* 3, at over 370-mph; and Nakajima's single-engine reconnaissance bomber *Myrt* 12 was rated at 390 mph.

By 1945, Japan succeeded in producing three fighters in the over 400-mph class.

MODEL 52—CARRIER-BORNE NAVY PLANE (ZEKE)

JAPANESE KAMIKAZE OR SUICIDE PILOT READY TO GO

"BAKA" ROCKET-PROPELLED KAMIKAZE SUICIDE BOMB

29

BOMBER PRODUCTION at the Heinkel factory at Marienhe, near Rostock, Germany, showed the remarkable manner in which German civil aircraft such as the Heinkel civil transport 1935, was converted into potent bombers like He-111H.

◀ **BLACK CAT** presaged the doom of the German Fighter Command. Pictured at left is an armament crew loading the 7.7 mm machine guns of an Me-109E. In production in late 1938, this Messerschmitt typified German design simplicity.

RESEARCH at the Hermann Goering Institute at Volken-▶ rode, Germany, aided much in the amazing progress made by the aviation industry in the field of high speed flight. The swept wing, delta configuration were stimulated by work here.

NAZIS PERFECT AIR BLITZ

Despite daring designs, early victories, Luftwaffe fails before allied onslaught

In the battle of France during spring of 1940, the German Luftwaffe hit its peak as a fighting air force. Never before had the world seen such air work as the Luftwaffe exhibited in support of Hitler's land armies. The Ju-87 *Stuka* dive bomber became the world's most publicized and feared airplane as it spearheaded the blitzkrieg, whining down to blast holes in Allied defenses. Through these lines roared German tank columns, constantly supplied with petrol flown forward by Luftwaffe transports. Roads became impassable for retreating Allied armies as German fighters strafed closely-packed refugees vainly fleeing the onslaught of war. The Luftwaffe appeared cruelly invincible.

England's gallant RAF cracked the fable of Luftwaffe invincibility. "Never have so many owed so much to so few," said Churchill. In the Battle of Britain, started as a Luftwaffe attempt to soften English defenses for invasion,

Goering's squadrons lost half their committed forces. The *Stuka* was withdrawn from combat, unworthy for such battle. German air crews suffered 90% more losses than England's "long-haired lads." The threat of invasion was over for England in late 1940 but the blood-letting of seasoned pilots proved too severe for Germany.

Hitler's disastrous Russian adventure, begun in 1941, also caused severe pilot losses. The Luftwaffe marshalled 3,000 aircraft to fight on the Eastern Front, but these were dispersed over some 2,000 miles of fighting line. Such attenuation meant that German pilots worked far harder and suffered greater losses to provide the same support they had given on the 250-mile front in France. By autumn of 1941, one third of the Luftwaffe forces on the Russian Front had been drained away. Losses stayed critically high.

By 1943, the Luftwaffe had become a defensive air force, standing guard over the gains

of earlier triumphs. German airplane designers concentrated upon night and day fighters, to intercept the ever-growing armadas of Allied bombers. At no time did Germany attempt to develop a big offensive force of heavy bombers. Yet, Nazi fuel supplies dwindled too fast under the accurate Allied attacks, and pilot ranks grew thinner. Germany ended the war with thousands of airworthy planes immobilized. Drastic losses of experienced pilots and lack of fuel to train new pilots properly left the once arrogant Luftwaffe helpless on German ground.

With its technical versatility and its daring designs, the German Air Force, while it lasted, set a pace for the world in the development of military aircraft. But, like the German nation at the time, it was badly led. Goering threw away seasoned pilots in the same manner as Hitler threw away the good will of men and nations. Neither could survive for long with such excess.

"VIPER" was designed as last-ditch jet plane to oppose Allied bombers. The *Viper* climbed to 30,000 feet in less than 60 seconds. After an attack, the pilot and engine parachuted to earth. Rockets in nose all were to be fired in one salvo.

FLYING WING twin jet fighter showed extent of development of all-wing aircraft by Horten firm. The Ho-9, above, was an experimental design for a day and night fighter. Flown in prototype as a glider, this plane (wings removed) was captured by Allies.

LAST DITCH BID for air supremacy was the Heinkel He-162A *Volksjager* (People's fighter). A single engine jet made from semi-strategic materials, this fighter was produced in record time. Design started Sept. 23, 1944, first plane flew Dec. 6, 1944. He-162A-1 was service version.

WILLY MESSERSCHMITT, airplane builder, and Hermann Goering, Luftwaffe chief, appear together at diplomatic party (above). Messerschmitt, in center, built gliders, bombers and fighters for Luftwaffe.

◀ **ERNST HEINKEL** was one of major aircraft designers of the German aircraft industry. The Heinkel concern was formed in 1922 by Dr. Ernst Heinkel and produced many notable bombers and fighters.

TOP BRASS of the German and Italian Air Ministries meet for first time in 1940. Shown are General Oberst Ehrhardt Milch, Gen. Giuseppe Valle of the Chief of Staff, Italian Air Force, Lt. Gen. Ernst Udet. ▶

RECONNAISSANCE in a Dornier 215 bomber is the mission of German pilot (above) being buckled into a parachute. Luftwaffe reconnaissance failed German armed forces after 1943.

AIR TRANSPORT of troops and materiel was a thoroughly developed phase of Luftwaffe activity. German blitzkrieg (lightning war) would not have been possible without mobility of air transport and proper type planes.

GIANT TRANSPORTS of the German Luftwaffe attempted to keep the armies on the north Russian front supplied with arms and food. These huge Messerschmitt Me-323 *Gigants* were easy targets.

FW-190A FIGHTER

HEINKEL HE-112 OF 1939

FOCKE WULF FW-189 "UHU" (OWL)

FOCKE WULF FW-187

ME-163B "KOMET"

ME-110 FIGHTER-BOMBER

ME-262A-i TWIN JET FIGHTER

JU-287 JET BOMBER

ME-109F STANDARD FIGHTER

DORNIER DO-335A PUSH-PULL

ARADO AR-234B-2 "BLITZ"

JU-88A-4 BOMBER

ME-410 ATTACK BOMBER

JU-90 CIVILIAN TRANSPORT

JU-87 "STUKA" DIVE BOMBER

JU-388K BOMBER

145

BATTLE OF BRITAIN

RAF, British morale thwart Hitler's invasion, make offensive possible

"The gratitude of every home in our island, in our Empire, and indeed throughout the world, except in the abodes of the guilty, goes out to the British airmen who, undaunted by odds, unwearied in their constant challenge and mortal danger, are turning the tide of world war by their prowess and by their devotion. Never in the field of human conflict was so much owed by so many to so few." —Rt. Hon. Winston Churchill, Aug. 20, 1940

COVENTRY RAID of German Luftwaffe on Nov. 15, 1940, virtually leveled the entire city. This disastrous raid only served as still another stimulus to all-out effort of RAF to rid England's skies of Nazi planes. Shown is the nave of Coventry Cathedral, once regarded as fine example of 14th century architecture, where services continued throughout the war in spite of its almost total destruction.

WAR PRODUCTION of the Bristol *Blenheim* Mk. I bombers at Speke, Liverpool, in the early part of 1939, was evidence of the growing might of the RAF. A cabbage patch only two short years before, this plant of Rootes Securities, Ltd. had 6,000 employees turning out the *Blenheim*. Powered by two Bristol Mercury VIII engines, these all-purpose bombers played a major part in RAF operations.

The long history of proud Britain had never, in modern days, faced so grave a threat of danger as that which followed France's capitulation to Germany in 1940. Only the Channel separated her from the enemy.

Military second-guessers have long concluded that if Hitler had staged a quick and massive invasion after Dunkirk, he could have brought a shaken empire to its knees. Instead, Hitler determined to soften England with disastrous air assaults, hitting simultaneously at transport, shipping, war production and civilian morale.

The British Air Ministry considers the Battle of Britain to have begun August 8, 1940, when Germany shifted her attack from Channel shipping to bombardment of the home island in daylight.

The Ministry chose to divide the battle into four phases. In the first phase, August 8-18, the principal objective was the disruption of Channel shipping, with land bombardments aimed at ports and coastal air facilities.

During this first phase, the Luftwaffe found Britain's defenses much more formidable than they had supposed. On August 15 the RAF *Hurricanes* and *Spitfires* marked up 180 German planes destroyed.

The second phase was calculated to have run from August 19 to September 5, with attacks concentrated on inland airdromes. The pattern of the raids indicated the intention of forcing defenses away from the Channel.

By Sept. 6, the Nazis were concentrating on industrial centers, particularly on London. On September 7th, a radical tactical change came with the first mass bombing at night. These nightly random bombings of industrial centers continued for weeks, with high civilian casualties and tremendous damage. Day bombing did not disappear, and when RAF defenses were deployed inland, the Luftwaffe renewed dive-bombing raids on ports.

In the last phase, beginning October 6th, daylight bombing almost disappeared; heavy bombers were abandoned for fighters and fighter-bombers.

During the 84 days of almost continuous attack ending October 31, Germany had lost 2,335 aircraft. RAF rosters tallied 375 pilots killed and 358 wounded as the cost of this essential delaying action, which kept the Nazis contained on the continent until new allies and new strength were available.

Over 14,000 British civilians perished, and 20,000 were wounded in this period, but morale continued high. The Hitler scheme had failed, British ships still used the Channel, and RAF bombers strew their own havoc.

AIR SUPERIORITY over the Channel and inside the occupied countries, to the limits of the fighters' range, was established by the Fighter Command by May of 1942. Shown above are (left to right) Air Marshal Sir Arthur Coningham, Air Vice Marshal Broadhurst and Air Chief Marshal Sir Arthur W. Tedder as they awaited return of *Spitfires* and *Mustangs* from scouting over European coast.

COASTAL COMMAND prepares to strike as De Havilland *Mosquito* F. B. Mk. VI's taxi out of dispersal areas before taking off on a sortie against German shipping off Norway. Escorting and protecting convoys, maintaining constant anti-submarine patrol, attacking enemy shipping were functions of Coastal Command. In 1944 they flew 66,362 sorties, dropped 1,411 tons of bombs and mines.

"BEAUFIGHTER" PARTY shoots up German convoy. One of the best pictures ever taken of an anti-shipping strike, photo shows *Beaufighters* of the Coastal Command attacking German "M" class minesweepers northwest of Borkum on Aug. 25, 1944. Photographed from lead plane, *Beaufighters* maneuver for attack.

EVERY INCH A FIGHTER was the famous Supermarine *Spitfire*. First prototype flew on Mar. 5, 1936, and by beginning of war, plane was ready for combat. First Mk. I types gave tremendous account of themselves during Battle of Britain, sharing honors with the *Hurricane*. Above is Mark 5A, produced in 1941.

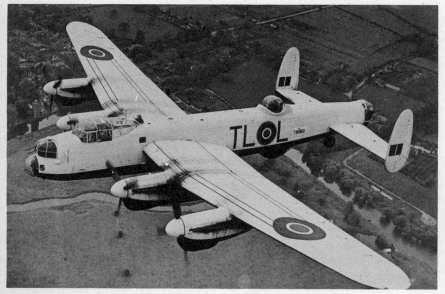

AVRO "LANCASTERS" were among the most versatile of British heavy bombers. This plane was capable of carrying the 22,000-lb. bomb and dropped first "blockbuster" on a railway viaduct at Bielefeld, Germany, Mar. 14, 1945. In 1942 Avro produced first *Lancaster;* in 1943 Canadian-built Mk.X's joined the RAF.

EAGLE SQUADRON returns from a fighter mission. Founders of this group were U.S. pilots, volunteers in the fight for freedom. Some went first to French Air Force before France fell. Others joined the RAF; some were in the 1940 Battle of Britain. At own request, these pilots banded together into Eagle Squadron.

BOULTON PAUL "DEFIANT" Mk.I

HANDLEY PAGE "HALIFAX" B.VI

BRISTOL "BEAUFIGHTER" Mk.X

WESTLAND "LYSANDER" Mk. I

D. H. "MOSQUITO" Mk. XVIII

SHORT "STIRLING" B. Mk. III

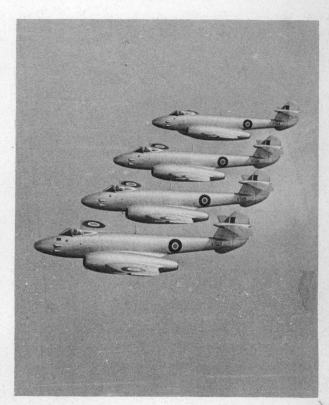

SHORT "SUNDERLAND' Mk.II

BRISTOL "BEAUFORT" T.B.Mk. I

HAWKER "HURRICANE" IIC

GLOSTER "METEORS" had the distinction of being the only Allied jet-propelled airplane to go into operational service during the war. The *Meteor* first flew in March, 1943, and shot down its first flying bombs on Aug. 14, 1944. *Meteor* Mk.4's shown above are powered by two Rolls Royce *Derwent* turbojets of 3,500-lbs. thrust each.

U.S. NAVY FLYING BOATS, though designed in 1933, performed vital patrol and rescue work. PBY amphibian, *Catalina*, was equipped to land on ice, land, or water. It was first to sight the fleeing battleship *Bismarck* (May, 1940), leading to its sinking.

◀ **AVIATION CADETS** at Randolph Field, Texas, trained seven months before flying a first-line combat plane. In 1939 both Randolph and Kelly Fields turned out 300 officers. Other air schools helped train 7,000 in 1940 and 12,000 more by late 1941.

LINE CHIEF MASTER SERGEANT J. T. Smith, ▶ held Air Corps record for 30 years service as instructor to fledgelings at Randolph Field, "West Point of the Air." World War II pilots owed much of their pre-battle training to enlisted instructors.

U.S. AIR EXPANSION
Growing military emphasis opens new plants

FIVE LINES OF BT-13's, the standard American basic trainer of World War II, show their peacetime markings as they line up for inspection at Miami. The *Valiant* used a 450-hp Pratt and Whitney engine, and was airplane in which air cadets were first trained to fly blind in bad weather using instruments.

CONTROVERSIAL "AIRACOBRA" rolled off Bell Aircraft's production line in 1940. Sleek, sport-like in appearance, its 1,325-hp liquid-cooled Allison engine was behind pilot. It was armed with deadly 37-mm cannon, had a maximum speed of 375 mph.

Though Europe's skies were dark with warplanes, U.S. aircraft factories continued to produce planes in modest quantities. European powers, it was apparent, were locked in a gigantic race for air supremacy. Few doubted Germany's intentions to secure "lebensraum" at any cost. Adolf Hitler reiterated in his frenzied utterances that only through land and airpower could Germany reach its destiny.

During 1939 some 2,000 military and transport planes were built in America. In its entire history the American aircraft industry had produced fewer than 45,000 planes of all kinds. On January 12, 1939, President Roosevelt requested that Congress vote a $300,000,000 Air Corps appropriation to be used in the building of 5,500 planes a year, with an additional 20,000 men in training to fly them.

A year later, Roosevelt asked Congress for $896,000,000 toward the building of 50,000 airplanes. Donald Douglas, speaking for the aircraft industry, wired "We can do it."

With this beginning, President Roosevelt, on Dec. 15, 1940, was able to commit the U.S. to its role as the "Arsenal of Democracy."

The burden of air power in America fell squarely upon the striking force of a few heavy, medium and light bombers, a few hundred fighters and combat training planes. Congress, meanwhile, fought heatedly over the Army's need for four-engine bombers.

Heightening the controversy were England's views. A leading British aeronautical magazine as late as 1940 said: "Any big bomber policy in Europe would be a tactical error of the first magnitude. Huge four-motor airplanes are fine targets on the ground or in the air . . . they would not survive long in a full-scale war in Europe." Operating groups within the U.S. Army Air Corps were more realistic. In September, 1940, the Air Corps ordered 512 B-17 *Flying Fortress* bombers. One month later, total defense appropriations passed $17 billion.

Slowly, at first, American factories began to produce military planes, armament and equipment. New factories and airfields were built. Existing plants were converted to wartime use while tooling and research facilities sprang up overnight. From 6,000 planes in 1940, U.S. production jumped to 19,000 in 1941.

INDUSTRY CHIEFS met as National Aircraft War Production Council, 1944, included (from left) G. Martin, H. Blythe (Goodyear), E. Breech (Bendix), D. Douglas, E. Wilson (United Aircraft), T. Ryan, F. Marchev, P. Johnson (Boeing), J. Kindelberger (North American), V. Emanuel (Aviation Corp.), L. Bell, L. Goad (Eastern Aircraft, GM), J. Ward, Jr. (Fairchild), R. Gross (Lockheed), H. Woodhead (Consolidated), L. Cohu (Northrop), G. Vaughan (Curtiss-Wright). Group served as liason between air industry and govt.

OUTDOOR AIRCRAFT assembly line of famed P-38 *Lightnings* ran full blast at Lockheed Plant. P-38's initially required 17,000 man-hours to build in 1941, but only 8,000 man-hours one year later. An accelerated program sent hundreds of these fighters over European skies.

FAST AND POWERFUL A-20 *Havoc* and *Boston* attack-bombers were built for Britain's defense in mid-1941. Night and out-of-doors construction like this at Douglas' Santa Monica, Cal. plant, typified the new "swing shift" methods of mass production.

THE BIG PUSH for arms to the Allies in 1940-1941 required day and night team work. Workers pushing the Lockheed *Hudson* (above) were among the 6,900,000 in U.S. defense plants by end of 1941. U.S. built 48,000 planes in 1942.

GREAT "LIBERATORS" await their turn in line before being flown by U.S. Ferrying Command on first leg of long series of flights to England. Thousands of rounds of ammunition, tons of bombs accompanied each ship. These four-engine bombers, as B-24's, later teamed with B-17's (*Flying Fortresses*) in destroying the might of Germany's war power.

ARMS TO THE ALLIES

Lend-lease leads to big U. S. build-up

By May of 1940, almost 2,000 planes had been sent to France and England. Production of planes and armaments for Allied Powers in Europe was greatly accelerated by orders received from Great Britain, later financed by the operation of lend-lease. Allied governments placed orders with American builders for 45,000 planes to be delivered in two years.

In March, 1941 the lend-lease bill was passed by a vote of 60 to 31 in the Senate, and 317 to 71 in the House. It permitted the United States Government to lend "defense articles" directly to Britain and many other nations whose defense was vital to the safety of the U.S. and the Western Hemisphere.

The United States began to build its own air power by providing orders that enabled the manufacturing industry to expand factory facilities, to tool up for mass production and to train workers in new skills. The Neutrality Act permitted the fulfilling of tremendous Allied contracts, stipulating that the countries involved pay for and transport the products. Thus, war needs abroad first brought mass production of aircraft to U.S.

AIR MARSHAL W. A. (Billy) Bishop, V.C., Canada's renowned World War I ace (see p. 88), was Canadian Air Ministry observer in European area.

FLYING TIGERS The first visible Allied air cooperation with China was supplied by the Flying Tigers, American Volunteer Group (AVG) of the Chinese Air Force. Led by Gen. Claire L. Chennault, seventy pilots created a legend in the skies over Asia. Between Dec. 18, 1941 and July 4, 1942, when they were disbanded and incorporated into the U.S. Army Air Force, the Flying Tigers were officially credited with the destruction of 280 Japanese planes. Some 1,500 Nipponese pilots and crew members died at the hands of the AVG, who lost eight pilots killed in action, two pilots and a crew chief killed on the ground and four pilots missing. Below right, Chennault shakes hands with member of a group of Chinese Nationalist pilots trained in the U.S. The American AVG commander shakes paw of his pet dachshund "Joe," after receiving the Distinguished Flying Cross from General G. E. Stratemeyer (l.), commander of the U.S. Army Air Forces in India and Burma. General Edgar Glenn, Chennault's Chief of Staff, looks on. Chinese mechanics (l.) took care of AVG's 55 precious P-40's.

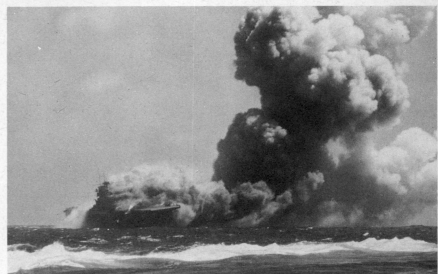

FOUR BATTLESHIPS WERE SUNK by Japanese carrier planes at Pearl Harbor. The *USS West Virginia* is shown here burning in foreground, the *USS Tennessee* beside it. Risking a strafing attack, the rescue boat crew has pulled in to pick up another man from the stricken ship. Although carrying less than full crews while in port, there were hundreds of men aboard when they burned and sank.

JAPANESE CARRIERS seen in artist's rendering (top photo), are the *Kaga* and the *Akagi* from whose decks torpedo and dive bombers took off to bomb Pearl Harbor. Of 1927-28 vintage, both were sunk by U.S. planes in the Battle of Midway Island. Jap torpedoes from a submarine brought the end of the U.S. carrier *Wasp* (lower photo), Sept. 15, 1942, while on escort duty at Guadalcanal.

PEARL HARBOR ATTACKED

Japanese air power scores heavily — bringing the U. S. into World War II

December 7, 1941, marked the coming of age of air power in the most positive manner for the United States. On that day, the Japanese First Air Fleet, in a maneuver planned during the summer of 1941, carried out a virtually perfect air strike against the U.S. Naval base at Pearl Harbor and the three Hawaiian Army Air Force Bases of Hickham, Wheeler and Bellows. During an hour-and-a-half attack, the Navy saw four battleships sunk, four others damaged; a mine layer and target ship were sunk; three cruisers, three destroyers and a seaplane tender were damaged; 2,086 officers and men were killed, an additional 749 wounded. Simultaneously, Japanese strikes against the Army air bases prevented effective retaliation, the Nipponese fliers destroy-

ing 64 planes, damaging 86 more. When the six attacking carriers turned west at the close of the strike, not a single American bomb nor torpedo had even remotely threatened them.

The crippling effects of the Japanese attack were so severe, ground forces could have been landed without air opposition and the entire Hawaiian Islands probably taken. Failure to do this was a major tactical error on the part of Japanese Imperial Headquarters. The terrible lesson of air power had been taught America with an impact that shocked the nation.

Pearl Harbor, however, was not the only American base hit from the air on December 7. Nine hours after the Hawaiian strikes started, land-based naval air units from Formosa began

attacks against U.S. air bases in the Philippines. Shortly after noon, Nipponese bombers made unopposed runs over Clark Field, destroying the communications center, hangars, shops, etc; then the attack planes followed with strafing runs, completing destruction of all planes but three of two squadrons of B-17's caught on the ground. Simultaneously, the fighter bases suffered heavy losses. By Dec. 10, only 31 pursuit planes remained operational; B-17's were reduced to 14. Eleven days later, the B-17's were forced back to Australia. A stunned U.S. read the war news and looked to its own coastal defenses. The Pacific had overnight become a crucial area and the U.S., for the first time in its history, recognized its own vulnerability to air attack.

CORAL SEA BATTLE fought in May, 1942, was the first engagement between U.S. and Japanese carrier forces. Both lost one flat-top each, American fliers sinking the *Ryukaku* or *Shoho*, Japanese sinking the *Lexington*, shown here.

BATTLE OF MIDWAY ISLAND, June, 1942, a heavy defeat for the Japanese, also was costly for the U.S. Navy. Every man, but one, of this heroic Torpedo Squadron No. 8 was lost. Survivor was G. H. Gay (kneeling, c.). Jap torpedo fliers sank carrier *Yorktown*; 4 enemy carriers were sunk.

GRUMMAN TORPEDO BOMBERS like these helped to sink the Nipponese carriers at Midway. Two Japanese naval task forces were turned back in that battle. Had the U.S. Navy and Army planes failed to stop them, Hawaii would have again been hit.

FLYING THE HUMP between China and India became the supreme test of the Air Transport Command's Curtiss *C-46 Commando* transports (l.). The U.S. AAF's ATC cargo and transport planes were modified commercial craft. Cargo planes had large doors, heavily reinforced landing gear and flooring. Transports had bucket seats or benches and smaller doors. The U.S. Navy's Air Transport Service (NATS) and the ATC both ran scheduled flights of troops, supplies, ammunition, medicine and wounded to nearly every section of the globe. A primitive oxen cart (c.) moves slowly across a field in China as an ATC transport roars in for a landing. Led by Chinese and U.S. Army Engineers, some 300,000 conscripted laborers (r.), toiled to clear fields, build air strips.

  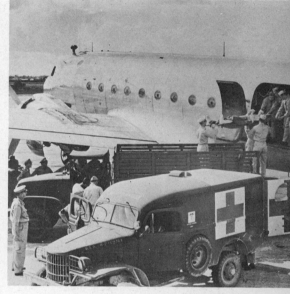

CORONADO FLYING BOATS of the NATS formed a global network of aerial highways. The burden of defending these unarmed and heavily laden PB2Y-3R's rested on the pilots and crews. Powered by four P-W engines, the *Coronado* had cruising speed of 191 mph .

NO NEW EQUIPMENT was available for foreign or domestic airlines in war days, so maintenance, like that shown being performed on Pan American *Clipper* above was emphasized to keep open routes like U.S.-Lisbon run. Most overseas routes were under military contract.

DOUGLAS C-54 *Skymasters* like this were basic airplane for long-distance hauls on military air supply lines and for evacuating the wounded to U.S. Airlines used C-54's widely until post-war models appeared.

THE NON-RIGID AIRSHIP L-2 arrived at its mooring at Lakehurst Naval Air Station, New Jersey, after a practice run over the North Atlantic in 1941. Blimps spent estimated 500,000 hours in the air during World War II.

◀ **CAPTURE AT SEA** of a Nazi U-858 submarine off the Atlantic coast by an M-type blimp was one of the numerous exploits of the Navy's Fleet airships. By 1944 airships were patrolling some three million square miles of ocean.

FIRST WOMAN PASSENGER AGENT, Mildred Bigelow, served T W A at Lockheed Air Terminal, Burbank, Calif. Millions of American women replaced men in vital jobs, were especially evident in the aviation industry. ▶

MASS PRODUCTION

The huge Ford Willow Run bomber plant near Detroit, Mich., like the majority of American industry, kept its highly complex assembly lines moving on a twenty-four hour schedule. New bombers at Willow Run (left) were moved on twin parallel production lines (background) before converging to a single assembly line. At this juncture the outer wings of the B-24 *Liberator* bombers were added (foreground). The big ships were then moved along the conveyer line to the point of final completion. In the process, 1,250,000 parts were put together for each *Liberator*. The backbone of a Boeing B-29 *Superfortress* (center) at Wichita, Kan. plant, was composed of the circumferentials and stringers. Parts comprising the bomber's skeleton were riveted before making the section ready for its outer skin. Women workers in the Douglas Aircraft plant at Long Beach, Calif. (right) gave their attention to the planes' shiny plexiglas noses. 12,355 bombers and 10,769 fighters were built during 1942.

DOUGLAS DB-7B, the twin-engine *Havoc* night-fighters were mass produced for Britain's RAF to use in North African theater. The P-70, or USAAF *Nighthawk* also were painted jet-black, flew over Germany.

CONTRAST in the skies is formed by Stearman PT-17 *Kaydet*, foremost American primary trainer of W.W. II and Boeing *Flying Fortress* as they cruise over Kansas plains. In buying out Stearman in 1938, Boeing became owner of plane's design; built 5,000 *Kaydets* during war.

FIREPOWER was the governing factor in the modified North American B-25H Mitchell bomber. Tail and waist gun positions, side gun packages and increased nose armament were added. The aircraft's 75-mm cannon was a spectacular innovation in the Pacific theater.

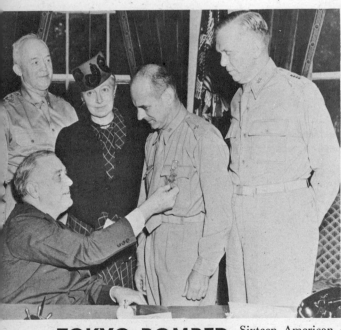

TOKYO BOMBED

Sixteen American carrier-based North American B-25 Mitchell medium-bombers took the Japanese populace by surprise in the bright noon light of April 18, 1942. Led by Colonel Jimmy Doolittle, USAAF, from the 20,000-ton aircraft carrier, *Hornet,* the 16 twin-engined bombers strafed and bombed the cities of Tokyo, Yokohama, Kobe, Yokosuka and Nagoya. President Franklin D. Roosevelt's humorous comment to the effect that Doolittle's medium-bombers flew from "Shangri-La," the mysterious Tibetan city of James Hilton's "Lost Horizon," added to the prevailing myth. Watched by Mrs. Doolittle, General Henry H. Arnold (l.) and General George C. Marshall, Chief of Staff, U. S. Army (r.), Brig. Gen. Doolittle received the Congressional Medal of Honor, highest U. S. award, from Pres. Roosevelt for the Tokyo raid. All of Doolittle's planes dropped their bombs, but they ran into foul weather and the airmen were forced to crash-land or bail out. Of the 80 fliers and crew members, 71 survived. Three captured fliers were beheaded by the Japanese. One of the injured fliers (above r.) crashed his ship on Chinese soil and was carried on cot used as stretcher and hidden in a Chinese home.

DAWN PATROL off Biscayne Bay by U. S. Coast Guard Martin *Mariners* kept up steady reconnaissance for Nazi submarines in the Caribbean Sea. The *Mariner,* already a vital cog in the USCG's air-sea rescue operations, did yeoman work in picking up hapless fliers crashing far out from shore. Coastal vessels, particularly small craft and out-bound convoys, operating in all kinds of weather, relied heavily on the Coast Guard's air facilities. After Pearl Harbor, U. S. Coast Guard aviation expanded three-fold. By 1944 the USCG used 195 aircraft: 146 transferred from the Navy, 49 registered Coast Guard aircraft.

FLYING MEDICS in a United States Army Air Force high-altitude chamber experienced the many ailments that combat fliers might acquire. Also, chambers aided in developing high altitude equipment.

GIANT PRODUCTION PLANTS such as North American Aviation (above), Consolidated Vultee, Douglas, Boeing, Grumman, Martin, Republic, Northrop, Lockheed, Bell, Curtiss, Ryan and other member aircraft manufacturing companies, acted in concert with the U. S. government's urgent call for planes. Army Air Corps appropriations at the turn of 1942 approximated $2,173,608,961. U. S. Naval Aviation appropriations in 1941 totalled $646,620,350 after original allocation had been augmented. By Pearl Harbor, aircraft output was eight times what it had been when war broke out in Europe in 1939.

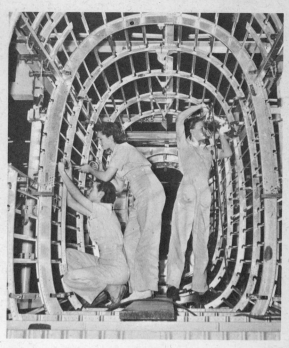

WOMEN WAR WORKERS in any plant were affectionately nicknamed "Rosie the Riveter." The percentage of U. S. women holding defense jobs rose to 33.9% in Dec. 1945 from a pre-war 25.8%.

WAR SKYROCKETS PRODUCTION

America's industrial might, growing under the impetus of the war in Europe, mushroomed after the Japanese bombed Pearl Harbor.

Engine production was the key to rapid expansion of airplane production, and the first money and priorities went to powerplant companies. Allocations for air frames came quickly.

At the time of Pearl Harbor, engine production was 12 times that of 1939; airframe construction had increased eightfold, and the dollar value of plane manufacture had tripled. Thirty combat types were being produced for the Allies, at their

expense, and the United States government had started its appropriations for expansion when the attack hit Pearl Harbor.

One of the early bottlenecks in plane building was the lack of trained workers. Companies had to set up their own training programs to turn unskilled workers into skilled. Engineers called into service in many cases were replaced by women. The industry faced the added handicap of having to pay wages frozen below the level of other industries.

Despite these handicaps, the aircraft industry

met and exceeded the goals set for it when President Franklin D. Roosevelt asked for and got almost 20,000 warplanes in 1941, and more than double that figure in 1942.

A potent force in reaching the tremendous goals set for airframe producers and engine manufacturers was the work of all kinds women learned to do, freeing men for the battlefront.

Between December 1942 and January 1944, the combined efforts of all U.S. aircraft companies produced 29,355 bombers, 38,873 fighters, 7,012 transports, 19,939 trainers, 5,604 others.

BELL P-63 "KINGCOBRA"

BELL YP-59A, FIRST U.S. JET

CONSOLIDATED PBY-4 "CATALINA"

LOCKHEED P-38L

B-17 "FLYING FORTRESS"

CONSOLIDATED B-24 "LIBERATOR"

GRUMMAN F6F-5N NAVY "HELLCAT"

CURTISS "HELLDIVER"

DOUGLAS A-20 "HAVOC"

NORTH AMERICAN B-25 "MITCHELL"

BOEING XB-29 "SUPERFORTRESS"

P-51 U.S. "MUSTANG"

155

THOUSANDS OF TONS of high explosive bombs (right) were stacked in ammunition bunkers at operational stations throughout the English countryside. With Hermann Goering's Luftwaffe unable to fight off strategic bombers of the Allied air forces, the cities of Germany suffered the heaviest "round-the-clock" air bombardments in history. From the outset of the war until May 8, 1945, American and British planes flew approximately 4,000,000 sorties against Germany. USAAF bombers, including *Flying Fortresses*, like the *Hell's Angels* (left), dropped a total of 1,500,000 tons of bombs on the Third Reich and German occupied areas, wrecking entire cities. Of all bombs dropped on Germany by the Allies in six years of war, 72% rained down during the last 10 months.

AIR COMMANDERS confer on progress of the war against Adolf Hitler's *Festung Europa*. Gen. Henry H. (Hap) Arnold (left), commanded the United States Army Air Force while Lt. Gen. Carl (Tooey) Spaatz (r.) then commanded Eighth Air Force.

U. S. OPERATIONS IN EUROPE

Allied bombs crush the axis

The participation of the United States in a "round-the-clock" aerial offensive against Hitler's "Fortress Europe" and German occupied areas, widened the scope of Allied raids. Royal Air Force *Stirling, Halifax,* and *Lancaster* bombers concentrated on night bombings, while U.S. B-17's and B-24's were employed for daylight precision raids. By mid-1943, by day and night, flights of 700 planes or more swept across the channel to strike Axis targets.

Chief target of the USAAF and RAF was the Ruhr Valley's industrial arsenal. The giant Krupp munitions works in Essen were paralyzed by repeated Allied aerial blows. Blockbusters hammered with monotonous regularity on Cologne, Dortmund, Stuttgart, Mulheim and Krefeld. Thirty-one Nazi cities had 500 acres or more destroyed: Berlin 6,437 (ten times as much as London); Hamburg 6,200; Dusseldorf 2,003; Cologne 1,994. One-fourth of the bombs dropped (about 650,000 tons) was directed at cities. About 305,000 German civilians were killed, 780,000 wounded and 7,500,000 made homeless. The shock effect was terrifying. Three hundred thousand persons fled the Ruhr area in May-June, 1943. Long distance bombers struck objectives as far as Trondheim in Norway and Crete in the Mediterranean. B-17's repeatedly raided the U-boat pens along the French Coast and ports of Kiel, Bremen, Emden, Wilhelmshaven in Germany.

The great 1944 offensive was climaxed in late July and early August when RAF bombers pounded Hamburg mercilessly. With one third of the city's homes destroyed, 60,000 or more people killed, little Joseph Goebbels told his diary—but not the German people—"A city of a million inhabitants has been destroyed in a manner unparalleled in history." Combined Allied air sorties dropped 800,000 tons on land transportation; 640,000 on industrial areas, 300,000 on military targets, 250,000 on oil and chemical plants, 190,000 on airfields, 48,000 on plane factories, and 410,000 tons on other targets, totaling in all 2,638,000 tons of destructive bomb force.

NAZI AIR BASES were felled one by one by the attacks of Lt. Gen. Hoyt Vandenberg's 9th Air Force. Northrop's P-61 *Black Widow*, parked in front of a shattered German control tower, was radar-equipped, and first plane designed as night fighter.

RADAR JAMMERS were crews like this above who specialized in dropping "chaff" dipoles, made of aluminum strips sized according to radar frequency. Use of "chaff" to shield attacking bombers was credited with saving 450 planes, 4,500 crew lives.

SMOKE MARKERS were used by these 8th Air Force B-24's when they hit Tours, France. The US AAF flew 2,362,000 combat sorties, lost 22,948 planes, dropped 1,500,000 tons of bombs, destroyed 39,691 planes, suffered over 120,000 casualties.

NORTH AFRICAN based *Liberators* of the 12th and 15th Air Forces hit targets in Italy and Austria as Allied planes bombed the Axis day and night from the west. On Aug. 13, 1943, the Messerschmitt factories near Vienna were raided. On May 31, 1944, 162 Libya-based B-24's (above) flew 1,000 miles to hit Concordia Vega oil refinery, Ploesti, Rumania.

BISMARCK LOOKS DOWN upon the ruins of Magdeburg, Germany, as civilians stroll the streets following the surrender of Germany. At 2:45 a.m., on May 7, 1945, Germany surrendered unconditionally to the Allies, ending the five years, eight months and seven days of conflict. The truce-signing ceremony took place in a schoolhouse in Rheims, France.

GERMAN FLAK clipped the wing of this careening 15th AF *Liberator* over Italy. The plane caught fire, lost one wing and an engine and plunged to earth. An early long-distance raid was made on Aug. 1, 1943, when 177 B-24's took off from Africa, flew southwest of Italy and across part of Greece, Albania and Yugoslavia, for bombing of Ploesti oil fields.

WALLS OF RUBBLE were all that remained of the proud city of Munich, Germany, as Michael Cardinal Faulhaber, Catholic Archbishop of Munich, officiated (above) in the celebration of the Feast of Corpus Christi, June 3, 1945. The German people knew in their own land the same kind of bitter devastation their bombs wrought in London, Rotterdam, Warsaw.

DER FUEHRER'S TANKS and turret assemblies in a Hanover factory were tossed around like toys in a play pen as bombs from 8th AF *Flying Fortresses* fell on March 3 and 14, 1945. Over Europe, the U.S. lost 9,949 bombers and 8,420 fighters, had 8,000 more bombers damaged beyond repair. The cost of dropping a ton of bombs on Germany was $28,000.

U.S. NINTH AIR FORCE fighter-bombers caught this German locomotive in the middle of a 300-ft. bridge spanning the Moselle River, wrecking both engine and span with well-placed bombs. Destruction of bridges and rail lines carrying supplies and troops to enemy positions was a decisive factor in stopping von Runstedt's counter-offense, Christmas, 1944.

ROUGH SAILING in the waters off Royan, France, hardly describes the destruction handed to Hitler's merchant marine. Low flying Royal Canadian Air Force pilots (above) smother a "Sperrbrecher" with a barrage attack of 20-mm cannon shells and rockets.

STREET SCENE in Tokyo reveals the ever-prominent safe, all that is left intact where a modern building once stood. By November, 1944, Saipan in the Marianas became a B-29 base from which 1,000 B-29's dropped 150,000 tons of bombs on Japan.

BATTERED Japanese planes in this Nagoya plant show how badly destroyed was Japan's aerial potential. Long-range B-29 *Superfortresses* began leveling Japan as early as June 16, 1944. The intensity of assaults increased until surrender, August 14, 1945.

WORK HORSE OF THE PACIFIC, the four-engine *Liberator*, takes off on another mission. Because of its greater range, the B-24 replaced the B-17 in the Pacific theater. The B-25 Mitchell (upper right) became the most versatile plane in island war: a reconnaissance ship, high and low level bomber, carrier plane, and, in models equipped with 75-mm cannon, flying artillery. Carrier air power of the U.S. Navy (lower right) increased nearly 1000 per cent during the war, some 110 flat-tops being in service on V-J Day. Since main axis naval strength rested with the Japanese, a majority of the U.S. carriers saw service in the Pacific.

OPERATIONS IN PACIFIC

Air power proves to be the deciding factor

During the opening phase of the war in the Pacific, from December 7, 1941, to August 1942, Japanese aggression was decisively successful. It extended the Nipponese Empire from Burma to Guadalcanal and included the entire Netherlands East Indies plus most of New Guinea. In each sector of that stolen area, Japanese air power seized and maintained air superiority, providing amphibious forces with ideal protection and tactical support.

At the outset, Allied forces were pitifully weak in air power throughout the Pacific. Nearly two years passed before their aircraft were made available in sufficient numbers to alter the Allied tactics from mainly a holding operation to an offensive one. The effectiveness of U.S. carrier air power was proven in the battles of the Coral Sea and of Midway Island; the effectiveness of land-based Army air power was proven in the Bismarck Sea battle. From these three operations, the Japanese Imperial Command learned that any further offensives beyond the 1942 perimeter were doomed to failure, since any amphibious forces they might send forth were certain to be turned back if not annihilated by either army or navy airplanes or both. When U.S. B-29 *Superforts* began strategic bombing of Japan itself in June, 1944, realistic military minds at Japan's Imperial Headquarters clearly saw that both air supremacy—and the war—were lost.

B-29's BOMB JAPAN. Systematically blasting 66 major cities, they accomplished an average destruction of 44 per cent. In Tokyo, more than 55% of the city was destroyed. B-29's also carried out an extensive aerial mining operation on Japan's harbors.

5TH AIR FORCE B-25's went in at masthead level to skip-bomb these Japanese ships in Rabaul harbor. The heavy cruiser was sunk along with two light cruisers, six destroyers, and eleven cargo vessels. Once a key Jap base, U.S. planes neutralized Rabaul.

DEATH DIVE of a Jap Kamikaze on the carrier *USS Hornet* is shown here. Also attacked by torpedo planes, the *Hornet* went down. During the last four months of the war, these suicide planes took a huge toll.

LOW LEVEL ATTACK is made by B-25 on Japanese destroyer escort off Amoy, China. With the acquisition of bases in the Philippines, AAF bombers forced Japanese shipping from oil-rich Sumatra and Borneo to a practical standstill. Ships caught like this inevitably were sunk by low-level bombing.

"USS SARATOGA" RECOVERED from seven hits sustained at battle of Iwo Jima and made her way back to Puget Sound Navy Yard under her own power. Termed the most extensively damaged vessel the Yard had received, the *Sara* was soon repaired and put back into service. Aircraft from this carrier took part in more strikes than those of any other ship.

END OF CV "FRANKLIN" (above, burning and sinking) followed a Japanese attack, March, 1945. She was taking part in softening up strikes against Formosa and other islands nearby as preparation for the massive assault against Okinawa which began April 1st. While Nipponese carrier operations had completely ceased following the great defeat in October, 1944 battle of Philippine Sea, land-based planes continued attacks.

U. S. NAVY "BAT," first fully automatic guided missile, was effectively used against Japanese shipping. Radar guided, the "Bats" had a length of twelve feet, a wing-span of ten, were launched from the wing of a Navy *Privateer* patrol bomber. Later obsolescent, "Bats" were another important first.

SILENT WEAPON of World War II was radar. The electronic "eye," developed by U.S., British, French and German scientists in the 1930's, was perfected for long-range detection and identification of airborne as well as surface objects. Above is radar plot room aboard carrier during operations in China Sea.

FLYING AMBULANCE is shown picking up wounded Marines on Okinawa, April, 1945. Swift evacuation by air became possible on the first day of the Okinawa assault when the Japanese air strip of Yontan was taken. Big C-54 Douglas transports like this removed hundreds of wounded men to base hospitals.

IWO JIMA AIRSTRIP, after capture in March, 1945, was put to use by U.S. Air Force. Twin-boom planes, foreground, are P-61 *Black Widow* night fighters; single-engine planes edging strip are P-51 *Mustangs*. In the distance famed Mt. Suribachi can be seen.

GROUND SUPPORT for infantry, an important phase of aerial warfare, is dramatized by the North American B-25 Bomber which is strafing Japanese dugouts in the jungle at Rabaul, New Britain, where heavy dual-purpose 75-mm anti-aircraft guns were hidden.

DIRECT HIT is made by 14th Air Force bombers. Burning target was important Japanese oil storage dump ► adjoining the city of Kowloon (lower left). American squadrons operating from China achieved an exceptional record despite meager numbers of planes and limitations of supplies coming by airlift over the Himalayan "hump." The ATC-developed air supply system later proved invaluable when used in the Berlin airlift.

ORK FOR DEFENSE
your way of life

information on DEFENSE JOBS ...

EE YOUR LOCAL OFFICE.
TE EMPLOYMENT SERVICE

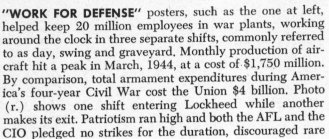

"WORK FOR DEFENSE" posters, such as the one at left, helped keep 20 million employees in war plants, working around the clock in three separate shifts, commonly referred to as day, swing and graveyard. Monthly production of aircraft hit a peak in March, 1944, at a cost of $1,750 million. By comparison, total armament expenditures during America's four-year Civil War cost the Union $4 billion. Photo (r.) shows one shift entering Lockheed while another makes its exit. Patriotism ran high and both the AFL and the CIO pledged no strikes for the duration, discouraged rare "work stoppages." Newspapers pooled news and photo facilities to give defense workers reports of war progress. U.S. Armed Forces swelled in 1944. More than 11 million wore uniforms of Army, Navy, Marines, and Air Force, while 19 million non-factory workers made up the nation's third-line of defense and 9 million farmers kept the nation and its armed services well fed. Acres of chicken wire (c.), painted cloth, fake houses, trees and scenery were wartime camouflage to hide aircraft factories from enemy attack. Coastal cities had "dim outs;" civil defense groups grew.

U.S. PRODUCES 96,000 PLANES

The total number of airplanes produced in 1944 reached 96,318 against 85,898 in 1943. In May, 1944 alone, more than 9,000 bombers, fighters, and aircraft were built—the all-time record and one-third more than the entire plane production of 1940. Manufacture in terms of number of planes decreased after June 1. But numbers no longer told the true story. Emphasis on heavy bombers, especially the *Superfortress*, had made airframe weight the essential indicator of the progress of airplane production. In 1944 more than 970 million pounds of airframe weight were accepted as compared with 657 million pounds in 1943. Of this total, 623 million pounds of airframe weight delivered in 1944 were in 35,000 bombers, and 219 million pounds were in 38,873 fighter and reconnaissance planes. America's gigantic production of aircraft, engines, propellers, spare parts and airborne equipment increased about 38% during 1944 as compared with peak production figures in 1943.

IN A SINGLE DAY in April, 1944, Boeing's airplane plant in Seattle, Wash. completed sixteen B-17 *Flying Fortresses* (above). These heavy bombers scored an unequaled combat record during W.W. II. The four-engined, air-cooled and turbo-supercharged B-17's were essentially high-altitude, long-range bombers designed for precision destruction of unrestricted targets during daylight. In all, 12,731 B-17's were built for the USAAF; 6,981 by Boeing, 3,000 by Douglas and 2,750 by Lockheed. The cost of the war in 1944, in planes, ships, and armaments, reached a new peak—$64 billion compared to $56,900 million spent for war equipment in 1943.

BOEING'S B-29 "SUPERFORTRESS," capable of well over 300 mph, was the spearhead of the USAAF's attack on Japan. The giant bomber's main landing gear assemblage (above) was lowered to join the fuselage bomb-bay section in a Boeing Company plant. Precision tooling made mass production possible. The B-29's huge 98-ft. fuselage stretched two-and-a-half times the length of a standard American railway freight car. 3,970 B-29's were produced during the conflict. U.S. 20th and 21st Bomber Commands, using B-29's escorted by P-47's and P-51's, dropped 171,000 tons of bombs on Japanese home islands of Honshu, Shikoku, and Kyushu during war.

REPUBLIC P-47N

CHANCE-VOUGHT F4U-4 "CORSAIR"

NORTHROP F-61 "BLACK WIDOW"

NORTHROP FLYING WING

VULTEE C-87

CONSOLIDATED PB4Y-2 "PRIVATEER"

MARTIN B-26B "MARAUDER"

B-29 "SUPERFORTRESS"

GERMAN ROCKETS

Hitler's final punch against the anticipated Allied invasion of Fortress Europe was the lethal V-1 buzz bomb (above) and V-2 missile. The long-range V-2 (r.), developed at the gigantic rocket center of Peenemuende, attained a speed of over 2,000 miles per hour. The V-1 bombardment of London (l.) lasted 80 days (June 13 to August 31, 1944) and killed an estimated 5,479 people. The V-2 attacks, aimed primarily against London and Antwerp, created considerable property damage and loss of life but were more sporadic. Although the German "wonder weapons" failed, they began new air age.

PARATROOP DROPS

Paratroops during World War II were developed into a new and highly effective type of infantry. Air-drop mobility often meant success or failure in crucial battle operations in both theaters of war—European and the Pacific. Typical large-scale drops such as the Anvil-Dragoon Operation (above), used in the invasion of Southern France, filled the skies with thousands of men who parachuted to strategic positions behind enemy lines. Largest airborne operation was Market-Garden, September, 1944, when more than 25,000 men dropped into Holland.

ENOLA-GAY, THE FIRST A-BOMB CARRIER

A-BOMB CLOUD RISING OVER HIROSHIMA

A-BOMB CLOUD RISING OVER NAGASAKI

VICTORY

Atomic warfare began on August 6, 1945, when the first atom bomb was released over Hiroshima. Three days later, a second A-bomb fell on Nagasaki, yet it was not due to use of atomic bombs exclusively that the Japanese government agreed to the cessation of hostilities on August 15 and signed the surrender documents V-J Day, September 2, 1945.

When Germany surrendered, May 7, Japan realized she would have to continue the war alone.

Premier Suzuki, Foreign Minister Tojo, and Navy Minister Admiral Yonai were in favor of immediate peace. But the other key figures of the Supreme War Council advocated fighting on, in the hope that new battles might provide a stronger negotiating position. The Potsdam Declaration of July 26 made clear that no compromise peace could be expected from the Allied Powers. Then on August 8, Russia formally declared war on Japan. *Superfort* air attacks had already reached massive proportions. Every major

city in Japan had felt their blows. On August 1, for example, 853 B-29's were in the skies over Nipponese targets, their bomb-load equal to more than 3000 B-17, B-24 bombers. Thus, by August 14, even the stubbornest militarist in Japan was ready to admit further resistance was useless. The Emperor called the cabinet together, requested an Imperial Rescript to be prepared accepting the Potsdam Declaration terms. On August 15, all hostilities ceased. The pressure of air power had forced victory without invasion.

LETHAL GUIDED MISSILES, GRADUALLY REPLACING CONVENTIONAL TYPES OF AIRCRAFT, REPRESENT MAN'S NEWEST CONCEPT OF AIR POWER.

Present Era

Sound barrier is shattered, jet fighters meet crucial tests of war in Korea, as U.S. air might stems tide of a third global conflict

SIR GEOFFREY DE HAVILLAND

Widely noted during and after World War I as the designer of the British DH-4, the warplane that "wouldn't wear out," Sir Geoffrey De Havilland was equally noteworthy at mid-century as producer of many jet fighters for the British Air Ministry, among them the first to break through the sound barrier. His firm was engaged in production of jet transports and various types of speed research craft.

I ACCOUNT it an honour to be asked to contribute to this issue of YEAR which devotes itself to the history of flight. One man's contribution to the progress of the past fifty years must inevitably seem small in an industry which today relies increasingly on specialized knowledge and unselfish team work among highly skilled men.

It was my good fortune that my early youth coincided with the birth of powered flight and taking my inspiration from the achievement of the Wright Brothers I started my experiments in 1908 and built my first successful aeroplane in 1910. In those days competition was keen and we worked as individuals, each man exploring his own line of thought and each learning as much from his failures as from his successes. They were years of trial and error far removed from today's exacting science.

Since then two wars have intervened and in England as in America the aircraft industry has seen many changes of fortune. It was in the lean years after 1919, when the firm which built D H aeroplanes during the war closed its doors, that the company was formed which bears my name. Happily the enthusiastic friends who rallied round me in those difficult days are still active members of our Board of Directors. It is to this fact as much as any other that I attribute the firm's successful growth.

At the close of the second world war aircraft production formed the largest industry in Great Britain but because of the concentration on military needs we lacked the transport aircraft to meet the needs of peace. The fine American airliners then available have since enjoyed a virtual monopoly on the air routes, and it is only now that the initiative and effort of British manufacturers are bearing fruit in the shape of the modern jet and turbo-propeller airliners, which are in the forefront of development and which are finding world-wide markets.

To my many friends in the United States I would say that we in England find their example as stimulating today as it was to me 45 years ago. My long association with the Industry has taught me that healthy competition is the only true spur to progress and I believe that a keen but friendly rivalry between the American and British aircraft industries will contribute materially to our joint prosperity and contentment thus providing our two great democracies with the most effective guard against those who would seek to destroy our way of life.

Geof Havilland

William B. (Bill) Bridgeman, 36, established world's rocket altitude and speed records in 1951, which remained unbroken for two years at 79,494 ft., 1,238 mph. Though not an engineer, he received an engineer's education while testing the Douglas Skyrocket and X-3 (see page 184). He learned to fly in the Navy in 1941 and earned the Distinguished Flying Cross, Air Medal and Purple Heart during World War II. After flying for a short time as an airline pilot following the war, he joined Douglas Aircraft Co. as a test pilot.

TEST PILOT WILLIAM BRIDGEMAN

O VER the last fifty years the techniques in the art of test flying have changed considerably. The day of pilot "note taking" with a cockpit knee board is rapidly disappearing. True, it will always be necessary to obtain quick qualitative information of this character but to obtain the kind of accurate data needed by the aerodynamicist today it has been necessary to develop more scientific methods of recording.

That the practices of Orville Wright, who performed the tests on the first powered aircraft, were sound is proven by the fact that some 50 tests were completed in the year 1904. It is interesting to note that the early test pilot relied heavily on information obtained from a scaled wind tunnel constructed to help determine the stability of the aircraft.

But here the similarity between the pioneering test flights and those which are so scientifically conducted today ends.

The Wright brothers had only four instruments which, though they were monitored faithfully, allowed little study of stability, except for a length of string mounted on the ship to indicate yaw. Today modern research craft are, of necessity, much more complex. Probably the most successful of these high performing research planes is the U.S. Navy's supersonic Douglas *Skyrocket*.

This ship is virtually a flying laboratory. A photographic flight recorder is used to record on motion picture film the reading of all the flight instruments. A pressure measuring system, consisting of an automatically recording manometer connects wing and tail at 400 points.

Control forces and stresses in the structure are measured by means of 904 electric strain gauges and are automatically recorded by an oscillograph. This means that a very complete and accurate data record is available showing drag characteristics, maximum lift and stall characteristics, buffet boundaries and stability and control trends. Flight boundaries throughout a very wide Mach number range are available. Because a rather substantial increase in Mach number was attained in the last stages of the testing, instrumentation was added to the glass wind shield, over the wing and in the fuselage to record the variation of structural temperature versus time, based on the increased Mach number variation, altitude variation and outside air temperature variation.

Telemetering is the latest advancement in flight test. Through this means, it is possible for a corps of engineers to interpret a pilot's every move though they are stationed safely on the ground thousands of feet below the maneuvering plane. Forces and stresses that might escape the pilot's detection become apparent to this staff of experts.

And so the science of test flying has successfully stayed abreast of the technological improvements of the industry and may it ever be true. For, as can readily be appreciated, only by testing an aircraft completely can its true limitation be found and can it be delivered to its purchaser to serve safely the function for which it was designed.

William B. Bridgeman

QUICK DEMOBILIZATION was the understandable demand from servicemen and civilians alike in 1945. Huge quantities of war materiel, en route to theaters of operation throughout the world, were left on battlefields or on the way. Most aircraft not sent abroad went into airparks to be "mothballed" or sold for scrap. Never the counterpart of the W.W. I *Jenny*, T-6 trainers, above, were too expensive for private use, went instead into commercial use or foreign service training.

AIRCRAFT FIRMS DEMOBILIZE

Industry falters, then expands in commercial lines, rebuilds for Korean crisis

The postwar belligerency of the Communist world soon began to impart uneasiness to the free nations. In retrospect, demobilization by the Allies came to be called "hasty." From a wartime peak of two and a quarter million men and women, the U. S. Air Force shrank to less than one-fourth of this. Employment figures in the aviation manufacturing industry fell from 2,101,600 to 219,000 persons. Military appropriations dropped to 1.6 percent of the wartime average.

The depletion of trained personnel, both military and civilian, disrupted newly-undertaken research in jet and atomic power, each of which brought a host of new problems. Because all weapons, aircraft in particular, age rapidly, their scrappage cannot be considered a total loss, but the chief blunder in "hasty" demobilization was the curtailment of research at a time of keen technological competition with both friendly nations and potential foes.

Caught between the loss of contracts and inflationary costs, airframe makers who turned to other products suffered losses. They could not, in general, compete economically with the established manufacturers of other goods. The postwar boom in private flying became a bust. They persevered, however, charged off losses wherever possible, and were partially consoled by the thought that they had kept their plants and crews together. For most, it was late 1950 before their prospects brightened.

In commercial transport aviation rapid postwar expansion found major airlines vying with each other for new liners and competing with new companies for war surplus transports. A new class of competition, non-scheduled air carriers, arose, pooling their equipment, operating over well-travelled routes, and becoming the chief factor in the spread of air coach travel. This low-fare service, developed in 1948 by Capital Airlines and soon adopted by "non-skeds," became strong competitive feature of air travel.

FROM MOTHBALLS TO COMBAT in record time, these World War II *Mustangs* made epic journey to Korea aboard *U.S.S. Boxer* in July, 1950, helped stem advance of North Koreans.

IMPROVISED INSIGNIA for R.O.K. forces was made by painting an ancient emblem, the monad, over the U. S. star on the fuselage of this F-51 fighter when turned over to South Korean pilots.

FIRST LINE COMBAT AIRCRAFT were short-lived. From "cocooned" reserves came hundreds of *Mustang* fighters and B-29 bombers to be completely rebuilt by overhaul-supply companies such as Pacific Airmotive, Temco, Grand Central.

DONALD W. DOUGLAS paused only briefly to adjust to slackened postwar demand for military craft. He soon became largest competitor for war surplus planes of his own previous make with the Super DC-3, DC-4 *Skymaster*, DC-6 and DC-7 above, right. A leader in commercial aviation since 1933, when first DC appeared, Douglas had built 11,000 twin-engine transports by 1945.

The C-54's (DC-4's) represented 44% of the world's war surplus transports. Through refinement, the DC-4 became DC-6 (1946) and DC-7 (1953). Wing span stayed the same, but fuselages lengthened 15 feet, horsepower rose from 5600 to 13,000, and passenger capacity doubled. Speed was almost doubled. Above (l.) Douglas receives Legion of Merit from French Gen. Jacques Martin.

DIVERSIFICATION OF INTERESTS placed Northrop Aircraft Corp. in high-speed research field with the X-4; in jet research field with Northrop "turbodine." Oliver P. Echols, new Northrop chairman in 1949, furthered company through operation of engineer and mechanics school, launched into guided missiles, bought Radioplane Co., makers of target drones. He is shown, above r., and at left with Whitley Collins, president of Radioplane, discussing target plane. In rear is F-89 *Scorpion*, all-weather interceptor.

HOWARD HUGHES, long known for mighty undertakings, made his greatest in the flying boat, above. Actually airborne only once, it was controversial project for many years. Hughes also developed a huge helicopter, made airborne radar gunsight, search equipment for USAF.

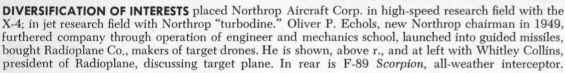

GLENN L. MARTIN'S company, oldest continuous maker of U. S. aircraft, persevered with long range naval patrol designs, made fast twin-engined feeder-line commercial transports, expanded to guided missiles. Maker of *Canberra* bomber (above with English pilots) as B-57 for USAF, Martin retired in 1952 after long career.

MODERN EMPHASIS on logistics of military transport brought Fairchild Airplane Corp. to develop cargo carriers *Packplane* and *Packet*. Latter, shown here in production, is versatile workhorse of U. S. and NATO forces, served in Berlin Airlift, Operation Haylift, and Korean War. It carries heavy load, lands on small fields.

YOUNG HELICOPTER DESIGNER Stanley Hiller, in plant at Palo Alto, Calif., made two-place *Model 360* 'copters for commerce, line patrol, fish scouting surveys, and crop dusting. Korean crisis brought them into use by Army. Production rate rose to three a week. One *360*, using its strong down-draft, harvested figs at an acre-per-minute rate. One of U.S.'s youngest designers, Hiller built first 'copter at 26.

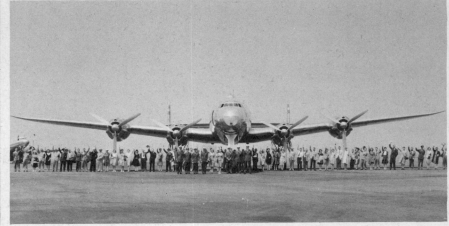

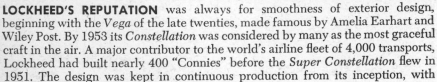

LOCKHEED'S REPUTATION was always for smoothness of exterior design, beginning with the *Vega* of the late twenties, made famous by Amelia Earhart and Wiley Post. By 1953 its *Constellation* was considered by many as the most graceful craft in the air. A major contributor to the world's airline fleet of 4,000 transports, Lockheed had built nearly 400 "Connies" before the *Super Constellation* flew in 1951. The design was kept in continuous production from its inception, with yearly increases in speed and range. The original load of the *Constellation*, above right, shows 57 passengers and a crew of nine; the *Super Constellation* carried up to 101 passengers. Most famous was the *Columbine* of President Eisenhower. Lockheed brothers began making flying boats in W. W. I, grew to a huge manufacturing concern in W. W. II. Above are pioneer employees at 40th Anniversary, B. R. Rodman, Allan Lockheed, President Robert Gross and John Northrop.

FAMOUS AS BUILDER of the wartime *Liberator* bomber, Consolidated-Vultee Aircraft Corp. tried postwar commercial field with a Model 240, a fast twin-engined feeder-line transport, shown on the assembly line above; 178 were sold to 14 different airlines and companies. Gen. Joseph T. McNarney, (l.), W. W. I squadron commander, succeeded Eisenhower as head of Occupation Forces in Germany in W. W. II, became postwar chief of Convair. With him is Reuben Fleet, founder of Consolidated in 1923. The company also built Navy's *Catalina* flying boats, some of which were still in service seventeen years after the design was first made. World's largest airplane, main instrument of Strategic Air Command in 1953, was Convair's B-36 intercontinental bomber, charged with making first air strike in event of war.

BELL AIRCRAFT CORP. made notable firsts in 40's and early 50's, produced first U.S. rocket plane to pass speed of sound, first helicopter to win Approved Type Certificate. The P-59 *Airacomet* used low powered jet engines, appeared in 1943. On Oct. 14, 1947, the X-1 high speed research plane broke sound barrier, and won Collier Trophy for Lawrence D. Bell. Model 47 helicopter obtained A.T.C. No. 1 in May, 1946. These utility helicopters attained everyday use as scouts for petroleum and power line crews, police work, crop dusting, fire fighting, air rescue. Larry Bell (r.), with one of over 10,000 war-built *Cobras* made for AAF and Russia (lend-lease), associated with Douglas, Martin during W. W. I, started own Buffalo plant in 1935; added at Ft. Worth, built more commercial helicopters in 1952 than all others.

BOEING BOMBER DESIGN stayed in the forefront with the world's first large swept-wing jet-powered airplane, the B-47, called a medium bomber. Later design was B-52, a scaled up B-47 (very large bomber class) for the Strategic Air Command. As speed rises, the problem of deceleration in landing becomes acute. Features of the B-47 shown here are the tandem landing gear, like a bicycle with outrigger wheels, under the engine pods and the parachute, to aid the brakes in stopping. Boeing began this line in 1935 when the first B-17 was built for long-range precision daylight bombing. This theme was the chief controversial point in the effectiveness of air power and was given its initial proof on August 17, 1942, when B-17 bombers struck at Rouen, France, deep in occupied territory. It culminated in the end of W. W. II with Boeing B-29 bombing raids over Japan. At center is Wellwood E. Beall, Vice-Pres. of Boeing, amid charts analyzing the corporation's activities, which include building double-decked *Stratofreighters*, (right), gas turbine research, in-flight refueling development. Boeing KC-97 tanker planes enabled strategic air forces to take off, fly part way, refuel in air, continue to their objective, greatly extending their range.

AIRCRAFT DESIGN advances required corresponding increase in power plant. Pratt and Whitney engine makers at East Hartford, Conn., put thousands of hours yearly into research. Most important result was increased life span of engines with horsepower many times that of a few years before. Types in manufacture included jet, turbo-propeller, and piston engines; later project was atomic power.

MAKERS OF F-86 "SABRE," North American Aviation, Inc. at Los Angeles by 1953 had produced more airplanes than any other company in the world. The T-6 Trainer, B-25 *Mitchell* bomber, and P-51 *Mustang* fighter all came from this plant. Production of P-51's rose to 22 per day during W. W. II. First F-86 was built soon after war ended, was continuously developed during postwar years and established a 14-to-1 kill ratio over Russian MIG's in Korea. Later model, the "D," shown at right is interceptor with all-weather equipment, radar, and rockets for armament, held world's speed record at 715 mph in mid-1953. It represented latest in automatic fire control wherein the pilot was guided by ground-based radar. At left are J. H. Kindelberger, N. A. chairman, and Gen. D. F. Stace, discussing acceptance of the 45,000th N.A.A. plane, an F-86E.

TACA INTERNATIONAL Airlines had a colorful and heroic history in bringing transportation to the world's most dangerous terrain. Beginning in Honduras in 1932, it grew to 3,469 miles from New Orleans and Mexico City to San Jose, Costa Rica, carried everything from butter to heavy machinery. Maintenance is strong point with TACA. Here airliner engines are overhauled at New Orleans base.

U.S. CORPORATE-OWNED AIRCRAFT grew to a record 9,500 in the postwar years, flew very few less miles than the scheduled airlines, a total of 442 million in one year. They were aided by overhaul supply companies like Pacific Airmotive Corp. of Burbank, offering service facilities. Business aircraft represented $175 million investment in 1953, annually spent $1 million for fuel and maintenance.

SHREWD MANAGEMENT, good facilities brought Temco, short for Texas Engineering and Manufacturing Corp., into picture as builder of sub-assemblies for major airframe concerns between 1946 and 1953. In 1947 they absorbed the Globe *Swift* production, obtained overhaul contracts for mothballed F-51's above, at beginning of Korean War. Temco made own fighter-trainer design for U.S. Air Force.

CRIPPLING LOSSES SUSTAINED by KLM during W.W. II left world's second oldest airline with almost no facilities and but three war surplus *Dakotas* (DC-3's). Since then, the headquarters have been rebuilt (above), the air fleet replaced by four-engine airliners and facilities reestablished at Schiphol, Amsterdam. Koninklijke Luchtvaart Maatschappi routes extend chiefly to the East Indies, first flown (1927) by U.S. businessman Van Lear Black on chartered trips.

CLIPPER "AMERICA," following the famous *China* Clipper by fifteen years, joined Pan American Airways on its West Coast-Hawaii route. In November, 1935, the *China Clipper* established the first leg of the airline's round-the-world route of 100,000 miles, by making the first commercial major ocean crossing (p. 121). In 1953, 234 U.S. flag aircraft carried 1.3 million passengers to and from the U.S., surpassing by more than 300,000 the number carried by ships.

MILITARY AIR TRANSPORT SERVICE, or MATS, merged AAF and Naval commands on July 1, 1948. Using their own planes and others borrowed from airlines, MATS put over Berlin and Korean Airlifts, runs scheduled world routes. Above, MATS C-54.

POSTWAR AIRLINES
U.S. and foreign air travel soars to record high

The most spectacular rise in a civil transportation medium the world had ever seen began with the cessation of hostilities in 1945. Even logistics of the military transport service, with routes flung around the world, could not equal the pent-up demand for passenger and cargo service. In three years domestic route mileage increased from 8,000 to 28,000 miles; 100,000 route miles were flown by U.S. flag carriers; passenger traffic showed increases of 15-25 percent each year.

Air freight came into its own. Starting from 15 million ton miles in 1946, it grew to 21 times that in 1953. (Even so it was but one-tenth of 1 percent of total U.S. freight movements, pointing the way to an almost endless expansion.) In merchandising, shipment of goods by air reduced packing, warehousing and mark-down losses, proved economical for many businesses.

Another postwar development was coach travel with its lower fares, made possible by "high density loading," i.e., increasing number of passengers, cutting crew members, etc. Pioneered by the major airlines in 1948, it was used largely by the non-scheduled lines, ultimately adopted even by trans-Atlantic carriers.

U.S. manufacturers supplied 90 percent of the new transport planes put into service between 1945 and 1953, all of piston-engined type. With all of the development work on jet engines, they were still not considered economically feasible for domestic airline use.

Financially speaking, air travel had moved up to an all-time high by 1949; at the same time deliveries of new planes, expansion of facilities and personnel brought record losses. But within two years most lines were operating in the black.

TRANSPOLAR COMMERCIAL flight became a reality in late-1952 when Scandinavian Airways System flew DC-6's over the Pole. Hjalmar Riiser-Larsen of Norway is shown with plane named for his Arctic achievements.

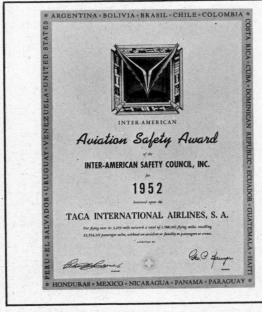

INTER-AMERICAN SAFETY AWARD went to TACA for 11th year of perfect safety, flying 22,554,121 passenger miles without accident. Western Hemisphere airlines set 1952 record of 0.38 fatalities per 100-million passenger miles to 0.43 for trains, 2.4 for autos.

MEALS HAVE BEEN INCLUDED as part of the fare aboard airliners since United Air Lines opened the first flight kitchen at its Oakland station in December of 1936. Keeping it hot or cold revolutionized food handling. View shows interior of British European Airways plane.

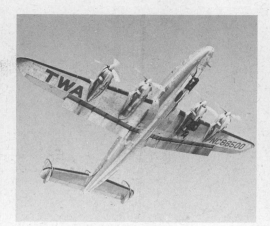

POSTWAR EXPANSION of Braniff-International Airways, the formerly transverse continental airline, extended route to Buenos Aires, later linked Chicago-So. Africa in 1 day.

COCKPIT INTERIOR of American Airlines DC-6 shows orderly array of instruments required in airliner operation. Constant research implemented flights' safety, reduced crew effort, and improved flying efficiency.

TRANS WORLD AIRLINES began overseas service Feb. 5, '46, spread to India same year. Direct U.S.-Rome line aided pilgrimage in Catholic Holy Year, 1950. It came of age in 1951, then second longest airline, 32,000 mi.

UNITED AIR LINES inaugurated *Stratocruiser* service from Hawaii to mainland in 1950 giving Honolulu direct link with 87 stateside cities.

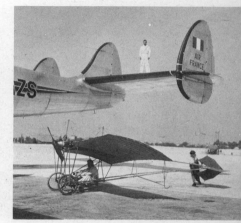

WARTIME FLYING TIGER personnel started cargo line in 1945, swiftly became a major freight carrier in U.S., operated over Los Angeles-New York mainline; flew Pacific airlift to Korea.

SLICK AIRWAYS, likewise using war surplus transports, moved into third place with Flying Tigers; operated scheduled domestic routes, hauled chartered freight on foreign routes.

TRANS-CANADA AIR LINES used Canadian version of Douglas DC-6 planes. Above, Lt. Gov. J. A. D. McCurdy of Nova Scotia points to photo of *Silver Dart* he made, 1909, when flying with Glenn Curtiss.

AIR FRANCE *Constellation* towers over replica of Santos Dumont *Demoiselle* of 1909. Nationalized Jan. '46, Air France's routes were to colonies, Middle East, West Africa.

NATIONAL AIRLINES inaugurated international route in 1946 with ceremonies at Tampa, Fla. Initial flight to Havana, Cuba, was commemorated with plaque, speeches by officials.

CHANGES IN CUSTOM were seen in Indo-China. These first hostesses of Air Viet-Nam opened new opportunities for Vietnamese women aboard DC-4 liners.

TRADITIONAL DRESS and modern mingle at Tokyo International Airport. Japan Air Lines Co., Ltd., operated DC-4 aircraft over Eastern routes to Philippines, China.

AIRWAYS INDIA used surplus *Dakotas* (DC-3) to aid flood and earthquake stricken areas, organized supply service. Cargos of food and medicines were flown in and inhabitants evacuated during crisis in job of outstanding public service.

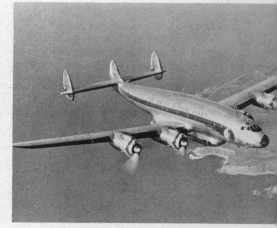

CENTRAL AIRLINES took delivery of Beechcraft *Bonanzas*, marking first time single engined aircraft were permitted for scheduled passenger service since the early '30's.

WESTERN AIRLINES, the nation's oldest, covered 13 states and Canada with 5,000 route miles, continued one of best airline records for safety and profitable operation. Above is Convair 240, replacing wartime equipment.

NORTH CENTRAL AIRLINES, formerly Wisconsin Central, christened new planes aided by President Fran Higgins, Lynn Mohr, TV's Tommy Bartlett.

EASTERN AIR LINES under Eddie Rickenbacker, made postwar replacement of its fleet with *Constellations* and Martin 404's. "Speedpak" under belly of *Constellation* was developed for cargo.

DE HAVILLAND "VAMPIRE" and its many variants have seen service in the forces of ten nations. Above is a group of F. B. Mk.6's, powered by the DH *Goblin* 3 jet of 3,300 lbs. thrust made under license in Switzerland. First *Vampire*, the DH-100, flew on Sept. 20, 1943, but none had seen combat by war's end.

ASSEMBLY LINE at the Vickers Armstrong plant at Surrey, England shows the new *Viscount* Type 701 in full production. These 40-48 passenger airliners were powered by four Rolls Royce *Dart* 504 turboprop engines and were the first aircraft with this type of power plant to go into scheduled flight operations.

DE HAVILLAND COMET was awarded its certificate of airworthiness, the first in the world to be awarded a turbojet-powered airliner, on Jan. 22, 1952. Delivery of the *Comets* to British Overseas Airways Corp. began in February, 1952, six months ahead of schedule. World's first scheduled jetliner service with *Comets* was inaugurated by B.O.A.C. on May 2, 1952, when a DH *Comet* Series II (above), powered by four Rolls Royce *Avon* engines, started from London on flight to Johannesburg, S. Africa.

BRITISH AVIATION
Comet jetliner marks new era of air transport

In the field of military aircraft production, postwar research emphasized high-speed aerodynamics to evolve airframes capable of handling the powerful gas turbine engine. At the same time, Britain's wartime lead in the development of gas turbines established her as the creator of some of the world's most powerful and efficient turbojet and turbopropeller engines. Continued production of the Gloster *Meteor* and De Havilland *Vampire* variants served to stock the RAF and Royal Navy's squadrons.

When the development of high performance planes reached the stage where sonic flight was safely attained (1948-to-1950 period), the Air Ministry embarked on a military production program which included seven super-priority jet-fighter types of the most advanced design: the Fairey *Gannet*, Hawker *Hunter*, Supermarine *Swift*, Gloster *Javelin*, Avro *Vulcan*, Handley Page *Victor* and the Vickers *Valiant*.

Use of the delta-wing configuration in many postwar experimental craft was so effective that two of the planes selected for production were of pure delta-wing design. The swept wings of the *Hunter* and *Swift* and powerful boost of the Rolls Royce *Avon* brought the world's speed record to Britain in September, 1953. However, the record was regained by America in the flight of the Douglas XF4D-1 *Skyray* at El Centro, Calif., on Oct. 3, 1953, when Lt. Comdr. J. B. Verdin flew an average of 753.4 mph.

Neville Duke's 723 mph on September 7 and Mike Lithgow's 737.3 mph on September 25 over the Libyan desert demonstrated the capabilities of two top British jet fighter planes.

In British transport aviation the *Comet*, barely five years from the original design stages, was in regularly scheduled service on B.O.A.C.'s routes to South Africa, India and the Far East. Vickers *Viscounts* and the new Bristol *Britannia* were pioneering turboprop airliner service. A revolution in air transport in one decade (1945-1955) would see British turbojet and turboprop airliners in service on every continent.

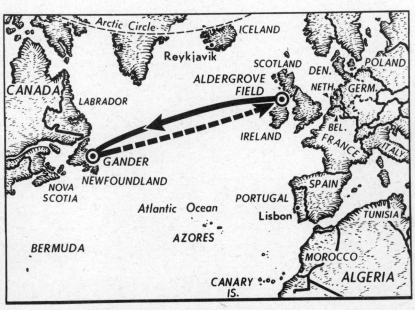

NEVILLE DUKE, English jet pilot, made headlines in 1953 with Hawker *Hunter* (p. 169), displaying skill on measured course, and other test flights.

ATLANTIC ROUND TRIP by an English twin-jet *Canberra* bomber on Aug. 26, 1952, set a new record for the east-west crossing and was the first time in history that a double crossing was made in one day by the same aircraft. Flight out from Aldergrove, Ireland, with W. C. Beaumont at the controls, took 4 hrs., 33 min. F. L. Hillwood made return in 3 hrs, 25 min.

FARNBOROUGH SHOW each September brings latest developments of British aviation industry to the public for display. Shown above is group of delta research craft at the 1951 event. Delta in foreground is Boulton P-111; behind is Avro 707-B.

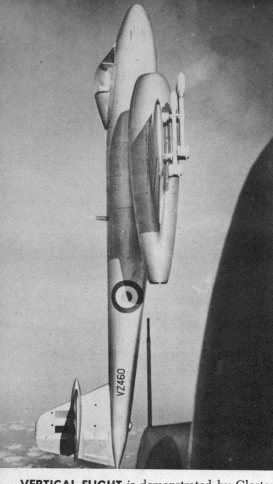

FAIREY GANNET AS Mk-1 of Royal Navy is powered by *Double Mamba* turboprop.

HAWKER P-1052 was ordered into top priority production for NATO air force.

CANBERRA B. Mk-2 bomber is powered by two Rolls Royce *Avon* turbojet engines.

SUPERMARINE SWIFT F. Mk-1 is like type ordered into top priority production.

VERTICAL FLIGHT is demonstrated by Gloster *Meteor* F Mk-8 fighter. Powered by two Rolls Royce *Derwent* turbojets, this plane was only Allied jet to see operational service in W.W. II.

WESTLAND WYVERN Naval fighter with Armstrong Siddeley *Python* turboprop first flew March 22, 1949.

GLOSTER JAVELIN GA-5 is world's first twin-engined, delta-wing fighter aircraft, first flew Nov. 26, 1951.

SONIC SPEED of the Hawker P-1067 *Hunter* was demonstrated on Sept. 7, 1953 when Neville Duke flew the *Avon*-powered fighter four times over 3-km. course at record speed of 727.6 mph.

ALL-WEATHER FIGHTER is the De Havilland DH 110 powered by two Rolls Royce *Avon* engines. On test since Sept. 26, 1951, this unusual craft had attained the design aim: satisfactory transonic characteristics in two-seat radar-equipped speedy plane.

WORLD'S LARGEST DELTA made its maiden flight on Aug. 30, 1952 from the Woodford Airfield of the A. V. Roe Co. Known as the Avro *Vulcan*, this huge jet bomber was ample demonstration of the faith placed in delta wing by British aircraft industry.

CRESCENT WING BOMBER, the Handley Page HP 80, made its first flight at Boscombe Down on Dec. 24, 1952. Powered by four *Sapphire* turbojets, the *Victor* was the world's first with a crescent wing and the most powerful then ordered by the RAF.

AVIATION INDUSTRY LEADERS gathered at Boscombe Down on Dec. 16, 1947, to witness the first public demonstrations of the Armstrong Whitworth AW-52 flying wing. Shown (left to right) are Mr. J. Lloyd (chief designer), Mr. T. O. M. Sopwith (Chairman, Hawker Siddeley Group), Sir Ben Lockspeiser (chief scientist, Ministry of Supply), and Mr. H. M. Woodhams (Director and Gen. Mgr. of Armstrong Whitworth). First flown on Nov. 13, 1947, this twin *Nene*-powered tailless monoplane was purely experimental.

BRITISH CRACKED THE SOUND BARRIER with the De Havilland DH-108 experimental jet-propelled tailless monoplane. First 108 flew on May 15, 1946, and second prototype was equipped with retractable wing slots to assess the high speed characteristics of the wing. This plane (TG306) carried Geoffrey R. DeHavilland to his death on Sept. 27, 1946, when it apparently disintegrated at or near the speed of sound. Geoffrey (above right) was the eldest son of the founder of the De Havilland Co. and was chief test pilot. The third DH-108 was No. VW-120 (above left) which set a 100-km closed-course record of 605.23 mph on April 12, 1948 with pilot John Derry flying. Derry exceeded speed of sound Sept. 16, 1948.

"SHOOTING STAR," the Lockheed F-80, was the first U.N. jet in Korea. Although it was the most outstanding fighter at start of hostilities and the first MIG killer, this 600-mph plane was replaced by faster, more potent *Sabre* jet.

HUGE CARGO PLANES like this C-119 *Flying Boxcar* were vital in maintaining U.N. troops in Korea with supplies and equipment. Another transport, the C-124 *Globemaster*, carried 50,000-lb. payload 3,300 miles, could fly 200 troops.

WOUNDED MARINES are transported to aid stations by a Sikorsky HO3S helicopter. For the first time, the "copter" played a major role in warfare, rescuing downed pilots, directing artillery fire, carrying riflemen to front line positions.

WAR IN KOREA

SABRE jets tally 14–1 kill ratio over MIGS, show superiority of U.S. planes

The Korean War became a testing ground for modern military aircraft when jets went into full-scale combat for the first time. Communists and United Nations countries at first withheld their latest developments, jockeying for position in the event the conflict exploded into an all-out war. But as the fighting progressed, innovations in air weapons came forth from both sides, disclosing tremendous technological advances over the most spectacular aircraft of World War II.

On June 25, 1950, the North Koreans, with the aid of Russian technical training and military supplies, attacked South Korea. Two days later President Truman, with United Nations' sanction, ordered U.S. combat units to the defense of South Korea. U.S. factories once more went into large-scale military plane production and the 150-planes output per month in 1950 increased to 1,000 per month by 1953.

At the beginning of hostilities, American planes went into combat from established U.S. bases in Japan. The *Invader*, a light bomber, and the lone jet fighter of the Fifth Air Force, the F-80 *Shooting Star*, were early entrants, along with such veterans of World War II fame as the *Superfortress*, and F-51 *Mustang* fighter.

These planes ruled the skies in Korea, but Communist ground forces continued to move ahead, capturing Seoul, the capital of South Korea, and pushing U.N. forces into a small area

in southeastern Korea near Pusan, the largest Korean port. However, the coordinated air superiority of U.N. forces soon paid off. Constant bombing disrupted Communist supply lines and stopped Red advances long enough to permit U.N. ground forces to regroup and expand the size of their forces while they increased their military supplies. Soon after General MacArthur's strategic Inchon landing, Sept. 15, 1950, the Reds were pushed out of South Korea.

THE "SABRE" JET was credited with 800 out of 1,000 MIG's destroyed. The North American F-86 F's, with a 14-to-one kill ratio over the MIG's, effectively protected U.N. bombers from Red jets.

When Intelligence reports indicated Russian MIG-15 fighters in Canton and Shanghai in July, 1950, the U.S. Air Force quietly shipped the 4th Interceptor Group, under command of Col. John C. Meyers, to Japan. This group was equipped with F-86A *Sabre* jet fighters, which held the world's speed record for fully equipped military aircraft, a flashing 670.98 mph. On December 22, 1950, *Sabres* shot down six MIGS, and the jet air war was under way. In 1951 an improved *Sabre*, the F86E appeared over the Korean battlefront and, in 1952, the F-86F came into use. Royal Canadian Air Force supplied planes in the "E" series and the *Avon Sabres* built in Australia were also based on the "E" series. The Aussies' 77th Fighter Squadron was equipped early in 1953 with the British Gloster *Meteor*.

U.N. jet fighters were largely responsible for the success of the propeller-driven bombers by ably defending them against MIG attacks. Pilots reported that the lighter-weight MIG could outclimb, outspeed and out-maneuver the *Sabre* above 30,000 feet. The *Sabre's* 16,000 lbs. as compared to the MIG's 12,000 was due to equipment designed for pilot safety as well as greater fuel capacity, superior gunsight and armament. The record of 801 MIGS destroyed to 58 *Sabres* after three years of war, would indicate the *Sabre's* superiority. The MIG may have flown better but the *Sabre* was a superior weapon.

"TWIN MUSTANG," the F-82G long-range fighter, was first to encounter and destroy a North Korean plane. Note pod between fuselages which houses its radar, electronic "eye" found on night fighters.

DREADED GASOLINE-JELLY mixture, napalm, replaced fuel in this Marine *Corsair* F4U-4 night fighter's auxiliary dropable tank. When the extra fuel was not needed, tank was filled with napalm and dropped as incendiary bomb, causing untold destruction.

MORE THAN 200,000 LBS. OF BOMBS were dropped on North Korean target in air raids. ▶ Strategic bombing of railroads, troop concentrations, power plants and dams allowed U.N. ground forces to at first hold off and then advance on an army many times its own numerical strength. A direct hit (right) near Seoul helped disrupt Chinese retreat after MacArthur's Inchon landing.

OUTSTANDING HEAVY BOMBER in Korea, as in W.W. II, was the Boeing B-29 *Superfortress*. Armed with 20-mm cannons and 50-calibre machine guns, its range was 4,000 miles, its bomb load, 20,000-lbs.

AIRCRAFT CARRIERS played an important role in Korean War because of maneuverability to within striking distance of anywhere on the peninsula. Above, from the deck of *USS Valley Forge*, a Douglas AD *Skyraider*, loaded with three 2,000-lb. bombs, takes off.

"BELLYING IN" for an emergency landing is a B-26 *Invader*, its hydraulic system damaged so that landing gear could not be fully lowered. This Douglas light bomber, with a maximum speed of 345 mph, range of 1,525 miles, 6,000 lb.-bomb load, was in Korea from the start of hostilities.

RUSSIAN FIGHTER LA-11   **GIANT TRANSPORT, TUPOLEV TU-70.**   **JET MODEL 150, SIMILAR TO U.S. B-47**   **JET GROUND ATTACK FIGHTER**

RUSSIAN PLANES

Russian aircraft developments in the post World War II era were shrouded in secrecy. Intelligence reports, however, indicated that the Reds were not lagging behind the U.S. in technological progress. They, too, were experimenting with rocket fighter aircraft at speeds up to 1700 miles per hour and altitudes of approximately 100,000 feet.

The successor to the MIG-15 of Korean War fame was the MIG-17, a twin engine jet fighter with top speed of about 650 mph, service ceiling 50,000 ft. It was designed for interception and all-weather operations. MIG designer, Mikoyan, also was credited with the development of the MIK-21, a twin-engine jet ground attack fighter with swept wings and tail. Russ equivalent to the U.S. B-47 was a tactical bomber known in the West as *Model 150*. Designed by former German Junker's design engineer, Dr. B. Baade, its speed was reported to be in the 650-mph class, service ceiling about 46,000 feet. Little was known about the 650-mph IL-28 medium jet bomber except that it could carry the A-bomb.

CAPTURED IL-10 "FLYING TANK"   **MIG-15 JET FIGHTER**   **TWIN-ENGINE MIG-17, MIG-15'S SUCCESSOR**   **LAVOCHKIN JET FIGHTER**

THE "SAVAGE," AJ-1 attack bomber powered by one jet and two piston type engines, was designed for high altitude missions from aircraft carriers. Its wings and horizontal tail surfaces could be folded for stowage below deck. Shown are North American-built *Savages* on USS *Midway*.

SIX JATO ROCKETS added to the normal 14,000 hp of this huge U.S. Navy transport, the 180-passenger Lockheed *Constitution*, reduced normal take-off distance approximately 25%. JATO rockets were used on carrier-based planes, enabled jet aircraft to take off successfully on the length of the flattops, a feat often otherwise impossible.

MILITARY PLANES
Jets with bigger bomb loads link sea-air, land-air fighting

By the time of the Korean Truce, July 27, 1953, the race between nations for supremacy in military air power had reached a peak. Keen competition during the Korean war had precipitated an era of rapid advances in military aircraft.

In warfare, the propeller-type plane had become obsolete except in specialized cases. At a maximum speed of around 400 mph, it could not compete with jet propulsion speeds of 600 mph and up. Straight wing jets, once so spectacular, were also quickly superseded by the faster, more efficient swept wings, which were better able to cope with supersonic forces. Fighters and bombers gained greater range with successful air-to-air refueling of jet planes.

With the advent of the atomic bomb, a fast interceptor became necessary for the defense of coastlines against bomber attack. The result was the development of a supersonic all-weather plane with powerful engines, rocket take-off and concentrated instantaneous firepower capable of destroying the largest bombers.

Among the most advanced military aircraft in existence at the 50th anniversary of powered flight were the B-52 *Stratofortress* heavy bomber; supersonic fighters, Air Force's F-100 *Super-Sabre;* Navy's delta-wing *Skyray*.

ATOMIC BOMB CARRIER, the 70,000 lb. Douglas A3D-1 was the largest carrier-based plane built as of December, 1952. In the 650-mph class, built for use on large carriers such as the 60,000-ton *Forrestal,* it was Navy's first swept-wing jet attack bomber.

MARTIN XB-51 was the first plane after World War II to be designed specifically for the destruction of military targets in cooperation with ground forces. The three-jet bomber is shown on its initial flight at Martin Airport, Baltimore, Maryland, during 1949.

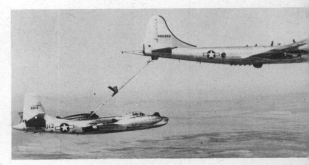

FIRST AIR-TO-AIR REFUELING of a U.S. jet bomber was accomplished when North American RB-45C *Tornado* took fuel from a Boeing KB-29P tanker using a "flying boom." The experimental "rendezvous" took place over the California desert early in 1951.

DUBBED "ABLE MABLE" by appreciative Navy men was the Martin AM-1 *Mauler* dive-torpedo-bomber. It is shown here with load carried April 8, 1949, when it flew at total weight of 29,332 lbs. and set a world's record for single-engine plane payload.

TWO NAVY "FURIES," the swept-wing FJ-2 and its predecessor, the FJ-1, fly in formation. Built by North American, the FJ-2 carrier-based fighter had many of the features of the *Sabre Jet,* was in the 650-mph class, with a range of 1,000 miles and 45,000 ft. ceiling.

TO THE BANSHEE goes credit for the first emergency pilot ejection in U.S. This twin-jet F2H-2 McDonnell fighter and reconnaissance plane was the highest flying (52,000 ft.) and the fastest (630 mph) Naval plane in the Korean War.

"SPEED: SUPERSONIC in level flight; service ceiling: 50,000 ft." was the performance record of the F-100A *Super Sabre*. A great technical step over the Korea-famed F-86 *Sabre*, the newer North American jet fighter made its first flight on May 25, 1953.

"PANTHERS" make a pass over *USS Princeton* in Korean waters. This Grumman F9F-2 was the first Navy jet plane in Korean combat. A 600-mph fighter, it was used to fly air patrols, armed reconnaissance, rocket, bombing and strafing missions.

F-84E "THUNDERJET," successor to Republic's famed W.W. II *Thunderbolt* was the Air Force's first jet fighter-bomber. Its speed was 630 mph, combat radius 1,000 miles. Here it carries clusters of 32 5-inch, high-velocity rockets it used in Korea.

STRATEGIC MOVEMENT of large numbers of troops and heavy equipment, such as tanks, bulldozers, trucks, made paramount the use of planes like this Boeing C-97 *Stratofreighter* in Korea. Here, a plane is stowed in the fuselage.

SUB HUNTER Lockheed P2V-5 *Neptune* was equipped with device in "stinger tail" for seeking out enemy submarines and carried rockets, depth bombs, and mines to destroy them.

NIGHT ESCORT for the USAF B-29 *Superfortresses* was the Navy's F3D-2 long-range jet fighter, the *Skyknight*(above). This Douglas plane was valuable also for reconnaissance duty. It was assigned both to carriers and to shore-based Marines in the Korean War and was used to patrol "Mig Alley" at night.

"STARFIRE," Lockheed's F-94C jet fighter-interceptor, was designed to guard U.S. air approaches from A-bomb attack.

PRIMARY MISSION of the Northrop F-89D *Scorpion* was protection against bomber attack. A single hit from one of the rockets blasted from this twin-jet, all-weather interceptor would destroy large bomber.

AVERAGE COST OF A FIGHTER in W.W. II was $58,000; in 1953, $233,000. Sharing the blame for this big increase were inflation, smaller orders and electronics for a superior airplane. The W. W. II *Mustang* (r.) weighed 9,650 lbs., carried six 50-calibre machine guns, flew at speed of 440 mph as compared with the 18,000 lbs., 24 2.75" rockets and 700-mph speed of the F-86D *Sabre* jet (l.) in the Korean theater.

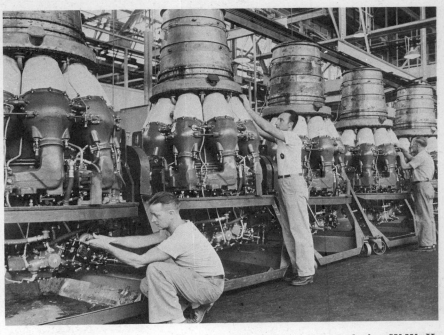

FASTEST DECADE IN HISTORY, 1940-50, was made possible by the successful development of the aircraft turbine power-plant, which almost completely revolutionized aviation. So universal was the military acceptance of the jet engine that all the newest combat warplanes in the early 50's were jet powered. Even commercial airlines planned to switch from internal combustion to jet engines within a few years. Although the world did not learn of it until after W.W. II, the German Heinkel Aircraft Co. produced the first flyable jet engine in 1939. At left are shown two General Electric J-47 jet engines installed on mammoth B-36 bomber. A later J-47 engine was reputed to develop nearly 6,000 pounds thrust. At right is Pratt and Whitney J-48 turbojet engine undergoing final inspection.

TECHNOLOGICAL ADVANCES

Research produces gas turbine power plant, new fuels, improved radar

Despite a half-century of unparalleled development and progress, aviation in 1953 presented as mystifying and stimulating a challenge to engineering enterprise and ingenuity as it did to Wilbur and Orville Wright in 1903. But while two men and a contraption called a flying machine made aeronautical history in those days, the vast corporations, thousands of machines, hundreds of thousands of men, and billions of dollars necessary for continuing the era started by the Wright Brothers clearly indicated that the similarity of the two periods was less practical than emotional. In 1953, the brain children of creative imagination were born in well-equipped and lavishly-outfitted research laboratories and huge industrial plants, not the backyard tool plexity greatly increased costs, it also brought

shed or garage of the Wright Brothers' era.

The astounding degree of technological progress in the field of aeronautics during and after World War II was reflected most vividly in the field of jet and rocket-powered guided missiles. Reaction-type engines had eclipsed for all time the old standbys: the steam engine, the steam turbine, and the gasoline engine. Under the stimulus of electronic developments, the perfection of guided missiles had progressed to where they incorporated the intelligence of a low-order automaton with a one-track mind able to hunt, track, intercept, and kill.

The translation of designs for high-performance missiles, aircraft, and rocket and jet engines from the drawing board to reality imposed a staggering load on production activities, for a nation's air power strength is measured not only in qualitative excellence but also by its ability to produce quantitatively. With the inauguration of heavy press programs in the United States and other countries, the aircraft industry took its biggest industrial step in history.

In addition to production machinery, aviation's phenomenal progress introduced many new materials whose adaptation created new burdens in the research and development of production processes. The introduction of many of these new materials was for the purpose of solving the high-temperature problems inherent in jet engines and supersonic airframes. The amazing growth of the plastics industry, spurred on by the needs of aviation, became one of the modern miracles of mid-century America.

The most intriguing aeronautical trend during the late 40's and early 50's was the acceptance of the delta-wing geometry as a basic design configuration for supersonic airframes. Pioneered in Germany during World War II by Lippisch, and developed to a workable aircraft by Convair in the postwar XF-92A, the delta configuration reached a current zenith in the sleek Avro 698, Britain's four-jet bomber. British enthusiasm for the delta was further demonstrated by unprecedented orders of the Gloster *Javelin* interceptor. In the United States, Convair and

Douglas had done the majority of delta research in the aircraft industry. The high-speed delta was prophesied as the last major aerodynamic design change before the eventual elimination of the pilot altogether and the accepted debut of guided missiles as synonymous with, and the champion of, modern air power.

Although modern technology and creative imagination were always coming up with something new and startling to upset all previous guesses and speculation, mid-century aviation was certain of one fact. The "sonic barrier," first officially shattered by the bullet-shaped X-1, was doomed to become a mere curio to the chroniclers of aeronautical history. Aircraft would become faster and faster and faster . . .

CONCENTRATED POWER of modern gas turbine powerplants is highlighted by this cutaway of the Pratt and Whitney J-42. The *Airacomet*, produced by the Bell Aircraft Corp., was the first airplane equipped with an American gas turbine powerplant.

FANTASTIC COMPLEXITY is shown by this photograph of the interior of the Douglas DC-6B cockpit. Although modern mechanical and electrical complexity greatly increased costs, it also brought about increased safety and greater comfort in air.

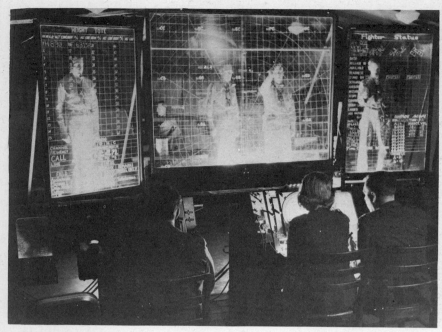

VAST RADAR NETWORK has been developed to protect American harbors, cities, and industry from surprise atomic air attack. The picture above shows training at the Aircraft Controllers School, Tyndall Air Force Base, Panama City, Florida. Huge plotting boards, in background, are used to track enemy aircraft.

WORLD'S LARGEST WIND TUNNEL is located at the Ames Aeronautical Laboratory, Moffett Field, San Francisco. This huge research apparatus is used to test low-speed flight characteristics of high-speed airplanes and large experimental supersonic models. The Republic F-84 is being "flown standing still."

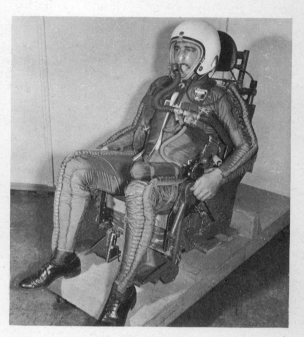

NEW EYES FOR TRANSPORT PILOTS are shown above in the form of a radar unit installed in the nose of a DC-3 transport. This wartime development gives the pilot "eyes" that can see 150 miles through darkness, fog, other obscuring weather conditions.

IMPORTANCE OF PETROLEUM to the advancement and maintenance of the aviation industry did not begin to be appreciated until World War II. Tons of high-grade aviation gasoline were required to keep Allied aircraft in the air, and the petroleum industry responded with unprecedented speed. The sea of gasoline required to maintain a successful war effort was provided. A Phillips Petroleum Co. refinery, located at Sweeny, Texas, is shown above. The alkylation units of the refinery are pictured at the left.

HIGH ALTITUDE PRESSURE SUIT provides airmen with protection in stratosphere flight. It is worn deflated and then inflates automatically when cabin pressurization is lost. It was developed by ARDC's Aero Medical Laboratory at Wright Field, Ohio.

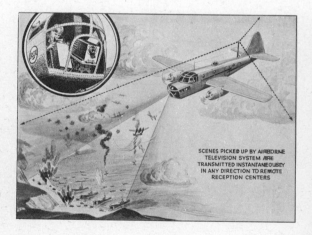

LOCKHEED QF-80 JET DRONE is shown in takeoff position at Indian Springs Air Force Base just before its flight through a radioactive cloud. The Dept. of Defense issued a statement that this flight was first use of jet drones in continental nuclear tests.

AIRBORNE TELEVISION CAMERA for wartime use was unveiled in 1953 by RCA. In addition to its military utility, RCA spokesmen foresaw the beginning of revolutionary television news coverage from cars, boats, planes and helicopters. Other uses included the replacing of test pilots in experimental supersonic aircraft, television sight for plane and marine navigation, and serving in factories as "eyes" to watch processes which might either be inaccessible or too dangerous for men. Thousands of the TV units were built by RCA for the armed forces. Special adaptations of this TV camera guided pilotless bombers, gliders, rocket projectiles, aerial bombs, missiles, and explosive-crammed crash boats.

WILLIAM P. LEAR holds the F-5 Automatic Pilot which makes possible the safe flying and landing of jet fighters in all kinds of weather. For the development and production of the F-5, enterprising William Lear received coveted Collier Trophy in 1949.

THE NEEDLE-NOSED "SKYROCKET" was equipped with both turbojet and rocket motors. In September, 1953, with Lt. Col. Marion E. Carl, USMC, at the controls, the *Skyrocket* attained the highest altitude (83,235 ft.) ever recorded by a piloted airplane. In the picture above, the swift *Skyrocket* has just been released from a B-29 mother plane. Three *Skyrockets* were built by Douglas for Navy, NACA.

NAVY'S AIR WEAPON, the Convair XF2Y-1 *Sea Dart*, was the world's first delta wing seaplane. With the development of the jet-powered sonic *Sea Dart*, the fighter plane re-entered the water-based field, an area from which it was conspicuously absent for many years. The *Sea Dart* was launched on San Diego Bay, December 16, 1952, and made its spectacular test flight on April 9, 1953.

WORLD'S SPEED RECORD was shattered by the Douglas-built F4D *Skyray* on October 3, 1953 when Navy Lt. Comdr. James B. Verdin piloted. the craft 753.4 miles per hour over California's Salton Sea.

DOUGLAS' "SKYSTREAK" was one of the earlier research aircraft developed for NACA's high-speed flight program. The extension of the NACA program called for the development of the *Skyrocket* and X-3.

THE FAMOUS X-1 made the first recorded flight beyond the "sonic barrier" on October 14, 1947, driven by a Reaction Motors rocket powerplant. The X-1 was put on display at Smithsonian Institution.

THE DESIGN THAT FAILED as a heavy bomber, the 213,000-pound Northrop *Flying Wing* is shown high over Southern California's desert. The USAF cancelled the project in favor of conventional types.

MOVABLE WING SWEEPBACK during flight is a unique feature of Bell's X-5. In the picture above, the wings have been moved to a rearward position which permits greater speeds at high altitudes.

SHAPE OF THE FUTURE is displayed by Convair's XF-92 delta wing research interceptor. Believed to be the prototype for Convair-built warplanes, the delta configuration has gained wide acceptance.

NORTHROP'S X-4 was the result of USAF's flight research program. Tested at Edwards Air Force Base, Calif., the X-4 was designed to explore flight characteristics existing in the high sub-sonic zone.

THE "FLYING PANCAKE" was a radical-type Navy fighter, designated the V-173 built to incorporate high and low speeds in the same plane. The airplane's speed ranged from 40 to 425 miles per hour.

A PARASITIC JET FIGHTER designed to be launched from a bomber during flight, the McDonnell XF-85 is powered by a J-34 Westinghouse jet engine. The little hornet-like fighter uses no landing gear.

176

PRIDE OF CANADA as aviation advanced was the magnificent aviation establishment of A. V. Roe Canada Ltd. Forming an integral part of Canada's aeronautical self-sufficiency, A. V. Roe came to be regarded as the center of gravity of the whole pattern, for within its boundaries were built the RCAF's latest jet fighter, the CF-100 *Canuck,* and the jet engine used to power it, the Avro *Orenda.* In the picture at left, the big fast all-weather jet interceptor is shown taking off from an RCAF field using jet-assisted take-off (JATO). The CF-100 was built to complement the F-86 *Sabre* as the RCAF's standard day fighter. At center is shown the Avro *Jetliner,* the first jet-propelled airliner built in the western hemisphere. The sleek *Jetliner* could carry fifty passengers at a cruising speed of better than 420 mph. Further development of the *Jetliner,* however, was postponed in favor of increased military activities. At right are shown the personnel and planes of Squadrons 427, 413 and 434 during departure ceremonies at RCAF Station, St. Hubert, prior to take-off for Zweibrucken, Germany. By successfully producing a jet transport, jet fighter, and turbojet engine, Canada took her place with the world leaders of, and contributors to, the Jet Age.

GROWTH OF AIR POWER IN CANADA, SWEDEN, FRANCE AND ITALY

CREAM OF AERONAUTICAL ACHIEVEMENTS in Europe often came from Sweden, whose progressive aircraft industry gave the Royal Swedish Air Force some of the finest airplanes in the world. In 1953, the RSAF could operate about half as many jet aircraft as the whole NATO Central European Command. Sweden's developments made her one of the best armed nations in the air. At left is shown the Stal *Dovern II* turbojet. Second from left is the delta winged Saab 210, an experimental design powered by an Armstrong Siddeley *Adder.* Second from right is the Saab 29, dubbed the "Flying Barrel." The standard jet interceptor of the RSAF, the Saab 29's top speed was in excess of 650 mph. Saab A-32 *Lance* (r.), a prototype all-weather fighter, has top speed of 700 mph.

AMERICAN DOLLARS were used to help France rebuild her air power. An encouraging sign that foreign financing was beginning to show results was the fact that in 1952, for the first time since W.W.II, French-built planes began to go into squadron service. At right is the *Mystere 4,* of the fighter series, built from Marcel Dassault's drawing boards in 1953, and leading contender to bolster French strength in the air. At left is the S.O. 9000 *Trident* research plane with two wingtip-mounted turbojets. With a rocket motor installed in the tail, the *Trident* was expected to attain a speed of Mach 1.6. Second from right is the SIPA 200, the world's first jet light private airplane. Second from left is the S.O. 4050 *Vautour* twin-jet, designed as night fighter and ground support plane.

DR. ERNST HEINKEL and son Karl take pictures at British air show. The famous aircraft designer awaited expected rebirth of German air industry.

THE ECONOMY AXE cut the props from under Australia's ambitious air-power build-up program. Australia's biggest program in 1953 was the manufacture of English Electric *Canberras.*

ONCE FAMED IN AERONAUTICS the world over for advanced thinking in aerodynamics and design, the resurgent Italian aviation industry was showing signs of rebirth. Above is the Fiat G-80, Italy's first jet trainer.

THE INFANT INDIAN aircraft industry was taking first steps to give India an air force. The picture above shows the final assembly hangar for British *Vampire* jet-propelled fighters.

AVIATION PIONEER Frank Coffyn makes his first flight in a helicopter. Under the tutelage of the Wright Brothers, Coffyn soloed in an airplane in 1910 after two-and-one-half hours of instruction. Serving as pilot for Coffyn's initial helicopter ride (above) is Stanley Hiller of Hiller Helicopters, Inc.

JET-POWERED HELICOPTER rises from the earth on its first test flight. With a rotor length of 125 feet, the Hughes XH-17 was one of the largest helicopters built in its time. Two mighty turbojet engines enabled this workhorse to lift and carry massive equipment such as artillery, bridge sections, and vehicles.

ANTI-TORQUE ROTORS mounted aft on the Bell HTL-4 Coast Guard helicopter provided a reaction to the torque of the main rotor. This type of device was usually employed by the Bell, Sikorsky, and Hiller helicopters while Piasecki and Kaman design used dual, contra-rotating rotors (bottom left photo).

HELICOPTERS

Widely used in Korea, rotating wing craft reach practical stage

RESCUE MISSIONS were one of the many duties of helicopters. Most navies used helicopters to pick up pilots from the ocean after a mishap. This U.S. Navy Piasecki HUP-2 has retrieved a fighter pilot after an aborted take-off from an aircraft carrier. Hovering ability made 'copter essential carrier equipment.

The ability to ascend vertically and hover in the air has been one of man's earliest visions. Even the versatile Leonardo da Vinci made sketches of a human powered aircraft with a vertically mounted airscrew. The period between the conception and ultimate fulfilment of the desire to mock the humming bird was hundreds of years because of the lack of a light and compact engine. When a suitable engine became available, the designers devoted their full attention to the inherent torque and stability problems.

Torque, the tendency of the helicopter air frame to rotate in a direction opposing that of the rotors, was counteracted in several ways. The earliest approach was a combination of two concentrically mounted coaxial rotors, the torque of one rotor cancelling that of the other. Or the two opposite rotating rotors may be centered in different positions such as the tandem arrangement of the Piasecki aircraft or the intermeshed arrangement of Kaman planes.

Successful construction of small reaction engines such as ram or pulse jet engines provided another method of eliminating torque. Mounting the jet engine on the rotor blade tip transmits only a small amount of torque caused by bearing friction to the fuselage.

The credit for flying the first practical man-carrying helicopter goes to German scientists. While others had raised themselves from the ground, their maximum height had not exceeded five feet. Dr. Heinrich Focke's Fw-61 made many notable flights just prior to World War II. It was flown in the Deutschland Hall in Berlin to show its stability and control.

However, helicopters of the United States furnished the impetus that has provided the world-wide acceptance of the helicopter. Much of the credit for this work was due Russian-born Igor Sikorsky. His first attempt to construct a helicopter in 1909 was unsuccessful. Just prior to World War II, he returned to this type of aircraft. The result was the VS-300, the first usable helicopter to be produced in America.

"FLYING BANANAS" illustrate one of the methods used to resist the rotating forces induced to the fuselage by the revolving rotors. The twin rotors of the Piasecki YH-21 turn in opposite directions, thus checking the torque of each. Helicopters may be classified by the means used to reduce torque.

TIP-MOUNTED PULSE jet engines supplied the power for the XA-5 *Top Sergeant* built by the American Helicopter Co. Lighter and simpler structure, as well as omission of torque problems, were the main advantages of this type of design. Loud noise was the principle drawback to the use of pulse jets.

FIRST TRANS-ATLANTIC helicopter flight was made by these Sikorsky H-19A's. To complement their long range, these Air Force helicopters could carry eight litters or ten pasengers. The commercial version, the S-55, was in wide use as mail transports and as personnel carriers for large business enterprises.

JACQUELINE AURIOL, daughter-in-law of the President of France, suffered near-fatal injuries in a plane crash, but recovered and went on to break the woman's speed record in a *Mystere* jet, 1952. Her helicopter instructor here is Richard Buyers.

RECORD-BREAKING flight story of Bill Odom in his Beech *Bonanza* is pictured graphically on the side of his low-wing metal monoplane. The cruising range of the private airplane was increased by the use of external fuel tanks mounted on wing tips.

HARMAN TROPHY is presented to Jacqueline Cochran by President Harry Truman for her wartime service in aviation. Miss Cochran, a foremost aviatrix of the first fifty years of aviation, served as an outstanding saleswoman of aviation to the public.

PRIVATE PLANES

Used in business and pleasure; 'mass market' is yet to come

The average man's desire to fly was greatly amplified by aviation's rapid advance during World War II. Heretofore unheard-of feats became routine as the result of necessity.

Many service-trained aviators, whose military flying had served only as an appetizer, returned to civilian life with the desire to continue flying, if only as a means of relaxation. Supplementing this large source of pilots were the thousands of veterans who acquired flight instruction under the GI Bill of Rights.

During this increase of pilots and aircraft, the number of air fields available to the private pilots was diminishing. Few airports could resist the real estate boom in view of the ups and downs of the aviation business.

After an initial boom, the market leveled, and only manufacturers with excellent management and products emerged. Many of the prewar private plane manufacturers could not make the grade and withdrew. Beech, Cessna, and Piper were left with the lion's share of the market for private aircraft.

Of the many companies that suspended production, the Ercoupe was the most interesting. With a simplified control system, their plane was directed entirely by the control wheel. It was an easy airplane to operate, but it appeared that the majority of pilots desired an airplane that required more skill to fly.

Though the flying "Model T" had not presented itself, the prediction was prevalent that when economic conditions should warrant it, a "flying machine" would be in every garage.

COMPANY-OWNED airplanes form the world's largest air fleet. The availability of surplus transports after the war, and their subsequent use, convinced many companies of their practicability. Here is the plushly equipped interior of a C-47 "Flying Office."

DEMONSTRATING the reliability of the modern day light planes, Woody Jongward and Bob Woodhouse broke the world's endurance record with the time of 1,124 hours in the air. They refueled the Aeronca *Sedan* by passing gas and oil from a moving auto.

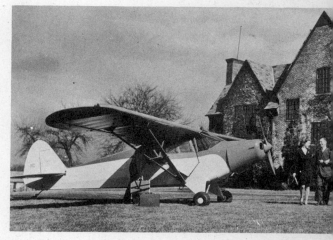

PERENNIAL LEADER of the light aircraft industry, Piper airplanes could be found almost anywhere in the world. The first airplane produced by this company flew in 1929 and, with the airplanes built by Aeronca, opened a new era for the light planes.

LIGHT PLANES provide a relatively cheap means of travel. Stable yet maneuverable enough to give the pilot the feel of flying, many different types of light planes have been built. Shown are Piper *Cubs*, a mid-wing Buhl *Pup*, and metal-skinned Luscombes.

REPUBLIC "SEABEE," produced by the builder of the memorable *Thunderbolt* fighter of World War II, introduced a four-place amphibian for the boom in postwar flight activities.

V-TAILED BEECH "BONANZA" was one reason that Beech Aircraft became a leading producer in the private plane field. Their earlier stagger-wing biplane was still used in 1953 as pleasure craft.

DELUXE PRIVATE AIRPLANE, the Ryan *Navion,* first flew in 1946 as a North American product. Ryan purchased all rights to the *Navion* in 1947 and continued producing until the Korean war when it ceased civil aircraft production.

CESSNA AIRCRAFT presented six new airplanes for the postwar flyer. Founded in 1927, Cessna had produced many popular types.

BLOCKADED BERLIN was a crucial focal point in the Cold War. The United States, through the use of air power, showed an ability to carry out its promises to the people of Berlin without precipitating global war. This Western countermove when Russia closed off all land routes to Berlin's Western Zones was probably the turning point in winning the allegiance and friendship of the West Germans. At left, an airport safety beacon stands incongruously among the graves in the cemetery beside Berlin's Tempelhof Airfield, where German buildup began in 1933. Over the ruins of their city, the airlift began Nov. 18, 1948, when planes like the Douglas C-54 above flew food from Fassberg in the British Zone to Tempelhof and Gatow fields over blockade. Weather made trips perilous.

AVIATION SERVES HUMANITY

Berlin airlift thwarts Russ blockade; hay-lift, spray dusting aid farmers

The United States recovered from its demobilization scramble following the end of World War II to discover that world peace was in fact far from reality. Instead, global strife continued in the guise of a new type of aggression commonly called the Cold War, and the "big stick" in the free world's arsenal became the USAF Strategic Air Command. Equipped with the atomic bomb, the U.S. array of high-flying aerial dreadnaughts was acknowledged during the late 1940's and early 1950's as the primary factor restraining the advent of a third World War.

On March 31, 1949, Winston Churchill publicly stated: "I cannot conceal from you the truth as I see it. It is certain that Europe would have been communized and London under bombardment some time ago but for the deterrent of the atomic bomb in the hands of the United States." This American predominance in strategic aerial might largely determined the free world's global strategy during the Cold War and was the most probable reason Soviet Russia resorted to its campaign of propaganda, infiltration, subversion, and promulgation of limited hostilities as in Korea, Indo-China and Malaya.

The decision that America first achieve strategic air dominance in the postwar military buildup undoubtedly saved the world for the time being from the terrors of World War III. The strategic air power of the U.S. upset the traditional weights and balances which Russia considered in her decision as to all-out war.

Before the advent of the air age and the theories of Mitchell, Seversky and Vandenberg, the dominant geopolitical influences could be channeled into either Mahan's sea-power doctrines or McKinder's land-power concepts. While Admiral Mahan believed that control and use of the sea was the primary pre-requisite for world power, finding his chief exponents in England and the United States, geographer McKinder thought that control over the largest mass of continuous land and population would guarantee world dominance for a nation.

McKinder's chief advocates were Imperial and Nazi Germany and Czarist and Soviet Russia. The two 20th century world conflicts demonstrated that sea supremacy had limited advantages when applied against land-based air power. Soviet Russia at the mid-century controlled most of the European-Asian continent; however, her power ebbed from its fullest tide and she hesitated to launch an all-out bid for world conquest.

The answer to this malfunctioning of traditional geopolitical axioms lay in the rise of a new kind of power created out of man's victory over the earth's atmosphere. Air power changed the equation and within a brief historical era, the

MANNA FROM THE SKIES feeds starving cattle in Nevada during the worst winter in 60 years. *Operation Haylift* provided an outstanding example of the integration of military air power to the needs of a desperate civilian community in time of peace.

warplane, particularly the atomic bomber, revolutionized military and political strategy.

America's military and political leaders envisioned that the chief hope for peace, inherent in strategic air power and a resultant aerial mastery over Communism, could be attained most successfully through a pattern of global air bases. Operating from airfields around the periphery of the Communist empire, the USAF Strategic Air Command helped "contain" Communism and achieved effective air supremacy of the world. Thus, in 1953, just 50 years after the Wright Brothers flew their "infernal contraption" over the sands of Kitty Hawk, both survival and victory were directly dependent upon a nation's success in the sky. The evolution of warfare, largely determined by the invention of weapons, had rapidly progressed during the half-century from the sea and land to the air.

But the genuine strength of strategic air dominance was not in death power but peace power. The slogan "Air Power is Peace Power" was not an empty gesture. The U.S. and the U.N. spearheaded the peaceful application of air power with programs like the Berlin Airlift, Operation Haylift, and Operation Magic Carpet. Operation Flit Gun consisted of modified C-46's equipped with huge bellows-type tanks spreading more than 100,000 gallons of DDT over large areas of Korea to kill millions of mosquitos and flies and thereby reduce disease and pestilence. A similar program was carried out in South America, Africa and Asia, where disease-ridden swamps and jungles—potentially rich agricultural and mineral land—could be reclaimed for crops.

The destructive potential of strategic air power, its ability to pulverize an enemy, was shown to be only one aspect of this titanic weapon. The peacetime application of air power was shown to be just as important and even more compatible with democratic objectives.

OPERATION MAGIC CARPET was a major American diplomatic triumph, restoring waning Western prestige throughout the Arab world. On "carpets" of Air Force transport planes, several thousand Moslem pilgrims, stranded in Lebanon because of lack of transportation, were airlifted to their sacred shrine at Mecca. This one gesture accomplished far more toward re-establishing friendly relationships with the Near East than money and propaganda could have done.

FLYING PARSONS in Central and South America found the airplane a useful instrument for spreading the gospel. Using small airplanes and landing strips cleared in the jungle, missionaries avoid the hazards of the trail, in addition to cutting time of their trips from months to hours. The missionary above, facing his airplane, is affiliated with the Missionary Aviation Fellowship. He has just landed his plane among the Chol Indians, deep in the jungle area of Mexico.

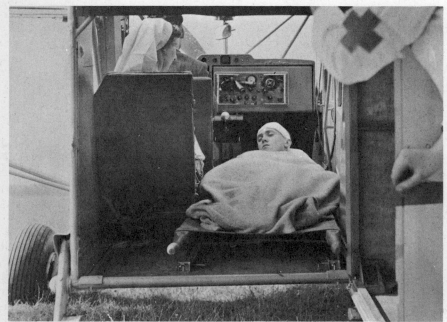

AIRCRAFT RESCUE WORK, mainly for the evacuation of sick and wounded, is an important humanitarian development of modern aviation. At left is the interior of an Auster ambulance-freighter, showing stretcher ramp and seat for attendant. At right, a Marine rescue team moves quickly to a waiting Bell Model

HTL-4 helicopter, its blades still swirling. These and other similar rescue craft were put into use in Korea. In addition to military operations, the airplane was applied in peacetime to such uses as traffic control, beach patrols, fire-fighting in mountain areas, aerial evacuation in stricken areas and crop dusting and seeding.

INTERNATIONAL CIVIL AVIATION Organization consisted of sixty member nations. With headquarters in Montreal, Canada, the Executive Council of this world organization met in virtually continuous session. The primary aim of the ICAO is the adoption of international standards and recommended practices and techniques which bring technical unity to the operation of expanding international civil aviation. The Executive Council of the ICAO is pictured above.

ADMIRAL BYRD'S FOURTH EXPEDITION to the South Pole and Little America during 1946-47 used six R4D's, launched from the deck of the aircraft carrier *Philippine Sea.* In the picture above, one of the R4D's comes in for a landing after a successful photo mapping flight. It is equipped with skis to make use of the snow-covered runways. Runway shown here is near the Byrd camp which was pitched on the shore of the famous Bay of Whales on the Ross Ice Shelf.

MODERN MILITARY GIANTS Thule Air Base was carved from the frozen wastes of Greenland with Denmark's help. Despite extreme weather, personnel, military supplies and equipment were flown in by air freighters such as the Douglas C-124 *Globemaster*, (foreground), and C-54 *Skymasters*, (background).

VITAL U.S. AIR BASES have been located in French Morocco. Through an agreement with General Franco, announced in October 1953, the United States received permission to build additional Spanish air fields, reinforcing the free world's air defenses in the Mediterranean area. From its bases in North Africa and Spain, the USAF could launch retaliatory air assaults against Russia.

BLACKBURN "BEVERLY" was one of Britain's largest air freighters. The big transport features an extremely interesting tailboom, unique among similar transports. Powered by four Bristol Centaurus engines, the 162-foot span freighter was produced for the Royal Air Force for cargo and troop carrying. Heavy equipment, like the bus shown above, could be loaded through the rear.

UNUSUAL XC-120 "PACK PLANE" built by Fairchild Aircraft Co. could release one cargo pod and pick up another. A modification of this pod, test-flown in 1952, was dubbed *Roadable Pack*, since it could be towed over secondary roads on truck-type wheels by a jeep or truck. With air freighters like the XC-120, and its "Flying Trailer" the U.S. might give logistic support to armies anywhere.

CONVAIR'S XC-99 was the world's largest land plane in 1953, capable of carrying 400 fully-equipped troops, or 100,000 pounds of cargo, or 300 litter patients with attendants. This huge transport had a top speed of more than 300 miles per hour and a maximum range of 8100 miles. Its six 3,000-horsepower engines, mounted in wings, developed as much horsepower as five locomotives.

BOEING'S C-97 *Stratofreighter*, in extensive use by the United States Air Force, was in quantity production at the Boeing plant in Renton, Washington, near Seattle. The big plane was interchangeable as a cargo carrier, troop transport, hospital ship, or aerial tanker. In conjunction with the Strategic Air Command's bombers, America's air transport fleet was a potent long-range striking force.

ONE GIANT SHRANK in comparison, when USAF's new heavy bomber, the B-36, parked alongside the veteran B-29 *Superfortress*, once the backbone of America's strategic air power. Although the B-29 had been considered the ultimate in strategic bombers, the B-36 atomic bomber pointed up the remarkable technological advancement in aeronautics in less than a decade after W.W. II.

AMERICA'S FOREMOST BOMBER for many years to come was prophesied for the B-52, successor to the B-36. Powered by eight Pratt and Whitney J-57 jet engines, the B-52 was first flown on April 15, 1952. The USAF demonstrated such confidence in the B-52 that it was literally ordered "off the drawing boards." Like its sister ship, the B-47 *Stratojet*, B-52 had a 35-degree angle wing sweep.

"U.S.S. FORRESTAL" type supercarriers bolstered America's strategic air might, their atomic bombers acting as long-range artillery to replace the 16-inch rifles of yesteryear's battleships. The ability of the United States to maintain powerful carrier task forces on the high seas, poised for instant retaliatory bombing attacks, was considered a strong argument against World War III, along with A-bombs.

CARRIER AT MIDNIGHT highlights the concentrated power of modern American warships. The dramatic photograph above shows a jet fighter, an F9F *Cougar*, just clearing the deck of the *U.S.S. Antietam* during one of the big carrier's training maneuvers in the Atlantic. The canted deck of this great aircraft carrier permitted simultaneous launching and landing of fighter planes.

CONVAIR'S B-60 was designed as an all-jet successor to the huge B-36. Flight tested on April 18, 1952, the giant B-60 was powered by eight Pratt and Whitney J-57 turbojets. The B-60 was 9 feet longer and 3 feet higher than the B-36, could fly faster and at higher altitudes, and carry a greater bomb load. Needle-nose appearance of the bomber originated from the use of a test boom, lent distinction.

FASTEST BOMBER IN THE WORLD was the distinction accorded the B-47 *Stratojet*, powered by six General Electric J-47 jet engines. In quantity production by Boeing, Douglas, and Lockheed, the speedy B-47 became the USAF's standard medium bomber. Since its first flight on December 17, 1947, the bomber was improved to the point where it could travel faster than many jet fighters.

RESEARCH VEHICLE FOR TOMORROW, DOUGLAS X-3 HYPERSONIC SPEED CRAFT USES HEAT-RESISTANT TITANIUM WINGS, TAKES OFF AND LANDS AT GREAT SPEEDS UNDER ITS OWN POWER

The Future

Active scientific research and interest of all age groups impel development of ships and equipment for the invasion of space

One of the more than one hundred German scientists who came to live and work in U.S. at the conclusion of World War II, Dr. Wernher von Braun is a leading authority on guided missiles. He played the principal role in development of Germany's V-1 and V-2 weapons at Peenemuende. He is now Chief of the Guided Missile Development Division, Redstone Arsenal, Huntsville, Ala.

THE ground work for guided missiles was laid during the first three decades of the 20th Century, when a few men with vision declared that it was possible to build rocket-propelled machines which could fly to the moon. Though man has not yet reached this ultimate goal, the first steps toward this ultimate goal have led to developments in the military field which no early rocket pioneer could foresee.

At the turn of the century, 35 years after Jules Vernes had published his novel, *From the Earth to the Moon* (wherein his heroes travel by cannon ball), Konstantin E. Ziolkowsky, a Russian schoolteacher, and Herman Ganswindt, a German lawyer, came up with the idea of using rocket power.

During World War I, an American physics professor, Robert H. Goddard, conducted experiments with a novel kind of powder rocket. He subsequently wrote a little booklet which, for the first time, proved in scientific terms the tremendous potentialities of rockets for upper atmosphere research. In 1923, another physics professor, the German Hermann Oberth, published the first scientific book offering proof of the feasibility of flights to other planets with rockets using liquid fuels.

While Oberth's book was being printed, Goddard was busy conducting some basic experiments with liquid-fuel rocket motors. In 1926, Goddard fired his first liquid-propelled rocket 184 feet.

The liquid-fuel rockets were simple affairs. Fuel tanks were pressurized with a tire pump, and they had no guidance system. The maximum altitude

DR. WERNHER VON BRAUN (C.)

reached by one of these rockets was 1200 feet.

In November, 1932, the author entered the services of the Ordnance Department of the German Army and continued his experiments at the Kummersdorf Army Proving Ground, 50 miles south of Berlin. Two years later he succeeded in firing two experimental A-2 liquid-fuel rockets to an altitude of 1.6 miles.

By 1936, the success of the work at Kummersdorf led the German Army and Luftwaffe to join forces in setting up a vast Guided Missile Center at Peenemuende on the Baltic Sea. Shortly before the outbreak of World War II, several A-5 rockets were successfully launched at this station. The A-5 was equipped with a guidance system employing gyroscopes, servo motors and graphite vanes im-

mersed in the rocket jet. These missiles, strictly experimental designs, reached altitudes of about eight miles when fired straight up.

The A-5 led the way to the A-4 missile, which later became famous as the V-2. The first V-2 was successfully launched on October 3, 1942. Quantity production began in 1943, and on September 7, the first V-2 was operationally fired at London, over a range slightly exceeding 200 miles. About 100 V-2's were shipped to the U.S. after the war and served as test equipment carriers for an extended upper atmosphere research program at White Sands Proving Ground, New Mexico.

In the postwar era, guided missiles rapidly became an important segment of the defense programs of all major powers. The threat posed by atomic bombs and high-flying jet bombers triggered the development of radar-guided anti-aircraft missiles. The potentialities of such missiles, in turn, led to the need for long-range guided missiles immune to interception by anti-aircraft missiles. The performance of such long-range missiles is rapidly approaching the point where it will be possible to fire a missile into an orbit wherein it would permanently circle the earth without any application of power. The next logical step would be the establishment of a permanent and inhabited space station in an orbit which would offer tremendous potentialities in the fields of science and global reconnaissance. Ultimately, such an "artificial satellite" could serve as a jumping-off station for trips into space. Rockets may finally do what the early pioneers thought they could: carry a group of explorers to the moon or one of the nearer planets.

Wernher von Braun

AUTHOR WILLY LEY

BEFORE making any technological prediction of "things to come," based on available knowledge and existing facts, let us imagine what seers might have predicted for the second quarter-century of powered flight based on developments up to 1928. The prognosticator could have foreseen that airplanes would grow to a carrying capacity of 100 passengers. He could have prophesied sufficient range for profitable transatlantic operation. He might have envisioned cruising speeds between 250 and 300 miles per hour, and probably would have predicted flight at high altitudes to avoid most weather phenomena.

Author, lecturer, rocket expert Willy Ley has been a leader in interpreting to the public development of guided missiles. He wrote the first scientific book about space travel in 1926, in his native Germany. In 1927, Ley formed with Hermann Oberth the Society for Space Travel and built many rockets. In 1935 he came to America and is presently Technical Consultant to the United States Department of Commerce.

Barring unexpected developments, as the jet engine proved to be, the third quarter-century of powered flight, seen from the end of the second, could be described by one observer as follows:

For short distances in densely settled areas, like the East Coast from Boston, Massachusetts to Norfolk, Virginia, and the West Coast between San Francisco and San Diego, the "helibus" is likely to become important. This would be a large helicopter for rapid commuter service. It may carry as many as 120 passengers and have a ground speed of as much as 150 miles per hour. It may be used for distances up to about 150 miles, its relatively low speed being unimportant as compared to the advantage of going directly into the central areas of the cities on the route.

Traveling ranges between 150 and 600 miles will probably remain the domain of airplanes as we know them, with refinements, of course. Distances of more than 600 miles will be the realm of the turbojet plane, developments of the *Comet* and

jet bombers. In addition to the turbojets needed for take-off and landing, ramjet engines may be employed for cruising, in spite of engineers' strong and justified tendency to shy away from airplanes with more than one type of engine.

Traveling ranges of more than 1,000 miles may well be served by passenger-carrying rockets capable of climbing at a steep angle and traveling most of the distance in the near-vacuum of the upper stratosphere to avoid heating by air resistance. The atmosphere between 12 and 25 miles altitude will stay virtually untraveled; beyond 12 miles altitude the air is too thin for turbojets and ramjets to "breathe" but still too dense for rockets to move horizontally at high speeds.

It is possible that, 25 years from now, some airplane types will have atomic power plants and unlimited range. Their external shapes, necessarily large, may resemble flying boats.

If developments continue and huge costs are sustained, a station in space may be established even before 1978, moving around the earth as an artificial satellite more than 1,000 miles above sea level.

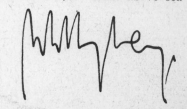

BATTERIES OF SUPERSONIC anti-aircraft guided missiles have gone into full-scale production. The *Nike*, shown above, is designed to protect strategic U.S. targets from enemy atomic air attack. Controlled from the ground by automatic computers, the rocket-powered *Nike* is equipped with the latest type warheads.

TWO-STAGE ROCKET reached 250 miles at White Sands, N.M., Feb. 25, 1949. The German V-2 carried a smaller WAC *Corporal* in nose to be fired 20 miles above earth. WAC missile reached record height, but steel fins were fused by heat generated by air resistance. Heat is major barrier to man's space travel.

ROCKETS AND MISSILES

Building of space ships capable of going to moon becomes a possibility

For centuries man had dreamed of voyaging to other planets. The first known interplanetary story was written in the second century, A.D., with propulsion to the moon via waterspout. Later writers envisioned trained swans, boats, guns, and even ram-jets as vehicles for their imaginary trips to the moon and other planets.

The invention of the rocket by the Chinese about 1200 A.D. provided the ultimate means of interplanetary propulsion. The rocket became the popular fictional motive force, and then appeared to be the actual motive power that might be used on the first attempts at space flight. The rocket works in a vacuum, and final speed of the rocket depends upon fuel weight ejected. In little more than 40 years Dr. Robert Goddard in the United States, and other men in Germany had turned the rocket from an unstable, erratic device into a controllable machine, developing

KIDS DRAG PARENTS to registration booth in Detroit, Mich., when $35,000, 35 foot model of TV's "Space Patrol" ship is attraction. Children had already preceded scientists in conquest of outer space.

tremendous thrust for its size and weight. With the advent of World War II, the rocket was ready for use as a destructive airborne weapon.

By mid-century, the sciences of propulsion and space travel had progressed to the point where Dr. Wernher Von Braun, Willy Ley and others had visualized man's first timid steps into vast reaches of outer space—destination moon.

The first problem was to escape the huge gravitational pull of the earth. An "escape velocity" of 17,500 mph was needed. Speeds less than this would exhaust rocket fuel before the rocket had reached the region of minor gravitational pull. Once this velocity was reached, the rocket could "coast" the remainder of its flight.

This vehicle would be a three-stage rocket, whose payload was a small rocket, fired after the first two stages had attained maximum velocity and been dropped. To project 36 tons of men and cargo into orbit would require a 7,000 ton, 265 ft. rocket, about the size of a light cruiser. The third stage would orbit about the earth, at an altitude of 1,075 miles. From this tiny, man-made satellite, scientific researchers would be able to observe the universe and carry on their experiments in space.

The second problem was the construction of a wayside station in the orbit. This man-made laboratory (p. 188), carried piece by piece into space by rocket ships, would circle the globe at 15,480 mph. It would serve as an assembly point for the actual space ship that would make the moon trip. Since the lunar ship would be assembled in zero gravity, and would experience only the weak, lunar gravity fields, it would be made of light, fragile materials, such as aluminum and plastic, and powered with a small rocket motor. Leaving the space station with a short rocket blast, it would coast to the orbit of the moon, meeting and passing directly around that planet, and then "falling" back to the space station. That eternal mystery, the unseen face of the moon would have been in full view during

the trip. Upon return of the lunar ship to the orbit of the space station, a second blast of the rocket motor would bring the ship to a halt near its departure point, completing the travel cycle.

Thus the first flight to the moon was envisioned. The feeling of many missile men was that such an undertaking would be premature, and end in failure; that the best way to achieve space flight was evolution of the current missile program, step by step. An evaluation for or against Dr. Von Braun's daring proposal would be made on the highest political and scientific levels, and most likely no public announcement of the final decision would be made.

The air age of the future lay in the atomic age already here. The earth had shrunk, its stratosphere had been touched and needed only to be invaded. Scientists of all nations worked toward that end, while the military waited.

SPACE SNOB pictured by "Punch" magazine, hints at problems of space traveller. Air Force believed rockets could navigate space, but were not sure human bodies or nervous systems could stand trip.

NAVY VIKING MISSILE launched from tender *Norton Sound* off Christmas Island, May 11, 1950 set new altitude record for single stage rocket of 106.4 miles. This research missile was prototype of future ship-to-shore weapons. With atomic warhead, missile of this type could raze enemy coastal city.

REGULUS MISSILE spouts cloud of smoke in flight launching from *Norton Sound*. The 30-foot craft, resembling conventional swept-wing jet fighters, could be launched from several type vessels, including a submarine. A recoverable version had a landing gear instead of a warhead, was used for training and test purposes.

RAM-JET MISSILE installed in 6'x 8' supersonic wind tunnel at Lewis Flight Laboratory of NACA, for purpose of evaluating flight maneuvering attitudes on jet engine inlet characteristics, underwent a prolonged series of tests. Supersonic wind tunnels were essential for many aircraft factories.

BRITISH SUPERSONIC ROCKET is fitted to the launcher in specially designed bay of *Mosquito* bomber. Released over the Atlantic at 36,000 ft., rocket was designed to record aerodynamic data and to telemeter the information to the ground observers during its brief two minute test flight.

FIRST OPERATIONAL MISSILE was the Martin B-61 *Matador*, shown at Caribbean facilities of USAF Missile Test Center, Cocoa, Fla. It was to be used by First Pilotless Bomber Squadron. *Matador* was boosted into air from moveable ramp by an auxiliary rocket, which was dropped after take-off when turbojet engine started.

PIONEER ROCKETEER Dr. Robert H. Goddard loads early model rocket-propelled *Bazooka* on Mount Wilson, Calif. during early summer of 1918. His book, "A Method of Reaching Extreme Altitudes," published in 1919 opened era of rocket research. Goddard died in 1945.

MOBILE LAUNCHING PLATFORM on railway flatcar was used for Nazi V-2 guided missile, fired upon England and Belgium during 1944-45. 100 captured V-2's were brought to U.S. and 70 were fired experimentally at White Sands Proving Grounds, in New Mexico.

RADAR TELESCOPE picked up radiations from distant galaxies to help man solve mystery of universe. Giant antenna transmits pulses to be reflected by moon and nearby planets for studies of interplanetary flight problems.

RYAN FIREBIRD air-to-air missile shown under wing of F-82 twin *Mustang* fighter. Rocket driven missile was designed to "home in" on moving target and explode upon contact. Guidance was by means of miniaturized radar navigational system carried in nose.

SWEPT WING EXPERIMENTAL craft was tested at Ames Laboratory, Moffett Field, Calif. Test wings were mounted on streamlined bodies to be dropped from high altitudes. Recording instruments inside fuselage provided data of fast plunge to earth.

◀ **AERODYNAMIC HEATING TESTS** were run on research rocket at NACA Research Station, Wallops Island, Va. Magnesium body, 14 ft. long was launched by twin booster rocket, which fell off at burn-out. Missile motor then ignited, producing top speed of 2,600 mph. Cameras and telemetering record flight.

MAN'S FIRST FLIGHT with ram-jet power, in early 1950, was made in a Lockheed F-80 *Shooting Star* with two ram-jet engines, one mounted on each wing tip. The 20-in. diameter engines were produced by Marquardt Aircraft Co. Plane reached operational height with jet engine, which was turned off for tests.

MONKEY SPACE TRAVELER was rocketed forty miles into space in missile. Airman 2C M. V. Ross (Lovett, Texas), left, and Erich Gienapp (Yellow Springs, O.) observe simian passenger in his cabin. Recorded results of these experiments gave information about human reactions to zero-gravity flight.

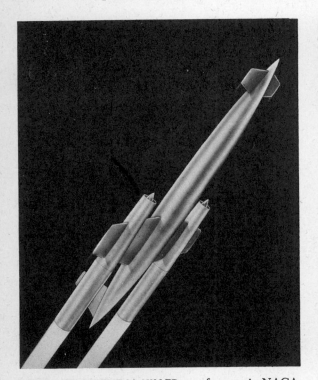

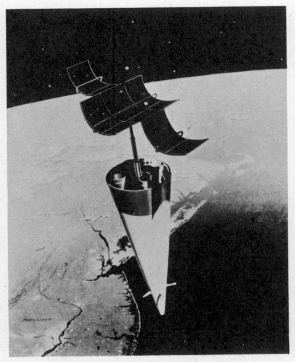

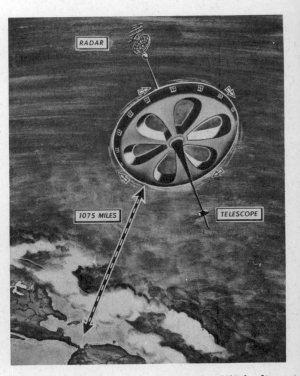

INTERCONTINENTAL KILLER was foreseen in NACA model of twin ram-jet guided missile of future. Flying through stratosphere at supersonic speed, guided by radio or celestial navigation, missile could deliver atomic payload to target halfway 'round the earth. Because of its high speed, defense against such a missile was thought to be practically impossible.

ROBOT SPACE STATION was dream of Dr. Werner von Braun, famous rocket authority. Station would be shot into 200-mile orbit about earth, travelling at 17,200 mph. It would contain three monkeys living in air conditioned cabin, and telemetering and television equipment to relay reactions of monkeys and equipment operation to observers on earth.

ULTIMATE DREAM of von Braun was 250 ft. diameter space station, orbiting 1,075 miles above earth in 2 hr. period. Three stage shuttle rockets would supply materials for station and provisions for crew. Scientific and political advantages of station would dwarf estimated cost of 4 billion dollars. Practical missile men were dubious of success of project.

The World's Outstanding Aeronautical Collections and Libraries

Compiled for YEAR'S PICTORIAL HISTORY OF FLIGHT by the Rev. John F. B. Carruthers, M.A., D.D., Chairman of the Institute of Aeronautical History Library, Claremont Men's College, Claremont, California, and Historian and Librarian of the National Aeronautics Association of the United States.

Library of Congress, Aeronautics Division, Washington, D.C. *Most complete collection in the world. Includes Tissander Tissandier's 18th Century rarissima and many others.*

Smithsonian Reference Library and Photographic Collection, National Air Museum, Washington, D.C. Paul Garber, Head Curator. *Extensive collection of aeronautical pictures, well-indexed.*

National Aeronautics Association Collection, on loan to Institute of the Aeronautical Sciences Library, New York City.

Institute of the Aeronautical Sciences, New York and Los Angeles. S. Paul Johnston, Director; John Glennon, Librarian. *Contains collections of Bella Landauer, William A. M. Burden, Paul Kollsman, Ernest W. Robischom and Sherman Fairchild Collection of aviation photographs.*

Huntington Library, San Marino, California. *Rich on history of early balloons. Includes Maggs Collection of 1923.*

U.S. Air Force Library, Maxwell Field, Alabama. Compiled by Col. Ernest Jones.

James Carruthers Memorial Collection, Institute of the Aeronautical History Library, Claremont Men's College, Claremont, California. *Donated by Rev. and Mrs. John F. B. Carruthers.*

Army Medical Library, Washington, D. C.

Gimbel Collection in association with Yale University, New Haven, Conn. *Strong on rare museum material.*

Harvard Library, Cambridge, Mass. *Includes Rotch and Weidner Library.*

Vail Collection at Massachusetts Institute of Technology, Cambridge, Mass. *Includes historic rarissima exclusive of the Engineering Library.*

Norwich University, Northfield, Vermont. *Endowed by Godfrey Cabot, strong on commercial aviation.*

New York Public Library, New York City. *Possibly the most complete of all city libraries on subject of aeronautics.*

Seattle Public Library, Seattle, Wash. *One of the largest public library collections on aeronautica, assisted by Boeing Airplane Co.*

Jefferson Memorial and St. Louis Public Library, St. Louis, Mo. *Contains contributions of Charles A. Lindbergh and others.*

Los Angeles Public Library, Los Angeles, Calif. *Excellent technological material and complete serials of aviation publications.*

University of Michigan Library, Ann Arbor, Mich. *Rich in aeronautical history items.*

New York University Library, New York City. *Excellent air law reference collection gathered by Dean Reppy and Alexander Klemin.*

San Francisco Public Library, San Francisco, Calif. *Most complete collection of propaganda leaflets dropped by air during the war.*

Hopkinson Library of Transportation and Hoover Library, Stanford Univ., Palo Alto, Calif.

University of California Libraries, at Los Angeles, and at Berkeley, *Emphasis on engineering and aerodynamics.*

U.S. Navy and Marine Library, Washington D. C. *Strong coverage of sea plane developments.*

Crerar Library, Chicago, Ill. *Mechanical art of flight and ephemera.*

Field Museum, Chicago, Ill. *Particularly rich in pre-history aviation data.*

Institute of Aeronautics Library, University of Illinois, Champaign, Ill. Leslie Bryan, Director.

Gillette Collection of the Brookins-Lahm-Wright Aeronautical Foundation, Burbank, Calif.

Royal Aero Club of England Library, London, England. *Strongest on books and prints; includes Cuthbert-Hodgson print collection.*

Aero Club of France Library, Paris, France. *Combined with Federation Aeronautique Internationale, Center of International Aeronautical Documentation, supported originally by Guggenheim Foundation.*

Bibliotheque Nationale, Paris, France. *Generally considered finest collection of rare prints and aeronautica in the world.*

Museum of the Air, Meudon, France. Charles Dollfus, Curator. *Most complete coverage of French aeronautica.*

Ellis Archives, Vancouver, B. C., Canada.

DaVinci Museum, Milan, Italy.

Caproni Museum, Rome, Italy.

Science Museum, Kensington, London, Eng.

Science Museum, Munich, Germany.

In addition to the above listed sources, most universities, aircraft manufacturers, airlines and aviation publications have libraries and collections on aeronautical subjects. Extensive aeronautical collections also exist in Argentina, Brazil, India, Japan, Russia, Spain and Holland.

INDEX

ERRATA

P. 11, bot.—"wearing winged sandals" should read "wielding a curved sword"; p. 13, bot.—"flight" should read "fight"; p. 20, bot.—"August 18, 1897" should read "October 12, 1897"; p. 28, mid.—"hobbled uncontrolled on its test run August 18, 1897, and crashed, ending Ader's dream of being the first to construct and fly a practical airplane" should read "succeeded several times in leaving the ground on its test run on October 12, 1897, but crashed two days later when a wing was damaged by wind"; p. 29, mid.—"*Aerodome No. 5*" should read "*Aerodrome No. 5*"; p. 30—"King George V" should read "King Edward VII"; p. 35, bot.—"Griffiths" should read "Griffith"; p. 59, bot.—"Wilbur Wright" should read "Orville Wright"; p. 64, bot.—"Volmoller" should read "Vollmoller"; p. 65, bot.—"Roy Knabenshue" should read "Philip O. Parmalee"; p. 68, top—"later type French Farman" should read "British F.E.2"; p. 69, mid.—"Lt. Loulois" should read "Lt. Foulois"; p. 91, mid.—"Bell Aircraft in 1939" should read "Bell Aircraft in 1935"; p. 100, bot.—"Douglas torpedo" should read "Curtiss R-6"; p. 104, mid.—"Boeing B-40A" should read "Boeing 40-B4"; p. 105, mid.—"Count Igor Sikorsky" should read "Ivan Igor Sikorsky"; bot.—"first airliner of the Imperial Airways" should read "early airliner of the Imperial Airways"; p. 108, mid.—date of Ellsworth and Balchen flight should read "1930", not "1929"; p. 113, mid.—"crew of the Russian built seaplane" should read "Russian crew of the ANT landplane"; p. 116, mid.—"baby daughter" should read "baby son"; p. 123, mid.—"Lockheed 10" should read "Lockheed 12"; p. 128, top—"Sikorsky produced first commercially useful helicopter, VS-300, (above), 1940" should read "Sikorsky, who produced the VS-300 (above) in 1940, led helicopter manufacture"; p. 137, bot.—"British Blenheim" should read "British Anson"; p. 139, mid.—"Feisler" should read "Fieseler"; bot.—"Gloster SS-9" should read "SS-19"; p. 144, top—"He-111H" should read "He-111K"; p. 145, bot.—"JU-388K" should read "JU-88K"; p. 157, top—"End of CV" should read "Near end"; "burning and sinking" should read "burning and listing"; p. 158, bot.—"Vultee" should read "Consolidated"; p. 163, top—"DC-6" should read "DC-6B"; bot.—"built first 'copter at 26" should read "built first 'copter at 19"; p. 169, top—"Hawker P.1052 was ordered into top priority production for NATO air force." should read "Hawker P.1052 was developed from the Hawker *Sea Hawk*, a Navy fighter."; p. 170, mid.—"Sikorsky HO3S" should read "Bell HTL-4"; p. 173, bot.—"F-86D *Sabre Jet* (l.) in the Korean theatre" should read just "F-86D *Sabre Jet* (l.)"; p. 178, top—"Anti-torque rotors" should read "Anti-torque rotor"; bot.—"Flying Bananas" should read "Flying Banana"; p. 185—"Dr. Wernher von Braun" not included in top picture.

SOURCES OF PICTURES

The following list credits the source of each picture used in YEAR's Pictorial History of FLIGHT. Credits are listed picture by picture for each page—left to right, top to bottom. Each picture starting a new row horizontally across a page is preceded by a dash (—); each picture following on the same line is preceded by a comma (,).

Names of cities in parentheses indicate the city of the original picture source.

Picture sources that appear quite frequently have been abbreviated as follows to conserve space:

BB—*Brown Bros. (N.Y.C.);* **Bett. Arch.** *Bettman Archives (N.Y.C.);* **Culver**—*Culver Service (New York City);* **Dept. Def.**—*Department of Defense (Washington, D.C.);* **FPG**—*Free Lance Photographers Guild (N.Y.C.);* **Fairchild Coll.**—*Sherman K. Fairchild Collection at Institute of the Aeronautical Sciences (N.Y.C.);* **Hist. Bild.**—*Historisches Bildarchiv (Bad Berneck, Ger.);* **IAS**—*Institute of Aeronautical Sciences (N.Y.C.);* **INP**—*International News Photos (N.Y.C.);* **LC**—*Library of Congress (Wash., D.C.);* **SI**—*Smithsonian Institution (Wash., D.C.);* **U & U**—*Underwood and Underwood (N.Y.C.);* **UP**—*United Press (N.Y.C.);* **USAF**—*U.S. Air Force (Wash., D.C.);* **USN**—*U.S. Navy (Wash., D.C.);* **WW**—*Wide World (N.Y.C.)*

2—North American
5—Aircraft Industries Association—Harris & Ewing
6—Douglas Aircraft
8—Huntington Library
9—SI—Ralph Upson
10—American Museum of Natural History, SI—SI—Culver, SI, Bett. Arch.
11—Bett. Arch., SI, Iraq Museum (Bagdad)—Historical Picture Service, Culver, same, BB
12—Bett. Arch.—Culver, Hist. Bild.—BB, SI
13—SI, Hist. Bild., Culver—LC, WW—SI
14—*Astra Castra*, Huntington Library—BB, LC
15—LC, Hist. Bild., SI—LC, SI, Huntington Library—same, same, SI
16—Huntington Library, WW—Bett. Arch., SI, Huntington Library—Frederick Lewis, same, SI
17—Bett. Arch., Hist Bild.—Huntington Library, New York *Sun*, LC—Hist. Bild., Huntington Library
18—Huntington Library—same
19—L'Aero Club of France (Paris), SI—BB, SI, SI,—BB, Culver, same
20—*Eighty Years of British Aviation*, SI—SI, Science Museum (London), BB—*Eighty Years of British Aviation*—Fairchild Coll.
21—Bett. Arch., Sovfoto—Bett. Arch., Sovfoto, same—Culver, SI
22—SI, BB—USAF, IAS—IAS, SI, BB
23—*L'Illustration*, Historical Picture Service—SI, BB, Bett. Arch. —IAS, WW
24—Bett. Arch.—same, Culver
25—Huntington Library, LC—Hist. Bild.—LC, LC
26—Hist. Bild., SI—Bett. Arch., BB, BB
27—SI, BB—Goodyear Tire & Rubber Co.—Hist. Bild., Fairchild Coll.
28—Fairchild Coll., SI—Fairchild Coll., SI—Fairchild Coll., Culver, European
29—Aero O/Y Finnish Airlines, same—Ernest Jones Coll. (Ford Museum and Greenfield Village, Dearborn, Mich.), BB, SI—BB, SI
30—National Cash Register Co.
31—© Karsh of Ottawa—USAF (Wright-Patterson Air Base)
32—BB, *Aero Digest*—National Cash Register Co.—BB, BB
33—SI—SI, Culver, *Aero Digest*—United Aircraft, same, same
34—Hart O. Berg Coll., same—National Cash Register Co., Hart O. Berg, Historical Picture Service—Hart O. Berg, same, same
35—INP, IAS—BB, IAS, USAF—Lord Brabazon of Tara (London), Short Bros. & Harland Ltd. (Belfast, No. Ireland)
36—IAS, INP—SI, SI—J. C. Hunsaker, Hart O. Berg, SI
37—U & U, WW—Culver, same, same—SI, Culver, IAS
38—Culver, BB—Henry Beaubois (Paris)—Fairchild Coll., Historical Picture Service
39—European, Historical Picture Service—European, SI, Fairchild Coll.—Fairchild Coll., *L'Illustration*, same
40—SI, SI—SI, SI
41—SI, Ewing Galloway—Nat. Arch., BB, BB—SI, BB
42—FPG, LC—LC, European—INP, BB
43—Curtiss-Wright Corp., SI—INP, U.S. Naval Academy Museum—USN, USN, Union Title Insurance and Trust Company Historical Collection (San Diego, Calif.)
44—Fairchild Coll., BB—BB, Henry Beaubois (Paris), IAS
45—SI, SI—Nat. Arch., European, *Flight* (Iliffe and Sons Ltd., London)—BB, Nat. Arch.
46—Fairchild Coll., BB, BB—BB—Fairchild Coll., European, BB
47—Fairchild Coll., BB, Fairchild Coll.—BB, European, Historical Picture Service—BB, Fairchild Coll., BB
48—Keystone, Fairchild Coll.,—European—BB, Bett. Arch.
49—BB, Fairchild Coll.—BB, BB—IAS, SI
50—Iliffe and Sons Ltd. (London), European—Iliffe and Sons Ltd. (London), IAS—BB, IAS
51—INP, USAF—USAF, BB—SI, Fairchild Coll.
52—BB, SI—BB, BB, European
53—Fairchild Coll., European—BB, BB,—BB, BB, BB—European, BB, BB
54—SI, BB—SI—BB,U & U, same
55—SI, U & U—BB, BB—BB, BB
56—Hist. Bild., BB, SI—BB, Joseph Nieto Coll. (San Antonio, Texas), same—SI, SI, BB—INP, BB, USAF
57—U & U, SI—United Aircraft, BB—U & U, Iliffe and Sons Ltd. (London), SI—De Havilland Aircraft Co. Ltd. (Hatfield, Hertfordshire, England), *Flight* (Iliffe and Sons Ltd., London)
58—Fairchild Coll.—U & U, SI, U & U—Nat. Arch., same
59—Frederick Lewis—same, same—same, INP, SI
60—Frederick Lewis, same—INP, SI—BB, Frederick Lewis, same
61—European, BB, Keystone—Frederick Lewis, Culver, BB—Frederick Lewis
62—BB, U & U, Fairchild Coll.—European, Fairchild Coll.—BB, SI, BB—U & U, Ernest Jones Coll. (Ford Museum and Greenfield Village, Dearborn, Mich.), same
63—USAF, *Flight* (Iliffe and Sons, Ltd., London)—B, Nat. Arch. —European, same
64—U & U, European, same—BB, U & U, Handley Page Ltd. (London)—European, BB, European—same, Hist. Bild., SI
65—BB, INP—European—SI, SI—Fairchild Coll., Erik Hildes-Heim Aeronautical Coll.
66—SI, BB—BB, Thomas Bros. Airplane Co. (Ithaca, N.Y.)—INP, Culver, SI
67—LC, U & U—Robert C. Hare Coll. (Los Angeles, Calif.), Vaughn Bell Coll. (Santa Monica Calif.), U & U—*Flight* (Iliffe and Sons Ltd., London), WW, Henry Beaubois (Paris)
68—USAF, Hist. Bild., Combine Photos—BB, USAF, European—Sperry Gyroscope Co., Dept. Def., USAF—BB, Fairchild Coll., BB
69—Keystone, Fairchild Coll.—USAF, European—U & U, USN—Nat. Arch., USAF—Nat. Arch., USAF, USAF, USAF
70—INP, BB—BB, Fairchild Coll., same—U & U, BB, SI, Keystone, Culver
71—INP, Frederick Lewis—Warren Bodie Coll. (Van Nuys, Calif.), Frederick Lewis, WW—Ernest Jones Coll. (Henry Ford Museum and Greenfield Village, Dearborn, Mich.), *Flight* (Iliffe and Sons Ltd., London), European—Fairchild Coll., Warren Bodie, same
72—Frank Coffyn (Hiller Helicopter Co., Palo Alto Calif.), same, SI—Culver, SI, Fairchild Coll.
73—BB, BB—Robert C. Hare—IAS, SI—Henry Beaubois (Paris), Ernest Jones Coll. (Henry Ford Museum and Greenfield Village, Dearborn, Mich.)
74—George Lawlor Coll., Combine Photos, European—BB, SI—INP, Fairchild Coll.—BB, USAF
75—SI—USN, U & U—Fairchild Coll.—Nat. Arch., Alfred V. Verville
76—Robert C. Hare
77—INP—Packard Motor Car Co.
78—BB, U & U—European—INP, LC, European
79—Imperial War Museum (London), Henry Beaubois (Paris) —Robert C. Hare, Joseph Nieto, Robert C. Hare—same, IAS —U & U
80—Robert C. Hare, same, same—SI, Robert C. Hare, same—IAS, Joseph Nieto
81—Robert C. Hare, Keystone—European, Frederick Lewis—Fairchild Coll., USAF, U & U—Robert C. Hare, USAF
82—Imperial War Museum (London), Robert C. Hare, Culver —Nat. Arch., BB—Robert C. Hare, same
83—Joseph Nieto, SI, Joseph Nieto—INP, IAS, Robert C. Hare—same, same, same—U & U, Nat. Arch., LC, Robert C. Hare
84—IAS, Historical Picture Service—LC, Robert C. Hare, European—Nat. Arch., Robert C. Hare—Goodyear Tire and Rubber Co., same, same
85—Historical Picture Service, Joseph Nieto, Robert C. Hare—same, BB—Robert C. Hare, U & U—Robert C. Hare, Nat. Arch.—BB, Robert C. Hare, same
86—U & U, U & U—Robert C. Hare, same, Nat. Arch.—U & U, Joseph Nieto—Imperial War Museum (London), USAF
87—Nat. Arch., BB—Robert C. Hare—same, same—Black Star, Robert C. Hare—*L'Illustration*, INP
88—INP, INP—INP, European, INP—Henry Beaubois (Paris), Nat. Arch., Elliot Springs
89—Joseph Nieto, Imperial War Museum (London)—same, same —Joseph Nieto, European—BB, SI, Imperial War Museum (London), Robert C. Hare
90—Combine Photos, Office of Postmaster General (Washington, D.C.)—Joseph Nieto, Robert C. Hare—same, same—BB, BB —Nat. Arch., SI, SI
91—Nat. Arch., SI—Fairchild Coll., European—Fairchild Coll., Joseph Nieto—U & U, USAF, Sperry Gyroscope Co.
92—*The Cleveland News*
93—Admiral Richard E. Byrd Coll.—Guggenheim Coll.
94—INP, European—INP—European, same, U & U
95—WW, *Flight* (Iliffe and Sons Ltd., London)—Handley Page Ltd. (London), Vickers Armstrongs Ltd. (England)—BB, European
96—U & U, BB—Douglas Aircraft, SI, European—WW—INP, INP —Boeing Airplane Co., BB, WW
97—USAF, USAF—Nat. Arch.—Warren Bodie, Fairchild Coll., Warren Bodie—same, same, Fairchild Coll.
98—Jack Canary Coll. (Pacific Palisades, Calif.), Vickers Armstrongs Ltd. (England)—Henry Beaubois (Paris), USAF—SI, Jack Canary—*Flight* (Iliffe and Sons Ltd., London), Vickers Armstrongs Ltd. (England)—Nat. Arch., *Flight* (Iliffe and Sons Ltd., London), SI
99—Joseph Nieto, LC—LC—LC—WW, George A. Page, Jr. Coll. (Reynoldsburg, Ohio), INP
100—Nat. Arch., LC—Nat. Arch.—Joseph Barry (Culver City, Calif.), Pratt & Whitney Aircraft
101—USAF, Fairchild Coll., BB—U & U, J. C. Hunsaker (National Institute of Technology, Boston), Joseph Barry—European, same, U & U
102—Ewing Galloway, same, WW—SI—WW, Ryan Aeronautical
103—WW, BB—WW, BB, WW—WW, WW, WW
104—WW, Joseph Nieto, Lockheed Aircraft, WW—Keystone, Boeing Airplane Co.—U & U, United Air Lines—SI, U & U, Pratt & Whitney Aircraft
105—Douglas Aircraft, same, same—Fairchild Aircraft, WW, Pan American World Airways—W. G. Armstrong Whitworth Aircraft Ltd. (England), Aero O/Y Finnish Airlines, WW
106—BB, John Sloan Coll. (Woodland Hills, Calif.), European—Air France, United Air Lines—Frederick Lewis, U.S. Post Office Dept.
107—United Air Lines, same—Western Air Lines—K.L.M. Royal Dutch Airlines, John Sloan, American Airlines—Historical Picture Service, Trans World Airlines, Pan American World Airways
108—BB, Admiral Richard E. Byrd—same, WW—BB—WW, WW, Lockheed Aircraft
109—Fairchild Coll., WW, BB—BB, European—USAF, INP, WW
110—INP, Bendix Aviation (Eclipse Pioneer Div.), George A. Page, Jr.—Union Title Insurance and Trust Company Historical Collection (San Diego, Calif.)—USAF, George H. Prudden (Lockheed Aircraft), Lockheed Aircraft
111—George A. Page, Jr., WW, Handley Page Ltd. (England)—U.S. Dept. of Agriculture, SI, Dayton Wright Co.—Warren Bodie, WW, WW
112—C. S. Jones (Academy of Aeronautics), U & U—same, WW—BB, BB, Fairchild Coll.—U & U, INP, U & U
113—INP, WW—U & U, A. M. Rochlen (Douglas Aircraft), Fairchild Coll.—Henry Beaubois (Paris), U & U—WW, USAF, USAF
114—WW, WW, USAF—U & U, same—WW, BB, George A. Page Jr.
115—Cecil B. DeMille Coll. (Paarmount Studios, Hollywood, Calif.), same, same—LC, C. S. Jones (Academy of Aeronautics), James W. Montee—L. Jansen (Ministere de Communications Regie des Vois Aeriennes, Brussels, Belgium), Wm. P. McCracken, U & U
116—WW, USAF, Fairchild Coll.—Jack Frye, Gilloon Agency, U & U—same, Capt. R. S. Barnaby, Wm. P. McCracken
117—BB, George A. Page, Jr.—*The Cleveland News*, Sovfoto—INP, U & U
118—Gilloon Agency
119—Sikorsky Aircraft—George A. Page, Jr.
120—Western Air Lines, same—Trans World Airlines—WW, United Air Lines, same
121—BB, Pan American World Airways—same—Northwest Orient Airlines, Pratt & Whitney Aircraft, INP—WW, European
122—BB, WW, United Airlines—IAS, Braniff Airways
123—WW, J. Ernie Adams (Auckland, New Zealand *Weekly News*) —T.A.C.A. (New Orleans), Trans-Canada Airlines—Aero O/Y Finnish Airlines, B. Marble (Douglas Aircraft), Black Star
124—U & U, Douglas Aircraft, WW—WW, Lockheed Aircraft, IAS
125—Douglas Aircraft, same—Beech Aircraft, BB, Keystone—Consolidated Vultee Aircraft, North American Aviation, Northrop Aircraft
126—European, U & U—W. G. Armstrong Whitworth Aircraft Ltd. (England), *Flight* (Iliffe and Sons Ltd., London), Independent Newspapers Ltd. (Dublin, Eire)—A. V. Schmidt Coll. (Tarzana, Calif.), Swissair (Zurich, Switzerland), Fairchild Aircraft—A. M. Rochlen (Douglas Aircraft), Pan American World Airways, Lockheed Aircraft
127—Black Star, WW, *L'Illustration*—WW—Black Star, WW, Imperial War Museum, (London), WW—Pratt & Whitney Aircraft, WW—Aeronautica Nacchi (Fiat Aviazione, Milan, Italy), same, same
128—United Aircraft, Fairchild Coll.—FPG, SI, INP
129—A. V. Schmidt Coll., BB—United Aircraft, SI, Sovfoto—Sperry Gyroscope Co., WW
130—Pratt & Whitney Aircraft, U & U—WW—U & U, WW, INP
131—U & U, Harris & Ewing—Frederick Lewis, WW—Culver, Western Air Lines
132—Culver, WW—Keystone—Gilloon Agency (New York *Daily News* photo), Sperry Gyroscope Co., WW
133—WW, INP, WW—INP, WW, INP—WW, BB, WW
134—WW, WW—U & U, WW, Pratt & Whitney Aircraft—WW, WW
135—Goodyear Tire & Rubber Co., Ewing Galloway—BB—WW—USAF, WW, WW
136—INP, WW—UP, INP—European, INP
137—Black Star, European, UP, European—WW, WW—INP, INP, European
138—U & U, Boeing Airplane Co., BB, Northrop Aircraft, Fairchild Coll.—USAF—Fairchild Coll., INP, INP
139—European, Sovfoto, same—INP, FPG, U & U—European, WW, Keystone
140—Dept. Def.
141—*Newsweek* Magazine—WW
142—Gloster Aircraft Co. Ltd. (Hucclecote, Gloucestershire, England), Warren Bodie, Guido Botta (Naples, Italy)—Bell Aircraft, Combine Photos, Hughes Aircraft
143—Sovfoto, same, same—same, same, same—INP, SI, SI—USAF, PIX, SI
144—Hist. Bild., WW, LC—SI, SI, Warren Bodie
145—Hist. Bild., Black Star, UP—INP, European, INP—Warren Bodie, Hist. Bild., European, same—USAF, WW, Jack Canary, USAF—USAF, Warren Bodie, same, USAF—Warren Bodie, U & U, Keystone (Munich, Germany), Warren Bodie
146—WW—Combine Photos—INP, Black Star
147—Imperial War Museum, Vickers Armstrongs Ltd.—British Information Service, WW—European, Handley Page, British Information Service, European—Keystone, INP, Short Bros. & Harland Ltd.—UP, WW, Hawker Aircraft Ltd.
148—BB, FPG, BB—Black Star—BB, AIA
149—Lockheed Aircraft, WW, Lockheed Aircraft—European, Royal Canadian Air Force photograph—USAF, WW, WW
150—USN, BB, USN—USN, WW, WW
151—Pratt & Whitney Aircraft, WW, WW—Consolidated Vultee Aircraft, WW, Pratt & Whitney Aircraft—European, FPG, same
152—WW, WW, WW—Douglas Aircraft, BB, Fairchild Coll.—Shell Oil Co., WW, U.S. Coast Guard
153—BB, North American Aviation, European—Bell Aircraft, Warren Bodie, Otto Menge, Lockheed Aircraft—BB, Sperry Gyroscope, Dept. Def., Ewing Galloway—European, North American Aviation, Boeing Airplane, USAF
154—WW, USAF—UP, WW—USAF, Fairchild Coll.
155—USAF, WW, European—WW, USAF, USAF—National Defense Photo (Ottawa, Ontario), Black Star, WW
156—WW, USAF, Pratt & Whitney Aircraft—Dept. Def.—USAF, USN, USAF
157—USN, BB—USN, USN, BB—USAF,Dept. Def, USAF
158—Dept. of Labor, Lockheed Aircraft, same—Boeing Airplane Co., FPG—Republic Aviation, Chance Vought Aircraft, Northrop Aircraft, same—Consolidated Vultee Aircraft, same, USAF, Boeing Airplane Co.
159—WW, WW—Dr. Wernher von Braun—European, USAF—USAF, USAF
161—DeHavilland Aircraft Co., Ltd. (England)—Douglas Aircraft
162—A. V. Schmidt—INP, Black Star, A. V. Schmidt
163—Douglas Aircraft, same—Northrop Aircraft, same, European —INP, Harris & Ewing, FPG
164—INP, BB, Lockheed Aircraft—Harris & Ewing, Bell Aircraft (Helicopter Div., Fort Worth, Texas)—Consolidated Vultee, Bell Aircraft (Buffalo, N.Y.)
165—Boeing Airplane Co., same, Harris & Ewing—Pratt & Whitney Aircraft, North American Aviation, same—T.A.C.A., Pacific Airmotive Corp. (Burbank, Calif.), Texas Engineering and Mfg. Co. (TEMCO, Dallas, Texas)
166—K.L.M. Royal Dutch Airlines (Amsterdam, Netherlands), Pan American World Airways—USAF—Norsk Telegrambyra's OG Klsjeavdeling A/S (Oslo, Norway), T.A.C.A (New Orleans), British European Airways
167—Braniff Airways, BB, Trans World Airlines, Boeing Airplane Co.—Flying Tiger Lines (Burbank, Calif.), Slick Airways, Trans Canada Air Lines, Air France—National Airlines, Air Vietnam (Saigon, Indo China), Japan Airlines Co. Ltd. (Tokyo, Japan), Airways (India) Ltd. (New Delhi, India)—Beech Aircraft, Consolidated Vultee Aircraft, North Central Airlines (Minneapolis, Minnesota), Lockheed Aircraft
168—DeHavilland Aircraft Co. Ltd. (England), European—British Overseas Airways Corp. (BOAS)—UP, WW, European
169—INP, Chas. Brown, Black Star, same—Glenn L. Martin Co., Vickers Armstrongs Ltd. (England)—Armstrong Siddeley Motors Ltd. (England), Black Star—DeHavilland Aircraft Co. Ltd. (England), Black Star, Handley Page Ltd. (England)—Combine Photos, DeHavilland Aircraft Co. Ltd. (England), same
170—USAF, INP, WW—North American Aviation
171—North American Aviation, Dept. Def., INP—Dept. Def., USN, Dept. Def.—UP, Sovfoto, UP, UP—WW, WW, WW, WW
172—North American Aviation, Lockheed Aircraft—Douglas Aircraft, North American Aviation—Warren Bodie, Glenn L. Martin Co.—North American Aviation, McDonnell Aircraft Corp. (St. Louis, Mo.), North American Aviation
173—Dept. Def., FPG—Republic Aviation—Lockheed Aircraft, Douglas Aircraft, Lockheed Aircraft—INP, North American, UP
174—Consolidated Vultee Aircraft, Pratt & Whitney Aircraft—Douglas Aircraft, Pratt & Whitney Aircraft
175—USAF, National Advisory Committee for Aeronautics (NACA) —WW, Phillips Petroleum Co., Dept. Def., USAF, Radio Corporation of America (RCA), Lear, Inc.
176—Douglas Aircraft, WW, Douglas Aircraft, same, USAF—Ewing Galloway, Bell Aircraft, Consolidated Vultee Aircraft—Northrop Aircraft, BB, Warren Bodie
177—National Defense Photo (Ottawa, Ontario), INP, National Defense Photo (Ottawa, Ontario)—Armstrong Siddeley Motors Ltd. (England), European, same—S.N.C.A.S.O., *Informations Aeronautiques* (Paris), same, same—Keystone (Munich, Germany), Australian Information Bureau (San Francisco, Calif.), Aeronautica Nacchi (Fiat Aviazione, Milan Italy), Hindustan Aircraft Ltd. (India)
178—Hiller Helicopters, WW, Bell Aircraft—WW—Piasecki Helicopter Corp. (Morton, Pa.), FPG, Sikorsky Aircraft
179—WW, Beech Aircraft, WW—Remmert Werner, Inc. (St. Louis, Mo.), BB—INP, FPG—BB, Beech Aircraft, Ryan Aeronautical, Cessna Aircraft
180—WW, UP—WW
181—WW, Missionary Aviation Fellowship (Los Angeles, Calif.)—Auster Aircraft Ltd. (England), Bell Aircraft—Admiral Richard E. Byrd, International Civil Aviation Organization (Montreal, Canada)
182—UP, WW—Blackburn & General Aircraft Ltd. (England), Fairchild Aircraft—Consolidated Vultee Aircraft, Boeing Airplane Co.
183—European, Boeing Airplane Co.—Victor Black, Sylvania Electric Products, Inc.—USAF, Boeing Airplane Co.
184—Douglas Aircraft Co.
185—WW—Willy Ley
186—Douglas Aircraft Co., WW—WW, "Reproduced by Permission of the Proprietors of *Punch*"
187—USN, United Aircraft—NACA, WW, Glenn L. Martin Co.—Mrs. Robert H. Goddard, Dr. Wernher Von Braun, United Aircraft
188—NACA, Ryan Aeronautical, NACA—Marquardt Aircraft, USAF, NACA, UP, WW